POETRY IN A GLOBAL AGE

POETRY IN
A GLOBAL AGE

Jahan Ramazani

The University of Chicago Press Chicago and London

The University of Chicago Press, Chicago 60637
The University of Chicago Press, Ltd., London
© 2020 by The University of Chicago
All rights reserved. No part of this book may be used or reproduced in any manner
whatsoever without written permission, except in the case of brief quotations
in critical articles and reviews. For more information, contact the University of
Chicago Press, 1427 East 60th Street, Chicago, IL 60637.
Published 2020
Printed in the United States of America

29 28 27 26 25 24 23 22 21 20   1 2 3 4 5

ISBN-13: 978-0-226-73000-4 (cloth)
ISBN-13: 978-0-226-73014-1 (paper)
ISBN-13: 978-0-226-73028-8 (e-book)
DOI: https://doi.org/10.7208/chicago/9780226730288.001.0001

The University of Chicago Press gratefully acknowledges the generous support of
the Buckner W. Clay Dean of Arts and Sciences and the Vice President for Research
at the University of Virginia toward the publication of this book.

Cover illustration: Martina Nehrling, *Found Gone* (2011). Acrylic on paper, 9 × 9 in.
© Martina Nehrling. Photograph: Courtesy of the artist (martinanehrling.com).

Library of Congress Cataloging-in-Publication Data

Names: Ramazani, Jahan, 1960– author.
Title: Poetry in a global age / Jahan Ramazani.
Description: Chicago ; London : The University of Chicago Press, 2020. |
Includes bibliographical references and index.
Identifiers: LCCN 2020013380 | ISBN 9780226730004 (cloth) |
ISBN 9780226730141 (paperback) | ISBN 9780226730288 (ebook)
Subjects: LCSH: Poetry, Modern—20th century—History and criticism. |
Literature and globalization.
Classification: LCC PN1271 .R36 2020 | DDC 809.—dc23
LC record available at https://lccn.loc.gov/2020013380

♾ This paper meets the requirements of ANSI/NISO Z39.48-1992 (Permanence of
Paper).

For Paul Armstrong, Jim Marshall, & David Wyatt,
& in memory of Mary Lederman,
life-changing teachers

CONTENTS

Introduction 1

1 "Cosmopolitan Sympathies":
Poetry of the First Global War 25

2 The Local Poem in a Global Age 51

3 Poetry and Tourism in a Global Age 77

4 Modernist Inflections,
Postcolonial Directions 101

5 Poetry and the Transnational
Migration of Form 117

6 Yeats's Asias: Modernism, Orientalism,
Anti-orientalism 133

7 Poetry, the Planet, and the Ecological Thought:
Wallace Stevens and Beyond 155

8 Seamus Heaney's Globe 177

9 Code-Switching, Code-Stitching:
A Macaronic Poetics? 193

10 Poetry, (Un)Translatability, and
World Literature 213

Epilogue. Lyric Poetry: Intergeneric,
Transnational, Translingual? 239

Acknowledgments 251   Notes 257   Index 309

A Polytemporal, Polyspatial Poetics

"I am a lead pencil," begins an essay that, if it were less widely known, might well seem the start of a poem.[1] After all, nonhuman beings often speak in poems: "I am a frog," begins one; "I am a lamp," begins another; "I am a lonely, woodland lake," begins a third.[2] In economist Leonard E. Read's "I, Pencil" (1958), a humble, everyday utensil, granted a voice by prosopopoeia, tells the story of its making. It recalls its genesis out of cedar felled in Oregon; milled in San Leandro, California, where it's also kiln-dried and tinted; combined with graphite mined in Ceylon (Sri Lanka) that has been purified with Mississippi clay and treated with candelilla wax from Mexico; lacquered (a technique originating in China and Japan); and plugged with an eraser made of rapeseed oil from the Dutch East Indies. It embodies the transnational movement and coalescence of money, labor, commodities, and skills. Although Read, a Cold War libertarian, wanted to show that a pencil's fabrication can't be centrally planned, already in the nineteenth century, when the groundwork of twentieth-century globalization was being laid, thinkers of a very different kind, Marx and Engels, had observed the increasingly "cosmopolitan character" of worldwide production and consumption, with "raw material drawn from the remotest zones" for products consumed "in every quarter of the globe" (*in allen Weltteilen*), including intellectual products such as "world literature" (*Weltliteratur*) that bespoke a "universal interdependence of nations."[3] What's true for Read's strangely articulate and self-reflexive pencil is no less true for the poem it writes. The making of a poem, as of a pencil, amalgamates, reshapes, and compresses materials that span large swaths of the globe.

Whether you're a Marxist, libertarian, or neither, you know that, since the Cold War, the flow of ideas, culture, and capital across national borders has only intensified, albeit with periodic counterforces of isolation and retrenchment. Just as an "American" pencil is more pencil than it is American, an "American" car can have a transmission made in Japan, an engine from China, all assembled in Mexico, where many of its parts may have originated. So too a Boeing 787, though ostensibly "American," results from a global supply chain linking Asian, Australian, European, and US parts and labor.[4] Such chains become most visible when disrupted, as during the coronavirus pandemic. But often "locality," writes Arjun Appadurai, "becomes a fetish that disguises the globally dispersed forces that actually drive the production process," such as a steel structure in Libya with elements "from India, China, Russia, and Japan, providing different components of new technological configurations."[5] We are less accustomed to thinking this way about poems. It hasn't helped that many of the most prominent global literary scholars, such as Franco Moretti, Pheng Cheah, and Pascale Casanova, have had little to say about poetry. But poetry—long lived and apparently ubiquitous—may have much to contribute to our rethinking of literature in an extranational frame. According to William Carlos Williams, "A poem is a small (or large) machine made of words," and even a nationalist machine made of words, techniques, and ideas, of rhythms, images, and stanzas, bears a multinationally heterogeneous array of traces.[6]

Those traces are also of temporally diverse origins. Another analogy might help us think afresh about a poem's elements of composition. Although Bruno Latour looks to neither the libertarian's invisible hand nor the Marxist's economic base, he, too, tracks the migratory meeting of sundry ingredients in the here and now:

> I may use an electric drill, but I also use a hammer. The former is thirty-five years old, the latter hundreds of thousands. You will see me as a bricoleur 'of contrasts' because I mix up gestures from different times? Would I be an ethnographic curiosity? On the contrary: show me an activity that is homogeneous from the point of view of the modern time. Some of my genes are 500 million years old, others 3 million, others 100,000 years, and my habits range in age from a few days to several thousand years.[7]

Poets, too, are bricoleurs. They enfold varied temporalities in the radially vectored language, techniques, forms, and rhetorical strategies of their work. If we were to submit almost any modern or contemporary poem for analysis to Ancestry.com, and if the units of analysis included allusions, techniques, etymologies, genres, forms, and rhetoric, the resulting pie chart, even if favoring one region in one era, would inevitably include others. Poems belong to their immediate historical moment and to the longer transhistorical skeins—generic, formal, tropological, etymological, environmental—that they twist together and remake to address their moment. Latour describes "form" as "what circulates from site to site," "something which allows something else to be transported from one site to another."[8] Rucked thick with form, poetry exemplifies this circulation and transportation, albeit intermittently impeded by linguistic and cultural difference. In recent years, literary studies has been fraught with contention over the nature of poetry's historicity. Opposing positions have been forcefully articulated by Virginia Jackson, who would demystify lyric as a New Critical anachronism, and Jonathan Culler, who embraces it as a transhistorical paradigm.[9] Although their nuanced arguments complicate the polarity, Latour can help us consider an alternative to either a strictly historicist or a formalist poetics: a polytemporal poetics. According to Latour, "every contemporary assembly is polytemporal"—hammer, drill, engine, pencil, poem.[10]

In a subsequent essay Latour returns to and elaborates the metaphor of the hammer, tracing the multiple temporalities it brings together:

> The hammer that I find on my workbench is not contemporary to my action today: it keeps folded heterogenous temporalities [*il garde plissés les temps hétérogènes*], one of which has the antiquity of the planet, because of the mineral from which it has been moulded, while another has that of the age of the oak which provided the handle, while still another has the age of the 10 years since it came out of the German factory which produced it for the market. When I grab the handle, I insert my gesture in a 'garland of time' as Michel Serres (1995) has put it.[11]

The physical properties of one of the books of poetry stacked on my desk—ink, paper, binding, glue—are obviously susceptible to such analysis. The ink can be traced back to its constituent vegetable or petroleum oils, pigments, and additives, purified and mixed in a factory by workers drawing on four and a half millennia of know-how; the paper to trees in a two-millennia-old process, updated and put into action by the paper mill's staff and machinery; but its unsewn binding goes back only to the 1830s, its hot-melt adhesion to the 1940s; and the modern publisher—an institution formed in the early modern period—was responsible for acquiring, editing, typesetting, marketing, and distributing it to the bookseller who sold it to me. Book historians could expand in great detail on the book's physical polytemporality, whether or not they were interested in the poetry inside it.[12] But the book you are holding in your hand (or reading on a screen) takes an approach grounded in poetics; and, even conceived primarily as a text, a poem folds within itself the heterogeneous temporalities of words, forms, rhythms, tropes, and genres.

In addition to these long and varied *durées*, Latour also sees in the hammer, as does Read in the pencil, a spatial plurality that defies geographic boundaries. So too, the constitutive bookmaking techniques mentioned above can be traced to a host of regions, if we consider just crucial bibliographic developments in ancient China and Korea, medieval West Asia, early modern Germany, early nineteenth-century Britain, and so forth, let alone the global sources of their physical elements.

> What is true of time holds for space as well, for this humble hammer holds in place quite heterogenous spaces [*des lieux tout à fait hétérogènes*] that nothing, before the technical action, could gather together: the forests of the Ardennes, the mines of the Ruhr, the German factory, the tool van which offers discounts every Wednesday on Bourbonnais streets, and finally the workshop of a particularly clumsy Sunday bricoleur. Every technology resembles what surrealists called an 'exquisite cadaver'. If, for pedagogical reasons, we would reverse the movement of the film of which this hammer is but the end product, we would deploy an increasing assemblage of ancient times and dispersed spaces: the intensity, the dimension, the surprise of the connections, invisible today, which would thus have become visible, and, by contrast, would give us an exact measure of what this hammer accomplishes today. There is nothing less local, less contemporary, less brutal than a hammer, as soon as one begins to unfold what it sets in motion; there is nothing more local, more brutal and more durable than this same hammer as soon as one folds everything implicated in it.[13]

Invoking an aesthetic analogue in surrealism's exquisite corpse, a form of serial, collage-like creativity, Latour imagines reversing the movement of the film (yet more surrealist echoes), tracing to various times and places the ingredients that constitute the hammer. At the same time, a Latourian reading of his own text might observe that it plays with and against Heidegger's ready-to-hand (*zuhanden*) hammer, Levi-Strauss's binary-straddling *bricoleur*, and Deleuze's labyrinthine folds (*plis*). Whether we're analyzing a hammer, poem, book, or essay, according to Latour, "we would have to draw bushy arrows in order to include" everything "acting in it at the same time," all the "faraway sites."[14]

To test the applicability of this polytemporal, polyspatial model to poetics, what happens when we substitute a specific poem for Latour's hammer? As we'll see, the poem a poet makes is no less globally enmeshed than are the physical, economic, and everyday spheres of the poet's life. But unlike a hammer, pencil, or other instrumental commodity, a poem not only embodies a complex genesis but also flourishes it, insofar as it foregrounds the immaterial materials, the words, forms, and sounds, of which it's made. If Read and Latour reveal for us the many unseen processes that go into the making of a tool, criticism can trace a poem's tessellation of intangible ingredients and histories—formal, generic, and verbal.

"Reverse Suicide," one of Matt Rasmussen's remarkable elegies for his brother in *Black Aperture* (2013), resonates with Latour's injunction to "reverse the movement of the film":

The guy Dad sold your car to
comes back to get his money,

leaves the car. With filthy rags
we rub it down until it doesn't shine

and wipe your blood into
the seams of the seat.[15]

The poem's confessionalism and even the diction of its opening line—*guy, Dad*—signal an American familiarity. But the first-time reader might be perplexed by the enjambed preposition "into"—don't we normally wipe things *up* or *away*? How and why would we wipe blood *into* a seat? Soon we realize the images must be running backward in time:

Each snowflake stirs before
lifting into the sky as I

learn you won't be dead.
The unsuffering ends

when the mess of your head
pulls together around

a bullet in your mouth.

If we were to reverse the movement of the film, as Latour suggests, and as the poem does at the diegetic level, we'd span multiple temporalities and spaces. The poem's conversational idiom and sharp enjambments come out of an American tradition identified with William Carlos Williams. But its reverse motion is unimaginable prior to film, a late nineteenth-century French invention often attributed to the Lumière brothers. Its ungainly coinage for the suicidal brother's psychic state after death's release—"unsuffering"—recalls English precursors from over a century earlier: Gerard Manley Hopkins's "unleaving" in "Spring and Fall," Thomas Hardy's "unhope," "unsuccess," "uncare," and "unblooms."[16]

At its end, the poem twins autumnal leaves and grief:

> You spit it into Dad's gun
>
> before arriving in the driveway
> while the evening brightens
>
> and we pour bag after bag
> of leaves on the lawn,
>
> waiting for them to leap
> onto the bare branches.

Even as poetry adapts and resists the media, discourses, and other "others" of its time—here, visual media and obituaries—it embeds within itself a long memory of the stuff it's made of.[17] Unlike Latour's hammer or Read's pencil, it both exemplifies and bears witness to its transhistoricity, more fully divulged in turn by criticism. This poem's elegiac play on the pathetic fallacy associating grief with autumn and mortality with fallen leaves, its elegiac wish to reverse time (here, literalized), its echo of elegiac couplets, and its apostrophe to the dead go back via anglophone poems to pastoral elegies of classical antiquity.

But at the same time as poetry endures, it changes. If couplet-like, this elegy's stanzas are, in the contemporary style, highly enjambed, enacting time's imagined backward flow. And in accord with the melancholic turn in the modern elegy, this elegy exposes the impossible fictionality of the longed-for redemption (leaves leaping onto branches).[18] Recalling the temporal juxtapositions of many elegies, the poem sets the cyclical time of diurnal and atmospheric processes against the temporality of a car, a gun, and a singular death. There may be nothing more historical in the sense of being time-bound and irreversible than the violent death of a loved one. A poem answers to the uniqueness of the present.

Yet it also answers to the recurrences within the present. A poem works on even the moment of death with a transhistorical toolkit.

Words like "shine" and "brightens," "leaves" and "snowflake," and "lifting into the sky" reverberate across a long elegiac history, updated here by juxtaposition with a contemporary idiom ("The guy," "the mess," "You spit"). At the still more particulate level, the poem's bare, elemental diction goes back mostly to Old English words of Norse or German origin ("filthy," "rags," "blood," "snowflake," "sky," "dead," "mouth," "spit," "gun," "driveway," "evening," "brightens," "leaves," "leap," "bare"), mixed with words from Old and Middle French ("guy," "car," "unsuffering," "mess," "bullet," "arriving," "lawn," "branches"). The lyric's psychological word, itself of French origin—"unsuffering"—stands out all the more against the blunt, matter-soaked terrain of the Germanic diction.[19] The grieving poet responds to a brother's death in a specific time and place—"there is nothing more local, more brutal and durable," writes Latour ("brutal" in the sense of violently sudden). At the same time, as Latour puts it, "There is nothing less local, less contemporary, less brutal," the elegy knit by a radial network of connections to other times and places. Although criticism sometimes veers toward either under- or overhistoricization, either under- or overlocalization, the complex temporality and spatiality of poetry are better suited to a translocal and polytemporal poetics.

Rasmussen's elegy might seem an odd example of poetry's poly-temporality and polyspatiality. Because we're used to thinking of post-colonial aesthetics as intensely and visibly hybrid, poems from South Asia, Africa, the Caribbean, the Pacific Islands, Black Britain, and else-where might be more obvious candidates.[20] A. K. Ramanujan's "Elements of Composition" traces the genesis of its composite lyric "I" to India, America, Britain, and Kenya, and to Hinduism, Islam, druidic religion, and Platonism, as well as various biological, chemical, elemental, and psychological ingredients from many times and places. Lorna Goodison's "To Us, All Flowers Are Roses" uncovers in the poet's internal and external Caribbean landscapes Ashanti, Irish, German, Spanish, Greek, Scandinavian, and other constitutive elements. If the flower catalogue—Spenser, Milton, Thomson—traditionally gloried in the variety of colors, scents, and shapes of flowers, Goodison turns this topos around, uniting all flowers in one but relishing Jamaica's toponymic polyglossia. In "Heir-loom Rose, for Maya," made up of one syntactically branching, prickly, twisting run-on sentence, Vahni Capildeo, a Trinidadian-Scottish poet of the South Asian diaspora who worked as a lexicographer for the *OED*, entangles the roses of English history ("you could even make wars under its banner, york or lancaster"), of India (known in Hindi as *gulab*, derived from the Persian for rose, *gul*, and water, *ab*), of Saint-Exupéry's *Le Petit*

Prince ("ombrageuse"), of Gertrude Stein ("rose exceeds/is in excess . . . of rose"), and of the British "empire, imperial as natural, pressing away the senses' write/right to come to the rose as is."[21] The roots and branches of such literary flowers are multinational, intertextual, and intertemporal.

But if the paradigm is to hold, it should also work for poetry of the global North. While postcolonial poems figure prominently in the ensuing chapters, so do putatively "British," "Irish," and "Canadian" poems, as well as "American" poems by T. S. Eliot (albeit in French), Marianne Moore (albeit humorously multinational), Wallace Stevens (albeit environmentally global), and others, from Lorine Niedecker to A. R. Ammons and Mai Der Vang. For those of us living in what is for now the world's most powerful nation, often susceptible to self-congratulatory exceptionalism, it may be especially important to remind ourselves (and our students, if we teach) of the myriad extranational and polytemporal elements migrating through culture's porous boundaries, instead of reinforcing the illusion that the literary or cultural artifact is a smoothly unitary mirror of the nation, a monadic reflection of the homeland and of its mononational citizen. The complexly polytemporal, polyspatial folds within poems can help alert us at the micro level to the transnationalism we more often conceive at the macro level of trade, finance, migration, and instrumental communications. They become visible once we reach across the nationally defined institutions that often frame literary recognition and study. I first read Rasmussen's poem in evaluating more than a hundred books nominated for the National Book Award for Poetry, an institutional space that limits entries, as do many syllabi and anthologies, to poetry by American citizens published in the United States. But no poetry seemingly *made in the USA* would likely comply with the Federal Trade Commission's requirements for commodities bearing its label: "all significant parts and processing that go into the product must be of U.S. origin. That is, the product should contain no—or negligible—foreign content."[22]

Attention to the specificities of poetry—form, genre, poeticity— necessarily exists in some tension with the national paradigm, as the pre- and cross-national vocabulary of poetics indicates: elegy, pentameter, persona, diction, metaphor, anaphora, chiasmus, epanalepsis, ottava rima, triolet, haiku, tanka, ghazal, masnavi, pantoum, blues. Just as Rasmussen's elegies have to be read in a broad generic and literary framework, you can't understand Terrance Hayes's creative deformations in his "American sonnets"—multiple voltas, contorted compression, fourteen unrhymed lines flush with internal echoes, address not to an unnamed beloved but to an assassin—without reading them against Italian and English norms.²³ Even when you localize, nationalize, and historicize poems, poetry's deep memory of literary form and antecedent and its linguistic and aesthetic sedimentation transport you willy-nilly across national and historical boundaries.

Whether postcolonial, American, or otherwise, each poem should be seen, like Latour's hammer or Read's pencil, as the product not of one nation, as in the conventional literary-historical paradigm, or of one time, as in a strict historicism, but of multiple intersecting histories and cultures. Asking "What Is Literary History?," a scholar surmised in the 1990s, "The paradigmatic model is the history of a national literature," "identified in part with the character of the nation or people."²⁴ But in the wake of the still-incomplete transnational turn in the humanities, many of us now emphasize that the supposed "character" of nations is at least in part a fiction—as indeed, after Freud, is the supposed unity of "character." "Peoples" and "people" are always already multiple internally and at the same time enmeshed externally, across geopolitical borders, by virtue of intensifying, if sometimes reactively impeded, flows of culture, ideas, media, technology, and capital—even when they don't, like Mina Loy and Derek Walcott, consider themselves mongrels.

In *A Transnational Poetics* (2009) I argued for an approach to poetry that highlights literary confluences, commonalities, and conflicts that cross national borders. Transnational and postcolonial studies of poetry have recently multiplied.²⁵ This book builds on the momentum and expands my earlier argument, examining the transnational dimensions of modern and contemporary poems in relation to current debates in and around world literature, world history, translation studies, tourism studies, ecocriticism, modernist studies, postcolonial studies, and lyric studies. The issues raised in these debates can help illuminate the specific ways in which poetry participates in global flows, planetary enmeshments, and cosmopolitan engagements, especially, though not exclusively, since the late nineteenth century, when, as outlined in the historical discussion below, the global movement of people, goods, cultures, ideas, and information accelerated and expanded.

No doubt the contemporary resurgence of nationalisms and nativisms, from the Americas to Europe and Asia, partly in reaction to voluminous global flows, has helped spur my and other scholars' transnational interests. As an American of Iranian and Anglo-Iranian parentage (Zoroastrian, Christian, mostly Muslim) who married into an Ashkenazi Jewish family, I'm deeply troubled by the more virulent and xenophobic forms of such ideologies. That said, I fully acknowledge at the outset that the nation—as a reality, concept, and ideology—isn't "over," won't disappear anytime soon, and continues to exert a powerful influence on literary cultures and their transmission. Location matters; nations matter; religious cultures matter. Literature does not float above the earth in some globalized vapor. T. S. Eliot's claim that poetry is "stubbornly national" has recently been revived to spotlight state sponsorship of poets, such as by the CIA during the Cold War.[26] Even if free-footed (in both senses of the term), poets are subject, like the rest of us, to financial incentives, state ideologies, border checkpoints, tariffs, protectionist laws, and immigration restrictions. While moving beyond methodological nationalisms, moreover, we should acknowledge that nations retain some usefulness as organizing concepts for transnational literary comparativism, provided we acknowledge their porosity, fluidity, and at least semi-fictionality. In my view, poems reward attention to both their located and mobile qualities, a balance that terms like "transnational" and "translocal" can evoke, highlighting how literary works often verbally and aesthetically stretch between divergent cultural sites watermarked by divergent temporalities. Admittedly, my emphasis—counterposed against ideological and methodological nationalisms and localisms—tends to be more on cross-border movement, but in some areas, such as the translation of lyric, I also highlight impediments to cross-cultural mobility. To avoid allowing the local or the global to become mystified abstractions, we should join Latour in "localizing the global and distributing the local."[27] On the one hand, a poem that appears to be rooted in a singular culture and history may have world-traversing strands that should be teased out. On the other, an apparently global poem may relocalize once distant realities, indigenize once alien influences, or vernacularize the once foreign as mother tongue. We'll see both dynamics at play across this book.

In short, our understanding of poetry, perhaps especially in its modern and contemporary varieties, should straddle nation and world, local and global, as illustrated by another poem. Returning us to the trope of the pencil, Terrance Hayes's "How to Draw a Perfect Circle" reflects on a lesson in blind contour drawing, associating the speaker's uninterrupted line drawing with his genetic and familial connections to a cousin, shot after stabbing a policeman in the eye. Whereas Read traces the coalescence of globally transmitted ingredients in a pencil, as does Latour in a hammer, Hayes's pencil follows an ever-looping line of connections, literally among the features of a model, figuratively among various emanating circles. His poem lavishly uses poetry's capacity for drawing like-nesses. Proliferating metaphoric resonances, it compares the circle of a contour drawing to various other circles: an eyeball, the moon, an onion, a war drum, the letter O in apostrophe and "Oh" in exclamation, subway doors opening and closing, God, and the circle of breath, love, and causa-tion: "Everything the eye sees enters a circle, / The world is connected to a circle: breath spools from the nostrils / And any love to be open becomes an O."[28]

The poem is grounded in the particulars of a local incident that made news in New York City and of the poet's familial connection with it.[29] It places the story's protagonists in an American racial history of violence, madness, and mutual destruction: "a black man stabs a black transit cop in the face / And the cop, bleeding from his eye, kills the assailant."[30] Yet refusing the mimetic, localist presentism of metro news, the poem's ever-widening circles also encompass Homer, recalling both the poet's legendary blindness and the blinding of the Cyclops, and the symbol of the Ouroboros, an emblem with a genealogy extending to ancient Egypt: "Everything is connected / By a line curling and canceling itself like the shape of a snake / Swallowing its own decadent tail or a mind that means to destroy itself."[31] As a poet, Hayes draws circles still more extensive and extravagant than he can as a draftsman, suggesting the multifarious con-nections between here and over there, one place or person and another. "The world comes full circle," Hayes declares, and if so, then the lines connecting the lines of an "American" poem like this one shouldn't be severed from the literary and cultural lines it traces from local to global, present to past.[32] In their different ways, both Hayes's and Read's pencils trace webs of connection that extend well beyond locality and nation, and in this, our own pencils may do well to follow their example.

A Global Age

When is "a global age"? A review of the massive social-scientific literature on globalization, only a fraction of which has been engaged by literary studies, suggests various options, including archaic, premodern, early modern, industrial age, modernist, and contemporary times. Which is the most appropriate historical framework for this study, even if they all inflect it in varying degrees? I briefly consider several possibilities, starting with the popular but narrow reading of the scope of "the global" as the apparently unprecedented period since the late twentieth century marked by the widening, deepening, and speeding up of worldwide inter-connectedness and interactions.[33] Focusing on how the world became a single, electronically integrated marketplace at the end of the Cold War (1989–91), this short-term view emphasizes the traversal and compression of the globe since then by more efficient long-distance transportation, greater transnational trade, and quicker and denser communication networks and platforms.[34] The presentist, economistic perspective on globalization (*globalisation* in French as distinguished from long-term *mondialisation*) underscores the rupture of the new—the Internet, the electronic mass media, digital consumer electronics, etc.

If we believe globalization begins with the Internet, we might think a study of poetry in a global age should be about digital poems composed in tweets and texts, transcribed and collaged from the Internet, posted on Tumblr and Instagram.[35] But such an approach would foreshorten our understanding of poetry's relation to globalizing processes, which, as we'll see, significantly precede the 1990s. Moreover, critics such as Marjorie Perloff and Jessica Pressman have increasingly recognized digital poetry's continuities with modernist poetry and before.[36] Even conceptual poet Kenneth Goldsmith concedes that the technique of rearranging found language, albeit today on the Internet, goes back thousands of years in the form of the cento.[37] And while poems now circulate digitally in vast numbers, including works examined in this book, print publication has hardly disappeared.[38]

Gayatri Chakravorty Spivak may be the most prominent literary theorist who takes the short-term view that consigns globalization to digitally mediated economics. She influentially argues that the globe is an "abstract ball covered in latitudes and longitudes," "the gridwork of electronic capital."[39] Unlike the planet, it isn't experiential; it belongs to the uniform, capitalist system of exchange: "The globe is on our computers. No one lives there."[40] But despite the undeniably powerful impact of electronic capital, world historians see in globalization a number of other long-lived strands, including the political, the cultural, the technological, the social, even the biological (e.g., the 1918 flu pandemic that killed more people than the war it followed).[41] The "manifold and multi-layered" connective processes that constitute globalization, states Sebastian Conrad, have "adhered to different and sometimes incompatible logics," "overlapping structures" that are often difficult to disentangle.[42] For Spivak, "Globalization takes place only in capital and data" and "is the abstract as such," while "culture is the irreducibly text-ile," "the concrete as such."[43] These sharply binary distinctions between globalization and culture, the globe and the planet, the globe and experience lead her to claim that "Globalization can never happen to the sensory equipment of the experiencing being."[44]

Literature and the fine arts suggest otherwise. Consider Agha Shahid Ali's "Lenox Hill," in which New York's sirens sound to a migrant's ear like "elephants / forced off Pir Panjal's rock cliffs in Kashmir."[45] Consider Lorna Goodison's "Where the Flora of Our Village Came From," which arrays the vibrantly colored and scented flowers, fruits, seeds, and languages imported into Jamaica from across the globe, partly through the slave trade:

> seeds and herbs of language to flavor English;
> those germinated under our tongues and were cultured
> within our intestines during the time of forced crossings.[46]

Or consider paintings by Gauguin, Matisse, Kandinsky, Picasso, and others in which the visual sensory field is dramatically transformed by contact with Polynesian, Japanese, Muslim, and African art. I agree with Spivak's admittedly overstated point about globalization as conceived by world-systems theory ("useless for literary study—that must depend on texture"), and in a later chapter I raise concerns along these lines about some forms of "distant reading."[47] Even so, the "text-ile" and "texture" of literary culture, now and in the past, can't be quarantined from globalizing processes. This point is crucial in answering the question of what the literary humanities can add to the thinking about globalization already available in the social sciences, if they're not merely to confirm what we already know. In my view, they can uncover how, why, and to what effect imaginative writers create textures, forms, and voices that embody and reflect on the experience of living transnationally and interculturally, in poems that make freshly visible and audible, that identify and memorably compress, what it looks and sounds and feels like to live in a global age.

Before equating the global with present-day "capital and data," let's remember that the poets were there before the economists. When Seamus Heaney uses the word *globe* in a poem like "Alphabets," as we'll see in a later chapter ("The globe has spun. He stands in a wooden O"), he conjures a meaning that, hardly restricted to digital longitudes and latitudes or circuits of finance capital, recalls the terrestrial globe of the world's most famous *theatrum mundi* ("He alludes to Shakespeare. He alludes to Graves").[48] It's by virtue of magic that Shakespeare's Oberon can affirm, "we the globe can compass soon"; by theatrical trick that Prospero can make "the great globe itself" seem to "dissolve"; and because of his seared conscience that Othello thinks "the affrighted globe / Did yawn at alteration."[49] Long before the sociologist Roland Robertson suggested that globalization is not only a material and objective process but also an intensified consciousness of the world as a whole, poets were vividly imagining and imaging the globe.[50] They can help us see the fundamentally imaginative work involved in grasping global totality and our place in it. They are "worldmakers," in the seventeenth-century term that Ayesha Ramachandran revives—a term that suggests the *poiesis* of the imaginative making of the world "beyond the events and material processes that were catalysts" for such making.[51] With its long and rich literary history, the concept of the globe shouldn't be surrendered to contemporary electronic data and finance. The globe is more than global capital.

On the opposite side of the debate over globalization's historicity is the idea of the *longue durée*. From this perspective, the globalized world didn't spring like Athena fully formed from the digitized head of the late twentieth century. World historians, Sebastian Conrad observes, have been challenging "the idea of a radical and epochal break with the past."[52] For them, as Michael Lang puts it, "contemporary global integration is both exaggerated and precedented."[53] Even political scientists who emphasize today's uniqueness—social media, instantaneous news 24/7, cellphone transmissions, interconnected financial markets— concede globalization's "ancient roots," well before tweets and bots, in age-old trade routes, exploration, colonization, travel, migration, and the spread of religions and technologies.[54] There is no single point of origin for today's globality since some of the processes behind it are polytemporal and multifaceted, including intercontinental trade (e.g., the Indian Ocean), migration (e.g., from ancient Africa into Europe and Asia), conquest (e.g., the Persian Empire), and spreading religions (e.g., Christianity, Buddhism, and Islam).[55] "Throughout history," note world historians Jürgen Osterhammel and Niels P. Petersson, "supranational networks and permeable borders were the norm."[56] An archaeologist has traced globalization through ancient Mesopotamian and pre-Columbian cities; a sociologist has uncovered a world system in the Islamic Afro-Eurasian middle ages.[57] In literary studies, Susan Stanford Friedman, Wai Chee Dimock, and Paul Jay take the long-term view. Friedman, for

example, traces precedents for cultural modernism's planetary interactions back to the Tang Dynasty and the Mongol Empire.[58]

What does poetry suggest about globalization and the *longue durée*?
Poetry's long-distance influences and traveling forms furnish the philosopher Kwame Anthony Appiah with ready examples of humanity's
ineluctable cosmopolitanism—Goethe's poetic inspiration by the medieval Persian poet Hafez, Shakespeare's adaptation of the Italian form of
the sonnet.[59] In Appiah's view, cross-cultural migration and interaction
have been more the rule than the exception in human history: "you could
describe the history of the human species as a process of globalization,"
so that "trying to find some primordially authentic culture can be like
peeling an onion."[60] Indeed, poems composed even before modernity
and in places other than the West thematize a human interdependence
across cultural, political, and geographic borders. Consider, for example,
the cosmopolitan humanism in Persian poetry, a tradition dear to long-
distance readers like Goethe and Emerson (returned to, alongside several other traditions, in a later chapter).[61] The thirteenth-century Persian poet Sa'di's famous lines from the *Golestān* known as "Bani Adam"
(بنی آدم) or "Human Beings" (literally, sons of Adam) appear in a carpet
that hangs in the United Nations Secretariat Building—literally a woven
text about humanity's interwovenness. Alongside the carpet is a plate
inscribed with a translation:

بنی آدم اعضای یکدیگرند	Human beings are members of a whole,
که در آفرینش ز یک گوهرند	In creation of one essence and soul.
چو عضوی بدرد آورد روزگار	If one member is afflicted with pain,
دگر عضوها را نماند قرار	Other members uneasy will remain.
تو کز محنت دیگران بی غمی	If you have no sympathy for human pain,
نشاید که نامت نهند آدمی	The name of human you cannot retain.[62]

So much for the idea that the modern West originates ideas of global
humanity and interdependence. The poem's genre-characteristic compression, sonically and figuratively emphasized, bodies forth human
interconnectedness. Another thirteenth-century Persian poet, Rumi,
as we'll see later, also draws on the cosmopolitan elements of Muslim
thought, especially pronounced in Sufism, to define himself as beyond
boundaries—a view also enabled by the vast reach at the time of Persian
language and culture from Asia Minor and Central Asia into the Indian

subcontinent. There have been different global ages in varying degrees. Hence the indefinite article *a*, not the definite *the*, appears in this book's title.

As distinct from the "archaic" and the "premodern" *longue durée*, another view of globalization takes as pivotal the late fifteenth to the sixteenth century—the time of Rabelais, Montaigne, Shakespeare, Donne, Cervantes—with the modern extension of European trade and empire into Asia, the building of the Ming, Ottoman, Safavid, and Mughal empires, the European exploration and conquest of the Americas, the beginning of the mass enslavement of Africans and their deportation to the Americas, the development of the printing press, and the spread of merchant capitalism and of global trading networks.[63] World historians illuminate these early modern networks by tracking the circulation of commodities from East to West, such as coffee from the Arabian peninsula to Europe and the Americas, and from West to East, such as chili from South America via European explorers to Asia, along with other long-distance traversals of cotton, tobacco, diamonds, silver, gold, mahogany, tea, and chocolate, as of the traders, preachers, adventurers, and warriors, the interpreters, experts, brokers, and intermediaries who "shaped globalization."[64] But while modernity and globalization are intertwined, as in Anthony Giddens's concept of modernity's disembedding and stretching of social relations, they aren't identical.[65] For Roland Robertson, early empires represent "miniglobalization," and globalizing processes began already in ancient times.[66] Even so, he argues convincingly that modernity amplified them, and so he dates the "germinal" phase of globalization from the early fifteenth to the mid-eighteenth century, followed by the "incipient" phase of the Industrial Revolution up to the 1870s.[67]

Poetry in a Global Age is informed by both short- and long-term views of globalization, but it sides with neither. For our purposes, short-term views may not adequately account for the continuities, long-term views for the departures. Instead, this book takes the historical span from the late nineteenth century to today as its focus. Because of the popularity of the short-term view of globalization as "an economic phenomenon mediated by cutting-edge digital technologies,"[68] it may seem strange to deem also "global" the period from the late nineteenth century into the 1920s, usually considered the core of the modernist era. But as we'll see in poems examined in this book, Thomas Hardy was tracing even a provincial's imaginative extensions to South Asia and the Americas; W. B. Yeats was poetically sailing East to multiple distinct Asias; Wallace

Stevens was conceiving of planetary enmeshment of the human and non-human; Marianne Moore was situating a national identity within a kaleidoscopic array of global cultures; Claude McKay was tensely twisting between global North and South; T. S. Eliot was representing himself as a series of globally dispersed subjects; and Ezra Pound was code-switching among an array of global languages. The history of modernist poetry is, as Jernej Habjan remarks more broadly of literary genres, "not only an example but also an embodiment of the history that we abstractly term *globalization*."[69] Or perhaps we might say that such poetry is both globalizing and metaglobalizing. It both instances and reflects on global processes, both participates in them and helps us apprehend them in all their connectivity and violence, integration and scattering, enmeshment and dispersal.

If poems seem insufficient evidence for a global modernism, sociologists, historians, anthropologists, and political scientists offer further support; they call the era variously the "take-off phase" of globalization, the "first globalization," "early globalization," "an era of extensive globalization," and "an earlier phase of globalization, characterized by the expansion of transportation and communication networks, the rapid growth of international trade, and a huge flow of capital."[70] This global era, as the world historian C. A. Bayly argues, was built on earlier patterns of entanglement, most immediately the innovations and changes of the nineteenth century, rooted in the Industrial Revolution that began in the eighteenth.[71] But by the nineteenth fin de siècle, the extensity of globalizing processes was much greater than it had ever been before in human history, spanning not one or two regions but much of the world, with linkages of greater speed, density, and intensity. Though not unprecedented, an expanded, deepened, accelerated globalization enmeshed much of the planet.

At the outset of this book, it's worth specifying the key historical factors at play. During the modernist period, the transport of goods and people changed dramatically in speed, distance, and volume because of steamships and railroads, then bicycles, cars, buses, and airplanes.[72] Communication crossed much greater distances at higher velocity and in larger quantities, with the development of transatlantic cable, the telegraph, the telephone, wireless radio, cinema, and mass-circulation newsprint. In politics and diplomacy, agreements on protocols and common procedures governing mediating technologies, such as telegraphic and signaling codes, made further global integration possible.[73] In 1884 the world was divided into twenty-four time zones, a convention adopted nearly everywhere, albeit with pockets of resistance, over the next thirty years.[74] The standardization of space and time increased the coherence of the world, with the apprehension of the simultaneity of events in various regions, however distant from one another. As attested and advanced by such landmark poems as Yeats's "The Second Coming," Eliot's *The Waste Land*, and Pound's *The Cantos*, the world was increasingly experienced as a single if heterogeneous place. Large numbers of people migrated, as witnessed in poems like Mina Loy's "Anglo-Mongrels and the Rose," Claude McKay's "America," Sterling A. Brown's "Odyssey of Big Boy," T. S. Eliot's "Mélange Adultère de Tout," and Charles Reznikoff's "Early History of a Writer." In 1913, around 10 percent of the world's population consisted of international migrants, relatively many more than in 2017, when about 3.4 percent lived outside their birth country.[75] The West's imperial powers took more of the world into its orbit, carving up and colonizing Africa, Southeast Asia, and India, and diplomatically coopting Japan and parts of West Asia.[76] International charitable organizations such as the Red Cross developed, and competitions such as the Olympics and the Nobel Prize were institutionalized. The intercontinental flow of goods, labor, and capital became massive, and economic integration and exchange reached levels that by some measures exceed those of today.[77]

In 1917, a sociologist at the University of Chicago, Robert E. Park, encapsulated these trends. A contemporary witness's account deserves to be quoted at some length:

> With the extension of international commerce, the increase of immigration, and the interpenetration of peoples, the scene changes. The railway, the steamship, and the telegraph are rapidly mobilizing the peoples of the earth. The nations are coming out of their isolation, and distances which separated the different races are rapidly giving way before the extension of communication.
>
> The same human motives, which have led men to spread a network of trade-communication over the whole earth, in order to bring about an exchange of commodities, are now bringing about a new distribution of populations. . . . One may illustrate, but it is scarcely possible to estimate the economic changes which have been brought about by the enormous increase in ocean transportation. . . . Whatever may have been the immediate causes of the world war, the more remote sources of the conflict must undoubtedly be sought in the great cosmic forces which have broken down the barriers which formerly separated the races and nation-

alities of the world, and forced them into new intimacies and new forms of competition, rivalry, and conflict.[78]

Whether or not this diagnosis of the war's origins is accurate, Park understood that the "great cosmic forces" of globalization were propelling their opposite. As Osterhammel and Petersson state, the First World War represented both "convulsively intensified interaction" and the destruction of "numerous long-standing networks," in a conflict joined by several million troops from India, Australia, New Zealand, Africa, Canada, and the United States.[79] As seen in the next chapter, poetry vividly enacts the war's cross-cultural intimacies and witnesses its catastrophic destructiveness.

One measure of globalization's intensity since the nineteenth century has been, ironically, the counterforce of localization and nationalization, evident not only in the outbreak of a globe-engulfing war but also in stricter requirements for passports, more stringent policing of international borders, and the nation-state's burgeoning power and investments, its greater efforts to shape collective memories and identities. Whether early in the twentieth century or in the twenty-first, revanchist nationalisms can't be understood outside the contexts of the global flows they seek to counteract. The belle époque was paradoxically a period both of intensifying cosmopolitanism and nationalism, globalization and state building. It witnessed the growth of the world economy and of the interventionist state, of economic interdependence and protectionism, of mass migration and restrictions on immigration.[80] Scholarship has characterized the exceedingly complex relation between the national and the global at that time in a variety of ways, which might be distilled thus: (1) the national as a reaction against the global; (2) the national as the building block that makes possible the larger integration of the global; (3) the global as undermining the national; (4) the national as a modular form that diffuses globally; and (5) the national as both homogenizing and differentiating the global.[81] Each dyadic formula highlights one aspect of a vexed, multifaceted relationship that shouldn't be oversimplified. Since at least the nineteenth century, after all, there have been cycles of globalization and deglobalization, sometimes both at once.[82] Although metaphors of globalization, as Lisa Lowe argues, often include circulation, flows, transfers, spread, and migration, world historians also rely on metaphors such as holes, lumps, barriers, friction, unevenness, inertia, obstacles, and blockages to remind us that globalization's reach doesn't extend uniformly into every corner of the world and isn't a predictable progression.[83] The processes of globalization are neither linear nor unitary. Maybe we should think of the global and the national, like other elements in Yeats's schematization of history, as interlocking and interdependent gyres, "Dying each other's death, living each other's life."[84]

Termini

Thanks are due—as W. H. Auden suggests in his "Ode to Terminus," the term from which "term" derives—to this "God of walls, doors and reticence," for "giving us games and grammar and metres," "rhythm, punctuation, metaphor," and even, we might add, works of literary criticism.[85] Singular *terminus*, plural *termini*: terms both impose limits and help us get somewhere. A terminus is a limit, and a terminal condition ends in death, but we also use the word *terminal* for a train station. This book's framing critical terms—*poetry, poetics, global, transnational, planetary, postcolonial, world anglophone*—are contested. Each such "terministic screen," in Kenneth Burke's metaphor, is a *"reflection," "selection,"* and *"deflection* of reality"; each "directs the attention into some channels rather than others," makes some things more visible while screening out the rest.[86] An adequate discussion of each would require a book of its own, but since this book is devoted above all to poetry, a preliminary glance will have to do. I won't dwell on the term *poetry* here because I began my previous book exploring the question "What is poetry?" and end this one with "What is lyric?"[87] As Alastair Fowler, Virginia Jackson, and others have shown, there are many evolving genres and subgenres of poetry, and we falsify that multiplicity if we collapse all poetry into lyric.[88] Even so, as they've also shown, poets and critics tended to blur those differences in the twentieth century, the main historical terrain of this study, with what is called lyric at its center. For now, suffice it to say that *poetry* can be thought of as interlocking discursive practices such as lineation, sonic repetition, and lexical heightening that, while neither exclusive to poetry nor transhistorically consistent, have been perpetuated and remade for millennia, partly through remembrance of past examples, and partly through self-defining interactions with other genres and discourses, such as song, prayer, the law, philosophy, and science. The term *poetry* selects certain ever-shifting generic features for attention but shouldn't be hypostasized, lest we obscure poetry's historical changes and inconsistencies. *Poetics* focuses above all on how this made thing, *poiema*, works— its textures, elements, and techniques—in this case, with particular consideration of how form and history speak to one another in a time of globalization.

What do the other key terms, as Burke suggests, screen in and screen out? As we've seen, when the words *globe*, *global*, and *globalization* are used in a narrowly presentist and economic sense, they tend to screen in present-day mobility, capital, and computer connectivity, screen out impediments and longer-term continuities. Thus, Spivak states, "I propose the planet to overwrite the globe," because we should "imagine ourselves as planetary subjects rather than global agents, planetary creatures rather than global entities."[89] But the differences between *globe* and its synonyms needn't be exaggerated. Just as *planet* can be used in the particular sense of Earth and the abstract sense of a large celestial body that orbits the sun, so too *globe* can apply to Earth or any spherical body. Not that these terms are identical. *Planet* screens in the collective life forms that Earth supports, a meaning that *globe* screens out; hence *planet* and *planetary* are especially apposite in ecological contexts. *Globe* screens in spherical, cartographic representation, not only what's represented, a meaning screened out by *planet*; hence *globe* may be more useful for highlighting the interplay between the world and the ball-like maps that help us imagine it. In light of these similarities and differences, a transnational literary paradigm may benefit from an inclusive terministic field that encompasses both *planet* and *globe*.

Words like *transnational*, *postcolonial*, and *world anglophone* also screen in and out. If we're willing to give up terminological monism—the quest for the perfect field-defining word—we can work with and between such inevitably tainted terms, stereoscopically employing multiple terministic screens. As Eric Hayot observes, "Placed alongside other concepts, differently powerful and differently limited, a concept's limitations and powers spring into light."[90] Whereas *global* lays the emphasis on spherical totality, the word *transnational* more effectively directs attention to the cross-border traffic between specific nations. But *transnational* has the liability of naming and hence perhaps reinforcing what it's meant to transgress. This same liability emerges as a strength if we consider that nations, scarcely rendered obsolete by globalization, remain potent cultural, political, and economic forces. Hence *transnational* may be a useful check on the potential for universalist vacuity in the term *global*, while *global* can help check the national ghost in the *transnational* paradigm. *Global*, *world*, and *world anglophone* now enfold literary critical work of the sort that has taken place under the umbrella term *postcolonial*. *Postcolonial* has the advantage of inscribing in the term itself the historical and political conditions under which many literary cultures emerged, whereas *world anglophone* risks dehistoricizing and depoliticizing its subject, distortively equalizing the various areas of the world it encompasses. But centering attention on European colonization, *postcolonial* sometimes shortchanges the *pre-*, *para-*, and *extra*-colonial, and risks subordinating form and culture to politics, checked by *world anglophone*. *World anglophone*, however, may otherize non–First World English-language literatures, if it's used in the sense not of "literature in English" but of "peripheral literatures in English," akin to the institutionalized use of the term *francophone*. It also marginalizes translation, multilingualism, and translingualism. Although English-language poetry is this book's center of gravity, it makes forays into poetry in other languages in its later chapters and examines the hazards and promise of coupling *poetry* with *world literature*. All these terms have their strengths and weaknesses, but as postcolonial writers have taught us, the literary enactment of historical struggle in language reworks that language and its inheritances without ever fully redeeming them. For all the flaws of whatever field-encompassing terms we choose, and for all our efforts to transgress and confound them, terministic screens, when self-critically deployed, can usefully discipline and focus attention. After all, without Terminus, metaterminological meditations might never reach their end.

"Go Litel Book"

This book takes multiple angles of approach to its impossibly large subject. Grounded in a formal and historical understanding of poetry in a global age, the chapters shift methodological gears depending on the questions they pursue and the poems they study. Successive chapters engage cosmopolitan theory (chapter 1), cultural geography (2), tourism studies (3), postcolonial and modernist studies (4), world literature (5), orientalist critique (6), ecocriticism (7), cultural anthropology (8), linguistics (9), translation studies and world literature (10), lyric studies (epilogue), and flexible combinations of the above. Within the scope of these heterogeneous emphases, each poem is seen, like Read's pencil or Latour's hammer, as formally and discursively entwining various histories, geographies, and cultures. The chapters are intended both to stand on their own and to contribute to the larger argument.

Without aspiring to comprehensiveness, *Poetry in a Global Age* raises a series of questions that are meant to select tranches of its larger subject for close analysis. Beginning with the first global war, I ask in the opening chapter, How do English, American, Irish, and Canadian poets enact "cosmopolitan sympathies" for their supposed enemies in wartime, and what can we learn from their border- and culture-traversing imaginative energies, solidarities, and vocabularies? On the other side of this historical threshold, the sequence of chapters subordinates chronology to concept, since I agree with world historians about the continuities across the long twentieth century, even as I attend to historical distinctions within it. Chapters 2 and 3 open onto broad questions of global poetics regarding place, referentiality, and globalization. Calling for a dismantling of the default framework of locality, chapter 2 asks, If poems by writers as various as Lorine Niedecker, James Wright, and Agha Shahid Ali are globally refractive despite seeming to be anchored in particular places, how should we conceive the relation of poetry to place under global modernity? Exploring poems by Elizabeth Bishop, John Ashbery, Philip Larkin, Karen Press, Arun Kolatkar, and others, chapter 3 asks, If modern tourism has been one of the most powerful forces reconfiguring the relation between local and global, how are poetry's ways of representing place complicit in, yet critical of and distinct from, tourist discourse? The next pair of chapters turns to issues of formal and literary migration, particularly between the global North and South. Mapping the relation between two geohistorical literary domains, chapter 4 asks, How do postcolonial poems by writers such as Press, Goodison, and Daljit Nagra intrinsically theorize their relation to modernism, and which of various extrinsic theoretical models—diffusion, singular modernity, writing back, creolization—are most productive in charting the relationship between modernism and postcolonial poetry? Further probing the relation between local and global in poems by Moore, Nagra, and others, chapter 4 asks, Can we track the circulation of both fixed and open forms in ways that refuse the one-way diffusionist, distant-reading model of world literature, which misses the poetry of the poetry and the interaction between local and imported poetic forms?

After these discussions of heterogeneous archives of modern and contemporary poems, the next cluster of chapters narrows the focus to three individual poets whose work raises questions that nonetheless have broad implications for a global poetics. Can a canonical Western poet like Yeats be rethought as both orientalist and anti-orientalist, as not only interested in but profoundly shaped by a variety of Asian cultures—Indian, Japanese, Arab, and perhaps surprisingly, via Byzantium, Iranian—and if so, what are the repercussions for modernism and orientalist critique? Can another canonical modernist, Wallace Stevens, be reread in terms of the global imaginative capacity that Timothy Morton calls "the ecological thought," an apprehension of enmeshment on a planetary scale, further explored by later poets from Auden to Jorie Graham and Juliana Spahr? And is the poetry of even a seemingly deeply rooted poet like Seamus Heaney traversed by all five of Appadurai's global flows, and if so, what does this suggest about the relation of poetry to the world-making imagination?

The final pair of chapters re-widens the lens, encompassing a still broader literary archive. Chapter 9 pushes the boundaries of an anglophone literary study, asking what kind of home poetry has provided for bi- and multilingualism from Pound to Lorna Dee Cervantes and Craig Santos Perez; how we should think about the code-switching that's particular to poetry; and what we can learn from the analysis of poetry about code-switching, and from the analysis of code-switching about poetry. Stepping outside the book's linguistic and historical frame, the last chapter ranges across poetry in a number of different languages and times to rethink the place of poetry in the novel-dominated field of world literature, asking, Can we disaggregate the facets of (un)translatability and develop a more nuanced position than either the translation-friendly or the hard untranslatability thesis? Finally, the epilogue asks, How can we understand "lyric" without imposing on it either a too restrictive or a too universalist definition, while allowing for its transnational, translingual, and transhistorical dimensions?

Another study of the same subject would have pursued other paths and selected other poems. I had originally intended, for example, a chapter on digital poetics, but after much research, I decided its scope still remains too limited on a global scale—a situation likely to change rapidly in the coming years. To help knit the chapters together, this book returns repeatedly to close formal-historical analysis of poems and to certain poets who function almost like refrains, including Yeats, Hardy, Eliot, Stevens, Press, Larkin, Heaney, Ali, Nagra, Kolatkar, Goodison, and Walcott, but opens out onto a wider array that could have been expanded indefinitely. Long after most of us have been forgotten, these and other poets will help future readers understand what it was like to live in, and be inspired to write the poetry of, our global age.

CHAPTER 1

"COSMOPOLITAN SYMPATHIES": POETRY OF THE FIRST GLOBAL WAR

Despite the unprecedented scale of the human slaughter in the First World War, many of us continue to look a century later for signs of something beyond the death drive—the sheer murderous aggression Freud saw in it; beyond the nationalist and imperialist warmongering that proved catastrophic.[1] Little wonder that the Christmas truce of 1914—spontaneous outbreaks of fraternization along parts of the Western Front—plays an outsize role in the popular imagination. When the renovated Imperial War Museum in London reopened in 2014, it devoted a section to pictures and memorabilia from the episode. A few years earlier, the British poet laureate, Carol Ann Duffy, had recounted it in "The Christmas Truce," published in both *The Guardian* and a short illustrated book.[2] As she tells it,

> Men who would drown in mud, be gassed, or shot,
> or vaporised
> by falling shells, or live to tell,
> heard for the first time then –
> *Stille Nacht. Heilige Nacht. Alles schläft, einsam wacht* . . .
>
> *Cariad, the song was a sudden bridge*
> *from man to man;*
> *a gift to the heart from home,*
> *or childhood, some place shared* . . .
> When it was done, the British soldiers cheered.[3]

Incorporating song, the poem reflects on itself in the mirror of a sister genre. Like a poem, a song can be a *"bridge / from"* person to person across cultural and political differences. For each singer, it's affectively rooted in local or childhood experience but extends across time and space. In Duffy's account, song forms that are often mobilized to fortify dividing lines between warring sides paradoxically unite the so-called enemies:

> A Scotsman started to bawl *The First Noel*
> and all joined in,
> till the Germans stood, seeing
> across the divide,
> the sprawled, mute shapes of those who had died.
>
> All night, along the Western Front, they sang,
> the enemies –
> carols, hymns, folk songs, anthems,
> in German, English, French;
> each battalion choired in its grim trench.[4]

Did singing end the First World War? Hardly; and Duffy's wry rhymes in this passage seem to know it. As Seamus Heaney put it, "no lyric has ever stopped a tank."[5] Generated by the subalterns, the Christmas truce was quickly nixed by the generals, who couldn't countenance song-fueled outbreaks of solidarity across enemy lines. Millions more were killed in the years that followed. But the episode offers a glimpse into one of the many potentialities of song: though often an instrument of state and military power, it can also summon carnivalesque and connective energies that extend beyond the nation.

On the centenary of the Christmas truce, another remarkable depiction of it appeared, this time before a mass audience. The supermarket chain Sainsbury's, in collaboration with the Royal British Legion, made a lavish three-minute-and-forty-second Christmas advertisement that dramatizes the spontaneous truce. Like Duffy's poem and the Imperial War Museum's exhibit, the ad recalls British and German troops joining each other in carols on Christmas Eve and emerging the next morning from the trenches to share greetings, photographs, souvenirs, food, small gifts, and football games.[6] But while the TV commercial attracted millions of viewers, some questioned the ethics of selling a brand and commodities like chocolates by coopting the memory of a war that had killed millions.[7] And contrary to the massive literary, photographic, material, and historical archive of the First World War, the Sainsbury's ad occludes the war as war, despite aspiring to historical authenticity in its bilingualism, costuming, food packaging, and other details. It shows no bodies ripped open by gunfire or shells, no soldiers gagging as they die from poison gas, no one treading trenches that brim with rats and mud. By contrast, Duffy's poem, steeped in the language of First World War poetry, not only celebrates the magical interlude (a Berliner "was the first from his ditch to climb. / A Shropshire lad ran at him like a rhyme") but also spotlights "a rat on the glove of a corpse," "Men who would drown in mud, be gassed, or shot, / or vaporised / by falling shells," and "the sprawled, mute shapes of those who had died."[8] Sainsbury's commercial was hardly the first to seek financial gain by tapping into an idealism that wipes away the grimmer realities of history. Yet for all its distortions, this TV ad, like poems, songs, museum exhibits, historical books, and other recent remembrances of the Christmas truce, may have performed useful cultural work in making widely visible the solidarities between combatants on opposing sides of the First World War. Other, more nuanced, less exploitative representations may allow a fuller recovery and reexamination of these trench-spanning impulses—among them, poems written during the First World War by soldiers, officers, and civilians. Neither whitewashing in their idealism nor myopic in their realism, they provide a complex exploration of a structure of feeling for the enemy at a time of global war. They also reveal that, however compelling we may find the Christmas truce, such sentiments were hardly restricted to a single historical episode.

Isaac Rosenberg and the Rat's Leap

The word *cosmopolitan*, revived in the mid-nineteenth century and often used either to reproach or to compliment the nonpatriot, famously appears in Isaac Rosenberg's "Break of Day in the Trenches" (1916).[9] Rosenberg apostrophizes a rat that has touched his hand:

> Droll rat, they would shoot you if they knew
> Your cosmopolitan sympathies.
> Now you have touched this English hand
> You will do the same to a German
> Soon, no doubt, if it be your pleasure
> To cross the sleeping green between.[10]

Paul Fussell's judgment of Rosenberg's "Break of Day in the Trenches" as perhaps "the greatest poem of the war," or at least one of the best, still finds broad assent in Great War scholarship.[11] But in one of several departures from Fussell's groundbreaking book *The Great War and Modern Memory* (1975), recent criticism has begun to address the global dimensions of a global war—for example, recovering the experience and cultural expression of soldiers from the dominions and colonies, as of observers elsewhere far from the Western Front.[12] Rosenberg's poem reminds us that for all the traditional emphasis on the English upbringing and values behind much well-known war poetry, even such quintessentially "English" war poems sometimes also have a transnational reach, if we take seriously their "cosmopolitan sympathies."

Not that Rosenberg's "Break of Day in the Trenches" is representative. Most Great War poetry is either nationalist or pan-imperial, famously exemplified by Rupert Brooke's anglicization of earth and heaven in "The Soldier" and John McCrae's bellicose torch toss in "In Flanders Fields." Poetry is no more inherently internationalist than song. Independence fighter Ho Chi Minh, dictator Saddam Hussein, and convicted war criminal Radovan Karadžić all wrote poems, sometimes of a belligerently nationalist kind. But some First World War poets seized on and developed the cosmopolitan potentialities of poetry. Their poems are cosmopolitan in the sense not of airily transcendent detachment from bonds but of grounded attachments that span specific cultural and national differences, or what Bruce Robbins calls a "located and embodied" cosmopolitanism and Kwame Anthony Appiah a "partial" or "rooted cosmopolitanism."[13] These poems illuminate the felt or experiential basis for some of the more abstract forms of cosmopolitanism. They demonstrate that even as war impedes transnational connections, it can also be, paradoxically, a catalyst for meaningful cross-cultural encounters and reflections, for, as Jürgen Osterhammel and Niels P. Petersson say of this war, it both destroyed economic, cultural, and other networks and fostered "convulsively intensified interaction."[14] While the antiheroism of Great War poetry has been amply discussed, its overlapping but distinct capacity for imaginative solidarity across enemy lines, if often acknowledged, remains less fully explored. Appiah, Richard Rorty, Martha Nussbaum, and other philosophers have usefully conceptualized such cosmopolitan fellow feeling, but they have tended to privilege prose fiction as an especially potent vehicle for it.[15] First World War poems by Rosenberg and others demonstrate that lyric, balladic, and other forms of poetry can also function as literary spaces for enacting, and reflecting on, transnational imaginative solidarities. They anticipate what Paul Gilroy calls a "vital planetary humanism": in place of the view that "we are all sealed up inside our frozen cultural habits," they provide a "workable precedent for adopting a more generous and creative view of how human beings might communicate or act in concert across racial, ethnic, or civilizational divisions."[16] Drawing on the theoretical work of Gilroy, Rorty, Nussbaum, Appiah, and Freud, but above all attending to the poetry, I explore the ways in which Rosenberg and other poets of the Great War not only state but linguistically, formally, and thematically enact their cosmopolitan sympathies. Their poems speak to our both nationalist and globalist moment a century later and set an important example for writers such as Duffy, Seamus Heaney, and Yusef Komunyakaa. To give due attention to the poetic specificities, textures, and ingenuities of this body of work, to the poems as poems, I focus on a handful of examples, beginning with Rosenberg's poem.

Instead of touching his ears in "Break of Day in the Trenches," as Apollo touches Milton's shepherd's in "Lycidas," Rosenberg's whiskered muse goes straight to the hand that writes the poem, this living hand that, as in Keats and Whitman, reaches to us across differences of time and culture. Long before Art Spiegelman's *Maus*, Rosenberg appropriates the anti-Semitic trope of Jews as vermin—threatening transgressors of geographic boundaries, as of the borders between the living and the dead—just as he revalues the dangerously subversive "cosmopolitanism" then often ascribed to Jews.[17] Much as the rat leaps both English and German hands, so too the English word *rat*—thought to be onomatopoeic of a gnawing sound—seems to be cognate with both the German *Ratte* and the Anglo-Norman and Old French *rat*.[18] *Rats*, as in *ratsnlokh* for rat hole, is also a word in Yiddish, the High German language of Jews that was Rosenberg's mother tongue and his only language before he went to school.[19] In the etymological depth sounding and cross-lingual play that poetry often performs, Rosenberg's rat enacts "cosmopolitan sympathies" at the level of both signifier and signified. Like his insistent assonance, the word *rat* crosses the "sleeping green between" Allied and Central Powers, English and German, Gentile and Jew.

Perhaps seemingly in tension with the ideas of the global or cosmopolitan, some of the best recent criticism on First World War poetry, such as the work of Santanu Das and Tim Kendall, has drawn attention to the poetry's sensual, tactile, and local immediacy, and critics often judge war poetry inferior insofar as it deviates from documentary detail.[20] To some extent Rosenberg's poem fits the docupoetic framework: its title situates it in a specific time ("Break of Day") and place ("in the Trenches"), further accentuated in the first line, "The darkness crumbles away," which employs the present tense and pinpoints the precise moment between night and day. As Roland Robertson and Bruno Latour indicate in different ways, the global is always embodied and experienced locally, with what Latour calls "unexpected connections starting from local points," and this includes a soldier's experience of a global war.[21] But the poem quickly juxtaposes with its spatiotemporal exactitude a planetary space-time that sucks the moment into a vast continuum: "It is the same old druid Time as ever." Since the first transcripts are hand-dated June 1916, "druid Time" may refer to a specific day, the summer solstice celebrated at dawn by the druids, but the modifiers "same old" and "as ever" place this instant in a pattern of cosmic return.[22] In the first two lines, the poem straddles local immediacy and infinite recurrence, the here-now and the global anytime, before the rat's leap in the next lines resituates the poem in the tactile world of the trenches—initially called "a live thing" as if to suggest a momentary uncertainty about how to interpret this sensory experience. Bringing Celticism into the poem, the word *druid*, from a Latin word of Celtic origin for wizard, has an associative relation to the "queer sardonic rat." Long affiliated with druidism, bards in Ireland were traditionally thought to have the power to rhyme rats to death—an association between rats and Irish incantatory rhyming embedded in canonical works by Shakespeare, Jonson, Pope, and later by Yeats.[23] Wryly turning this topos on its head, Rosenberg makes his rat not the antithesis of poetry but its quintessence. The free-verse habitat he builds for his rat eschews the rat-killing toxicity of rhyme. Celtic, German, English, Yiddish—the polyglot rat carries the poem's cosmopolitan sympathies across the trenches and beyond.

As we've seen, Rosenberg's poem has one foot, so to speak, in the immediate, sensory, documentary details of a midsummer dawn encounter with a rat in a trench in France and another in the deeper time and vaster space of poetic allusion, etymological play, and cross-cultural travel. In Latour's terms, while precisely located in place and time, it is also polyspatial and polytemporal. It exemplifies poetic reportage of here-and-now haptic sensation and ocular witness, but words and phrases also extend the scope of the lyric—"same old druid Time as ever," "cosmopolitan sympathies," "the shrieking iron and flame / Hurled through still heavens." Even a locally plucked poppy can take on an extralocal and extranational significance. "In Flanders fields the poppies blow," McCrae wrote in the "war's most popular poem," as Fussell called it; but while that poem puts the poppies to belligerent use (the poppy-surrounded dead urge the living to "Take up our quarrel with the foe") and helped make them a nationalist symbol, Rosenberg recruits these same flowers for cosmopolitan sympathy.[24] As Neil Corcoran observes, the speaker's pulling "the parapet's poppy / To stick behind my ear" is an aestheticist gesture, the act of a dandy.[25] Poppies in Rosenberg's poem aren't the property of a warring side: "Poppies whose roots are in man's veins / Drop, and are ever dropping," he writes; his trope of blood-fed poppies, his buried pun on "in vain," and his mimetic enjambment ("veins / Drop") associate the poppies with human mortality, regardless of culture, creed, or nation. In the poem's final two counterbalancing lines, the speaker both brags of having rescued a poppy and ironically deflates any hope of escaping death: "But mine in my ear is safe— / Just a little white with the dust." Biblical "dust unto dust" encrusts the would-be-immortal flower, almost as if mortality were a kind of confectioner's sugar. Having drawn himself into an intimate apostrophe to an earthbound rat instead of a Romantic skylark or nightingale, the poet seems to have learned from the rat's mordant humor ("you inwardly grin as you pass"). Playing on the ancient association of flowers not only with mortality but also with poems, Rosenberg deflects any partisan meaning from the safe-seeming but death-encrusted poppy, as from his cosmopolitan rat.

Cosmopolitanism, in short, animates the poem at multiple levels: thematically, in its meditation on a shared human mortality; affectively, in its self-declared imaginative empathy; etymologically, in its cross-lingual play on "rat"; sonically, in its boundary-leaping assonance and punning; imagistically, in its border-crossing tropes; and allusively, in its linkage of what happens locally in the trenches to global space and deep time. The poem's publication history adds yet another layer to its transnationalism: recommended by the American expatriate "imagiste" Ezra Pound to Harriet Monroe, the poem journeys out of the trenches and into print in the Chicago journal *Poetry* in 1916.[26] Once a lyric like Rosenberg's made it past the barbed wire of physical impediments and military censorship, it could travel swiftly by virtue of its compactness. War poems like Rosenberg's—condensed, etymologically self-conscious, cross-nationally allusive, at once tactile and abstractive—reach toward the "human solidarity" that Richard Rorty sees as being achieved "by imagination, the imaginative ability to see strange people as fellow sufferers."[27] "Solidarity has to be constructed out of little pieces," writes Rorty, and Appiah concurs that it "isn't principle" or "a theoretical understanding of us as having a commonly understood common nature" that's the basis of cosmopolitanism but "particulars," "some small thing" that we share.[28] Rosenberg imagines his way across no-man's-land through particulars of language, sound, and image. He wrote in a letter, "I never joined the army from patriotic reasons. Nothing can justify war."[29] His and other First World War lyric mobilizations of the "little pieces" of linguistic play and sensual detail, yoked to space-skidding technique, evoke the possibility of trench-crossing solidarities.

Thomas Hardy, the Interlingual Weave, and Cross-national Mirroring

Although language was central to British, German, French, and other European nationalisms,[30] some First World War poems—highlighting the complexity of the interlingual weave out of which they are woven—turn in the opposite direction. In these poems, language figures as a signifier not of the mononational culture that must be preserved but of the cosmopolitanism embedded in English. As a Yiddish-speaking Jew who came late to English and who was taunted by other soldiers as an outsider ("why do they sneer at me?" he asks in "The Jew"), Rosenberg had ample reason for skepticism toward the mononational and monolingual ideal.[31] It is no less problematic for an Englishman of Anglo-Saxon stock who sets linguistic cosmopolitanism against narrowly nationalist dogmas of culture. The speaker of Thomas Hardy's "The Pity of It" (1915) finds in the phrases spoken by both the English and the Germans evidence of a common humanity and shared history that the war denies, developing an insight already implicit in "Drummer Hodge" (1899). In "The Pity of It," a title borrowed from Shakespeare's famous Moor, Hardy recalls having heard in the Dorset countryside "many an ancient word / Of local lineage like 'Thu bist', 'Er war', // 'Ich woll', 'Er sholl', and by-talk similar."[32] "Little pieces" (Rorty) or "particulars" (Appiah) that evidence human continuity, Low German words in England's West Country dialect—words that English soldiers "speak" on the field of battle as they clash with their supposed opposite—prove the interwovenness of the two cultures and the perversity of the conflict. Nor are these words recent imports or impositions from a foreign land. They have survived for centuries in the English countryside, since the spread in the early middle ages of Saxons into Britain. In the recent debate over whether globalization has a long history or is peculiarly modern, Hardy provides support for the long historical view, even as his own arguably modern consciousness of that long history also supports the reverse position. From the poem's perspective, the long-lived intercultural contact the words evidence is grounded in the "local" space of the lanes, fields, and farms that have changed little since the Kingdom of the West Saxons, or Wessex. Far from being opposites, regionalism and cosmopolitanism are for Hardy inseparable: the beloved countryside, though often held to distinguish the English from their foes, contains ancient deposits of migration and cross-cultural connection, of polytemporal and polyspatial enmeshment, that defy warmongering divisiveness.

In the sestet, Hardy personifies his outraged and sorrowful response to nationalist oversimplifications as a Heart that condemns those "who flung this flame / Between kin folk kin tongued even as are we." The syntactic and phonetic weaving of the word "kin" through the line becomes a visible and audible sign of the imbrication of the war-divided peoples. The phrase "kin folk kin tongued" is the culmination of a series of alliterative pairs that enact the theme of kinship and reinforces the impression of echoic or mirrorlike resemblance, as in Anglo-Saxon verse ("loamy Wessex lanes," "field and farmstead," "local lineage," "month's moon," "gangs whose glory," "flung this flame"). The adaptive Petrarchan rhyme scheme further contributes to the poem's sonic enactment of verbal kinship, most obviously in rhyming the English words "afar," "similar," and "are" with the Low German (or modern Saxon) "Er war." The sestet once more recalls "Er war" in the anagrammatic phrase that ends the third stanza, "are we." Visually split for emphasis, the sestet intones a curse in the last stanza, repudiating the German militarist "gangs" responsible for "threats and slaughters" but extending beyond them: it condemns "Whosoever" the makers of war may be to infamy ("Sinister, ugly, lurid, be their fame"), repudiation ("May their familiars grow to shun their name"), and oblivion ("And their brood perish everlastingly"). Having celebrated the extranational ingredients that make up a national language (though artificially circumscribed), the poem affirms the Germanic imprint on English as outliving nationalisms that seek their survival by violence. Since our thinking is entangled in words, Hardy's poem suggests that a narrowly nationalist view is likely contradicted by the cross-nationalism of the medium through which it is conceived. Heightening poetry's attention to the etymological layers sedimented in language, a writer like Hardy practices what we might call an etymological cosmopolitanism.

Hardy's poem entered the public sphere and even had a small place in the contentious debates over nationality and language during the war. In a letter sent with the proof of "The Pity of It," he glosses the "gangs whose glory threats and slaughters are" as "the group of oligarchs & munitionmakers whose interest is war" and who "have stirred [the German people] up to their purposes."[33] In a later letter, he states that the poem's claim that the Germans were a "kin folk kin tongued" was "indisputable," despite the fact that "letters attacking me appeared, denying it!"[34] Later he wrote to his wife for his biography: "Fussy Jingoes, who were hoping for knighthoods, attacked H for his assumption & asserted that we had no sort of blood relationship with Germany: But the Germans themselves, with far more commonsense, translated the poem & approved of it, & remarked that when relations did fall out they fought more bitterly than any."[35] Proud that his poem disproved assertions of national purity, Hardy also relished his poem's traversal of no man's land into Germany—an example of how a regionally rooted poem can travel, even in wartime, across national boundaries. Not that a few "Fussy Jingoes" were the only Britons who wanted to suppress their linguistic and kinship ties with the Germans. During the war, the once-beloved idea of the English and the Germans as cousins had become an embarrassment at the highest levels of the British state.[36] Now it was an inconvenient fact that the warring King George V and Kaiser Wilhelm II were first cousins—both of them grandsons of Queen Victoria. George V's father was a member of the House of Saxe-Coburg-Gotha, as the British royal family was known, but the king and his family in 1917 replaced that name with Windsor to disguise their German kinship. Poetry, with its deep attention to linguistic traces and crossings, functions for Hardy as a verbal space in which to reveal what politics would obscure—the irrepressible German in the English language and hence the deep interwovenness of the two peoples and cultures.

In addition to these specific filiations between the language, history, culture, and blood of the combatants, poets also explored the more general human and psychological connections between the warring sides. Such poems figure opposed combatants as prospective drinking companions, fellow sufferers, mirror images, alter egos, doppelgangers, and brothers. Although the use of such motifs could be seen as sentimental—tender-heartedness obscuring the alterity of the German other—it needs to be understood in the context of still more fantastical representations of the German soldier as irremediably monstrous and bloodthirsty. Even if battlefield attempts to whip up hatred for the enemy tended to be ineffective and soon faded, "frequently overwhelmed by feelings of empathy,"[37] some versifiers echoed and stoked propagandistic worries that "the Hun is at the gate" or, in the words of the leading poem of a 1915 anthology, addressed the Kaiser as a "loathsome, monstrous, most unholy thing."[38] Under these circumstances it was up to other poets to explore the shared humanity of the other side. Hardy reflects in a 1917 letter on German prisoners working in his garden: "They are amiable young fellows, & it does fill one with indignation that thousands of such are led to slaughter by the ambitions of Courts & Dynasties."[39] After visiting a hospital with wounded English soldiers and a nearby German prisoner-of-war camp at Poundbury, he concluded that the two scenes were sadly intertwined: "Men lie helpless here from wounds: in the hospital a hundred yards off other men, English, lie helpless from wounds— each scene of suffering caused by the other!"[40] In "Men Who March Away," published a month after the war began, he seems to upbraid himself in the voice of marching soldiers for his "musing eye," "doubt and dolorous sigh," and "much pondering," but Hardy knew he didn't "do patriotic poems very well—seeing the other side too much," and his best war poems played a role in exploring cross-cultural connections and resemblances that war making denies.[41] This affordance of poetry isn't limited to any one side or language. First World War scholarship has identified in some German and French poems an "awareness of shared suffering," even if other poems are no less jingoistic than their English counterparts: one's supposed enemy is what one poet paradoxically calls "mein Bruder Feind" (my brother enemy).[42] Poetry's facility at double- and even multisided thinking makes it suited to the "imaginative ability to see strange people as fellow sufferers" (Rorty), a capacity ascribed by Rorty to the novel, and by Martha Nussbaum especially to the realist novel: "it exercises the muscles of the imagination, making people capable of inhabiting, for a time, the world of a different person."[43] War poetry also works these muscles of the imagination.

During the Second Boer War, Hardy had already explored this theme in a dramatic monologue that directly influenced the trench-traversing cosmopolitanism of some First World War poets, "The Man He Killed" (1902). It answers "the narcissism of minor differences" with what Gilroy calls, adapting Freud, "the invaluable solidarity of the slightly different."[44] Seemingly speaking to friends in a pub, the former soldier in that poem reflects that he and an enemy soldier could have been drinking mates. But having been divided by nations into opposing infantries "And staring face to face, / I shot at him as he at me, / And killed him in his place."[45] The chiastic syntax of "I shot at him as he at me" helps establish, like "face to face," a mirrorlike relation between the two combatants that contravenes the soldier's efforts to justify the killing. So too does the connotation that haunts the idiom "in his place"—that he might as easily have been the one killed. The poem's middle stanza brilliantly captures the contradiction between the soldier's effort to impose a syllogistic logic on his action (I must kill all foes; he was a foe; therefore I killed him) and his recognition that the enemy is a falsifying construct, that he and this other soldier have more commonalities than differences:

> 'I shot him dead because—
> Because he was my foe,
> Just so: my foe of course he was;
> That's clear enough, although
>
> 'He thought he'd 'list, perhaps,
> Off-hand like—just as I—
> Was out of work—had sold his traps—
> No other reason why.'

Humane doubt ripples beneath warrior certitude in the stuttered "because." Instead of conveying confidence, the assertive language betrays itself in the mildly absurd marching assonance of "my foe, / Just so: my foe," the repeated declarative "he was," the syntactic inversion in "my foe of course he was," and the assertions of obviousness in "of course" and "That's clear enough." After the cross-stanza enjambment dramatizes the soldier's hesitation ("although"), his warm insight into shared humanity collides with the icy machinery of war, splintering his syntax in a spray of dashes ("Off-hand like—just as I— / Was out of work—had sold his traps—"). In the final stanza, he tries to laugh off the contradictions of war as "quaint and curious," but the seemingly dismissive phrase echoes the grief- and eventually madness-stricken narrator of "The Raven"; the disjunction between murderous violence ("You shoot a fellow down") and fellow feeling (a person "You'd treat if met where any bar is, / Or help to half-a-crown") isn't easily resolved.[46] Through the parallelisms and elasticities of poetic technique and the rich particulars of recognition, Hardy builds up the "little pieces" of human solidarity across the sharp divisions of war.

Robert Service's Demotic Cosmopolitans

During the First World War, other poets took up the theme of potential drinking buddies forced by war to kill each other. Although the topos of camaraderie and friendship has often been remarked as a salient feature of wartime poetry and prose,[47] these poets turn it inside out—extending human solidarities across the national divisions that were meant to contain them. Robert Service, a poet often referred to as the Canadian Kipling or the Bard of the Yukon, witnessed combat

as an ambulance driver, a stretcher bearer, and a reporter for Canadian
newspapers, such as the *Toronto Daily Star*, which printed his often vivid
accounts of suffering on the Western Front. In "A Song of the Sandbags,"
another dramatic monologue by a soldier, this time reflecting as bullets
whiz past, the speaker addresses his friend Bill in rollicking rhythms
suited to a drinking song—perhaps oddly at first, but in keeping with the
poem's finale. The poem concludes with a rousing hope for a day "when
war will cease, / When 'Ans and Fritz and Bill and me / Will clink our
mugs in fraternity"—a cross-national braiding of names that Carol Ann
Duffy would resume nearly a hundred years later in her poem about the
Christmas truce ("Harry, Hugo, Hermann, Henry, Heinz . . .").[48] For
Service, a Canadian poet who never gave up his British nationality, the
wished-for community of the transnational pub replaces the imagined
community of the nation. As in poems by Hardy, Owen, and other wartime writers, the cross-national solidarity is partly constituted around
opposition to the rich and powerful who "made" the war ("them as lies
in feather beds while we kips in the mud" and "them as makes their for-
toons while we fights for 'em like 'ell").[49] "Cosmopolitan solidarity from
below" is Gilroy's phrase for such engagements of humble origin, "articulating cosmopolitan hope upward from below rather than imposing it
downward from on high," unlike the high-altitude, high-register cosmopolitanism of the elite and powerful.[50] Or, to literalize Homi Bhabha's
phrase, it is a "vernacular cosmopolitanism," spoken in the language and
rhythms of a commoner "Hunkerin' down" as shells burst overhead.[51]

From its beginning, the poem captures the oddity of people killing
their likenesses—a sameness emphasized by repeated comparatives
("just the same as," "as much as"):

> And though I strafes 'em good and 'ard I doesn't 'ate the Boche,
> I guess they're mostly decent, just the same as most of us.
> I guess they loves their 'omes and kids as much as you or me;
> And just the same as you or me they'd rather shake than fight;
> And if we'd 'appened to be born at Berlin-on-the-Spree,
> We'd be out there with 'Ans and Fritz, dead sure that we was right.[52]

A key line pivots at the balladic caesura between its four beats boasting
a capacity for murderous violence ("And though I strafes 'em good and
'ard") and three undoing the presumed justification ("I doesn't 'ate the
Boche"). In another kind of pivot, the speaker imaginatively projects
himself into the minds of German soldiers who see him as the enemy

and who have similar domestic loves, showing up the fundamental arbitrariness ("if we'd 'appened") of military and national division. In recent
decades, certain strands of postcolonial, anthropological, and affiliated modes of scholarship, prizing difference, have sometimes rejected
notions of human commonality across cultural lines as falsifying. Appiah
worries about "a professional bias toward difference" that treats "cross-
cultural sameness" as "the null result."[53] Gilroy also worries that "invocations of incommensurable otherness command such wide respect"
that "much of what passes for radical and critical thought rests on the
notion that the very aspiration toward translocal solidarity, community,
and interconnection is tainted."[54] A poem such as Service's should give us
pause: an overemphasis on cultural difference can sometimes serve violent and militarist agendas, while the capacity to imagine oneself as the
enemy other may be vital to thinking beyond the divisive nationalisms
that breed war. Poems with cosmopolitan sympathies can, in Gilroy's
terms, "help in seeing how we might invent conceptions of humanity that
allow for the presumption of equal value and go beyond the issue of toler-
ance into a more active engagement with the irreducible value of diversity within sameness."[55]

In another dramatic monologue in ballad meter, "Only a Boche,"
Service represents in intricate and engrossing detail an Allied soldier's
process of imagining his way into a single German soldier's experience.
Although his blue uniform and exclamations mark him as French, most
of what he says and does could as easily be English or Canadian. The
title captures his initially dismissive and condescending response to the
wounded man he has helped rescue from the front lines: "what's the use
of risking one's skin for a *tyke* that's going to die?"[56] Contractions ("we'd,"
"what's," "he's"), interjections ("I say"), and exclamations ("what a time
we had!") help create the immediacy of offhand, casual speech (109).
But as Gilroy writes in another context, the soldier-speaker is eventually "able to grasp the common humanity that binds him shamefully to
the prisoner's fate."[57] A moment of intimate contact with the wounded
body ("we were wet with blood and with sweat!") marks the beginning
of a transition toward recognizing this member of the other tribe as kin:
"We carried him in like our own" (109). Tense shifts from past to present
("Now there he lies in the dug-out dim"), when the Allied soldier starts
to play bridge and listens to the wounded man's deep breathing (110). Service represents the card players in painterly detail, with the candlelight
falling on the clay walls and "faces bristly and grim" (110). But it is the

candle beside the wounded soldier that draws the Allied soldier, and he stands still—mimicked by the repetitive, stand-still verse—and stares:

> And his face is white in the shabby light, and I stand at his feet and
>   stare.
> Stand for awhile, and quietly stare, for strange though it seems to be,
> The dying Boche on the stretcher there has a queer resemblance to me.
>
> It gives one a kind of a turn, you know, to come on a thing like that.
> It's just as if I were lying there, with a turban of blood for a hat,
> Lying there in a coat grey-green instead of a coat grey-blue,
> With one of my eyes all shot away, and my brain half tumbling through;
> Lying there with a chest that heaves like a bellows up and down,
> And a cheek as white as snow on a grave, and lips that are coffee brown.
>   (111)

This "turn" in the soldier's contemplation of his opposite occurs appropriately at the midpoint of the poem, as he swivels from seeing the German as other to seeing him as his double. Words like "turn" and "resemblance" are especially relevant to the specificities of poetry—verse (from the Latin *versus*, "turning"), trope (from the Greek *tropos*, "turn")— and indeed the speaker who first sensed the German might be "like our own" now sees him more immediately as the mirror image of himself. Poetry's tools seem well suited to such reflections on cross-cultural resemblance. In this poem, metaphor and simile play an intimate part in the soldier's process of conjoining himself with his alter ego. The intensification of the figurative language ("chest . . . like a bellows," "cheek as white as snow," "lips that are coffee brown") not only vivifies the descriptive language with imagistic detail but also suggests an Allied soldier whose consciousness is drawing ever closer to his opposite, seeing him no longer as an anonymous churl or "*tyke*" but as an immediate human presence.

Still more intimate resemblances proliferate when the soldier recognizes that the wounded man wears a wedding ring "like me," and that he has a locket "around his neck, as around my own," with a woman's face on one side and the angelic faces of three girls on the other. The soldier feels competitive with this other ("He has beaten me; for me, I have only two"): Service indicates that the opening toward cosmopolitan sympathy isn't without its difficulties. But the ensuing stanza, in which the soldier muses on this dying man, "Crushed in the mutilation mill, crushed to a smeary clod," leaving "anguish" behind among his loved ones, reveals at least as much sorrow over the wounded victim's approaching demise (112). Having intensely humanized his opposite, the soldier returns to playing cards, as if in an effort to block out the thought of the dying man. In the midst of war, an attitude of cross-state solidarity is fragile, always at risk of collapsing under the weight of countervailing forces. The penultimate stanza repeatedly reverses the direction of the soldier's thought: with its multiple uses of "but," it flips between the idea of the wounded man as like himself—relief at not having been "The man who gave him his broken head, the sniper who fired the shot"—and the idea of him as other, reinforced by divisive clichés: "War is war, and he's only a Boche" (113). But as he curses the bizarreness of war ("*Mon Dieu! Quelle vache de guerre*"), the card game from which the wounded man has distracted him becomes all the more clearly a figure for the arbitrariness of war's divisions and the chance of its outcomes (113). Although Service has received less literary-critical attention than other war poets, "Only a Boche" and "A Song of the Sandbags" are vivid dramatizations of a soldier's tentative breakthrough to the shared humanity of the enemy other. Transnational solidarity isn't pregiven, grounded in a metaphysics of human equality and rationality; rather, it's built up, in Rorty's terms, out of "little pieces" like the locket and wedding ring; in his words, it's "the ability to see more and more traditional differences (of tribe, religion, race, customs, and the like) as unimportant when compared with similarities with respect to pain and humiliation—the ability to think of people wildly different from ourselves as included in the range of 'us.'"[58] When suffering is conceived on too vast a scale, writes Susan Sontag, "compassion can only founder—and make abstract"; the concrete image is more likely to open us to "the pain of others."[59] Service's poetry enacts the imaginative birth and extension of such human solidarity.

Wilfred Owen's Strange Doublings

If Service's poetry is seldom examined in any detail, Wilfred Owen's "Strange Meeting" is probably the best-known example of a war poem of cosmopolitan sympathies. Like other poems I've discussed, it instances what Gilroy calls "'vulgar' or 'demotic' cosmopolitanism," finding "value in the process of exposure to otherness," "through proximity to strangers."[60] Whereas the high modernists Eliot and Pound developed their polyglot literary cosmopolitanism out of anthropological, philosophical, and philological excursions, war poets like Owen built their "vulgar" or "vernacular" cosmopolitanism out of on-the-ground contact and imaginative connection with the enemy "other." Ultimately, these two distinct strands of early twentieth-century poetry intersect in opening up the nation- and culture-crossing affordances of poetry. Owen's "Strange Meeting" shares with other war poems and other modernist works the motif of the enemy doppelganger or alter ego. In its deployment of the motif, "Strange Meeting," like these other war poems, unwinds what Desmond Graham calls "the central concept of militarism, that of the enemy."[61] Its dreamlike qualities invite comparison with Freud's nearly contemporaneous thinking about the doppelganger in his 1919 essay on the uncanny. Discussing E. T. A. Hoffmann's use of the doppelganger, Freud writes of a kind of telepathic process whereby "the one possesses the knowledge, feeling and experience in common with the other, identifies himself with another person, so that his self becomes confounded, or the foreign self [*das fremde Ich*] is substituted for his own—in other words, by doubling, dividing and interchanging the self."[62] In Owen's poem, as in Hardy's and Service's, the double is someone the soldier has been taught to regard as the enemy to be killed, yet also someone whose inner thoughts and feelings seem fused with his own. In keeping with the Freudian uncanny, the doppelganger is at once strange and familiar, friend and foe, homely (*heimlich*) and unhomely (*unheimlich*). Although some of Freud's essays more directly consider the First World War, his famous piece on the uncanny—with its examination of how the "foreign self" can be swapped with one's own—helps illuminate an important aspect of the psychology of war.

"Strange Meeting" is often seen as something of an anomaly in Owen's corpus: it has few documentary details of the sensory experience or vocabulary of trench warfare. Instead, it deliberately foregrounds its identity as visionary artifice. "It seemed," begins the poem, its first words emphasizing the "as if" of poetry, "that out of battle I escaped / Down some profound dull tunnel, long since scooped / Through granites which titanic wars had groined."[63] This is an exercise of the poetic imagination, and removal from the battlefield allows reflection on central questions about poetry's relation to war and killing. The underground tunnel as a site for human solidarity has a long history: warring medieval knights, if their tunnels met from opposite directions, fought but then embraced their foe as brothers-in-arms.[64] Owen's speaker tunnels his way toward his dead alter ego, the man he killed, and the string of assonances ("Down some profound dull tunnel, long since scooped") sonically enacts that tunneling. The groaning and moaning pararhymes (*groined/groaned, grained/*

ground, moan/mourn) create a dirge-like sonic field in which the soldiers meet. The discordant harmonies of Owen's pararhymes also suggest the doublings of the uncanny: the sound is the same, yet not quite, like the alter ego in relation to the speaker. So too images and words repeat, but with a difference, as in these nearly duplicative lines: "And by his smile, I knew that sullen hall,— / By his dead smile I knew we stood in Hell." Words with positive connotations ("smile," "hall") twist in another direction ("sullen hall," "Hell"). The other soldier lifts his hands "as if to bless," apparently endowed with the heavenly power of consecration, yet his blessings are oxymoronically placed in hell. Similarly, the exceptionally rich intertextual echoes of poetry, from Homer, the Bible, and Dante to Wordsworth, Keats, and Shelley, which have been the main focus of critical commentary on the poem, create the uncanny effect of phrases almost already heard, as if in a sonic echo chamber. "Strange friend," the speaker hails his double, a phrase that encapsulates the familiarity yet strangeness of the uncanny and at the same time intertextually enacts it, as an echo of Tennyson's apostrophe to Arthur Hallam in *In Memoriam* 129. In sum, the poem is not just a narrative mimesis of a soldier's encounter with his alter ego across cultural difference: it encompasses this story in a resonant poetic arena that amplifies it at multiple levels— imagistic, sonic, verbal, and intertextual.

More than half the poem is devoted to the dead soldier's speech about his abortive hopes for poetry—as expression of Romantic longing for the immortal embodiment of his feelings, both "glee" and "weeping," and as witness to the truth and sorrow of war, "the truth untold, / The pity of war, the pity war distilled." The enemy soldier's statement of poetic principles bears a close resemblance, of course, to Owen's—in his draft preface and elsewhere—and so we read it as an ars poetica, an inset statement of literary aspirations concretely realized in this very poem. By placing his ars poetica in the mouth of an enemy soldier, Owen flouts the logic of military confrontation and cultural differentiation. Implicitly, this poem is both the fulfillment of that soldier's unfulfilled dream and an expiation for having killed German soldiers equipped not just with guns but with imaginations. Since the enemy soldier-poet cannot cleanse the blood-clogged machinery of war and cannot pour out his spirit through poetry instead of wounds, it is up to his addressee to take up where his alter ego left off.

"I was a German conscript, and your friend," reads the final verse paragraph in draft. Although it omits the national specification, the revised line is even blunter in its self-confrontation:

'I am the enemy you killed, my friend.
I knew you in this dark: for so you frowned
Yesterday through me as you jabbed and killed.
I parried; but my hands were loath and cold.
Let us sleep now. . . .'

In a miracle of poetic miniaturization, Owen compresses the torment of being a "conscientious objector with a very seared conscience," straddling in one line "enemy" and "friend," the brutality of killing and the intimacy of apostrophe.[65] The unusual phrasing of "frowned . . . through" (instead of, say, "frowned at") turns a fighting soldier's subject-denying look into a violent piercing, the existential correlative of his piercing a body with a weapon. After the high literary reverie of the poem's middle section, the word "jabbed" jabs through the diction with a sudden violence. Like the phrase "slashed and dumped" at the end of Seamus Heaney's "The Grauballe Man," the words "jabbed and killed" suggest a physical brutality that ultimately exceeds the compass of art.[66] Owen's poem attempts to think and feel its way across or underneath what Rosenberg called "the sleeping green between," yet at the same time, in its harsh summoning of military violence, it tallies the difficulty of ever merging with one's uncanny double. As we already saw in Service's "Only a Boche," the wartime path to transnational solidarity is fraught.

Heaney, Yeats, and Irishing Owen

In a First World War poem written long after Flanders guns fell silent, Heaney follows up key implications of Owen's enemy-befriending poem and can thus help extend the discussion of cosmopolitan sympathies, both to the war's poetic aftermath and across the Irish Sea. In an essay on W. H. Auden's poetry, Heaney singles out "Strange Meeting" to make the case for Owen's influence:

> Pararhyme, Wilfred Owen's technically simple but emotionally complicating innovation, had been applied by Owen most systematically in the poem "Strange Meeting" which dramatized an encounter between doubles and lamented the collapse of trust in progress and all such melioristic notions. Owen had further declared that "All a poet can do today is warn." So, poetically and historically, it is proper that Auden's poem of admonition ["Venus Will Now Say a Few Words"] should also employ pararhyme and thereby echo the earlier one.

The verse lines, therefore, reach like sounding lines down to the mud of Flanders, back to that "conscientious objector with a very seared conscience." Owen's joining up, his training of recruits to kill and be killed, the terrible strain which he inflicted on himself by maintaining a patriotic courage in face of personal revulsion and trauma—all this did not release him from the recognition that nothing would be improved by his sacrifice. This too made Owen a true precursor of the Auden of "Spain," the poet who connived in what he deplored, that which he would at first call "the necessary murder" and then, in a more generally lenient revision, "the fact of murder."[67]

Key words in this remarkable passage connect Heaney's work to Owen's and to an Owen-influenced Auden: the phrase "the poet who connived in what he deplored" recalls the tensely conflicted speaker of Heaney's "Punishment," "who would connive / in civilized outrage" while recognizing his tribal complicity.[68] Like "Strange Meeting," much of Heaney's poetry of the Troubles both acknowledges strong bonds within a cultural group and at the same time works toward recognizing the humanity of the other, acknowledges its complicity in violence and yet attempts to enact cross-cultural fellowship. His mention of the "terrible strain which he inflicted on himself" recalls a poem of Heaney's more specifically anchored in the First World War, "In Memoriam Francis Ledwidge," at the end of which the speaker addresses the Irish republican poet fighting on behalf of the British Empire. Heaney hints at the transformation of the emotional and political strains of such self-divisions into the musical strains of verse: "In you, our dead enigma, all the strains / Criss-cross in useless equilibrium."[69] It is telling that Auden should be the mediating figure between Heaney and Owen. Auden's "In Memory of W. B. Yeats" brilliantly fused Owen with his Irish antithesis, the poet who had haughtily dismissed him as "unworthy of the poets' corner of a country newspaper" and "all blood, dirt & sucked sugar stick."[70] Auden's elegy brings together the seemingly irreconcilable attitudes, I argue elsewhere, of Owen's pity ("the seas of pity lie / Locked and frozen in each eye") and Yeats's tragic joy ("With your unconstraining voice / Still persuade us to rejoice").[71] So too Heaney's "In Memoriam Francis Ledwidge" makes peace between Owen and Yeats. "Strange Meeting" is clearly the paradigm for the cosmopolitanism from below of the poem's ending: "You were not keyed or pitched like these true-blue ones / Though all of you consort now underground." However divided they may have been by nationality and politics, in death the British and Irish troops belong to a postmortem, postnational community below the earth's tensely divided surface. Earlier in the poem Heaney Irishes Owen's war-groined under-earth:

> I think of you in your Tommy's uniform,
> A haunted Catholic face, pallid and brave,
> Ghosting the trenches with a bloom of hawthorn
> Or silence cored from a Boyne passage-grave.

Heaney layers the trenches of the Western Front with a mythical Celtic Otherworld sometimes imagined as underground, the Stone Age passage tombs of the Boyne Valley, and the site of the 1690 battle that proved fateful for Protestant-Catholic relations in Ireland for centuries to come. Fighting on behalf of the British Empire, the Irish Catholic soldier—his "haunted" face "Ghosting the trenches"— is already almost otherworldly in his agonized displacement.

Although the poem has been accused of a distortive Irish republican bias, such views are complicated by the prototype for Heaney's out-of-sync Catholic: a Protestant soldier who also died in the First World War. Heaney models his soldier on Yeats's Irish airman, imagined as soliloquizing on the verge of death ("Those that I fight I do not hate, / Those that I guard I do not love").[72] Like the Protestant airman, Major Robert Gregory, the Catholic infantryman fights without hating his supposed enemies and without devotion to the empire he supposedly fights to protect. In his collocation of Yeats and Owen, Heaney reveals how the soldier of "An Irish Airman Foresees His Death" resembles the nonhating combatant who encounters his German double in "Strange Meeting." Like the soldier elegized in "In Memory of Major Robert Gregory," who as an artist "had the intensity / To have published all to be a world's delight" but died before he could, Heaney's First World War soldier has more potential than realized success as a poet.[73] Not accidentally Heaney quotes not Ledwidge's poetry but his prose. As David Goldie observes, "one has to dig deeper to uncover . . . a distinctive, complicating Celtic element" in Ledwidge's poetry, unlike his prose.[74] For the Heaney of the Ledwidge elegy, as for the Owen of "Strange Meeting" and the Yeats of the Gregory elegies, a war poem also functions, strangely enough, as an ars poetica. The Irish airman exemplifies a principle of the Yeatsian lyric: to arrive at a state of mind that has the intensity, freedom, and sprezzatura of a heroic figure encountering death. In Owen's "Strange Meeting," as we've seen, the enemy soldier ventriloquizes Owen's first

poetic principles. And in Heaney's Ledwidge elegy, the tensile equilibrium of poetry is projected onto the elegized soldier-poet. The word
"useless" has been read as a pejorative, as if Heaney were despairing over
Ledwidge's self-division and alienation, but the assertion "all the strains /
Criss-cross in useless equilibrium" might encapsulate something important about poetry for Heaney: in it, he affirms the purposiveless purpose
of art, as Kant called it, the refusal to submit the conflicted texture of
his poetry to political or national causes. Not that Heaney's poetry is
altogether apolitical. Part of the power of a poem such as the Ledwidge
elegy is its ability to make peace between old wartime antagonists, such
as Owen and Yeats, an Englishman and an Irishman, as Owen and other
First World War–era poets such as Hardy, Rosenberg, Service, and Owen
had done before him. Engaging literary ancestors from the era of the
First World War, Heaney's elegy foregrounds poetry as a space in which
cultural and national differences can be straddled and negotiated. Poetry
can be an intercultural force. Yeats and Owen may not have known they
were one another's doppelgangers, but in its complexly allusive texture,
Heaney's poem enacts a strange meeting between these seeming antagonists, who, like the Irish and British soldiers or like the German conscript
and his strange friend, consort in a topographical inversion of Mount
Olympus.

Mary Borden and the Limits of Poetic Cosmopolitanism

Of course the poetic cosmopolitanism I've been tracing isn't without
its limitations. These cross-national solidarities may have global rever-
berations but they are still largely enacted within a European and North
American sphere. None of these poems aspires to solidarity with, say, a
Turkish soldier in the Ottoman army. Despite the African, West Asian,
South Asian, and other non-European involvements with the war, our
published poetic archive is largely European. Moreover, these solidarities are largely between men. When the speaker of Siegfried Sassoon's
"Glory of Women" extends his sympathies across no man's land, it is an
emphatically male comradeship that the poem has established, in contrast to the women who have stayed home and nurtured their sons' fantasies of valor:

O German mother dreaming by the fire,
While you are knitting socks to send your son
His face is trodden deeper in the mud.[75]

Seeing the soldiers as fighting supposedly on behalf of women metonymically hinged to the motherland, Sassoon and other poets typically circumscribe their cosmopolitan sympathies by gender. Focused
on the antiheroic reality principle of inglorious death, Sassoon can't
allow himself to recognize poetic solidarities with the German mother's
"dreaming" and "knitting," and thus akin to the British mothers who
"mourn our laurelled memories" earlier in the poem. In his memoirs
Sassoon recalls an "impulse" to wipe the mud from a dead German's
"blond," "good-looking," "gentle face"; the intimate language of connection may be charged, as it is in some First World War poems, with a sensual energy.[76] Whether homoerotic, homosocial, or an ambiguous combination, such bonding isn't extended to women.

The mud in which the German soldier's face is trodden is the anti-
individuating element at the end of Sassoon's poem, as in much First
World War literature, such as Mary Borden's "The Song of the Mud,"
part of a three-poem sequence "At the Somme" published in the same
year as Sassoon's "Glory of Women" (1917). But as if in riposte to Sassoon's chiding of women for their ignorance of the enveloping mud,
this American poet, well acquainted with trench conditions by her running a French hospital near the Somme, amply demonstrates an awareness of the menace of the "frothing, squirting, spurting liquid mud."[77]
Borden's work helps qualify the notion that First World War poetic cosmopolitanism is exclusively male, as do other counterexamples, such
as Mina Loy's poem on a Viennese war casualty, "Der Blinde Junge." In
Borden's poem, the mud is described in accretive free-verse repetitions
as covering, spreading, coating, caking, soaking, mixing, crawling, filling,
sucking—among many vivid verbs and verbals that convey its supreme
force—until the mud is personified as a devouring monster:

> This is the song of the mud, the obscene, the filthy, the putrid,
> The vast liquid grave of our Armies—
> It has drowned our men—
> Its monstrous distended belly reeks with the undigested dead—
> Our men have gone down into it, sinking slowly, and struggling and
>   slowly disappearing.[78]

Borden's fluid, recursive, ever-expanding and contracting lines evoke
the environmental catastrophe of the war as obliterating human distinctions. Although "our" may well suggest primarily the Allies, the final
poem in the sequence, "The Hill," explicitly extends that empathy to the

other side: Borden focuses on a German prisoner who stumbles forward: "I could see the pallid disc of his face thrust forward and the exhausted lurching of his clumsy body. I could feel the heaviness of his despair," and "it seemed to me that his hate was like a curse crawling through the grave of our nation."[79] Here again, the poet's cross-cultural affinities are circumscribed: they do not extend beyond Europeans to the Black, turbaned horseman who is driving the German prisoner forward. Racialized differences may have been even harder to traverse than were intra-European national divisions.[80] That said, Borden's poem does cross the divide between enemy combatants, as in the other examples we've explored. And at the center of the sequence's poetic cosmopolitanism is the nondifferentiating force of the mud, an environmental disaster resulting from the wartime human devastation of the earth's surface. In this, Borden anticipates a recent shift in postcolonial studies away from an emphasis on difference and incommensurability and toward what Paul Gilroy, Dipesh Chakrabarty, Ian Baucom, and others have identified as a human species vulnerability in the face of planetary environmental destruction.[81] Already on the battlefields of the First World War, Borden glimpses a human commonality that will become ever more evident in later stages of what will be called the Anthropocene.

* * *

There are various ways of taking the measure of the global dimensions of the first global war. One approach, as Santanu Das has urged, is the recovery of the literary and cultural output of parts of the world that contributed enormous numbers of soldiers to the war, including 1.4 million Indians, as well as the work of poets from the dominions.[82] Another is to observe, as does Edna Longley, the extranational connections of many of the key poets: "Rosenberg's and Sassoon's Jewishness (at opposite ends of the class-spectrum) should be reckoned with, as should [Charles] Sorley's Scottish, [Robert] Graves's German-Irish, and [Edward] Thomas's Welsh parentage," and indeed Sorley's "To Germany" and Thomas's "This Is No Petty Case of Right or Wrong" have much in common with the poems I've been discussing. Longley writes, "Owen *et al.* were no less internationally minded than poets later called 'modernist,'" as evidenced by Sorley's seven months in Germany, Owen's two years in France, Thomas's alertness to the Irish Revival and Frost's American experiments, and Rosenberg's and Ivor Gurney's training in the international vocabularies of the visual arts and music.[83] A third approach would be to trace in rare poems such as Kipling's "Epitaphs of the War" the global expanse in the cultural and toponymic references, ranging from a "Hindu Sepoy in France" to Cairo, Halfa (Sudan), Canada, London, Taranto (Italy), Thessalonica, and Stratford-upon-Avon. The couplet poem about the Hindu sepoy suggests both the limits ("This man in his own country prayed we know not to what Powers") and the possibilities ("We pray Them to reward him for his bravery in ours") of cross-cultural understanding during the war, particularly at a time when few poems evidence the extension of such understanding across the divide between colonizer and colonized or between global South and North.[84]

I have tried to supplement these approaches to the Great War with yet another, exploring formally and conceptually how poems enunciate, perform, and vivify cross-military cosmopolitanism. Perhaps the best way to sum up the significance of poetry of cosmopolitan sympathies is to outline the key tenets of militarist nationalism that it subverts. First, instead of being the quintessence of evil, the abject who exemplifies all that is monstrous and dangerous, the enemy becomes, through the play of likenesses that has a special home in poetry, one's kin or mirror image. Second, instead of representing the soldier as fighting for his national culture's uniqueness, cosmopolitan war poetry breaks down the narcissism of minor differences and rhymes soldiers across national lines. Third, instead of representing a soldier as vindicating his culture's superiority by his rightful victory over his opponent, such poems dissolve any notion of one nation's higher claim to honor, freedom, justice, righteousness, and poetry by showing the opposing soldiers to be, in Service's words, "just the same," for all their differences—examples of what Gilroy calls "the irreducible value of diversity within sameness."[85] Although humanities scholarship has sometimes prized cultural difference over commonality, we mustn't lose sight of the importance of these poetic constructions of sameness within difference, as of difference within sameness (viz. simile, metaphor, rhyme); they exhibit what Appiah calls connections not *"through* identity but *despite* difference."[86] Setting works "in the service of planetary humanism and global multiculture" against the commonplace "that some cultural differences are so profound that they cannot be bridged," Gilroy writes that such "acts of solidarity articulate a practical riposte to the despairing twentieth-century voices that wanted to discredit this sort of gesture by arguing that the openness and undifferentiated love from which it derives is tainted, ignoble, and unpolitical."[87] This "spirit of connection," as he calls it, "might even be recycled and employed to transform our understanding of how translocal solidarity can work so that we are more informed, more sensitive, less intimidated, and more likely to act."[88] At times of resurgent xenophobic nationalism, it is worth remembering how wartime writers—true to the tools of their craft—have worked poetry's figurative, linguistic, imagistic, sonic, and thematic possibilities to establish connections between combatants. Their triumph is to have found ingenious ways to shape language and poetic form into tunnels that join what war divides.

CHAPTER 2

THE LOCAL POEM IN A GLOBAL AGE

Is there any cultural haven from the onrush of globalization? Poetry may be it, according to the statement of purpose for *Windfall: A Journal of Poetry of Place*:

> Against the current tide of globalization, we posit its opposite, 'localiza-
> tion.' . . . [O]ur identity is tied to place: We don't know who we are unless
> we know where we are. . . . Rootless, detached people are dangerous. On
> the other hand, sanity happens when people understand that where they
> are is who they are. . . . A poetry of place is a poetry which values locales,
> which sees and lets the reader experience what makes a place unique
> among places.[1]

The editors cite poems such as Dylan Thomas's "Fern Hill" and James Wright's "Lying in a Hammock at William Duffy's Farm in Pine Island, Minnesota" as prototypes, and since 2002 they have published hundreds of other poems of place. They present poetry, when uncorrupted by a "modernist" treatment of "the phenomenal world as though all places were interchangeable,"[2] as uniquely suited to an intimate relation to place, its rooted stability the opposite of the dislocated and deranged mobility of global modernity. To write a poem of place is to ground one-self in a cherished spot that confers and confirms self-knowledge, whole-ness, and uniqueness. Although Bruce Robbins doesn't mention poetry when he discusses the "anticosmopolitan jargon of the authentically particular and the authentically local," the allure of such ideas about the poetry of place is encapsulated in his remark about "the miniatur-izing precision of 'locality,' with its associations of presence and unique-ness, empirical concreteness, complete experience, and accessible subjectivity."[3] Lyric poetry miniaturizes by virtue of its compression, and when this intimate verbal locality is made to stand for the enclave of a physical locality—as mirrored in a fully present and singular subjectivity, and as given voice in a lyric speech-act—the correspondence would seem to provide a stay against the dislocative pressures and gigantic scale of globalization.

Loco-descriptive or topographical poetry—the poetry of specific places—has a long and distinguished history in English, including such prototypes as John Denham's "Cooper's Hill" (1642), William Wordsworth's "Tintern Abbey" (1798), and other representations of named landscapes, prospects, great houses, and ruins, among other locales, a subgenre or mode that goes back to antiquity and has also flourished in French, Italian, and other languages. Irish poets such as W. B. Yeats, Seamus Heaney, and Paul Muldoon have combined this subgenre with the *dinnseanchas*, the Irish tradition of the place-name poem. With Denham as his example, Samuel Johnson defined "*local poetry*" as "a species of composition . . . of which the fundamental subject is some particular landscape, to be poetically described with the addition of such embellishment as may be supplied by historical retrospection or incidental meditation."[4] Subsequent critics have often echoed Johnson's factual emphasis. According to Robert Arnold Aubin, "'topographical' poetry aims chiefly at describing *specifically named actual localities*."[5] Bringing the critical model up to date in a wide-ranging survey, Stephanie Burt shows that contemporary examples have much in common with poems written several hundred years ago. She distills the mode's "formal signals: the name of the place, often in the title, sometimes with a preposition— 'At,' 'Above'; deictics ('Here,' 'there,' 'now'); present tense (we stand, walk, ride along with the poet, right now); and a structure involving movement or perspective, following the eye or the body as it moves across or through the site."[6] Although a few critics, such as John Barrell and Bonnie Costello, have drawn attention to the extra-empirical aspects of topographical poetry, Burt elaborates the Johnsonian view in arguing that the authors of such poems "are drawn to fact" above all and flaunt their ability to "say something true about something real."[7]

Like war poetry and occasional poetry, topographical poetry would seem one of the varieties of post-Romantic lyric best suited to the reorientation of poetry studies since the 1980s toward what could be called loco-materialist approaches. Overturning the placeless, abstractive, aestheticist proclivities of the New Criticism, deconstruction, and associated methods, several different strands of poetry criticism have sought

to rejoin poetry to the particulars of historical place. Critical regionalism is one such approach. Books like *Identifying Poets: Self and Territory in Twentieth-Century Poetry* (1994), *A New Theory for American Poetry:
Democracy, the Environment, and the Future of the Imagination* (2004), and
Local Attachments: The Province of Poetry (2010) explore poems in relation
to the historical sites from which they emerge and that they describe,
whether in Scotland, Northern Ireland, London, the Lake District, New
York, the American Midwest, Saint Lucia, Australia, or elsewhere.[8] The
editors of the essay collection *Locations of Literary Modernism: Region
and Nation in British and American Modernist Poetry* (2000) propound the
examination of "the interface," the "relationships between modernist
poetry and place."[9] Because topographical or scenic poems are preoccupied with local particulars, they may be especially suited to such treatment. Influenced by ideology critique, a second critical stance, the new
historicism, is more skeptical toward the literary than is regionalism, but
it shares the premise that such poetry should be understood in relation
to discrete locations at particular times under specific conditions. One
of the most influential accounts of a loco-descriptive poem in recent
decades is Marjorie Levinson's pathbreaking reading of "Tintern Abbey,"
which examines Wordsworth's poem in relation to the site's social history, as found in guidebooks and other period documents. Although
Levinson shares the Johnsonian and regionalist idea of local poetry as
the empirical description of an actual place, she comes to the opposite
conclusion: as measured against other records of local fact, Wordsworth's
poetry is found wanting, its "determinacy" watery, its documentation of
the place's "socioeconomic conditions" deficient.[10] While lauding the
brilliance of Wordsworth's formal achievement, she faults his "erasure,"
"exclusion," "suppression," and "displacement" of the sociohistorical
facts of locality.[11] More recently, she has defended the new historicism
against the strictures of twenty-first-century "new formalist" critics.[12]
In seeking to elaborate and update loco-materialist critique for poetry
studies, Levinson and the new historicists share common ground with
some critics working in a third area, known as the "new lyric studies."
They, too, often foreground factual place and, conversely, the obscuring
of historical and referential specificity, especially by certain reading
practices. In her influential book on Emily Dickinson, Virginia Jackson
rigorously explores ways to "retrieve some of those material historical
referents" that New Critical readings have abstracted and effaced, such
readings "detaching" the poems "from whatever circumstances clung" to
the original act of address or reference.[13]

Whether praising poetry for its quintessential localism, like the editors of *Windfall* and regionalist critics, or faulting it and lyricist approaches for insufficient grounding in local fact, like some proponents of the new historicism and the new lyric studies, loco-materialist approaches have sharpened the real-world edge of poetry commentary. This has been a valuable corrective to some of the overly abstractive and dehistoricizing tendencies of poetry criticism. It can be illuminating to consider a poem in relation to the particulars of a place it names, addresses, and lyricizes—especially, as I argue below, if poetic place is pluralized rather than homogenized, understood to be multiple and intersectional rather than discrete and contained; it should be read as no less a locus of "contemporaneous plurality" and "coexisting heterogeneity" than physical space, to borrow the words of geographer Doreen Massey.[14] However, after several decades of loco-materialist work, a corrective to the corrective has emerged. Repudiating mimetic and restrictively historicist approaches, Jonathan Culler's *Theory of the Lyric* (2015), for example, argues that lyric may be less good at delivering an empirical knowledge of a time and place than it is at providing specific kinds of value, memory, performativity, and pleasure; and a number of other critics have recently been rejuvenating attention in poetry studies to lyric and to dynamic models of form.[15]

Valuing historical inquiry within the transhistorical study of genre and form, I limit my field of investigation to English-language poems of place mostly in the twentieth and twenty-first centuries, when global modernity has shaped the spatial imaginaries of the loco-descriptive mode. But in light of the form-centered countercorrective and Caroline Levine's argument that forms have specific "affordances," inherent potentialities and limitations, I would ask, Are the forms most characteristic of poetry as well suited to the documentation of place as are the forms typical of certain other genres, such as the naturalist novel, documentary prose, the guidebook, and journalism?[16] What is the downside of applying frameworks to poetry—whether in praise or critique—that privilege loco-materialist referentiality, determinacy, and indexicality? Aren't poetry's frequent metaphoricity, compression, and indirection, its formal corrugation and extravagance, and its rhetorical performativity and self-reflection likely to look evasive, selective, and misleading? Against such standards, will many poems seem deficient in straightforwardly mimetic or indexical reference, even when locally descriptive? Do such frameworks risk making it harder to delineate what poems achieve when not hewing to documentary norms? How might poetry complicate ontological and epistemological assumptions to the effect that localities are self-identical, bounded, and knowable from within? It may be time to explore such questions from the perspective of a polytemporal, polyspatial poetics and consider a different way of understanding poetry's relation to place, particularly as the transnational turn in the humanities reconfigures our understanding of how localities are enmeshed within the global.

Entangled Places in Place Poems

Let's begin with a particularly well-known example of a modernist poem of place:

> The apparition of these faces in the crowd;
> Petals on a wet, black bough.[17]

Bearing a place-situating title that resembles that of other loco-descriptive poems, Ezra Pound's "In a Station of the Metro" also has the mode's indexicality (the deictic "these") and its focus on the immediate experience of a specific, named place. But from a loco-materialist perspective, its extreme compression—after earlier attempts in thirty lines and then half that number—would seem an evasion of social and historical fact;[18] its metaphoric juxtaposition of faces with petals, a diversion from urban specificity; its figurative view of faces as an "apparition," a dissolution of the real into ghostliness. Who are these crowds of people in the Paris Metro, and what historical factors are mobilizing them, and what is the speaker's socioeconomic relation to them, and which station is this? (It's Concorde, according to Pound.)[19] On such questions, the poem is information-poor, despite recent efforts to contextualize it in the local history of the Metro.[20] While the poem summons a local placetime, its allusive engagements with ancient Western precedents (the leaf-like dead in epic underworlds) and East Asian art (petals on a bough) and literature (the adaptation of haiku) also dislocate it from the specific social, material, and economic conditions of early twentieth-century Paris. But these transhistorical and translocational displacements are integral to the poem as poem—a vehicle that affords rapid and radial imaginative movement. By virtue of its metaphoric density, long formal memory, allusiveness, verbal self-consciousness, concision and compression, selectivity and economy, and layering of different times and places, poetry—at least in comparison with realist novels, journalism, guidebooks, and histories—accords less fully with referentially determinate critical templates. If this is true even of a poem aspiring to "Direct treatment of the 'thing,'"[21] then what of poems all the more richly embroidered and extravagantly embellished, from Gerard Manley Hopkins and W. B. Yeats to Charles Wright and Lucie Brock-Broido?

A further obstacle for one-point readings of poetry in relation to place is the larger implicit field of reference out of which each loco-descriptive poem carves its attention. The Paris Metro, itself a global matrix, is but one of innumerable locales available to Pound, some of which infiltrate his poem. Even when poetry "values locales" and scrupulously attends to "what makes a place unique among places" (*Windfall*) or specifies a locale's "socioeconomic conditions" (Levinson) and "material historical referents" (Jackson), the horizon against which the minutely local is engaged and cherished—intensifying this attachment—is extralocal. As Massey observes, place is often defined by its "counterposition to the outside," but its "linkage *to* that 'outside' . . . is therefore itself part of what constitutes the place."[22] Consider the localist American prototype adduced by the editors of *Windfall*. The view seen from a hammock at a named farm in a small Minnesotan town in James Wright's poem ("Lying in a Hammock at William Duffy's Farm in Pine Island, Minnesota") is "a place unique among places" by virtue of not being the other places against which it is implicitly defined, such as large cities or areas outside the Midwest. The pleasure of the minutely detailed title and the poem's dwelling on a highly specified rural locale is in part a consequence of energetically holding at bay other sites, particularly the anomie of the globalized metropole. The local isn't a pregiven fact that exists only in relation to itself; it's a relational construct, the microcosmic obverse of the global, on which it obliquely depends. According to Bruno Latour, "no place is self-contained enough to be local,"[23] and despite the foolhardy effort to "'resist globalization'" and exist "without relations with the rest of the world," "being local and having an identity" cannot "possibly be severed from alterity and connection."[24]

Moreover, in poetry, which often has an especially long memory of form and language, a named and denoted place is frequently mediated through a tissue of radial connections to poems of other times and places. This is perhaps obvious in the *Windfall* editors' other exemplar of the poetry of place, Dylan Thomas's "Fern Hill," which evokes a Welsh farm and country house in no small part through the rich play of resonances with biblical, pastoral, Romantic, and other intertexts, let alone the high art poetry of its rhapsodic rhythms and artful syntax. But it is also true of so bare a poem as James Wright's. "Lying in a Hammock at William Duffy's Farm in Pine Island, Minnesota" provides access to a quintessentially Midwestern American site via the detour of classical Chinese poems. Wright said he was interested in "setting down the stages of a mood the way the old Chinese poets did sometimes" in a poem that was "clearly an imitation of that Chinese manner" and that, as Robert Bly noted, playfully borrows the Chinese convention of an elaborate title.[25] Pound was, of course, a leading conduit of East Asian poetic techniques into English via poems such as "In a Station of the Metro," which juxtaposes petals and a black bough, as Wright's first two lines juxtapose a butterfly and a black tree trunk: "Over my head, I see the bronze butterfly, / Asleep on the black trunk." The poem's surprising last line, "I have wasted my life," which Wright said he later discovered in a poem by the eleventh-century Persian poet Ansari, has been understood as a rendition of Arthur Rimbaud's "J'ai perdu ma vie."[26] Yet more intertextual echoes have been traced to Georg Trakl, Rainer Maria Rilke, Thomas Gray, and others.[27] Though Wright's poem may seem unwaveringly faithful to a specific place in its full self-presence, the lyric constructs that place through a polytemporal, polyspatial web of phrases, conventions, images, and techniques attached to other places, from classical China to modern Germany and France. It can be difficult to keep a poem fastened exclusively to a place; even as it evokes a site, it darts in multiple directions. As any one poem is enmeshed with other poems, and as any one place is bound up with other places, the combination of the two—a single place in a single poem—multiplies entanglements with numerous unseen places elsewhere.

Poetry Atlas

An especially graphic example of the indexical conception of poetry's relation to place is the website *Poetry Atlas: Mapping the World in Poetry*, and so it may be useful to pause over and critically examine it, chosen from among many proliferating digital sites for pedagogical, scholarly, and popular use that it resembles. *Poetry Atlas* is built around an interactive Google map of the earth, dotted with red pushpins, one for each place and its poems, as well as white quills and scrolls for nations and their poems. The home page has boasted: "Poetry Atlas is mapping the world with Poetry. Already we have thousands of poems about places. We believe that there is a poem about almost every place on earth. We are mapping this poetic geography for the first time."[28] Visitors are invited to submit favorite poems, the text of which will pop up with a couple of clicks of a mouse, beside a magnified map of the area and a pushpin. The website's pushpins literalize the conception of poetry as a form of "local attachment," in Fiona Stafford's valorizing term.[29]

As a visitor to the site, you can touch down in the middle of the Pacific Ocean, where the 1905 poem "Waikiki Beach" is attached to O'ahu, cross the ocean and the continental United States to the Massachusetts coast, site of Sylvia Plath's less cheerful "Suicide Off Egg Rock," before traversing the Atlantic to Thomas Hardy's poems set in Dorset and Cornwall, such as the toponymic elegy "Beeny Cliff." You can range all the way from Thomas Pringle's "Cape of Storms" at the southernmost tip of Africa to Joseph Horatio Chant's "The Taj of Agra" in India to Rudyard Kipling's "Buddha at Kamakura" in Japan. Countless poems are pinned to localities, which are assumed in aggregate to make up the globe. The pinning of each wriggling poem to a place enacts digitally and visually what is presumed to be poetry's indexical referentiality.

Yet the approach to and assumptions about poetry reflected in *Poetry Atlas* and other such sites have their limitations. Maybe the most obvious is the distortion involved in collecting hundreds of poems for European and North American countries and few for most countries in Africa, Asia, Latin America, the Caribbean, and Oceania (and those few often written by westerners), as if digitally mapping Macaulay's notorious opinion that "a single shelf of a good European library was worth the whole native literature of India and Arabia."[30] Needless to say, the disproportions are far greater than those produced by the Mercator projection. Take Iran, for example. Despite being the land of Ferdowsi, Omar Khayyam, Saʿdi, Hafez, Simin Behbahani, and other world-famous poets, Iran had but three poems in *Poetry Atlas* as of 2020, and they were written in the nineteenth century by a Briton and an American, while the poems attached to countries such as the United States, the United Kingdom, France, and Italy have numbered in the hundreds.

Yet even if these orientalist disproportions were righted by a slew of additions, intractable problems would remain. Poems may not be "about" places in the same way that a pin can be pushed into a real or digital spot or that GPS can calculate a position. On closer inspection, the poems in *Poetry Atlas* often defy the topographical singularity ascribed to them. If you should alight near Calcutta, for example, a Thomas Hardy poem pops up. Hardy wrote a poem about Calcutta?, you ask in astonishment. Well, not exactly. It turns out that the poem is also "about" many other places. In his poem "Geographical Knowledge," a sailor's mother scarcely knows her way around local sites near England's southern coast, such as Black-moor Vale and Yellowham Wood,

> But that Calcutta stood this way,
>   Cape Horn there figured fell,
> That here was Boston, here Bombay,
>   She could declare full well.[31]

To borrow Anthony Giddens's term for an effect of globalizing moder-nity, this mother's consciousness is "disembedded" from her local habitat by her attachment to the faraway sites where her son sails.[32] Rather than fixing a spot, such a poem stretches across global networks laid by power and commerce. Under modernity, place poems bear witness to the rela-tionality of each site to its global others, as in Henri Lefebvre's descrip-tion of the networking and interpenetration of spaces.[33] Pin a poem to a place and it's likely to squirm away. The poetic principle of alliteration, moreover, appears to be more important than geography in Hardy's pairing of sites like Calcutta and Cape Horn, Boston and Bombay. At least as central to the poem's attention as any extrinsic locus is the verbal locus of the poem itself.

Granted, Hardy's ballad, merely mentioning Calcutta, may not fit the traditional definition of a scenic or topographical poem and so may be something of an anomaly. But dozens of Yeats's poems in *Poetry Atlas* would seem to be perfect examples of the poem-as-synecdoche-for-locality, fastened to cities, towns, and provinces from Galway and Sligo to Dublin, and historical sites from the Hill of Tara to the Rock of Cashel and Thoor Ballylee. A pin bears down on Lough Gill in Ireland, and when we click on it, the text of Yeats's "The Lake Isle of Innisfree" appears, along with a picture captioned "*The magical Isle of Innisfree is a real island lying in Lough Gill in Sligo.*" When teaching at the Yeats Inter-national Summer School, I, too, have taken such pictures of the wooded isle; boating there with my wife and some students, I once even won a free Guinness for reciting the whole poem from memory. But the seem-ingly seamless join between poem and place has a few wrinkles. Henry David Thoreau's Walden, which Yeats acknowledged as his model for his lakeside idyll, is at the very least a transatlantic detour through which the poem wends its way in representing the Irish isle.[34] Should there be an inset photo in our Irish photo of Walden Pond? Should the pushpin have a second prong that spans the Atlantic? And what about a third prong in the opposite direction, across the Irish Sea, making this pushpin a tripod?

The poem's Irish pastoralism is inextricable from the urban English "pavements grey" against which it pits itself, in accordance with Adorno's conception of lyric as the idiosyncratic obverse of reification and commodification: the poem took its inspiration from Yeats's encounter with a fountain in a London shop window's ad, his Lough Gill imaginatively releasing those captive waters.[35] Moreover, for all its obvious national implications as a dream of Irish freedom, the longed-for autonomy is also a supranational dream about the self-sufficiency of the arts, vivified by the poem's interlaced sounds ("lake water lapping with low sounds by the shore").[36] This poem is not "about" Innisfree in the same way that the pop-up picture is. Indeed, it functions poorly as a pre-GPS technology for marking locality; a photograph or map might have been more useful than a poem when, many years after writing it, Yeats rowed a boat around the lake to show Innisfree to his wife, but finally had to give up, unable to find it.[37] Though named after specific sites, such poems are compromised in their geographic mapping function both by their enmeshment with places elsewhere and by their preoccupation with themselves.

Similarly, a poem that harks back to Yeats's lyric, Claude McKay's migrant's-eyed, window-gazing "The Tropics in New York," though pinned to Manhattan in *Poetry Atlas*, complicates the loco-descriptive paradigm by being split among its Irish and English models, its titular urban American setting, and the West Indian fruits and landscape for which it longs, let alone its creolization of British and Irish pastoral models and of the elegiac quatrain with Jamaican fruits:

> Bananas ripe and green, and ginger-root,
>   Cocoa in pods and alligator pears,
> And tangerines and mangoes and grape fruit,
>   Fit for the highest prize at parish fairs. . . .[38]

McKay's poem also tropicalizes an earlier poetic superimposition of places, Wordsworth's "The Reverie of Poor Susan," in which birdsong on a London street occasions a hallucinatory vision of a former rural life's mountain, trees, and mist—even "a river flows on through the vale of Cheapside."[39] In "The Tropics in New York," the interpenetrating spaces traverse still greater cultural and geographic distances. "What is acting at the same moment in any place," writes Bruno Latour, "is coming from many other places, many distant materials, and many faraway actors. If we wanted to project on a standard geographical map the connections established between [one site] and all the places that are acting in it at the same time, we would have to draw bushy arrows."[40] Poets like Wordsworth, Hardy, Yeats, and McKay were making visible the plurality and translocality of space well before its theorization by Latour, as also by geographers like Massey and Lefebvre, sociologists like Giddens and Roland Robertson, and anthropologists like James Clifford and Arjun Appadurai, whose insights can in turn help criticism retrace such poetry's spatial bearings.

Recalling Wordsworth and Yeats, McKay's poem helped propagate later Caribbean and Black British trans-loco-descriptive poems that lexically and formally span metropolitan England and a remembered Caribbean, as well as the American influence of the Black Arts Movement. In Guyanese poet Grace Nichols's "Island Man," not yet pinned in *Poetry Atlas*, a Caribbean emigrant wakes to what he thinks is the sound of waves, only to realize it's London traffic: he

> Comes back to sands
> of a grey metallic soar
> > to surge of wheels
> to dull North Circular roar.[41]

In the sibilants "sands," "soar," and "surge," Caribbean waters sonically flow together with London traffic.

In a global age, scenic poems have radial dimensions. Modernity intensifies the cross-locational propensities of poetry: even when describing a single site, a poem's allusions, formal structures, generic inheritances, affective work, and etymological self-consciousness spin outward. Poems differ from more straightforwardly mimetic genres in the density of their formal mediation. Little wonder that site-specific ballads written in the same time period often have more resemblances with one another, however widely dispersed their subject matter, than with other discourses or media marking the same site. And when a poet such as Kipling writes poems about places from Kamakura and Mandalay to South Africa and France (all pinned in *Poetry Atlas*), they are more akin to one another than they are to other poems about these places, such as poems written by longer-term inhabitants working out of other poetic traditions. The formal contrivance of poetry, its transnationally mediated relation to its subject matter, its verbal weightedness and reflexivity complicate its locational "aboutness." Sonically and sometimes visually overdetermined, long-memoried and densely layered, a topographical poem may be as much "about" how it sounds and looks, "about" the linguistic, literary, and generic history from which it evolves, as about a single spot. Although critics today are wary of the biographical fallacy, there seems little hesitation about the risks of anything like a locational fallacy. Yet locations and poems each lead their own distinct if intertwined lives, and the life of the poem, though often partly elucidated by the life of the place, shouldn't be collapsed into it any more than it should be into the life of the poet.

Gloco-descriptive Poems of the Global South

Let's consider in more depth some poems from the global South that have been hailed for their attachment to and preservation of the local, for their resistance to the dislocative pressures of modernity. In the postcolonial world, where modernity and globalization are often experienced as alien intrusions from former colonizing powers in the global North, poetry is sometimes seen as having an especially vital role in enshrining the authenticity of previously colonized localities. A contemporary collection of poems that has been praised along these lines is focused on one locale and even bears the name of a single neighborhood in south Bombay (Mumbai): Arun Kolatkar's *Kala Ghoda Poems* (2004). But even as it demonstrates localization, it also renders its complexities. The book opens with a highly localized poem about a traffic island as described in the imagined voice of a stray dog. This device extends the loco-descriptive poem, but it also ironizes it: "I like nothing better / than to lie down here, at the exact centre / of this traffic island // . . . that doubles as a parking lot."[42] From its start, the poem intensively specifies the local as an experiential space, "the concrete surface hard, flat and cool / against my belly," and at the same time gently questions the idea of poetry as the preserve of self-contained locality ("traffic," "parking lot").[43] Playing on the dislocations of the local, the poem is sited in this spot where "the equestrian statue / of what's-his-name / must've stood once," King Edward VII and his black horse, the "kala ghoda" after which the neighborhood was named, but that king is ironically a monarch from a distant land, and, in a further irony, his statue was relocated elsewhere half a century earlier.[44] Attentive to the historical warps embedded in postcolonial place-names, Kolatkar's poem suggests that this carefully described local site is here and not here, both located and dislocated from itself. Giddens writes that place under modernity is increasingly *"phantasmagoric"* because "locales are thoroughly penetrated and shaped" by "distanciated relations" and

"What structures the locale is not simply that which is present on the scene."[45] "The local site," writes Latour, "has been *made to be a place* by some other locus through the now silent mediation" of actions and materials.[46] Many modern and contemporary poems demonstrate globalization's enmeshment of the local with the foreign. But well before the accelerated globalization of place in the late twentieth century, colonialism's cross-hemispheric ventures had, in anticipation of global modernity, already displaced sites such as Kala Ghoda from themselves. In the amusing artifice of Kolatkar's poem, the canine speaker traces his matrilineal descent to the importation of foxhounds from England in 1864 and his patrilineal descent to the mythical dog beloved by Yudhisthira and apotheosized in the *Mahabharata*, a mixture not unlike that of this piebald city and this Sanskrit-chanting, rockdrill-resounding, modernist-sequencing poem. The poem's aesthetic thickening provides a more accurate set of coordinates for postcolonial space than a punctual localism could achieve, showing even the circumscribed space of a traffic island to be traversed by diverse cultural vectors from afar.

In an incisive reading of *Kala Ghoda Poems* that draws on Michel de Certeau, Anjali Nerlekar argues that Kolatkar's "vehemently local," "walking documentation of city spaces provides a resistant alternative" to a "top-down, panoramic gaze" and global cartographies.[47] Like a number of other recent poetry critics, she is anxious to show poetry to be on the side of the local over against the global, globality being associated with mobility, rootlessness, and neoliberalism. But while Nerlekar brilliantly teases out the local elements of the poem's idiosyncratic mapping of space, Kolatkar's "intensely local" portrayal of urban life also presupposes and vivifies the global, and its investment in the local is inextricable from its globalism. The longest segment in the book is the thirty-one-part sequence "Breakfast Time at Kala Ghoda," which returns to the stray dog's ("pi-dog's") traffic island. Before the poem can dwell on that spot, however, it frames it in global time-space. A large "clock displayed outside / the Lund & Blockley shop across the road," a British imperial inheritance that brought with it the standardization of time across widely separated zones, is emblematic of the worldwide frame that makes it possible for the poet to imagine his south Bombay experience in relation to faraway sites at exactly the same hour.[48] As Lefebvre writes, "the *worldwide does not abolish the local*."[49] Or as Robertson suggests, the global does not exclude the local but partly creates it; "the local is essentially included within the global," and "globalization, defined in its most general sense as the compression of the world as a whole, involves the linking of localities."[50] More, not less, visible against global space-time are local differences, such as in Tokyo:

> where they're busy polishing off
> sliced raw fish,
> sushi balls and tofu with soy sauce;
>
> and the emperor's chopsticks are poised,
> at this very moment,
> over Hatcho Miso, his favourite dish.
>
> In a restaurant in Seoul,
> a dog is slowly being strangled
> before it's thrown into a cooking pot.[51]

The poem adds to these cameos a man condemned to execution in Texas eating his last steak and cheeseburgers, someone cooking potatoes over llama dung in Peru, another person hanging reindeer meat in Alaska, cosmonauts finishing breakfast in a Russian spaceship, an elderly Jewish Holocaust survivor in Poland looking at matzos on a table, four dalits in rural India being forced by their upper-caste landlords "to eat / human excreta," and an array of Arab, Persian, American, and other cuisines being served in Bombay's restaurants.[52] It's within this dazzlingly transculinary and translocal context that the poem clears a space for its minute focus on breakfast at Kala Ghoda: various poor people arrive at the traffic island to eat idlis, or rice cakes, including a pegleg, a shoeshine boy, a paralytic, a legless hunchback, and "the Demosthenes of Kala Ghoda" (an epithet hardly limited to south Bombay).[53] When the street vendor opens the box to dispense her idlis, they are metaphorically transformed into an erotic spectacle, "an orgy, / a palpitating hill / of naked idlis // slipping and sliding" over each other.[54] Instead of being a "top-down, panoramic gaze" that the poem disavows, the global is shown to be the arena that allows the peculiarities of localities to emerge in their full particularity—whether those peculiarities are shimmering or grotesque, inviting or repulsive. Under modernity, a loco-descriptive poem is also a gloco-descriptive poem.

By definition the site of coexisting cultures and histories, postcolonial space is perhaps especially vivid in the transnationalization of loco-descriptivity. Although the great house poem has long purveyed rootedness, stability, and national tradition, often mirrored in the architecture of a poem, it becomes a different kind of loco-descriptive space for post-colonial writers to reinhabit. In "Small-Scale Reflections on a Great House," A. K. Ramanujan reads the great house not as securely enclosing within its walls a singular tradition but as microcosmically instancing India's and his own poetry's cultural and religious porosity:

> Things come in every day
> to lose themselves among other things
> lost long ago among
> other things lost long ago. . . .[55]

Here, as throughout the poem's layered and stretched syntax, the repetitive diction and prepositional series demonstrate this process of accretion. Library books, neighbors' dishes, genetic predispositions—they all come into the house and never leave, or if they do, they are sure to return,

> like the hooped bales of cotton
> shipped off to invisible Manchesters
> and brought back milled and folded
>
> for a price. . . .[56]

Under Victorian-era global capitalism, India is no self-sufficient preserve; it is thoroughly penetrated by Britain's exploitative demand for cotton it can import, process, and resell, and even the imperial heart of the cotton industry is pluralized ("invisible Manchesters"). The great house is a site through which goods, histories, and stories circulate; the intimately local, such as the Indian cotton that returns as "cloth for our days' / middle-class loins," is stitched together with colonial and postcolonial spaces elsewhere, as is this poem of recirculation, animated both by the Hindu idea of samsara and by modernist intertexts.[57]

Other postcolonial poems represent outdoor sites as no less syncretic and sedimented than such indoor spaces. In Lorna Goodison's "To Us, All Flowers Are Roses," the local Jamaican landscape is written over with the cultural deposits of a multitude of other sites, as demonstrated by place-names of African origin (Accompong), as also of Irish (Armagh), English (Stonehenge), Amerindian (Arawak), German (Berlin), Asian (Bamboo Pen), and others:

> There is everywhere here.
> There is Alps and Lapland and Berlin.

Armagh, Carrick Fergus, Malvern
Rhine and Calabar, Askenish. . . .[58]

Space, as Massey argues, should be conceived not as surface but as "a meeting-up of histories," its elements "imbued with temporality."[59] Whether in its residential, urban, scenic, or national register, the postcolonial loco-descriptive poem reveals the history layered in place, as also in the language and forms used to evoke it.

Gloco-descriptive Poems of North America

But the gloco-descriptive poem isn't exclusive to the postcolonial world. In topographical poems, North American poets, for example, also show the local to be porous and multilayered. Like other poems of place, A. R. Ammons's "Corsons Inlet" is named after a specific site that it describes, in this case in southeast New Jersey. But the idea of a bounded place that can be reproduced in mimetic detail comes under suspicion, albeit scientific rather than cultural. Global economic, human, and cultural flows, as we've seen, complicate ideas of loco-descriptivity; science also erodes the illusions of a bounded locality. From a scientific perspective, "in nature there are few sharp lines," so a place called Corsons Inlet cannot be set off from all other places, especially if the poet wants to make his work accord with the unboundedness of natural space:

> I have reached no conclusions, have erected no boundaries,
> shutting out and shutting in, separating inside
>   from outside: I have
>   drawn no lines:
>   as. . . .[60]

This last assertion about not drawing lines is delivered with a knowing wink as it cuts off at the end of the line, in syntax that flows and spills over line breaks. If natural places have "no / lines or changeless shapes," but are ceaseless process, "the working in and out, together / and against, of millions of events," then even the loco-descriptive poet who orders the world in free-flowing lines must acknowledge, "I have perceived nothing completely."[61] The toponym Corsons Inlet names a real place where the poet in real time walks and muses, but it is a place suffused with other places and times. Even as he revivifies the place poem, Ammons dissolves loco-descriptivity into Heraclitean flow.

Some poets may seem to resist this flow of the natural world by anchoring their work in the built and bounded environment of a city, as did Charles Olson in the Gloucester, Massachusetts, of *The Maximus Poems*, on the model of William Carlos Williams's *Paterson*.[62] Attentive to Gloucester's geographical features, early history, and human relationships, Olson's *Maximus* poems have often been seen as championing, as philosopher J. E. Malpas writes of other poets, "the place-bound character of human life and thought."[63] But despite Olson's seeming "localism" (a term he disavowed), he affirms, no less than Ammons or Heraclitus, that "a thing does flow,"[64] setting his city in a global time-space, both geological and human, that highlights the instabilities of place. In huge leaps from line to line, such as "just last week / 300,000,000 years ago" (19), his poetry dramatizes how widely separated places and times can unexpectedly converge and collide. The cover of the second volume of *Maximus* features a map of Earth before the continents broke apart and drifted, and Gloucester is seen in Olson's later poems as having moved northwest

> to arrive
> where she is   from her old union with Africa
> just where the Canaries lie off shore (601)

Surprisingly, Gloucester's neighbors include northeastern Africa and southeastern Europe. Far from being stably positioned, as on a site like *Poetry Atlas*, every place on Earth, seen in a geological time scale, is on the move. Proposing that we replace "nearness as the measure of things" with "distribution," geographer Nigel Thrift observes, "A multiplicity of 'scales' is always present in interactions."[65] The relentless dissolving, breaking, and spiraling of Olson's lines and associations poetically suggest the flow not only of land masses, as he indicates in a poem initially laid out in a spiral: "Migration in fact (which is probably / as constant in history as any _one_ thing" is pursued "by animals, plants & men … / –and gods as well" (565).[66] Just as continents, life forms, and beliefs migrate, his poems often migrate back in time from civilization to civilization, from contemporary Americans to English settlers, early Amerindians, Portuguese seamen, ancient Greeks, Egyptians, and Phoenicians. He uncovers a single city's global accretions of geology, flora, culture, language, and migration. As Malpas concedes, and as Olson's open-form *Maximus* poems demonstrate, places "interconnect with other places— thus places are juxtaposed and intersect with one another," and because

of their "open-ness" they "turn outwards to reveal other places and locations."[67]

In a late poem Olson identifies with stones, which instead of being
markers of self-contained places quickly turn out to be "generous
... walls," "roads," and "passage-ways," routes to places elsewhere (633).
Other poets may seem more intent on fastening their poems to the
rocky substantiveness of geological place. Gary Snyder frequently works
the analogy between rock and poem, and his early poems are often cut
like the mountainside trails he helped carve in the Pacific Northwest.
In "Milton by Firelight," localized in Yosemite National Park by the tag
"Piute Creek, August 1955," Snyder, as Michael Davidson puts it, "attempts
to return words to the condition of stone and to keep his eyes focused on
the sensual surface of things."[68] Milton's *Paradise Lost* is quoted but dismissed as "a silly story / Of our lost general parents, / eaters of fruit," with
no relevance to the rocky immediacy of this quintessentially American
natural scene, the "vein and cleavage / In the very guts of rock."[69] Con-
trasting that mythical generality with the hard specificity of rock and
of "green apples" (real, not just symbolic apples), Snyder ends the poem
by recycling but demythologizing his English predecessor's phrase
"a summer's day," here but a natural image. But of course the impression of natural stoniness is itself a literary trick; the intertextual contrast
with Milton's myths and language helps produce the illusion of straightforward materiality. Snyder's Yosemite site depends on the English literary text it supplants—yet another example of the complex interrelations between literary siting and citing. Moreover, Snyder borrows other
exogenous literary resources to describe the scene:

> Sleeping in saddle-blankets
> Under a bright night-sky
> Han River slantwise by morning.
> Jays squall
> Coffee boils

The Han River, featured in Tang dynasty poems, is superimposed on
American geography, ironically, to localize the description. The mini-
malist lines, pruned of definite articles and juxtaposing the natural ("Jay
squalls") and the human ("Coffee boils"), echo Chinese literary models.
Even Snyder's rocky poems evidence the disloco-descriptiveness of local
poetry at a time of global literary transmission and consciousness.

Like Snyder, another twentieth-century poet of place, the objectivist
Lorine Niedecker, is fascinated by the analogies between rock and poem
and by East Asian literary models, and, indeed, she received Snyder's collection *A Range of Poems* (1966), which included "Milton by Firelight" and
the rest of *Riprap*, as she was gathering materials for one of her finest
loco-descriptive poems, the sequence "Lake Superior."[70] This example
is worth lingering over, given the poem's large ambition and Niedecker's
reputation as a meticulous documenter of natural place. The sequence
begins:

> In every part of every living thing
> is stuff that once was rock
>
> In blood the minerals
> of the rock (1)

Although rock may seem a trope affirming the thingly specificity and stability of place, Niedecker, like Olson and Snyder, complicates this idea;
in her poetic sequence, rock is a trope of recirculation. "And his bones
of such is coral / raised up out of his grave" (3), she writes, reversing the
human-to-natural transmutation of Shakespeare's "Of his bones are coral
made."[71] In making new poetic bones out of the coral-like accretions of
earlier language, she associates the poetic recirculation of words with
the physiological recirculation of minerals. A rock, a human bone, and
a poem are all made up of countless ingredients recycled from faraway
places. Even if lovingly described in a poem, a rock-anchored place is
but a temporary resting site of minerals on a journey from elsewhere. In
notes written in preparation for her and her husband Al Millen's week-
long drive around the lake, she observes:

> A rock is made of minerals constantly on the move and changing from
> heat, cold and pressure.
> The journey of the rock is never ended. In every tiny part of any living
> thing are materials that once were rock that turned to soil. . . . In our
> blood is iron from plants that draw it out of the soil. Your teeth and bones
> were once coral. The water you drink has been in clouds over the moun-
> tains of Asia and in waterfalls of Africa. The air you breathe has swirled
> thru places of the earth that no one has ever seen. Every bit of you is a bit
> of the earth and has been on many strange and wonderful journeys over
> countless millions of years. (7)

Writing about the rocky specificities around Lake Superior, Niedecker finds herself ineluctably conjuring faraway places where its elements once resided, such as Asia and Africa. Close inspection both affirms the specificity of locality and erodes it by revealing its thorough interpenetration by global sites far away and long ago. Lake Superior is a geopolitical interstice, moreover, between Canada and the United States, as emphasized by a one-word line that enacts in-betweenness:

> The waters working together
>   internationally
> Gulls playing both sides (1)

The waters and gulls disregard artificial political borders. No place is unto itself: like every other lake or rock, body or breath, Lake Superior is a point of multiple intersecting vectors.

Niedecker highlights in language a permeability, recirculation, and global mobility similar to what she finds in rock: in both, seeming stability and identity give way to dispersion, mobility, and recycling. In a letter to Cid Corman in which she explained her budding interest in rocks, she called the Lake Superior region "a massive, grand corruption of nature. And of language . . . Indian, French, British—" (51). Similarly, she asserts in her notes, "The North is one vast, massive, glorious corruption of rock and language—granite is underlaid with limestone or sandstone. . . . And look what's been done to language!—People of all nationalities and color have changed the language like weather and pressure have changed the rocks" (11). Her poem excavates the American Indian (Mohawk or easterly Haudenosaunee, and Chippewa or Ojibwe), British, French, and other sediments laid in the historical geology of the language and culture of Lake Superior, as also implicitly in the poem. A place has not only spatial existence; it is also the layering of human and natural histories, and even a local writer such as Niedecker is, in a global age, alert to the confluence of worldwide elements in a seemingly discrete place. Her poem, by collaging accounts by Pierre Esprit Radisson, John Doty, Henry Rowe Schoolcraft, and other explorers, reveals itself to be made by the collection, corruption, and compression of these diverse sources, akin to the geological formation of the region. Even as it honors Lake Superior, this is not a poem that asserts the scenic boundedness or isolation of place: "Beauty: impurities in the rock" (2).

In her notes about venturing into the Canadian border city Sault

Sainte Marie, Niedecker records hearing French and British English, buying a pocketbook made in Hungary, and her husband's purchasing clothing of "Calcutta fabric (not at all expensive) made in Hong Kong. The word for the entire trip is International. From agate on. The journeying, the mixing and changing" (15). Global capitalism is but the latest among various forms of transnational movement and circulation. In the poem, agate, as a stone "named by the Greeks" and "seen on the priest's breastplate" in the Hebrew Bible and found by Lake Superior (7), is another trope for the "International . . . journeying, the mixing and changing" of rock, language, place, culture, and poem:

> Greek named
> Exodus-antique
> kicked up in America's
> Northwest
> you have been in my mind
> between my toes
> agate (4)

Here, immediate physical contact with place doesn't circumscribe or localize it. Niedecker knows that her physical and poetic feet kick up a stone that has signified variously in the ancient Mediterranean and Holy Land and now in her North American-sited (and -dispersed) poem.

Disappointed that the roadway around Lake Superior made invisible much of what she had hoped to see, Niedecker ends her place poem on an ironic note, suggesting that we are often elsewhere even in the places we visit and roll up into poems:

> I'm sorry to have missed
>   Sand Lake
> My dear one tells me
>   we did not
> We watched a gopher there (6)

Even as meticulously topographical a writer as Niedecker has to concede that our attention is often displaced in place, just as place—layered, mobile, multifarious—is often displaced from itself. Even at its rockiest, the minutely localized here is suffused with the multilocal elsewhere (aka "the global"), and once it is plunged in the "impurities" of language for

poetic representation, it provides all the more evidence for the "journeying, the mixing and changing" that fascinated this rock- and language-
obsessed poet.

Between Traveling Poetry and Loco-descriptive Poetry

Elsewhere I discuss what I call traveling poetry, or poems that enact geographic movement—poems that would seem to be the opposite of local
poems.[72] But as I've been trying to suggest, global modernity blurs the
differences between these two strands of topographical poetry—akin to
what have been classified as the prospect poem and the journey poem[73]—
and I conclude with a poem that deliberately confounds them, as well as
the "American" and "postcolonial" poetic strands I've artificially separated for purposes of discussion. Kashmiri American Agha Shahid Ali's
"I See Chile in My Rearview Mirror" has at least some of the qualities
of a loco-descriptive poem, as can be seen if we map the poem's journey
through literal places. Place-names, deictics, and the present tense
situate the poet in the American Southwest: "I'm driving toward Utah,"
he reports, and "There's Sedona, Nogales // far behind."[74] Nogales is on
the US border with Mexico, with Tucson to its north, and to drive from
Tucson, where Ali lived while teaching at the University of Arizona, is to
take Interstate 10 north to Phoenix, changing there to Route 17 north
to Sedona, with the Grand Canyon to the northwest. The journey continues: "And here the rocks / are under fog," presumably the Red Rocks of
Sedona, "the cedars a temple, / Sedona carved by the wind into gods" (97).
He has been "driving in the desert" in the Verde Valley, but by the time he
returns to the deictic "here" a few stanzas later, he places himself "here in
Utah" (98), having passed by ancient petroglyphs: "I'm passing skeletal /
figures carved in 700 B.C." on "these canyon walls" (97). The literal topography of the poet's journey can thus be extracted and mapped, with the
help of either paper or Google Maps. But the poem splices the factual
landscape together with the even more prominent rearview topography
of Latin America—with the driver's mirror functioning as both a spatial and a temporal metaphor for reflecting on the global South, even as
he journeys northward. This is where the idea of poetry as an empirical
mapping of place once again falls short. Going north is also going south;
moving outward and ahead in time is also moving inward and backward
in time. And whereas Jean Baudrillard writes of the experience of driving
through deserts in the United States as metaphorical of endless futurity
and the obliteration of the past in an instantaneous time,[75] Ali turns such

ideas on their head: as the car moves into the future (north), memories of the past are deepened (both the stone inscriptions and Latin American history). We might see the poem as modernizing Samuel Johnson's idea of the local poem as both descriptive of a "particular landscape" and a space for "historical retrospection." But although loco-descriptively sited in the American Southwest, particularly by deictics such as "here" and "these," the poem imaginatively stretches to other countries across the mirrored topography of the Americas: to Argentina, Paraguay, Uruguay, Colombia, Brazil, and Peru, all figured as colored spaces on a map (grimly elaborating the playfully fantastical evocations of Elizabeth Bishop's "The Map"), and above all to Santiago, Chile. The place named in the title is not seen from "above" or "at," nor is it seen from a stationary or commanding position: the poet's view of it is indirect and backward receding, oblique and figurative.

Ali's poem thus exemplifies the translocational nature of loco-descriptive poetry, particularly in a global age. Much more than a literal mapping of place, it vigorously exploits poetry's potent capacities for figuration, reflexivity, and indirection to evoke the interfusion of multiple inner and outer worlds. The haunting knowledge of the atrocities in Chile during the Pinochet era, a time of over three thousand deaths and disappearances, is made just as vividly a part of the poet's inner landscape as is the Southwest desert he drives through:

> Now from a blur
> of tanks in Santiago, a white horse
> gallops, riderless, chased by drunk soldiers. . . . (97)

Apocalyptic images, dreamlike colors, and political violence converge with a road trip. Ali imagines a victim and witness of the Chilean dictatorship who tries to catch a bus but misses it, "watches . . . blindfolded men" taken away in vans, and is then taken to the stadium used for prisoners in Santiago, before meeting his fate (97): "He has returned to this dream for his bones" (99). The poem is replete with mirrorings, evocative of the reflexivity of poetry, and the person in Chile seems the poet's mirror image; "driving, // still north, always followed by that country," the poet guiltily reflects on the fate of this and other victims of the dictatorship, the pun on "still" hinting at stasis despite physical movement (98). His alter ego suggests how easily their places might have been reversed, how easily the poetic "I" might have been in lieu of the ill-fated "he," had he been so unlucky as to end up in Chile under Pinochet or, for that matter, to have been in Kashmir at a time of political violence. The poem's imperfect rhymes provide a sonic equivalent for this skewed mirroring, while also intensifying the dreamlike quality of its interleaving of North and South America (*a blur / soldiers, B.C. / history, spiral / crystal, the window / Santiago, taken here / disappeared*) (97–98). A poet from a Kashmiri Shi'a Muslim background who grew up in New Delhi and worked in the United States, who writes in other poems about the atrocities in his homeland, Ali suggests that the local is inextricably braided with the global, that a poem can be literally sited in one place while figuratively stretched to others, that poetry is a literary space that—irreducible to the empirical mapping of singular and self-contained places—miniaturizes, intensifies, and multiplies the entanglements among widely separated sites.

It is easy to imagine counterarguments: Ali's poem and others I've considered confirm that "'topographical poetry' aims chiefly at describing *specifically named actual localities*"; or perhaps they show, to the extent that they shirk the task of faithful reproduction, how liable poetry is to prove incapable of its true calling. Both stances presuppose that local descriptivity is a fundamental norm against which individual works should be measured. By these lights, either Ali faithfully maps an area of the American Southwest, or he obscures it with a South American overlay. Either Niedecker precisely charts the topography around Lake Superior, or her attention to foreign flows distracts her from the region's socioeconomic realities. Either her and Snyder's use of Chinese models for stony concision helps ground their poetry in the uniqueness of the local, or it deflects immediate American fact. Maybe Olson documents a city, Ammons an inlet, Goodison an island, and Ramanujan a great house, or maybe their interest in the natural and historical circulation of distant places through these sites distortively blurs the local peculiarities. Maybe Kolatkar's poetry wards off global vacancy by focusing on a Bombay neighborhood, or maybe his framing of that place in a global space-time matrix abstracts the speaker from his complex relation to the poor. We could talk about Nichols, McKay, and Yeats either as signposting singular postcolonial places or as retreating into pastoral primitivism to shut out the destructive effects of urban modernity. We could honor James Wright's poem for its fidelity to a highly individuated site in the Midwest, or we could fault it for dehistoricizing and displacing the decayed American industrial heartland with Chinese, French, and modernist intertexts. We could hail Pound for his direct treatment of the thing (the Paris Metro), or we could interrogate him for suppressing sociohistorical facts by way of lacunae, figuration, and literary allusiveness. From such perspectives, the translocal approach I'm proposing for loco-descriptive poems either neglects their authentic reproduction of the singularities of singular places, or colludes in these poems' lyricization, their mystification and displacement of such places' material histories.

Although such loco-materialist arguments may continue to yield critical insight, they advance a model of the poetry of place—whether in the guise of appreciation or critique—that is ultimately insufficient to the complexities of poetic mimesis and formal mediation, perhaps especially under global modernity. Instead of empirical documentation of a limited historical space as the critic's implicit representational ideal, a transnational framework enlaced with a form-attentive poetics may be better suited to the long-memoried figurative and linguistic richness of poetic mediation, and to the layering and stretching of space by globalizing processes focalized by poetry. Anything less radially or peripherally visioned, anything more locally circumscribed, risks missing poetry's peculiar ways of articulating the translocalization of locality and so its reinvigoration of the topographical imagination for our time. If we assume that, "against the current tide of globalization," poetry does or should represent "localization"—a home for "the authentically particular and the authentically local"—we may miss how its intricate verbal and formal architecture is often interpenetrated by other spaces and other times, how it manifests the spatial pluralities that traverse, inhabit, and even constitute place. In a global age, poetry often embodies and illuminates the accelerated intermelding of the local and global; a poetic locus often makes legible the multiplicities enfolded within a singular geographic locus. It can do so by virtue of its metaphoric reach and formal elasticity, its compression and velocity and deep memory, its inhabiting of multiple spaces and times at once, and its proficiency at straddling discrepant sites, both real and imagined.

CHAPTER 3

POETRY AND TOURISM
IN A GLOBAL AGE

In the poem that opens Elizabeth Bishop's *Questions of Travel* (1965), "Arrival at Santos," the speaker addresses herself as a "tourist." She wryly glosses the term as someone who has "immodest demands for a different world, / and a better life, and complete comprehension / of both at last, and immediately."[1] Bishop calls into question the tourist's insatiable desire for difference, for transparency, for quick understanding of other cultures; these "immodest demands" differ, we might surmise, from a poet's more tentative and reflective methods of exploration. Yet the poet is self-critically addressing a fictive version of herself, and poetry, too, can involve a quest for alternate worlds. Writing or even reading a poem, we make a temporary departure and return, imaginatively traveling, as the *OED* says of the tourist, "for pleasure or culture."[2] We make a turn with a poem or with a tour, as suggested by the roots of the words *verse* and *tour*— *versus* from *vertere*, to turn, and *tornus*, a circle, or a tool for describing a circle—and we may find our world and ourselves defamiliarized upon return.[3] Ideally, the circuit we travel by poem or vessel unmoors us, desta-bilizes our preconceptions, renews our sensory engagements, and opens us afresh to ourselves and the world.

Although literary tourism arguably goes back to *The Odyssey*, the word *tourism* initially denoted transnational travel especially of upper-class young men for cultural edification, as in the eighteenth- and nineteenth-century Grand Tour. Tourism greatly expanded its social, geographic, and literary reach in the twentieth century, as modernity made mass travel ever more affordable. In groundbreaking studies of tourism, Dean Mac-Cannell discusses what he calls the "democratization of tourist desire"— its cutting across social distinctions—and even claims that the tourist is "one of the best models for modern-man-in-general."[4] If so, then how does poetry coincide with tourism and how are they distinct, especially in a global age of accelerated movement across vast spaces, when poets like Bishop all the more frequently double as tourists and tourists as poets? What can we learn about poetry from tourism and about tourism from poetry? Definitive responses to such questions may be impossible, but close examination of key poems may suggest possible paths toward understanding an important dimension of poetry in our time. In keeping with the interdiscursive analysis of *Poetry and Its Others: News, Prayer, Song, and the Dialogue of Genres* (2014), I bring together tourism studies with poetry studies, focusing on poems self-consciously entwined with tourism as their discursive "other."[5]

Complicities of Literary Tourism

Although few critics have explored the touristic dimensions of modern and contemporary poetry, let alone of poetry criticism and the teaching of poetry, the discourses overlap extensively, if sometimes tensely. Robert von Hallberg, Jeffrey Gray, and Anthony Carrigan have usefully considered world-wandering poets who thematize tourism,[6] but the formal, conceptual, and discursive points of connection between poetry and tourism are worth teasing out further, particularly given that tourism is one of the "most obvious forms of the globalization of culture."[7] As sociologists John Urry and Jonas Larsen observe, "There are not two separate entities, the 'global' and 'tourism'. . . . Rather they are part and parcel of the same set of complex and interconnected processes."[8]

If poetry sometimes functions as a kind of tourism, does this condemn it to the superficiality and degradation we often associate with tourism? After all, tourism studies has disclaimed the distinction by Daniel Boorstin and others of the traveler from the tourist—work vs. pleasure, active vs. passive, solitary vs. mass—that might once have been used to salvage poetry; tourism theorists now see such distinctions as part of a larger tendency to use "tourist" as a negative label and to deny one's own tourism.[9] "Tourists dislike tourists," remarks MacCannell, and they often "point out the tawdry side of tourism and the ways it can spoil the human community, while hiding from themselves the essentially touristic nature of their own cultural expeditions."[10] "Let's face it, we all are tourists!," exclaims an Iranian student he quotes.[11] Urry and Larsen add that the boundaries between tourism and other social and cultural practices have increasingly dissolved, so that "people are much of the time 'tourists' whether they like it or not," including poets and their readers.[12]

Even so, all forms of tourism shouldn't be collapsed into one another. Frequenting multinational all-inclusive resorts that channel most of their profits away from the host site, create only low-wage service jobs, and damage and degrade the natural environment isn't the same as cultural or ethnographic study abroad, or relating a "foreign" excursion in literary form, or reading or teaching poems, plays, and novels from different parts of the world—though these, too, may ultimately be in a broad sense "touristic." If we all are tourists and, as MacCannell adds, "we are tour guides,"[13] some forms of touristic activity are more destructive and superficial, others more self-reflexive, self-critical, and potentially educative. Inexplicitly pivoting on his earlier disavowal of distinctions like "tourist" vs. "traveler," even MacCannell asserts in a later study: "The ultimate ethical test for tourists is whether they can realize the productive potential of their travel desires or whether they allow themselves to become mere ciphers of arrangements made for them."[14] Poetry also tests one's abilities to transmit or transform, to copy or remake inherited arrangements.

Perhaps the best-known indictment of tourism, Jamaica Kincaid's bitter and astute *A Small Place*, could ironically be seen as fostering another kind of tourism, imaginatively transporting readers to Antigua and inviting them to interrogate the harmful effects of their involvement in the tourist industry and indirectly in government corruption. Her attack on airplane-flying, hotel-staying, beach-combing mass tourism presupposes a self-critical literary tourism—readers who, following her in her narrative to Antigua, will be able to reflect on these other, more noxious forms of tourism. After excoriating tourists as ugly and evil, she rhapsodizes over Antigua in a paradoxically touristic evocation of the small place as seemingly unreal in its natural beauty, lines ironically picked up later in an *Essence* magazine piece promoting travel to Antigua: "Antigua is beautiful. Antigua is too beautiful. Sometimes the beauty of it seems unreal. Sometimes the beauty of it seems as if it were stage sets for a play, for no real sunset could look like that; no real seawater could strike that many shades of blue at once"—and so on, with the blue sky, the white cloud, the sunlight, and the darkness of the night.[15] Rebuking the unthinking tourist reader at the beginning of her book, Kincaid nevertheless implicitly carves out a rhetorical space for another kind of tourist experience—historically and politically savvy, literary and

self-aware, ironic and imaginatively probing, and open to cultural difference and awed by natural beauty, both of which she attempts to convey
in her lyrical prose.

Indeed, not to allow for such distinctions is to risk abandoning travel
beyond one's backyard and forsaking, too, tourism's readerly analogue, literature from around the world, confining oneself to a national literature
to avoid contamination by tourism. Yet under advanced globalization,
even "home" or a "homeland" is a site where "foreign" products, images,
and ideas meet.[16] And adherence to a "national literature" also inescap-
ably involves tourism of other times, ethnicities, regions, and classes
within the "nation." Postcolonial and global literary critics sometimes
shunt their touristic complicities off on novelists, poets, and dramatists.
Graham Huggan offers a smart but broad-brush critique of "the postcolonial exotic," with its "strategic exoticism" and "staged marginality,"
its "global market-value as a reified object of intellectual tourism."[17] But
instead of criticizing the literature for safely packaging otherness, as if we
literary critics were exempt from such charges, perhaps we should take
our cue from the literature's knowing and self-critical response to its own
tourism. Even Jamaica Kincaid writes a travelogue of her tourist experience of walking and gathering seeds in Nepal, *Among Flowers*, thrilled by
the natural beauty but also often annoyed by the local porters and Sherpas
who accompany her, having become one of those "people from rich countries in the process of experiencing the world as spectacle."[18]

Poets have often acknowledged in nuanced ways their vexed implication in tourism, even as they have criticized forms of it that are imperialist
and damaging. Derek Walcott is the obvious example.[19] He repeatedly
railed against the way Caribbean islands "sell themselves" and against the
industry's commodification of Saint Lucia, particularly tourist developments that have defaced the Pitons, twin volcanic peaks on the island's
southwestern coast. In his Nobel lecture, he describes how "the benign
blight that is tourism" is infecting all of the Antilles, and he implicitly sets
the cultural depth and historical memory of poetry against it: "But in our
tourist brochures the Caribbean is a blue pool into which the republic
dangles the extended foot of Florida as inflated rubber islands bob and
drinks with umbrellas float towards her on a raft."[20] Effacing Caribbean
history and culture, the tourist brochure represents the islands as time-
lessly fixed in superficiality and service. So too in *Omeros* Walcott places in
his Saint Lucian inferno "the traitors // who in elected office, saw the land
as views / for hotels," permitting horrendous exploitation of the island's
natural beauty.[21] His character Hector dies in a crash after forsaking his

fishing canoe for a tourist van, and Helen quits a demeaning job waiting tables at a resort hotel, though she eventually accommodates herself to a different hotel job that allows her to retain at least some human and cultural dignity. Yet despite his denunciations, Walcott acknowledged that his extended North American stays and class status made him somewhat of a tourist in his own country: when I "come down here," he said, "perhaps literally I'm a Tourist *myself* coming from America."[22] In *Omeros* he glances at himself in the opening portrait of Philoctete, who "smiles for the tourists, who try taking / his soul with their cameras," even as the fisherman ruefully reflects on his wound's poetry-like foldedness and recalcitrance: "'It have some things'—he smiles—'worth more than a dollar.'"[23] But of course the poet will tell the story of this wound and reap profits from the sale. Elsewhere in the poem, he criticizes himself for wanting "the poor / to stay in the same light so that I could transfix / them in amber," for "the hypocrisy / of loving them from hotels."[24]

In this ambivalent semitourism, Walcott is hardly alone. Robert Chi observes of the Pacific Island writer Albert Wendt, he "has positioned himself as a go-between, becoming a tour guide (both personally and textually) in the cultural 'interzone.'"[25] Similarly, Cathy Park Hong assumes the voice of a polyglot tour guide to a dystopian city in the desert in *Dance Dance Revolution* (2007). And Ara Shirinyan, in a flarf collection of Internet searches in *Your Country Is Great* (2008), both ridicules and revels in touristic clichés about countries around the world, such as these lines from "Andorra Is Great":

> Andorra is great place to do some winter sports,
> they have lovely high mountains
> you to ski or snowboard.
> In the summer time you can go hiking[26]

Such self-ironizing literary tourism, which recognizes its complicity in mass tourism yet also distinguishes itself from some of its forms and effects, provides a more nuanced approach than is to be found in sweeping critiques, in which the tourist is always someone else.

Poet-Tourists in the Global North

Before returning to other postcolonial examples that are less widely known than Walcott, I closely examine three canonical North American and English poems that ponder poetry's touristic complicities. These poems were written in successive decades of the mid-twentieth century when tourism grew exponentially as an industry of mass culture, as cheap air transportation became readily available—a trend that continued with an increase worldwide in international tourist trips from about 25 million in 1950 to 1.4 billion in 2018.[27] Elizabeth Bishop explores the syntax and visuality of tourism in "Over 2,000 Illustrations and a Complete Concordance" (1948); John Ashbery, the escapist fantasy and clichés of tourism in "The Instruction Manual" (1956); and Philip Larkin, the erotic idealism of both poetry and tourism in "Sunny Prestatyn" (1964). While increasingly critical of tourism as a discourse and industry, all three poets recognize in tourism something of a twisted mirror of their poetic procedures. As exemplified by all three works, postwar poetry grapples with its entanglement in tourism, even as it champions its distinctness.

Bishop famously encapsulates the parataxis of tourism in the line "Everything only connected by 'and' and 'and.'"[28] That is, the tourist turns from this sight to that sight to another, and these experiences are not hierarchically subordinated to one another or to some larger meaning or purpose that integrates them; instead, tourism is built on seriality in time and space, like the lexical and syntactic brickwork mortaring together "'and' and 'and.'" As an anthropologist remarks in another context, "Tourism produces a syntagmatic narrative strung together by conjunctions."[29] Bishop's line most immediately refers back to how she has just strung together several tourist vignettes in the second verse paragraph of "Over 2,000 Illustrations and a Complete Concordance," including places she visited as a tourist in global travels from 1936 to 1941, before her sixteen-year stay in Brazil:[30] "And at St. Peter's," "And at Volubilis," "And in the brothels of Marrakesh" (58). The serial "'and' and 'and'" quality of this well-known tourist passage comes more fully into view if we notice a feature of it that has passed unremarked: that it leaps back and forth intercontinentally with every new location, intensifying the sense of perpetual *dis*location. The "and" or equivalent in each case is transatlantic: Bishop begins in North America, with the Narrows at St. Johns, Newfoundland, and then leaps to Europe, namely St. Peter's in Rome, then jumps back across the Atlantic to Latin America, in Jalisco, Mexico, crosses the Atlantic again to North Africa with the Roman ruins of Volubilis, Morocco, then traverses the Atlantic south to north, to the British Isles, with a stop hosted by an Englishwoman at Dingle harbor in Ireland, and finally returns south to the Maghreb, winding up in Marrakesh and its environs. Bishop might have said everything only connected by "ocean" and "ocean." Her verse paragraph exemplifies traveling poetry in the compression and rapidity of its geographic movement. Bishop's poem speeds up and intensifies tourism's insatiable roving, and in so doing, she puts on display a structuring drive behind tourism—the propulsive desire for another place, and another, and another.

Some of these tourist experiences distantly echo the first verse paragraph's illustrations of the Holy Land, but they lack any metaphysical principle of order.[31] Whereas the biblical illustrations represented every scene as, in effect, "caught in the coils of an initial letter," tied to the divine Word, and whereas everything seemed subordinate to the controlling godhead—a courtyard engraved "like a diagram," the "birds / suspended on invisible threads above the Site"—the tourist sights have been emptied out of any higher ordering principle (57). Unlike the "'and' and 'and'" syntax that can also be found in the Bible, subsumed to the hypotaxis of a divine meaning and plan, the heterogeneous sights beheld by the secular tourist—more vivid and less predictable than the Bible scenes—have no inherent relation to one another or to a higher meaning. The sightseer is drawn on journeys by the standard tourist attractants: nature's beauty or grandeur in the bleating goats jumping up cliffs at St. Johns or the volcanoes of Mexico; famous religious and architectural monuments, such as St. Peter's Square; nature mixed with ancient history in the poppies erupting through Roman mosaics at Volubilis; dining experience, including an English tea in Ireland; and sex and sex work— the belly-dancing, pock-marked prostitutes in Marrakesh.

But the last vignette also exposes the potential for existential dread in postreligious travel. As in "In the Waiting Room," it is a frightening encounter with foreign otherness—in that poem the "horrifying" breasts of women of non-European origin—that threatens annihilation of the subject.[32] Here, the terrifyingly empty tomb is presumably decorated with Muslim calligraphy in Arabic ("carved solid / with exhortation"), its illegibility to the North American tourist reinforcing the sense of the letter unstuck from a metaphysical ground: she sees the void as opening like a mouth that threatens to devour ("yellowed / as scattered cattle-teeth") (58). But in contrast to the biblical illustration's "Arabs, plotting, probably, / against our Christian Empire," securely boxed into the category of alien others (57), this Arab guide isn't an orientalist stereotype; he is a named person whose ironic gaze the speaker partly shares: "In a smart burnoose Khadour looked on amused" (58). The north-south encounter, of North American poet-tourist with Moroccan tour guide, leads into the poem's final dialectical synthesis.

Bishop doesn't retreat from the vulnerability of secular, unsettlingly cross-cultural travel into the security of a bookish Christian framework that she has already dismissed as musty and predictable, "tired / and a touch familiar" (57). Instead, she attempts to synthesize spiritual insight, stripped of deity and dogma, with the worldly and expansive visuality of travel. In its culminating chiasmus, the poem secularizes the biblical scene of the Nativity, humorously renamed a "family with pets" (59), and at the same time spiritualizes the sightseeing core of tourism, so that looking becomes an end in itself, a source of wonder: when the imagination suffuses sight, perhaps in both senses of the word as *vision* and *place seen*, it apprehends "an undisturbed, unbreathing flame" that is partly of its own making (58)—an image that descends from Walter Pater's "hard, gem-like flame."[33]

> Why couldn't we have seen
> this old Nativity while we were at it?
> —the dark ajar, the rocks breaking with light,
> an undisturbed, unbreathing flame,
> colorless, sparkless, freely fed on straw,
> and, lulled within, a family with pets,
> —and looked and looked our infant sight away. (58–59)

The final dark-yet-light setting revises and combines the end of the first verse paragraph, in which God was said to "ignite" the scene (57), and the end of the second, with its dusty, deathly void. Similarly, the poem's last line tellingly returns to the "'and' and 'and'" repetition, but lifts it to a higher level of imaginative sight, in a line that metaphorically transfers speechlessness (Latin *infans*) from the "infant" Jesus to the poet. Through poetry, the speaker aspires to upgrade sightseeing to an imaginatively luminous experience that both recuperates and exceeds childlike sight. If the poem suggests that travel can be flat and disconcertingly fragmentary, and that religious orthodoxy can be schematic and restrictively homogenizing, Bishop situates poetry between tourism and religion, aspiring to combine their strengths—the experiential liveliness of travel and the awe of revelation.

What are the implications of Bishop's poem for poetry's relation to tourism? In the postwar period, both tourism and poetry tend toward a loosely jointed parataxis in their horizontal approaches to the globe. Both have a strongly ocular dimension, enacting an insatiable desire to see more of the world, to seek out sources of wonder, to extend and enliven experience beyond the "tired and . . . familiar." Both enact the

desire for, and the serial alienations of, encounters with cultural difference. Both presuppose the possibility of rapid movement from one site
to another across large distances. But they aren't identical. Bishop shows
off the greater compression of poetry (multiple crossings of the Atlantic
in a single verse paragraph), its freedom to traverse different vocabularies
from the sacred to the profane, and its heightened self-consciousness
about its procedures. She upgrades merely physical vision into awe
through imaginatively intensifying similes—"Collegians marched in
lines, / . . . like ants," "the dead volcanoes / glistened like Easter lilies,"
a tomb "yellowed / as scattered cattle-teeth" (58). Activating the mind's
eye, the poem also lives in the ear, as when Bishop's line endings subtly
hint at the sonic parallelism of rhyme, such as the sequence *lay/volca-
noes, lilies/Jalisco, poppies/eyes* (partly when evoking a jukebox) (58). Nor
is the poem's overall structure merely paratactic, since it moves dialectically toward synthesis: while unloosing poetry from religious constraint,
Bishop endows its imaginative sight and flamelike intensity with quasi-
spiritual potential.

   John Ashbery commented that "Over 2,000 Pictures and a Complete
Concordance" "epitomizes Miss Bishop's work at its best" and is "mar-
velous," "possibly her masterpiece," adding that after twenty years, he was
"unable to exhaust the meaning and mysteries of its concluding line."[34]
The attraction of Bishop's poem for Ashbery should be evident: few
poets cruise more rapidly than Ashbery across such a vast array of sights,
states, and discourses, with everything connected as if only by "and" and
"and." Toward the end of the fantasized tourist excursion of his "The
Instruction Manual," the speaker exclaims, "How limited, but how complete withal, has been our experience of Guadalajara!,"[35] a formulation
akin to Bishop's diagnosis of the tourist's wish for a different and better
life and "complete comprehension / of both at last, and immediately."
The desire for completeness, delivered through synecdoche—a person
or costume or building that exemplifies Mexicanness or Brazilianness—
characterizes the semiotics of tourism. As Jonathan Culler observes,
"The tourist is interested in everything as a sign of itself, an instance of a
typical cultural practice," seeking out "signs of Frenchness, typical Italian
behavior, exemplary Oriental scenes," and so forth.[36] But despite its vertical, synecdochic axis, both Bishop and Ashbery emphasize tourism's
horizontal or metonymic sprawl as well. The main conduit of such signs
is ocular, and so like Bishop, who writes "I saw" and "looked and looked,"
Ashbery repeatedly deploys the verb *see* with ancillary chiming (and perhaps a buried pun on the Spanish *sí*) in "The Instruction Manual": "*Ci*ty

I wanted most to *see*, and most did not *see*, in Mexico! / But I fancy I *see*"
(5, emphasis added). As Urry and Larsen argue in *The Tourist Gaze*, "the
organising sense in tourism is visual."[37] But whereas Bishop's tourist voy-
ages back and forth across the ocean to see new places (and secondarily
to hear, touch, and taste them), Ashbery's is an armchair tourist, traveling
to Guadalajara as a fantastical escape from the dull labor of writing a
"manual on the uses of a new metal," an effort to forget, as Jamaica Kincaid says of the tourist, "a life of overwhelming and crushing banality and
boredom."[38] Ashbery's poetry in itself could be said to suggest armchair
tourism as well, unleashing language to travel here and there and everywhere, across discrepant spaces and vocabularies.

Even so, for all the poet's affinities with the would-be tourist, "The
Instruction Manual" also satirizes this daydreaming speaker in particular and tourist discourse in general. If Bishop's poem salvages touristic looking as the basis for a secular poetic art, Ashbery makes the sight-
centered discourse of tourist brochure and travelogue the basis of his
poem while affectionately parodying it. Decades after Joyce fabricated
the "Nausicaa" episode of *Ulysses* out of the overwrought and sentimental
language of so-called ladies' magazines, and decades before Shirinyan
gathered and edited tourist searches in *Your Country Is Great*, Ashbery at
midcentury cuts up and reassembles clichés, tropes, and topoi of tourist
discourse in a way that draws the reader in and yet at the same time flat-
tens the language on the page, that makes us collude with the speaker's
fantasy and yet prompts us to inspect his words and phrases. Witness the
creaky use of contrived exclamations—"City of rose-colored flowers!"
(5); sentimental formulae—"His dear one, his wife" (5); and set phrases—
"holiday mood" (5), "in the American fashion" (5), "sincere eyes" (6).
There is, as MacCannell writes of tourist spaces, a front and a back, the
latter the site of a "staged authenticity" revealed by Ashbery's tour-guide
speaker:[39] "Let us take this opportunity," he entreats, "to tiptoe into one
of the side streets," where an old woman "welcomes us" and talks about
her son (6); but since this interior is so predictable and formulaic, we
never get beyond the surface. Parodying while indulging tourist ocularity,
the poem is like a painting that foregrounds the penetration-resistant
flatness of its surface, especially since the most vivid feature of the poem's
tourist discourse is its array of colors. Individually, these help create the
illusion of a narrative space, but cumulatively, they draw attention to the
poem's construction of this space, seeming like so much paint as paint on
a canvas: the tourist gaze takes in the "rose- and lemon-colored flowers"
(5), the flower girls, each "In her rose-and-blue striped dress (Oh! such

shades of rose and blue)" (5), a nearby "little white booth where women in green serve you green and yellow fruit" (5), and so on—deep blue clothes, a white hat, a "rose, pink, and white" shawl (5), let alone the racializing language of a lover with an "olive cheek" and a "dark-skinned lad" (6, 7). These latter references participate in the speaker's orientalist projection of generalized otherness, which seems to (con)fuse spheres of cultural difference—"The band is playing *Scheherazade* by Rimsky-Korsakov" (5).

Another key feature of the poem's language is its emphasis on touristic immediacy, established in time and space. Temporally, the poem places us in the moment of unfolding events, as if it were a minute-by-minute report: "The band is playing" (5), "The couples are parading" (5), "Here come the boys!" (6). This immediacy is heightened by the self-authenticating effect of the narrative frame, in which the tourist-narrator suggests his access is occasionally impeded: "I have lost sight of the young fellow with the toothpick. / Wait—there he is—on the other side of the bandstand" (6), and "I try to hear what they are saying" (6). The narrator pretends to have "written, as it were, to the moment," in Samuel Richardson's phrase for the epistolary style.[40] Spatially, the poem makes prominent use of deictics, as in the anaphoric series of lines beginning "There is"—"There is the rich quarter," "There is the poor quarter," "There is the market," "And there is the public library," and "Look! There is the square we just came from" (7). "There" is a vividly different space, an escape from entrapment in dull necessity, from technical writing as a cog in the capitalist machine.

But by flattening and foregrounding the prefabricated phrases and ideas out of which this dream world is made, the poem calls into question any sharp distinction between the realm of self-divided drudgery and that supposedly other world, the alterity of the "complete" space elsewhere. The poem doesn't exempt itself from the touristic procedures that it parodies and illuminates. It is about not writing an instruction manual, and yet it is also itself a kind of instruction manual—for writing poems, making them up out of the bits and pieces of tourism's prefabrications. Here, as in the postmodernist pastiches of Shirinyan's *Your Country Is Great*, the poet is like what Maxine Feifer describes as the "post-tourist"—a person who sees tourism as a series of games that can be played, finding as much pleasure in the fake or imagined or Internet-searched experience as in the supposedly authentic thing.[41] Although both Bishop and Ashbery take pointers from tourism, Bishop conceives it ideally as equipment for seeing freshly, without preconceptions, while for Ashbery it is a tissue of preconceptions, like the weave of discourses that his poetry shows us time and again can be deftly rewoven but cannot be escaped. Even though his office worker may want to forget about "the uses of a new metal," the innovative use of new and old metals in transportation technology had been speeding tourists to Mexico in ever greater numbers.[42] With mass tourism rapidly expanding from the 1940s to the 1950s, Ashbery's approach to tourism is more critical than Bishop's, evacuating its "staged authenticity" and flattening its surface/depth divisions, even as it recognizes its own complicity in tourism's seriality and voracious desire-for-newness.

Philip Larkin also entwines poetry with tourism to explore interdiscursive commonalities as well as differences. Although his approach to tourism is all the more skeptical, likely reflecting a third postwar decade's increasing wariness of the burgeoning industry, even he uncovers points of intersection. Having originated mass tourism in the nineteenth century, particularly the seaside holiday, Britain witnessed enormous growth in the industry in the late 1950s and the 1960s, a period when the government also formalized its involvement in promoting tourism. At the same time, mass tourism came under increasing scrutiny: international travel organizations started to discuss how to limit tourism's damaging effects, and popular publications began to draw attention to the "negative impacts from tourism."[43] Larkin's "Sunny Prestatyn" responds critically to the mediation and shaping of desire by both tourism and poetry. The poem opens with the language of a tourist ad: "*Come To Sunny Prestatyn* / Laughed the girl on the poster."[44] While the poem may seem to be incorporating an entirely alien discourse, set off in italics, the command to "Come" has long opened many a lyric poem, filling the double columns of ten pages of *Granger's Index to Poetry*, from "Come all ye" and "Come all you" and "Come hither" to "Come let us," "Come listen," "Come thou," and "Come ye" and "you."[45] The poem's vexed response to the tourist ad shouldn't blind us to the apostrophic rhetoric shared by poem and ad—what Roman Jakobson calls "conative" language oriented toward the addressee, as in the vocative and the imperative.[46] Some traditional poems beginning "Come" entreat an audience, though Larkin's poem, in which the fictionalizing frame suspends the command from its normal communicative function, inserts a gap between the ad's and the poem's audiences. Other poems beginning "Come" are entreaties to the beloved, and ingredients of the blazon tradition figure in this poem as well—face, eyes, lips, breast. Like such poems, the poster is erotically suggestive: the body of the "girl" seems sexually joined with the natural and built environment—"a hunk of coast, a / Hotel with palms," with a play on "hunk" and "palms," the latter rhymed with "arms." Like love poetry, tourist advertising is grounded in a grammar of seduction. "Advertising images are structured around, and work through, mobilising and triggering the spectator's desires and fantasies through 'spatial fictions,'" Urry and Larsen observe; commercial tourist photography assumes that "People desire to be seduced and such images are artfully constructed to seduce."[47] Both love poetry and tourist advertising engage, stimulate, and even produce desire. In poetry, unlike the tourist ad, the seduction process is often framed, rerouted from communication between seducer and seduced into a fictionalized seduction process whose seemingly secondary audience, the reader, is often the real one, able to observe and reflect on the erotic address staged in the poem. A love poem is both seductive and meta-seductive. Address, the vocative, eroticized language, parts of the body, seduction—from its beginning, "Sunny Prestatyn" suggests poetry's discursive intersections with tourism, even as it demonstrates a self-reflexivity that is often stronger in poetry than in tourist advertising.

Larkin takes the framing of love poetry's eroticism one step further by imagining a fierce resistance to, and interruption of, the touristic seduction process. Discussions of "Sunny Prestatyn" have revolved around whether or not the poet participates in the defacement of, and sexual violence against, "the girl on the poster," raising vexed questions about his sexual politics. Larkin himself remarked that he wanted "to provoke" a reaction of "shock, outrage at the defacement of the poster and what the girl stood for," seeing the disfigurement as both "funny" and "terrifying."[48] Joseph Bristow is probably right that the poem "operates in parallel to the graffiti that it also condemns. The poet's distance from Titch Thomas is both far and near."[49] One way of clarifying this complicity—without resolving the matter of Larkin's personal predispositions—is to recognize the likeness between the touristic promise of idyllic beauty and the poetic tradition of love poems that the poem also engages. Intrapoetic and extrapoetic, the act of defacement is directed toward the excessive idealism of both touristic and traditional poetic discourse. This is hardly the only one of Larkin's poems to take down poetic idealism: "Lozenge of love! Medallion of art!," he exclaims of the moon in the poem "Sad Steps," only to pivot on the word "No."[50] In "Sunny Prestatyn," Larkin effectively scrawls graffiti on both poetic and touristic romanticism in ways that are disturbing. The poet's hand may be implicated in the vandalism by the phrase "scored well in" (a marking with parallel lines), the verbs "scrawls" and "Autographed," and the embedding of the word "verse" in the phrase "great transverse tear." But if, in the narrative the poem tells, the vandals act out of rage at false and ridiculously elevated dreams, the poem as poem vandalizes the high poetic tradition. The first stanza's allusion to poetic address, its tight rhyme scheme, and its artful phrasing ("tautened white satin," "breast-lifting arms") set up expectations for a kind of poetic decorum that Larkin flouts by willfully intruding crude and vulgar diction—"slapped up," "snaggle-toothed and boss-eyed," "Huge tits and a fissured crotch," "A tuberous cock and balls." This verse is indeed transverse. In literary-historical terms the poem unleashes rebellious energies against a particular kind of lyric idealism, as also against its kin, the language and strategies of tourism.

Incorporating tourist discourse and revealing its likenesses to poetry, Bishop, Ashbery, and Larkin all acknowledge that tourism verges on poetry, poetry on tourism. Bishop shows tourism and modern secular poetry to share a hunger for fresh and nontranscendental vision, suggesting it is possible to upgrade tourism's visuality into an aesthetic principle. She also sees tourism and poetry to be joined by their paratactic seriality, as does the quintessentially "and"-and-"and" poet, John Ashbery. But whereas Bishop thinks of tourism as a resource for "infant sight," Ashbery conceives of it as a collection of discursive strategies and clichés. He more sharply satirizes exoticist travelese, though he also acknowledges it as the inescapable fabric of the contemporary manufactured encounter with other places, other cultures, other peoples. Of these three poets, Larkin takes the most aggressive approach to tourism, which is simultaneously a self-critical response to the lyric traditions on which his poetry was weaned. But even he shows the shared terrain—the beckoning invitation, the seductive use of the female body, the erotic idealism. "The term 'tourist' is increasingly used as a derisive label for someone who seems content with the obviously inauthentic," writes MacCannell.[51] These poets share in the broad critique of tourism—its empty fragmentation, commodifying clichés, and sexual objectification—but in their metatouristic poems, they concede at the same time that even the poets among us are on the tour bus, often searching for sources of imaginative renewal. In a global age, we can't easily escape tourism; but poetry—alert to its madeness (*poiesis*) and its making of its worlds—may be one means by which we can negotiate our linguistic and ethical participation in it.

Poet-Tourists of the Global South

For postcolonial poets, the intersections between poetry and tourism are still more disconcerting, given the many ways in which tourism economically and culturally extends the ghostly afterlife of imperialism. After the crumbling of British, French, and other European empires, peoples from Northern metropolitan centers returned to the former colonies, bearing more cameras and sunscreen than guns and Bibles, still exploiting human capital and natural resources on a staggering scale. Tourism is often said to be perhaps the largest industry in the world, accounting for about a tenth of world GDP, and multinational corporations that exacerbate inequities between wealthy and poor countries occupy a large share of this economic sector.[52] Having already glanced at a Caribbean poet, let's turn to an African and an Indian poet and explore their fruitfully vexed engagements with the tourist as antagonist and alter ego.

If you look up the publications of the South African Jewish poet Karen Press and see that one of her books, published by a small South African press, is titled *Echo Location: A Guide to Sea Point for Residents and Visitors* (1998), you might well suspect that, hard up for cash like many poets, she wrote a guidebook to this Cape Town suburb.[53] After all, it was published at a time when, after decades of stagnation in its tourist industry under apartheid, South Africa had hopes for a turnaround.[54] From a look inside the book, you discover instead that Press has collaged signs, news clippings, historical accounts, menus, and other found materials with lyrics and narrative poems into a poetic sequence that excavates the uncomfortable racial, sexual, legal, and personal history of the place—not the usual stuff of tourist guides. Her pseudo-guidebook emphasizes graphically on the page this variety of genres and discourses: some poems look like standard free-verse lyrics, but others are centered on the page in all caps like a plaque (17), arrayed as single, discontinuously numbered lines from a library catalogue, often cut off mid-word (26–27), printed in columns and boxes like pieces in a newspaper or a game (35, 73), or numbered as "Rules Binding on All Owners and Residents" of a building (42–43). These rules include prohibitions on noise, visible laundry, makeshift window coverings, animals, storage, gambling, and garbage, the latter hilariously specified as "rubbish, dirt, cigarette butts or boxes, chocolate papers, food scraps, odd bits of paper etc" (42). A culinary guide to the many different cuisines available in Sea Point runs along the bottom of the page. Linguistically, the poem swerves from its baseline Standard

English into overheard snippets of spoken dialect, Yiddish, Afrikaans, and Xhosa. Disrupting the monologic norms of the guidebook genre (*A Guide to Sea Point* . . .), which tends to blend neutrally informational discourse with the suasive appeal of advertising, the book splinters in an unsettling formal and linguistic variety—visual, sonic, discursive—that frustrates any desire for easy semantic access or place-consuming comprehension.

Press's "guide" doesn't market Sea Point as a uniquely desirable location; it uncovers the history of exclusions across several centuries that made it a site of white privilege for "residents and visitors." Blurring the lines between settlers and tourists, "residents and visitors," Press suggests that tourists are the latest in a long line of predominantly white European arrivants. In one found poem, "Recreation," the Dutch governor grants a petition to build a country club in 1766 on the assumption that any non-European claimants to the land are nonpersons ("knowing that it cannot prejudice the interests of others") (18). In another found poem, drawn from the next century, "A Most Desirable Location," auctioneers selling neighborhood properties in 1839 brag:

> None of the lower classes of the population
> either coloured or white,
> reside within the limits of the Municipality
> except those in service and residing
> with the several proprietors. (40)

Yet another found poem from the twentieth century, "Indecently Hilarious," recalls the termination of train service to Sea Point in 1929:

> Next morning, labourers from Langa and Ndabeni
> arrived at the station, bewildered to find no train
> to take them to their work at Sea Point. (21)

The "residents and visitors" to whom such a titular "guide" would normally be addressed belong to the racial and class groups that aren't shut out, are assumed to have mobility, and are the opposite of such nonpersons, lower classes, racial others, and laborers. Although "every native of every place is a potential tourist," as Jamaica Kincaid puts it, "some natives—most natives in the world—cannot go anywhere. They are too poor. They are too poor to go anywhere. They are too poor to escape the reality of their lives."[55] "The Wedding Was at Paddavlei" metaphorically evokes the simmering force of these exclusions and repressions. It tells of a Jewish wedding north of Cape Town at which a "groom's stamping on the glass" breaks open a hole: "The frogs burst through the floorboards," going "bananas, leaping / onto everything," possibly "insane with shock" after a hundred years of "exile" (an ironic allusion to the multiple exiles that brought Jews to South Africa) (87). Although the tourist guide rhetoric of the menu running at the bottom of the page is all about inclusiveness and diversity—the variety of national cuisines to be found in Sea Point—Press plays instead on the ironies of exile and highlights the exclusions on which this "whites only" social space has been founded. Her collaging of historical found texts across several centuries demonstrates how language has functioned at different times to screen out, negate, even dehumanize various people as nonpersons.

Least secure in this milieu are the nannies, maids, and other working people of color, whose spatial boundaries are the most easily and routinely violated, as in the poem "Glimpses of Women in Overalls" about an "off duty" nanny:

like children, fearing any moment
the door bursting open:
why did you
where is my
who said you (52)

To a greater extent than Bishop, Ashbery, or Larkin, Press draws attention to the divisions by class and race presupposed by the standard tour "guide" for "residents and visitors." The implied audience of such guides isn't a maid or nanny, whose location is seldom in her control and is often subject to violation, as highlighted by the abruptly enjambed and unpunctuated fragments of questions; rather, it's someone assumed to have relative freedom in choosing where he or she will reside or visit—or burst in.

Unlike the author of a guidebook, written from a seemingly impartial perspective, Press implicates herself in this history of white privilege of Sea Point's "residents and visitors." Another of her found poems, "Here We Go Again," recalls the evacuation of "coloured" and Indian families from Tramway Road by means of "Proclamation 190 of 1957," during the period of intensified geographic segregation under apartheid (57–58). But white children attending a primary school nearby are ignorant of this violent history of exclusion, "instructed to stay away from Tramway Road /

but never told why" (57). In some of her lyric poems about growing up in
Sea Point, Press signals the indifference of white teenagers to the social
repressions on which their world is based. Cousins returning from a tour
of Europe in 1968 wear psychedelic clothes that seem all the more out
of place because their London-bought purple wool jackets and velvet
hats are ludicrously ill suited to the climate: "It was 30°C and they looked
ready to faint" (22). Press conveys the narrowness of these supposedly
world-wise teens, who can't see past their preoccupations with sex,
clothes, money, and beaches. Including herself in this experience of racial
privilege, Press writes in first person plural,

> We pay for the view,
> enormous sums for the smallest glimpse
> of the border. (95)

The landscape was already "sliced into parlor views" in the nineteenth
century (20), and she is one of the inheritors of this violent expropriation of land. But if the view is an experience of timeless plenitude that
requires the repression of history, Press keeps recalling the history that
made it possible: "we are all in this place because somewhere else / sad-
ness and money converged" (50), "our uninhabitable past / pulling us
back" (95). Toward the start of the sequence, Press, who has also written
science textbooks,[56] adduces a lyrically scientific vision of flux and flow
against which all the subsequent barriers, exclusions, and slicings seem
unnatural: "We hang here, inquisitive carbon-based life forms," reads
the book's opening quotation, "knowing that every atom of carbon now
in our bodies was once in the interior of a star" (10). Against this permeability, the tourist dos and don'ts in "Tips for Visitors," all meant to
shore up boundaries, seem ludicrous: "Carry your keys in a separate
pocket," "Never sit alone in a park," "Count your change" (60). Press's
Echo Location is and isn't a "guide to Sea Point": it piggybacks on tourist
tips, plaques, menus, and other standard ingredients of tourist discourse,
tightly clamping poetry to its sight-locational other. Yet it also exposes
the sometimes violent policing of place that makes it available to privileged residents and visitors. The sequence evokes touristic discourses of
locality and yet thwarts touristic norms by its disorientingly heterogeneous collage of found and made materials, its recovery of the historical
languages of racial exclusion that make a place accessible to some and
not others, and its self-implication and self-critique of authorial respon-

sibility. Such self-interruptive para-tourism can serve as an ethical and intellectual model—actively rethinking place and travel in historical time, and pushing the reader to do so as well, without either pretending to be exempt from tourism or passively submitting to its consumerist proclivities.

Like Karen Press, Arun Kolatkar wrote a long sequence of poems that both approaches and resists being a guidebook introduction to a place: his *Jejuri* (1976) is named after a temple town some distance from Mumbai, a site of pilgrimage and tourism.[57] As a secular Indian visitor to a pilgrimage site, Kolatkar represents himself as an insider/outsider, knowledgeable about the site and its associated rituals and sacred objects, yet remaking it through a cubistic array of viewpoints, vocabularies, and forms. As in Press's pseudo-guide, this sequence's perspectivism complicates touristic homogenization and transparency: poems explore Jejuri from the viewpoint of a priest, a devotee, the poet's skeptical brother, a sixteenth-century Bhakti reformer, and ancient mythical characters, as well as a dog and her puppies, a rat, even a dung beetle. The kaleidoscopically multiform sequence also combines the paradoxes and ecstasies, bareness and heterodoxy of Bhakti poetry with Euromodernist techniques drawn from Dada, Imagism, and Objectivism, occasionally shadowed by the blues.[58] In form and style, the sequence jumps from the epigrammatic to narrative, the descriptive to song, second-person address to third-person narration, concrete spatialized poem to lyric inwardness. The variety of focal and formal perspectives undoes the priority of any, offering instead a playfully plural and idiosyncratic guide that calls attention to its fashioning and multiplicity. A poem in fourteen words, "The Doorstep" wryly plays two angles against one another, as if in a kind of rabbit-duck gestalt illusion: "That's no doorstep," asserts the poem, "It's a pillar on its side" (45). But is it a pillar, as the body of the poem asserts, or a doorstep, as the title asserts? The poem treats such questions as undecidable. It invokes but undoes the norms of what tourism theorists call a "sight marker," such as a sign or plaque, constituting a location as a place to be seen.[59] Like the sequence at large, this marker splinters into irreconcilable constructions of a supposedly bounded, tourable, self-identical place.

Irony in the sequence is pervasive and destabilizing not only at the micro level but also at the macro. The strongest structural irony is implicit in the chiastic crossing of the sequence's two major sections, the first part set in the temple complex, the second in the railway station. Stereoscopically defamiliarizing Jejuri, Kolatkar wryly deploys secularizing language to describe religious temples in the first part and, in the second, religious language to describe the secular train station and natural environment. Like Bishop's poem about her travels, Kolatkar's sequence, exploiting poetry's double-visioned capacities, secularizes the spiritual and spiritualizes the secular. When the tourist arrives at the train station, as if dragging the spiritual language from the temple complex with him, he describes the indicator as "a wooden saint" (69), the mangy station dog as "the spirit of the place . . . // doing penance" (70), the tea stall salesperson as a "novice" who "has taken a vow of silence" and conducts "ablutions" and "ceremonies" (70), the station master as believing in "the doctrine / of the next train" (71), and knowledge of when the next train is due as requiring sacrificial "slaughter" (72). By contrast, in the first section, it is the stone and bronze materiality of the temples and their contents that the sequence emphasizes. Perhaps the most "spiritual" moment in the temple sequence is an encounter with a butterfly, though without the aid of myths or religious narratives: "There is no story behind it. / It is split like a second. / It hinges around itself." It exists only in the immediacy of the present, and the moment of its disappearance is registered in a visual and verbal pun:

> Just a pinch of yellow,
> it opens before it closes
> and closes before it o
>
> where is it (52–53)

The "o" suspended at line's and stanza's end is the "o" of the broken word "open," the "O" of poetic vocative, the "oh" of astonishment, and the o (zero) of absence—all of which are summoned in the playful enjambment and the elided syllable "-pens," an omission that, while verbally, semantically, and visually enacting openness, silently speaks the poet's pen.

Sometimes the sequence deliberately courts tourist discourse but, at least in one instance, only to burst out of it. Aware that he has been a kind of tourist in this temple town, the departing speaker self-mockingly slips into touristic enumeration:

> You leave the little temple town
> with its sixty three priests inside their sixty three houses
> huddled at the foot of the hill
> with its three hundred pillars, five hundred steps and eighteen arches. (67)

Kolatkar parodies tourism's grounding in the psychology of collection—here, of experiential sites, as elsewhere of material souvenirs, postcards, pictures, videos.[60] Such cataloguing continues until the verse suddenly explodes out of touristic numeracy—explodes itself, language, the page—representing in modernist concrete poetry the harvest dance of a dozen cocks and hens in a field:

```
                n                        a
up            a   d      do  n         a n         uP    &      d
                              w          d
                   d              u
          &    wo       a      p       a d     do       &    u
        a        n      n               n        w            p
         n              d                   n      n
        d     u    an        o    &    u        d    d n    a d   u
              p    d        w          p     an    o     n      p
                           n                   p
        d                                                 P
          o       &  u      n d     d w      d    u  an       own  &
           w           p   a        o n     n   a            d   d   & &
        n                                          d
        an     uP    a      uP       a d    w    a d    n     uP
          d         d n              n    d on     n   a d
                                          n
```

FIGURE I Extract from Arun Kolatkar, *Jejuri*, in *Collected Poems in English*, ed. Arvind Krishna Mehrotra (Highgreen, UK: Bloodaxe, 2010), 68.

The movement of words, though mimetic of the birds' jumping, by virtue of spatialization also foregrounds the poetic page itself, in a sudden formal departure from the rest of the sequence. Halfway between the temples that afforded no religious revelation and the railway station that fails secular norms of modern efficiency, the speaker has an ecstatic vision uncontainable by either religious tradition or secular modernity—a vision perhaps best suited to poetry.

> And there you stand forgetting how silly you must look
> with a priest on your left shoulder as it were
> and a station master on your right. (68)

Earlier in the sequence, Kolatkar tracked by other means another kind of directional movement in his poem "Water Supply." Although we might expect a sequence entitled *Jejuri* to guide us step by step through the temple complex, the semitouristic speaker eschews travel-guide protocols by allowing his attention to be diverted:

> a conduit pipe
> runs with the plinth
> turns a corner of the house
> stops dead in its tracks
> shoots straight up
> keeps close to the wall
> doubles back
> twists around
> and comes to an abrupt halt
> a brass mouse with a broken neck (45)

The poem delights in following the twists and turns of a pipe as phenomenologically tracked by the poet's eye, the mobility emphasized by the short lines and lack of punctuation—modernist techniques adapted from William Carlos Williams and Gary Snyder. Focusing on the pipe instead of the historic temple complex, the poem dramatically calls attention to its own verbal energy and formal sinuousness, the pleasure of following the bends in the lines as though the bends in the pipes: it "turns a corner" sharply with every *versus*, each line launched with another propulsive verb, and the syntax "twists around" until it slams into the metaphor of the pipe as broken-necked mouse. While articulating the site's dilapidation and the speaker's dry-pipe faithlessness, the poem also asks us to read it not as a mere sight marker but as a poem, reveling in its idiosyncratic dynamism in language and form. Far from guiding us step by step through the shrines and their supporting structures, the sequence interrupts tourist transparency and consumption and foregrounds the poetry's linguistic iconoclasm and exuberant Bhakti creativity, its modernist adaptations and multiform perspectivism, its playful redundancy and punning and graphic materiality.

Poetry as/against Sight Marker

One way of reading location-affixed poems like Kolatkar's and Press's would be as a sight marker, or more specifically, an "off-sight marker," akin to a souvenir or postcard, framing a place as significant, as distinct from an "on-sight marker," such as a sign or plaque.[61] Applying MacCannell's stages of "sight sacralization," we could say that a poem as marker names the place, frames or elevates it, enshrines it, makes it mechanically reproducible in the form of a printed or digital text, as well as socially reproducible—cities, villages, sights honored by their literary representation.[62] Because many poems are compressed and memorable, they can be especially effective as mobile markers, which can be read, recited, and circulated. If so, then the poetry critic or teacher—myself included—becomes a specialized tour guide who adds another semiotic layer to this mediation of globally arrayed localities, such as those poetically pinned in the website *Poetry Atlas*. Each place is irreducibly local, affixed to singular geographic coordinates, set within a global network of interrelations. "Through internationalisation," remark sociologists Urry and Larsen, "tourist sites can be compared with those located at home and abroad, especially via the internet. . . . All potential objects of the tourist gaze can be located on a scale and compared with each other."[63] The tourist apparatus atomistically localizes all sites but at the same time ironically homogenizes them as rough equivalents.

But as I've tried to suggest, it would be a mistake to reduce poems to sight markers of single locales, regions, or nations; to read through their formal corrugations in search of referential transparency and locational authenticity; to assume they harbor the same kind of informational and promotional discourse as tourist guides. We should read such place-making poems not as sight markers but as translocal matrices of production and reference, formally and allusively enmeshed with the marked sight and with places elsewhere. Poems often recognize their touristic complicities—as seen by virtue of their visuality, parataxis, or seductive strategies, in Bishop, Ashbery, and Larkin, or their social privilege and insider-outsider mobility, as in Press and Kolatkar—at the same time that they parody and contravene tourism. As seen in this chapter and the previous one, even site-specifying poems should be read as poems—works, unlike a sight marker or brochure, that frequently splice and splinter reference, that are alert to their formal and verbal histories and to themselves as verbal artifacts that actively remake the world. If a first step toward changing tourism is recognition of our participation in it, poetry and literary studies have—alongside sociology, anthropology, and cultural geography—a role to play in self-critically engaging and rethinking it. Touristic poems are also metatouristic, reflecting on their conditions of possibility.

Uncomfortable though it may be to acknowledge, metatouristic poems help render visible the kinship between cultural tour guides and those of us who read and study literature comparatively, globally, or transnationally. To admit as much may be difficult, as it is for me personally. Whether living in West Asia or Europe, traveling in East and South Asia, Africa, or the Caribbean, I have been pained by the specter of tourists with scant historical or cultural understanding of the worlds they enter, even as I've also often found myself falling short, however assiduous my efforts to learn. As critics and students of literature, we should work to avoid the superficiality of some forms of tourism and certain kinds of world literary study, closely and respectfully engaging the cultural, formal, social, and linguistic specificities of individual works and their contexts. But the resemblances shouldn't be denied. Like cultural tourists, readers of global poetry make departures and returns in their horizon-widening journeys and periods of stay. Like travel to cultural sites, reading world poetry is usually at least in part a leisure activity, performed, to recur to the *OED*'s phrase for tourism's aims, "for pleasure or culture." Like cultural tourists, readers of critical works and anthologies encounter their field through the mediation and framing of signs, and just as tourism is a collecting activity, so too is anthologizing (etymologically, flower gathering). In our global age, when national frameworks no longer seem sufficiently capacious, we have to admit, if we're interested in transnational approaches, that poetry and our pedagogical engagement with it aren't innocent of touristic contamination. We should heed the cross-cultural nuances and self-reflective energies of the simultaneously touristic and post-, meta-, extra-, para-, even antitouristic poems we read. Such works can help teach us, whether we're traveling by page or website, by ship, car, foot, or plane, to encounter global localities with awe and irony, imaginative engagement and peripheral vision, self-critically attentive to our complicity in touristic modes of desiring, looking, collecting, and to how language and history frame, construct, and layer our interconnected worlds.

CHAPTER 4

MODERNIST INFLECTIONS, POSTCOLONIAL DIRECTIONS

Modernism and postcolonialism are, as seen across this book, two of the strongest areas of global literary achievement. But how to understand their relationship?[1] If we believe, as some have argued, that modernism is an extension and cultural manifestation of Western imperialism, then the two literary movements might seem inherently at odds.[2] It's possible, as noted in a later chapter, to see Yeats as performing orientalist exoticism,[3] just as it is to see Eliot's *Waste Land* and *Four Quartets* as exploiting Indian sacred texts,[4] Conrad's *Heart of Darkness* as fictively enacting colonialist racism,[5] Picasso's cubism as plundering African and Oceanic masks and sculptural forms. If so, the notion of either "postcolonial modernism" or "modernist postcolonialism" would seem to be a contradiction in terms.

In my view, the geocultural, political, and historical divergences between modernism and postcolonialism are such that they shouldn't be collapsed into one another as a uniform cultural formation, but neither should they be seen as antithetical. Recent scholarship has been showing that they are deeply intertwined: postcolonial writers adapt modernist techniques; modernism is fueled by encounters with non-Western cultures; and postcolonial and modernist writers work from the shared historical ground of a worldwide modernity.[6] Critics have been revealing continuities between Rushdie's fiction and Joyce's, Monica Ali's and Virginia Woolf's, Arundhati Roy's and E. M. Forster's.[7] They have shown that Derek Walcott and Kamau Brathwaite indigenized Eliot's poetics in Caribbean spaces, and that postcolonial and modernist writers engaged each other in cross-racial networks in radio, publishing, and other cultural institutions.[8] They have uncovered in Arab, African, and Caribbean novels preoccupations with capitalist modernity.[9] And while we'll see elsewhere in this book that orientalism and exoticism play a role in the work of Yeats, Stevens, and others, we'll also observe countervailing anti-orientalist and ecocosmopolitan strands in Euromodernism.

How does postcolonial poetry in particular converge with and diverge from modernism? How do postcolonial poems understand their relation to modernism? And what literary-historical models are most productive in mapping their relationship? To approach these questions, this chapter alternates between two vantage points: it explores the relation between postcolonial poetry and modernism both intrinsically, from within self-theorizing poems, and extrinsically, from the higher altitude of conceptual paradigms for transnationalism. That is, it closely examines poems that thematize the relation between postcolonial poetry and modernism, and it reconsiders the global analytic models that schematize it. Instead of surveying postcolonial writers' responses to and continuities with modernism, I explore what further light a few postcolonial poems might shed on this relationship—poems that bring us to the heart of the matter by directly engaging modernism. Because poetry, if it is to be read as poetry, demands close attention to language and form, I concentrate on two initial examples, from South Africa and the Caribbean, before considering a series of general models for modernist-inflected postcolonialism, and then conclude with a third poem, this one Indo-British. My wager is that postcolonial works that reflect on their modernist inheritances may be especially helpful in probing this relationship, one of the most important for understanding modern and contemporary poetry in a global frame.

This Is Not a Modernist Poem, or Is It?

The title of my first example, "This is not a riot policeman," wittily entwines modernism with postcolonialism. As published in South African Jewish poet Karen Press's collection *Bird Heart Stoning the Sea* (1990), the poem was annotated: "The title is drawn from a painting by René Magritte of an apple, entitled 'This is not an apple.'"[10] Like his similar painting *The Treachery of Images* (1929, *La trahison des images*), which famously includes the words "Ceci n'est pas une pipe" (This is not a pipe), the Belgian surrealist's oil painting bears words on its canvas that interrupt the painting's representational illusion. Each painting is thus a painting of an apple or a pipe and a painting of words about the painted image of the apple or pipe not being a real apple or pipe. Self-consciously "drawn from" Magritte's example, Press's poem would seem to evidence continuity between modernism and postcolonialism, as does the colonialism-interrogating, Beckett-inspired fiction of fellow white South African writer J. M. Coetzee: it transfers the modernist questioning of representational images from painting to poetry and from Europe to apartheid-era South Africa. Modernism is being transnationally and intercontinentally stretched.

As if ocular epistemology would suffice, the poem begins with a command.

Look:
three sweet blue riot policemen
standing watching the goldfish in the Gardens
somebody loves these bastards

But of course readers of the poem cannot literally "look" at the policemen looking at the goldfish, and so, as in Magritte's surrealist paintings and other modernist works, representational norms are both enacted and questioned. Also as in Magritte's and other modernisms, the images are uncannily vivid, colorful, sharply drawn. Magritte pushes realist illusionism so hard that he unmakes it, and so too Press's policemen, delineated by their coloristic contrast with the goldfish, seem suspended between the real and the imaginary.

But—and this is where the poem may begin to mark a postcolonial difference—Press is not questioning representation for its own sake or for its generalized shock value (*épater les bourgeois*). Rather, she suggests that in South Africa under apartheid, the real seems surreal, strangely difficult to imagine—that the brutality and the humanity of the police defy comprehension. Relocalizing Magritte, she gives a political edge to his conceptual twisting of the boundaries between the real and the imaginary. Granted, the antifascist painter's art may have been partly intended to subvert a bourgeois ideology grounded in ideas of stable things, but Magritte objected to overtly political art and the confusion of art with political action.[11] In place of a modernist unsettling of the conventional consumption of art—calling into question whether these signifiers are tangible, visible policemen rather than verbal signs—Press's defamiliarization shows up the irrationality of reality under a colonial police state. The seeming innocence ("sweet") of policemen looking at goldfish is difficult to reconcile with their vicious acts, and to think that they are ordinary beloved persons ("somebody loves these bastards") is hard to square with their being relentlessly violent. The tension in Magritte's paintings

between conventional reality and its defamiliarization is transferred here
to the disjunction between the policemen's humanity and their violence.
This postcolonial poet adapts modernism's violation of representational
norms—from Picasso and Braque to Magritte, and from Stein and Eliot
to Joyce—to probe the representation-warping contradictions of apartheid.

But the differences should not be overdrawn. As already indicated,
antibourgeois thinking informs Magritte's art. And if Press is sharpening
modernism's political edge, she is no less preoccupied than the modernists with aesthetic craft. She uses the resources of poetry to convey a
strangely idealist realism like that of Magritte's suspended apple or pipe,
seemingly real but out of time, hanging in space against a blank background: the repeated participles "standing watching," the assonance of
"three sweet," the alliteration of "goldfish in the Gardens," the syntactic
repetition, the seemingly innocent figures. The policemen "with their
sharp moustaches / and their smooth, fat cheeks" seem almost like dolls,
the sharpness of their moustaches juxtaposed with the plumpness of
their cheeks. Heightening the contrast between care and cruelty, Press
distills life under apartheid in a few pellucid images, including words
redolent of fairytale: "somebody takes the wicked blue cap off at night /
and strokes the poisonous brow." When violence enters directly into the
poem, it, too, is suspended in stylized language:

> How they must hate
> something, to beat and beat
> at women's breasts and the heads of children
> until they bleed and crack

Enjambing "hate" to make the emotion seem all the more frightfully
unfocused, Press alliterates and repeats (*beat, beat, breasts, bleed*), and
she abstracts the policemen's victims in elemental images of bleeding
female breasts and children's cracked heads. When she closes the poem
by repeating and varying the beginning ("fat, furious riot policemen /
watching the goldfish in the Gardens"), the police surveillance seems
ridiculous yet all encompassing. With an unpunctuated starkness, Press
redeploys the modernist sense of the irrationality of the seemingly
rational to conjure the world of a postcolonial police state. Like Coetzee's fiction, her poetry—far from agitprop, documentary, or socialist
realism—often has a dreamlike surreality. But even as it abstracts and
stylizes, even as it surreally suspends animation, a poem such as "This is

not a riot policeman" engages a more fully embodied social and political world than do Magritte's time-and-space-defying images. Modernist-inflected postcolonialism, as illustrated by Press's poem, builds on modernist defamiliarization but intensifies its social and political critique.

A Euromodernist Quest Transplanted in Jamaica

The terms by which Press's poem seems to distinguish the postcolonial from the modernist may well be expected, since so-called postmodern literature, coming after high modernism, is often described as politicizing and de-universalizing modernism and since postcolonial writing is often conceived as intensely political. But do they apply across the board? Let us look at another contemporary postcolonial poem that is equally deliberate about its relation to a modernist interlocutor. Jamaican poet Lorna Goodison's "Quest" recounts how a Caribbean schoolgirl—the poet's personal experience cast in the third person—responds when she hears a teacher read Eliot's "Journey of the Magi." Other postcolonial poets have testified to the catalytic role Eliot played in their poetic development, including Derek Walcott and most famously the Barbadian Kamau Brathwaite, who despite his revolutionary, Afrocentric poetics credited the conservative Anglo-Catholic royalist with introducing into Caribbean poetry "the notion of the speaking voice, the conversational tone."[12] Brathwaite's poems evidence the impact of Eliot's satiric couplets, jazz rhythms, disjunctive tone, vernacular diction, multiple personae, and apocalypticism. Like Brathwaite, Goodison describes hearing Eliot rather than reading him, thus assimilating him to Caribbean orature, but her emphasis is quite different from Brathwaite's.

According to Goodison's "Quest," Eliot's "Journey of the Magi" played a pivotal role in a Caribbean schoolgirl's awakening to adulthood and to poetry:

> At age twelve, six days
>   into the start of a year
>   this girl was seated
>
> in a whitewashed classroom;
>   dreaming herself outdoors
>   and up Lignum vitae trees
>
> and heard a teacher read:
>   "A cold coming we had of it."[13]

In this initiation scene, a girl at the threshold of change finds her day-dream infiltrated by a new language and imagery. The poem is precisely fixed in time by the January 6 feast of the Epiphany that celebrates the visit of the magi to baby Jesus, and by the girl's age and the school calendar (when Goodison was twelve in 1959, Jamaica was part of the West Indies Federation—like the schoolgirl, on the verge of independence). It is also firmly located in the space of the classroom and the local environment (the Lignum vitae is indigenous to Jamaica and bears its national flower). But the girl unmoors herself from space-time coordinates, floating imaginatively outside the confines of the stark classroom, and this dreaminess helps open her to being further dislocated by Eliot's poem—from Jamaica to a colder climate, and from her escapist fantasy to an unknown poet's and the magi's dreams.

In the steplike, variable trimeter tercets that enact her stepping from one world into another, she says she "went on a journey // with men whose names / or what they went in search of / never revealed." By omitting the auxiliary verb "was" before "revealed" (not so in manuscript), Goodison accentuates the mystery of this quest and sounds the West Indian tongue, a hint picked up in the next creolized verb, "rung," which even rhymes with "tongue":

> She only recalls that when
>   a prefect rung the lunch bell
>   she was wrenched from the ride
>
> with those men on a quest
>   and that she tested on her tongue
>   the words "refractory"
>
> and "silken" as adjectives for herself,
>   as hints for her own journey; girl exited
>   room with vaulted ceiling, disoriented.

The schoolgirl's estrangement echoes the magi's disorientation in Eliot's poem, feeling "no longer at ease" in the kingdoms to which they return after witnessing Christ's birth.[14] But whereas the magi's disorientation, presumably like Eliot's upon his conversion, is primarily religious, Goodison's is imaginative. Centrally concerned with the biblical quest story, as mediated by Lancelot Andrewes's Christmas sermon ("A cold coming we had of it"), Eliot's 1927 poem also echoes Guadeloupean-born Saint-John Perse's long poem *Anabase* (1924). Eliot was translating it at the

time and called it a "series of images of migration" in Asia, cross-cultural
movements that figure in part his own displacement through his conversion to Anglo-Catholicism.[15] Goodison's imaginative migration on the
back of Eliot's words and wandering magi thus adds yet another layer to
the cross-cultural mix of a modernist poem already entwined with the
Caribbean—and with the ancient story of a march to Persia and back by
a Greek mercenary army supporting Cyrus the Younger in Xenophon's
Anabasis. Bearing out Eliot's claim "that genuine poetry can communicate before it is understood," the schoolgirl—stimulated and deracinated
by the otherness of Eliot's somewhat opaque, syncretic modernism—
embarks on her own poetic migration.[16] Instead of responding, as does
Brathwaite, among other postcolonial writers, that "the imported alien
experience of the snowfall" in British poems has "little to do, really with
the environment and reality of the Caribbean," and that in Caribbean
education, "People were forced to learn things that had no relevance to
themselves," Goodison's schoolgirl is inspired by that climatic and environmental alienness to strengthen the alternative-world-creating power
of her imagination.[17]

Already evidenced by the transitive use of the verb *dream* ("dreaming
herself outdoors"), the schoolgirl's imaginative capacity takes on a more
specifically verbal and protopoetic texture as she tests and tastes a new
lexicon. An alliterative and internally rhymed sequence of words—"*quest* /
and that she *test*ed on her *t*ongue"—both bespeaks poetic awakening to
the sensual materiality of words and demonstrates it, signifiers felt in
their weight and texture, or what the linguist Roman Jakobson dubbed
"poeticity" or the "poetic function."[18] As she tries the words on herself,
they point in opposite directions that the poem reconciles: both "refrac-
tory," as in Goodison's self-directedness and resistance to fashion, and
"silken," as in her seamlessly incorporating Eliotic diction, Jamaican
Creole, and other ingredients. Adjectives belonging to marginal figures
in Eliot's poem—camels and girls—Goodison reassigns to herself. She
enacts a kind of reverse exoticism, in which modernism is the mysterious
other that stirs the poetic imagination. It is less a tool that sharpens and
stylizes a social and political art, as in Press, more a source of inspiration
and evocation, closer to the suggestiveness prized in the symbolist strand
of modernism. As we probe postcolonial engagements with modernism,
we mustn't collapse the plurality of modernisms any more than that of
postcolonialisms. Through its verbal and narrative disorientations, its
translocational bridging of distant geographies, this modernism helps
the poet develop an imagination that spans local experience and unfa-

miliar cultures elsewhere. Witness her poem's confluences of tropical warmth and cold snows, Standard English and Creole, Jamaica and biblical Asia, Anglo-American Eliot and Franco-Guadeloupean Perse. Like Eliot's poetry, Goodison's turns among different verbal, geographic, and cultural realms, a code-switching and translocal poetics, but Goodison's has a more overtly personal dimension than Eliot's, if placed within Caribbean cross-culturalism. Whether personalizing and translocalizing an already syncretic but purportedly impersonal art, as Goodison does, or historicizing and politicizing the disjunctive knitting together of dream and reality, as Press does, modernist-engaged postcolonial poems enact both continuities and differences between these cultural formations.

Models of Postcolonialism cum Modernism

With these self-theorizing poems in mind, let's exchange our close-up poetry zoom for a wide-angle conceptual lens and consider four general models for the relation between modernism and postcolonialism. While it's important to discern the intricate verbal and formal strategies by which specific poems engage with modernism, we also need to find a way to talk about such literary-historical relations in the aggregate, and here conceptual paradigms prove indispensable. A first way of theorizing the relation of postcolonialism to modernism is the idea that Western modernist inventions and techniques spread from the metropolitan center to the postcolonial peripheries, a variety of diffusionism.[19] In our two examples, Magritte's surrealism spreads to apartheid-era South Africa, and Eliot's syncretic modernism to 1950s Jamaica. Metropolitan modernism diffuses outward, whether because it seems formally advanced and inventive, or because an uneven world system makes for outflows from rich to less powerful regions, or because peripheral cultures establish their cultural authority by proving themselves according to Western standards, or because Western works have the advantage of colonial mechanisms of distribution, such as the British Council, which disseminated Eliot's recordings into the Caribbean and elsewhere. The West-centric diffusionist model has, however, a number of disadvantages. First, it attributes all the creative and inventive power to the metropolitan sites.[20] But modernism is already permeated by the supposed peripheries to which it is thought to have diffused, as evidenced by the impact of African and Oceanic art on Picasso, Islamic art on Kandinsky and Matisse, East Asian writing on Pound and Stevens, East, West, and

South Asian philosophy, theater, and art on Yeats, South Asian sacred texts on Eliot, and African and Latin American cultures on Langston Hughes. When postcolonial writers take up so-called Western experiments, as Laura Doyle remarks, "they are sometimes 'borrowing back' those styles" through the detour of the West.[21] As we saw in the example of Eliot's "Journey of the Magi"—influenced, inter alia, by the migratory work of a writer from Guadeloupe—the center has already been peripheralized. Eurocentric diffusionism occludes the mutuality, dialogism, and interdependence of modernism and postcolonialism. Second, it denies postcolonialism any significant agency. The receiving culture is imagined as being influenced, shaped, remade by the diffusing culture. But as Gayatri Chakravorty Spivak puts it, "the sources of literary agency have expanded beyond the old European national literatures."[22] And as Anthony Giddens states of globalization, "This is more than a diffusion of Western institutions across the world, in which other cultures are crushed."[23] Highlighting "the multiform varieties of individual and collective agency available" to postcolonial subjects, Kwame Anthony Appiah disputes the "deeply condescending" idea that they are "tabulae rasae on which global capitalism's moving finger writes its message"; instead, they are "constantly inventing new forms of difference."[24] As we have seen, Press remakes Magritte's time-space-suspended surrealism when she South Africanizes and politicizes it, and Goodison enacts a rather different journey from Eliot's when she Caribbeanizes, personalizes, and more emphatically translocalizes it. Postcolonial transformation may be no less inventive than is modernist innovation, itself based partly in the transformative impact of non-Western materials.

In diametric contrast to Euro-diffusion is a second model, which the title of a primary textbook in postcolonial studies puts succinctly: *The Empire Writes Back*, an abbreviation of Rushdie's remark "the Empire writes back to the Centre."[25] Western modernism doesn't spread across the postcolonial world; instead, the postcolonial world rejects it and other alien, Eurocentric, colonial impositions. Struggle, resistance, decolonization, decoloniality—according to multiple variations on this model, postcolonial peoples and literatures are in a cultural battle with the metropolitan center, refusing to be interpolated into Western aesthetics, values, and systems of knowledge. Achebe's rejection of Conrad's modernism as racist is prototypical, and a range of postcolonial poets with nativist leanings, such as Brathwaite, Louise Bennett, and Okot p'Bitek, would seem to exemplify such resistance. This model grants agency to postcolonial writers, acknowledges differences between their socioeconomic circumstances and those of poets from the metropole, and recognizes the political stakes of their self-assertion. But poems such as Press's and Goodison's at the very least complicate this model. To see Press's politicizing of Magritte's surrealism and Goodison's de-depersonalizing of Eliot's modernism as armies clashing by night is to exaggerate the conflict, imposing a nationalist political paradigm seldom sufficient to the complexities of literary enmeshment. As Appiah shows of Afrocentric nativists, even postcolonial poets who defy Western modernists are in dialogue with what they oppose.[26] And many others self-consciously embrace, coopt, develop, riff on, and borrow from them—not only poets we've already discussed but many others including Christopher Okigbo, A. K. Ramanujan, Arun Kolatkar, M. NourbeSe Philip, Craig Santos Perez, let alone nonanglophone writers such as Léopold Senghor, Nicolás Guillén, and Aimé Césaire. Finally, the "writes back" model presupposes essential differences between modernism and postcolonialism, even though modernist literatures are inextricably interwoven with African, Asian, Oceanic, Caribbean, Latin American, and other cultures. As Arif Dirlik puts it, "We are all modern now, whether we like it or not."[27]

If the "writes back" model exaggerates the cultural and political differences between postcolonial writers and the modernists, another model sees both modernist and postcolonial literatures as more or less the same, in that they constitute a shared response to global capitalism. The "fundamental meaning of modernity," according to Fredric Jameson, is "worldwide capitalism."[28] On this account, the political violence of colonialism is a secondary effect of forcing peripheral societies into a capitalist world system dominated by the center, in accord with Immanuel Wallerstein's world-systems theory. Propounding this view, Neil Lazarus criticizes Edward Said and other postcolonialists for whom "'imperialism' is typically cast as a *political* dispensation" more than an economic one, involving "military conquest, alien governance, systematized top-down violence, social asymmetry, cultural and symbolic domination."[29] Lazarus and his coauthors write that texts from around the world "should be considered together because they all bear testimony . . . to the 'shock of the new', the massive rupture effected at the levels of space-time continuum, lifeworld, experience and human sensorium by capitalist modernisation."[30] The advantage of the concept of a "singular modernity" is that it reveals the economic structures that traverse the distances between global North and South. And many postcolonial writers, like the modernists, respond vigorously to capitalism's melting of all that's solid into air. Walcott's lament over the tourist despoliation of Saint Lucia, Okot p'Bitek's critique of the importation of Western fashion and technology into East Africa, Louise Bennett's satire on the commodification of national symbols in Jamaica—these and many other examples demonstrate a sharp postcolonial critique of the excesses of capitalism. But this model also risks homogenizing vastly discrepant cultural, political, and historical circumstances, as well as literary works, conscripting them into documenting and allegorizing global capitalism. Notwithstanding refinements to the base-superstructure model, the cultural and political dimensions of colonialism, as well as responses to it, are seen as economically driven. Works such as Press's "This is not a riot policeman" and Goodison's "Quest," neither of which has any interest in commodification or the world economic system, slip into insignificance. More nuanced, less monolithic models allow for the many different facets of modernity and empire—economic but also social, governmental, bureaucratic, technological, cultural, and political.

A fourth and last model, rejected by proponents of the singular modernity concept, is alternative modernities and modernisms, and closely related ideas of cultural appropriation, indigenization, vernacularization, creolization, or hybridization. According to this paradigm, various cultures reshape modernity and modernism in assimilating them to their regional or local circumstances.[31] Jameson mocks the "cultural" notion that "you can fashion your own modernity differently, so that there can be a Latin-American kind, or an Indian kind, or an African kind, and so forth."[32] And Lazarus dismisses "various recent attempts to pluralize the concept of modernity" as "both unnecessary and misguided."[33] But whereas singular modernity and diffusionism stress standardization and homogenization in history and culture, pluralist concepts help to bring out heterogenization. Rather than positing postcolonial regions as passive recipients of a diffused modernism or an imperial capitalism, they attribute creative energy to the adaptation of modernism, whether in response to local or global exigencies. They credit the possibility of a Jamaican, a South African, an Indian, or an Oceanic creolization of modernism—each related to but distinct from the others. Both Appiah and Arjun Appadurai represent globalization as a process not only of homogenization but also of heterogenization. What arguments about homogenization, Americanization, and commoditization "fail to consider," writes Appadurai, "is that at least as rapidly as forces from various metropolises are brought into new societies they tend to become indigenized in one or another way: this is true of music and housing styles as much as it is true of science and terrorism, spectacles and constitutions."[34] We might add poetry to his list: "T-shirts, billboards, and graffiti as well as rap music, street dancing, and slum housing all show that the images of the media are quickly moved into local repertoires of irony, anger, humor, and resistance."[35] But this model also has its drawbacks. For all the attention to cultural heterogeneity, it risks oversimplifying each indigenizing culture, by virtue of the contrast between indigenizing and indigenized cultures. And each of these "cultures" needs to be internally differentiated. After all, Jewish South African Press's hybridization of modernism looks nothing like Soweto-born Lesego Rampolokeng's hip-hop, homiletic "sermons" in poetry, with their violently scrambled imagistic sequences, and Goodison's lyric Caribbeanizations of Eliot's modernism diverge from Brathwaite's *Waste Land*–indebted multiple dramatic personae speaking in different voices of apocalyptic loss and transformation. By the same token, the modernisms being indigenized are as heterogeneous as Magritte's surrealism and Eliot's religious-conversion-era modernism, Ezra Pound and Langston Hughes. And both the indigenizing and the indigenized cultures are always already permeated by multiple cross-cultural influences. Other liabilities of the indigenization model include the possible exaggeration of dialogic exchanges in asymmetrical relationships, and the possible overestimation of the social or material effects of culture (so-called culturalism). Still, this fourth model has the advantage over econocentric models of a vocabulary more responsive to the literary specificities and intricacies of works such as poems, and it allows for continuities and distinctions between modernism and postcolonialism.

Convergences: Testing the Models

Now swapping out the wide-angle for a close-up lens, let's examine one last postcolonial poem that, like our African and Caribbean examples, flaunts its engagement with modernism and so may help test the hermeneutic viability of these various conceptual frameworks. Written by a "Black" or "Asian" British poet of Indian Punjabi parentage, Daljit Nagra's "A Black History of the English-Speaking Peoples" is cast in the same stanza pattern as W. H. Auden's "Spain," a modernist poem that it quotes and alludes to repeatedly.[36] What do we learn about the conceptual models by looking at them anew from the perspective of this poem? And what do we learn about this and other modernist-inflected postcolonial poems by applying these various critical templates?

The poem provides ample support for diffusionism. Indeed, the modernist poem on which Nagra's is patterned even describes civilization as a historical process of "diffusion": "The language of size / Spreading to China along the trade-routes; the diffusion / Of the counting-frame and the cromlech."[37] As W. J. Perry argued in *The Growth of Civilization* (1924), to which Auden's poem is indebted and which Eliot reviewed, even though "the great civilizations are often assumed to be independent products of development in isolation," their arts, crafts, and inventions have dispersed and spread among one another.[38] If ever there was a literary exemplar of diffusion across countless works of postcolonial and diasporic literature, it is Shakespeare, his plays disseminated from the Globe to every region of the globe, and "A Black History of the English-Speaking Peoples" begins with a Black actor's performance of Shakespeare in London—"A king's invocations at the Globe Theatre" (50)—before declaring that the Globe (or globe?) may be the poet's muse.

Demonstrating diffusion, the poem plays on Shakespeare ("brave new verse"), refers to Conrad's *Heart of Darkness* ("the Livingstone spirit turned Kurtz"), quotes Tennyson, Arnold, and Macaulay, as well as modernism's postcolonial affiliates Walcott and Heaney, but its strongest formal and intellectual precedent is Auden's "Spain." Like that poem, it is built out of stanzas in an anvil shape, with two five-beat lines, an indented third line of three beats, and a fourth line that returns to five. Like Auden's poem, Nagra's is in parts that focus on past, present, and future. Both Auden and Nagra reflect on origins—how we got where we are, whether in the midst of the Spanish Civil War or in a multiethnic, globalized Britain. More important, Nagra embraces Auden's complex view of ethical responsibility in history—the modernist subject's self-division as morally complicit in wrongdoing (war for Auden, empire for Nagra). Although Auden abhors the Fascist Nationalists—associated with fevers, fears, invasions, greed, firing squads, and bombs—he doesn't idealize the left-wing Republican struggle he supports: fighting for them involves "the deliberate increase in the chances of death, / The conscious acceptance of guilt in the necessary murder."[39] Nagra quotes the phrase "necessary murder," famously denounced by George Orwell and later disavowed by Auden, transferring it from the Spanish context to Britain's imperial wars. But even though Nagra's redeployment of it has an ironic edge, and even though he questions the empire's civilizing mission and criticizes its "imperial gusto" (50), he concedes: "My forebears played / their part for the Empire's quid / pro quo by assisting the rule and divide of their ilk" (51). The witty enjambment of "quid," resulting in a cross-lingual pun, calls attention to the material motives of the poet's extended family. Just as Auden recognizes killing for a noble cause in a supposedly just war as a form of murder, Nagra's divided sense of himself is as both victim and victimizer, from an Indian family that helped perpetrate imperialism even as it bore its scars.

But doesn't the empire write back to the center? Surely, starting with the title: the poem announces a postcolonially resistant relation to Western culture in its Blackening of Winston Churchill's multivolume *A History of the English-Speaking Peoples*, a work that contemptuously belittled India and Indians. While "aligning" himself with Gandhi, the poet bitterly recalls a condensed version of Churchill's abusive reference in 1930 to the Indian anticolonial leader as a *"half-naked fakir"* (52). For all its allusions to Shakespeare, the poem, "Coming clean," turns on player and playwright, "this king at the Globe, whose head seems cluttered / with golden-age bumph," a metaphor that associates him with imperial waste (52).[40] And for all his reverence for Auden's "Spain," Nagra's citation of "necessary murder" ties his English predecessor's work to the logic of imperialism—the legitimation of killing in the service of "the light of learning" (50).

What about postcolonialism and modernism as reactions to, and encodings of, worldwide capitalism? Here again Nagra's poem lends support. It ends with the poet strolling along the Thames and remembering the history of an empire, including "flotillas of tea and white gold / cotton and sugar"—a history of violent expropriation of goods and labor ("sweetness-and-light // blood lettings," in an ironic turn on Arnold) that coincides with the history of worldwide capitalism (53). When he looks "ahead," both physically along the Thames and figuratively to the future, what he sees may be cause for some hope (the lovers) but also for dismay:

> Till what's ahead are the upbeat lovers who gaze
>   from the London Eye
> at multinationals lying along the sanitised Thames. (53)

The history of British imperialism has culminated in multinational corporations, which perpetuate the empire's earlier patterns of exploitative accumulation, yet sanitize that history (in the pun on "lying"), banishing all evidence from sight. The London Eye resumes the poem's earlier Shakespearean image of being "bound to the wheels / of global power" (52), updating Lear's wheel of fire and fortune's wheel as bondage to the vagaries of capitalism. This giant eye is panoptic yet blind to the long history erased by global capital. Implicitly, the poet's role is to recover that history, to remember and attest to its insistence even in the present,

and one way of doing so is to think back critically through English literature's complicities in empire even while extending that poetic tradition.
At poem's end he recovers a literary artifact of empire, Tennyson's poem
about the Indian Rebellion of 1857, "The Defence of Lucknow," which
celebrates the heroic defenders of the British residency under Indian
siege: *"Every man die at his post!"* (53). The ancestral literary house into
which this Indian-descended poet is writing himself, which once lion-
ized as heroes those who defended British space against Indians, helped
prepare the way for the reign of global corporations, now and into the
foreseeable future ("what's ahead").

What about indigenization? Here again Nagra's poem provides ample
corroboration. "A Black History of the English-Speaking Peoples" inge-
niously indigenizes Auden's civic modernism for the purposes of a Punjabi Briton's vexed relation to his literary inheritance—a poetics of complicity given a "Black" twist, akin to "masterful" Paul Robeson's mastery
of Shakespeare (51). Like the Black Shakespearean performer, the poet
assumes a somewhat archaic language, a high literary register that he lovingly mimics and subtly mocks. Nagra resembles the "dark pioneer" in
Tennyson's poem who tunnels his way with a pickaxe into the British
residency—or in this case into British literary tradition.[41] Self-critically
wondering if he hopes the "academy might canonise / his poems for their
faith in canonical allusions" (51), presumably in works such as the book
you are reading, Nagra combines insider and rebel, perpetuator and
opponent, mimic and insurgent. He asks in a line of iambic pentameter
that both bespeaks and instances hybridization:

Is my voice phoney over these oft-heard beats?
Well if my voice feels vexatious, what can I but pray
      that it reign Bolshie
through puppetry and hypocrisy full of gung-ho fury! (51)

In a vexed, angry, pumped-up, humorously theatrical voice, Nagra performs the English literary tradition he is part of, yet restively parts
from. Inheriting Auden's Eliot-derived poetics of self-division and self-
criticism, Nagra pronounces them not sotto voce but through a postcolonial megaphone that, like the three exclamation marks in his book's title,
projects rollicking mockery and self-mockery. He Blackens, indigenizes,
hybridizes, and postcolonizes modernism.

What do we learn, in short, about these critical models from Nagra's
poem? That each can highlight an aspect of such poetry—its diffusionist

inheritance of modernism, its writing back to modernism, its critical response to worldwide capitalist modernity, and its postcolonial hybridization of modernism. Because the stakes in postcolonial studies are often seen as political, debates over theoretical models have an especially sharp edge. But despite what may seem irreconcilable differences in the abstract, conflicting interpretive models turn out, when brought into dialogue with a complex and multidimensional work of poetry, to be surprisingly compatible as tools for practical criticism. Perhaps a pluralist model such as indigenization is more fully vindicated than monocausal models, such as singular modernity and diffusionism, since it accords with poetry's multiplicity; but all these models illuminate an important aspect of a diffusionist yet anticolonial, anticapitalist yet hybridizing, anti- yet pro-modernist poem. Postcolonial metamodernist poems such as Press's, Goodison's, and Nagra's are uncontainable by one or another conceptual model, revealing the folly of trying to force so complex a literary-historical relationship into a single paradigm. Whatever the allure of theoretical noncontradiction and rigor, the messily eclectic use of multiple hermeneutic filters—distant and close, formal and historical, modernist and postcolonial—may be the most productive way of exposing a poem's multidimensionality, the intellectual, emotional, aesthetic, and worldly complexity that makes us want to read it again—and again.

CHAPTER 5

POETRY AND THE TRANSNATIONAL MIGRATION OF FORM

Imagine, if you will, rewritings of Wallace Stevens's first line of "Anecdote of the Jar," recasting it in a global register as an allegory of the migration of form: not "I placed a jar in Tennessee," but "I placed a sonnet in India," or "I placed a film in Iran," or "I placed MTV in China," or "I placed a novel in Africa."[1] Or perhaps "I placed haiku in America," or "I placed Safavid architecture in India," or "I placed African masks in Paris." Forms—shaping aesthetic patterns, structures, configurations—travel from one part of the world to another. "Precisely because they are abstract organizing principles," observes Caroline Levine, "shapes and patterns are iterable—portable. They can be picked up and moved to new contexts."[2] As modernity has sped up and intensified such movement, an insistent question for globalist cultural scholarship is, as already seen in the previous chapter, how to understand this movement and its effects. Stevens's amusing allegory may help conceptualize the encounter between foreign form and local environment. In the case of the jar, the introduction of an alien form is transformative:

> The wilderness rose up to it,
> And sprawled around, no longer wild.
> The jar was round upon the ground
> And tall and of a port in air.

The internal rhyme of "Surround" with "around," "round," and "ground" sonically dramatizes the jar's in-forming mastery of the once wild native environment. It's almost as if native peoples were worshiping a newly arrived god ("rose up to it"). In a largely unrhymed poem, the final stanza's triple end rhyme with "air" emphasizes and mocks the new

form's assumption of "dominion everywhere. / The jar was gray and bare."
In keeping with long-standing representations of the American South
as exotic, its lushness and wildness continuous with the global South's,[3]
this environment is untamed and unruly (a "slovenly wilderness") until
the ordering principle of the jar arrives and takes control. The intruder's
unnaturalness ("gray and bare") may result in sterility ("did not give of
bird or bush") but is also the source of its power over the local environment. In a poem that represents an alien form's imperial takeover of a
wilderness, the poem's own form—quatrains in tetrameter, comically
simple diction, encircling phonemes—bears some resemblance to the
jar's. But the poem also marks its difference in the sonic and imagistic
ironies it directs at the jar's inflated sense of its significance.

Foreign Form and Local Content—A Paradigm for Poetry?

One of the most pervasive models for "world" and "global" literature has
been the formula *foreign form and local content*. New literature issues, we
are told, from the introduction of a jarlike foreign form into a local environment. Franco Moretti, who frequently makes use of this paradigm
in his studies of the novel, cogently distills it in "Conjectures on World
Literature" and other essays collected in *Distant Reading* (2013). Scholars
such as Ted Underwood, Andrew Piper, and Katherine Bode have developed and refined less schematic and more humanistically inflected varieties of "distant reading," "cultural analytics," or "computational reading,"
but when it comes to the circulation of form in world literature, Moretti's
work remains foundational and so continues to be worth interrogating,
along with that of Pascale Casanova and of some surprisingly like-minded
non-Western critics.[4] Moretti draws on Fredric Jameson's reading of the
Japanese novel and on Immanuel Wallerstein's world-systems theory to
propose what he calls "a *law of literary evolution*: in cultures that belong
to the periphery of the literary system (which means: almost all cultures, inside and outside Europe), the modern novel first arises not as
an autonomous development but as a compromise between a western
formal influence (usually French or English) and local materials."[5] Borrowing from various critical studies to track "the wave of diffusion of
the modern novel" on four continents over two hundred years, Moretti
asserts that "when a culture starts moving towards the modern novel, it's
always as a compromise between foreign form and local materials," "west
European patterns and local reality."[6] He modulates Jameson's binary law
as "more of a triangle: foreign form, local material—*and local form*. Sim-

plifying somewhat: foreign *plot*; local *characters*; and then, local *narrative voice*."[7] Even so, as he discusses further examples, the abstractive formal dimensions of a text are almost entirely associated with the Western metropole and raw materials with the peripheries. If you are interested in the history of world, not national, literature, you are going to see Western waves, their "uniformity engulfing an initial diversity: Hollywood films conquering one market after another (or English swallowing language after language)."[8] *Engulfing, conquering, swallowing*—like Stevens's jar, the foreign form takes dominion over the local wilderness.

Moretti is preoccupied with the novel, but what happens to the foreign form/local content paradigm when put to the test with other genres, such as poetry? In response to previous critics who have raised this question, Moretti cites the spread of Petrarchanism, and in my view, modern and contemporary poetry offers some further confirmation.[9] As the model would predict, poetic forms sometimes travel one way to new environments and are loaded with local materials, if "local" is used in Jameson and Moretti's elastic sense that includes the subnational, national, and regional, as opposed to the "foreign" or "global." A number of anglophone poets from around the world could be ventriloquized thus: "I placed the sonnet in Jamaica" (Claude McKay); "I placed epic in Barbados" (Kamau Brathwaite); "I placed terza rima in Saint Lucia" (Derek Walcott); "I placed dramatic monologue in Uganda" (Okot p'Bitek); "I placed projectivism in Oceania" (Craig Santos Perez); and so forth. As we saw in the previous chapter, poets of the global South directly engage with and reflect on their inheritances from metropolitan modernism, and I've argued elsewhere that Caribbean, African, and Indian poets adapt modernist syncretism, fragmentation, heteroglossia, and other formal principles to their local environments: witness the diverse Caribbean and Kashmiri uses that Kamau Brathwaite and Agha Shahid Ali make of T. S. Eliot's modernist strategies.[10] Nor is this pattern exclusive to anglophone works. To cite examples culled from *The Oxford Handbook of Global Modernisms*, three critics show that Algerian, Palestinian, and Turkish poets access the oral, older modern, and Islamic aesthetics of their own traditions through the symbolist poetics of Baudelaire, Rimbaud, and Mallarmé.[11] Following colonial patterns of cultural influence, francophone and anglophone modernist poetic forms were exported from the West to the so-called peripheries. Although Casanova, criticizing Moretti, proposes the terms "dominant and dominated" instead of center and periphery, and "structure" instead of system, she, too, advances diffusionism.[12] In her account of Nicaraguan poet Rubén Darío's *modernismo* as a variant of symbolism, for example, she sees him as having performed "the deliberate Frenchification of Spanish poetry, down to the phonemes and syntactic forms."[13] Wielding symbolic power entails the transfer of literary forms from the site of greatest cultural capital to disempowered "local" sites, such as Latin America. Thus far, it would seem the foreign form/local content model has much to show for itself in theorizing world, planetary, or global literature.

But poetry also reveals the paradigm's one-sidedness and other inadequacies. First, the jar's "dominion" over the slovenly local wilderness is in part a methodologically produced illusion. The model of the Eurocentric wave doesn't merely reveal monolithic diffusion from the West; it occludes countercurrents. Consider Moretti's view that "after 1750 the novel arises just about everywhere as a compromise between west European patterns and local reality."[14] Doesn't the rest of the world have any "patterns" of its own? Moretti quotes Jameson as discussing the fit between "the raw material of Japanese social experience and the abstract formal patterns of Western novel construction."[15] But this literary-critical paradigm is in danger of "re-inscribing a hegemonic cultural centre," in the words of Alexander Beecroft, despite the aspiration to globalize literary studies.[16] That is, it risks reinforcing an imperial episteme in which the West is associated with control and conceptual order and the east with "raw material," as if local content resembled the land, sugar, labor, and spices expropriated under colonialism. Even Moretti's more nuanced triangle assigns technique to the West and consigns the rest to voice. Whether the novel, which writers such as Chinua Achebe, Salman Rushdie, and Marjane Satrapi meld with long-lived local narrative and pictorial traditions, or poetry, which has local and often ancient forms in many different parts of the world, the "peripheral" culture brings more to the table than local content and voice. In the creation of cubism, African and Oceanic art contributed not just raw materials but abstractive forms that were generative for modernist pictorial and sculptural styles. At the same moment, Kandinsky's study of Muslim Arab art, ornament, and calligraphy in Tunisia helped propel his turn to abstraction. Through imagism and subsequent literary movements, Chinese and Japanese formal principles became integral to the juxtapositional and compressed structure of modernist poetry. South Asian culture plays a crucial role in modernist perspectivism, as in works such as E. M. Forster's *A Passage to India* and Eliot's *The Waste Land*. West, East, and South Asian cultural forms, as we'll see in the next chapter, profoundly shaped Yeats's poetry. "Forms are the abstract of social relationships," Moretti claims, "so, formal analysis is in its own modest way an analysis of power."[17] If so, then to represent Western forms as "engulfing" and "swallowing" local sites and agents is to grant those "peripheries" little power, either symbolic or conceptual. "The West, for Moretti," as Susan Stanford Friedman writes, "is the site of discursive creation, while the non-West is 'local materials,' a center/periphery binary that ignores the often long histories of aesthetic production among the colonized."[18] Casanova grants more agency to writers from "dominated" cultures in seizing cultural capital, but she, too, assumes that form typically travels from the European center outward.

Perhaps more surprisingly, the foreign form/local content paradigm plays a major role in loco-centric statements that may seem to contradict it. The so-called *bolekaja* critics ("Come down let's fight!" in Yoruba), for example, argued that some African poets, in anticipation of Moretti's wave metaphor, "trim their sails to the modernist squalls from the West."[19] Unduly influenced by the "wild and purposeless experimentation of some decadent Western poets," these African poets such as Christopher Okigbo and Wole Soyinka are said to import an "obscurantist cesspool" of difficult forms—arcane diction, contorted syntax, writerly instead of oral structures, privatist instead of communal language—into an environment where they did not belong.[20] Even as the *bolekaja* critics argue African poetry should be based in indigenous oral traditions, thus recognizing the prior existence of forms outside the West, they dichotomize foreign form and local content, seeing them as incompatible.

Similarly, Brathwaite argues in *History of the Voice* that Western forms such as the sonnet and iambic pentameter, having traveled to the Caribbean and other parts of the former British Empire, are ill suited to non-European environments and experience. Jamaican Claude McKay "allowed himself to be imprisoned in the pentameter," Brathwaite claims; in keeping with Moretti's triangle of foreign form with local content and local voice, "the only thing that retains its uniqueness"—that is, the only locus of Caribbeanness in such poems—"is the tone of the poet's voice," as heard in sound recordings.[21] But even as Brathwaite contends that poets should look not to the sonnet but to calypso and other local folk forms for inspiration, and even as he concedes the crucial role that Eliot's speech rhythms played in helping him and other poets creolize their poetry, he relies on and reinforces the binary of foreign form and local content. The pentameter, in his view, "carries with it a certain kind of experience, which is not the experience of a hurricane. The hurricane does not roar in pentameter."[22]

But such dichotomizing of foreign form and local content oversimplifies. As if in retort to Brathwaite's lecture, Walcott's frightening and tumultuous "Hurucan," a poem that uses the local Taino (Arawak) root of the English word, begins:

> Once branching light startles the hair of the coconuts,
> and on the villas' asphalt roofs, rain
> resonates like pebbles in a pan. . . .[23]

If it does not roar, this hurricane at the very least rumbles in the pentametric variations of these lines. And elsewhere, in Walcott's *Omeros*, the hurricane roars in loosely adapted terza rima, a form forged in Dante's fourteenth-century Tuscany. Or rather the hurricane sighs, zithers, rattles, winds, thuds, and lurches:

> all the village could do was listen to the gods in session,
>
> playing any instruments that came into their craniums,
> the harp-sighing ripple of a hither-and-zithering sea,
> the knucklebone pebbles, the abrupt Shango drums
>
> made Neptune rock in the caves. Fête start! Erzulie
> rattling her ra-ra; Ogun, the blacksmith, feeling
> No Pain; Damballa winding like a zandoli
>
> lizard, as their huge feet thudded on the ceiling,
> as the sea-god, drunk, lurched from wall to wall, saying:
> "Mama, this music so loud, I going in seine,"
>
> then throwing up at his pun. People were praying. . . .[24]

This hurricane, propulsively riding the momentum of Dante's interlinked rhyme, also rages in the outrageousness of Walcott's puns ("hither-and-zithering" as well as "in seine"), the onomatopoeic effects of alliteration ("rattling her ra-ra"), the strong rhythms ("made Neptune rock in the caves"), the hard enjambments ("zandoli // lizard"), the abrupt shifts in syntax, and the rolling hexameters. With other postcolonial poets, Walcott has adapted, remade, and refreshed terza rima, pentameter, hexameter, and other such "alien" forms. After all, if the hurricane could not roar in pentameter, then presumably neither could Western poets bespeak their experience in haiku, tanka, ghazal, pantoum, and other such imported forms. Tell that to Ezra Pound, Adrienne Rich, Paul Muldoon, and Evie Shockley. Despite the diffusionist wave, formal currents cross.

When Moretti and other theorists argue for the one-way global spread of the Western novel, their distantly read examples don't always support the terms of their argument.[25] In one footnote, Moretti quotes the critic Ken Frieden as saying that "Yiddish writers parodied—appropriated, incorporated, and modified—diverse elements from European novels and stories."[26] If so, then far from being engulfed by the European novel, Yiddish writers actively remade it in accordance with their own narrative traditions and techniques. In another footnote, he quotes Jale Parla as saying that "the early Turkish novelists combined the traditional narrative forms with the examples of the western novel," so Turkish writers, it turns out, themselves have form, not only local content or voice, and their inherited narrative forms transform the European novel.[27] Yet another quotation embedded in a footnote raises questions about the model it ostensibly validates: the first Dahomean novel, according to Abiola Irele, "is interesting as an experiment in recasting the oral literature of Africa within the form of a French novel," but here again, two discrepant forms are being fused, not a form and a content, and the result is a change in both.[28] Moretti makes some allowance for "diversification," but he sees "convergence" and "diffusion" as paramount from the eighteenth century onward.[29] Although postcolonial "hybridity" is often criticized, it and related ideas of creolization, vernacularization, indigenization, and inter- or transculturation are, as I suggested in the previous chapter, more capable of registering the intricate meldings of transnational forms than is the foreign form/local content model of diffusion.

"Distant reading" has the advantage that it can survey developments across not just a handful of canonical novels but an enormous corpus, "the other 99.5 per cent."[30] Moretti is right that literary scholars base their claims about a genre's evolution on a small number of examples. But consider what made this small subset of canonical works distinctive in the first place. When largely forgotten works are compared with critically favored examples in the same genre, in many cases the less-well-known works more passively replicate the formal codes and conventions than their better-known counterparts. More aggressively remaking genres, poems by Stevens, Moore, Yeats, and Eliot stand out against the bulk of poetry published in early twentieth-century literary journals.

Little wonder that foreign-form diffusionism finds itself confirmed in panoramic surveys. The governing tropes of Moretti's scientific model aren't neutral but skewed toward normativity, ill suited to close contact with works that actively trouble and twist inherited forms.

Distant Reading or the Disaggregation of Form?

What further limitations does the particularly form-intensive genre of poetry reveal and what alternatives might it suggest? For one thing, Moretti's approach to "distant reading" is especially incongruous with the study of poetry, since if you're reading poetry only at a distance, you're not reading it as poetry. Subsequent advocates for computational literary study, such as Andrew Piper, have understood that "bifocal" reading is necessary in order to "move into" a poem while also seeing it within a general framework, although there are as yet few readings of this kind.[31] Poetry has been associated more than any other genre with close reading partly because of the small-scale intricacies and textures that help constitute poems and that risk disappearing when works are viewed at a remove. Besides, the assumption that form can be extracted from content is anathema to poetry, in which form and content are more thoroughly melded than in perhaps any other genre. For many poets, as Robert Creeley declared, "Form is never more than an extension of content."[32] *How* a poem says what it says is no less essential to its identity as a poem than *what* it says. Indeed, in a great deal of poetry, the main idea—I love you, I mourn my loss, I am in awe of nature—isn't especially original; it's the linguistic, formal, and imaginative freshness and vividness that make many a poem.

Further, the multifacetedness of form in poetry calls for nuanced analysis. As we've seen, Jameson refers to the novel's "abstract formal patterns," and Moretti substitutes "foreign *plot*" for "foreign form"; but if the equation of "form" with "plot" simplifies the novel—which has other vital elements down to the level of syntax and sentence—it tells us even less about poetry. A survey of the plot or argument of thousands of poems says little about them as poems. Moretti's Stanford Literary Lab subsequently applied computational methods to the smaller-scale aspects of novels, such as the syntax and verbs of sentences, insofar as they can be correlated with an overarching genre or style, and other scholars have brought micro-level computational analysis to poetry: Andrew Piper, for example, has scrutinized the use of periods in African American poetry.[33] But if we're interested in tracing the transnational circulation of large-scale form, one way of salvaging distant reading for poetry is to consider poetic genre the macro-level equivalent to novelistic plot. Mapping the global migration of the sonnet, ballad, haiku, sestina, ghazal, and other such forms has long been an aspect of literary history ("form is precisely *the repeatable element of literature*," Moretti states), and much more such mapping remains to be done, perhaps assisted now by digital tools.[34] But as we track these migrations at the macro level, we need to keep in mind that a poem's fixed form is often only a part—not necessarily determinative—of what is going on in the work's multiple layers. "Epic in loosely adapted terza rima" could be said to be the "form" of Walcott's *Omeros*, but as we've seen, this scarcely begins to suggest the array of formal elements mobilized in the poem, from the mixing of discursive registers between creolized English, French-based patois, and Standard English to paronomasia, chiasmus, and personification of a hurricane in the guise of African Caribbean and classical gods. The same goes for works in "open forms." The "form" of Allen Ginsberg's "Howl" is to be found not only in its macro-level open structure but also in its insistent use of anaphora ("who . . ."), ellipsis ("Zen New Jersey"), mixed registers of diction ("who studied Plotinus Poe St. John of the Cross" and "Let themselves be fucked in the ass"), asyndeton ("yacketayakking screaming vomiting whispering facts") and polysyndeton ("facts and memories and anecdotes and eyeball kicks and shocks of hospitals and jails and wars"), oxymoron ("hydrogen jukebox"), zeugma ("waving genitals and manuscripts"), allegory ("Moloch!"), metonymy ("unshaven rooms"), personification ("negro streets"), long, cascading, rhythmically loaded lines (indebted to Whitman and the Bible), syntactic parallelism and compression, and a whole array of sonic devices such as alliteration and assonance.[35] If form is understood capaciously, as the "iterable," "portable," "repeatable" aspects of literature that shape, pattern, and configure it, the form of a poem is no less its figurative language, rhythm, tone, syntax, registers of diction, and so forth, than it is its overall structure. The evolutionary tracking of a single "device" such as the detective clue, albeit a smaller-scale unit than genre, hardly seems adequate to this multitudinous formal array.[36] Form needs to be pluralized and disaggregated in the analysis of its migratory patterns.

Another way of breaking up the monolithic foreign form/local content paradigm, or FFLC, would be to consider alternative configurations. There may also be works of foreign form and foreign content, or FFFC, such as Eliot's *Waste Land*, Pound's *Cantos*, Olson's *Maximus Poems*, and Walcott's *Omeros*—poems that draw on formal resources from various parts of the world and that reach for a planetary scope. In addition, there may be local form and foreign content, or LFFC, as exemplified by Louise Bennett's poems in orally performative Jamaican Creole but addressing midcentury news of the Nazi invasion of Europe. Perhaps Agha Shahid Ali's ghazals are also "local" in form insofar as they are written in a monorhymed structure widespread in the Muslim Indian subcontinent into which he was born, and "foreign" in content, insofar as they take in war, imperialism, and so forth on a worldwide scale. There may even be local form and local content, or LFLC, as in Bennett's patois poems about local emigration, poverty, politicians, race relations, and so forth, or in Brathwaite's "Rites," a tour de force in West Indian Creole about a 1948 cricket match at Kensington Oval in Bridgetown, Barbados.

But as we trace such local-foreign configurations, we must acknowledge that poetry's complex tessellation often makes it difficult to distinguish FFLC from FFFC in any hard-and-fast way, and each from LFFC or LFLC. Let's not forget that all FFFC poems have "local" bearings, such as the Whitmanian models behind Pound and Olson, or the Saint Lucian code-switching in Walcott; that Bennett's poems, if seemingly LFLC and LFFC because strongly Jamaican in orality and language, are still organized by British ballad stanzas, while their foreign news is always screened through local preoccupations and their local experience impinged on by distant pressures; that the local form in Ali's LFFC ghazals looks back to not only Urdu but also Persian and Arabic sources, welded to Eliotic modernist disjunctiveness and syncretism, and their foreign content bears traces of a localizable Kashmiri Shi'a background; and that the use of Caribbean vernacular in Brathwaite's LFLC "Rites" and other poems is indebted to anglo-modernism, and their local content is transatlantically striated by the Middle Passage. If Brathwaite's LFLC can be flipped around into FFLC or LFFC, Ali's LFFC to FFLC, Bennett's LFFC and LFLC into their mirror opposites, and even Walcott's FFFC can be seen as its chiastic obverse, then these mirror-image initialisms point up the slipperiness of "foreign form and local content" and its variants. A pluralized, four-part tracking structure is surely more promising than the monolithic FFLC schema, representing a first step toward a more flexible and multidimensional model for charting global aesthetic flows. But even as we deploy it, we must bear in mind that, owing to the complexities of poetic form and of local-global enmeshments, most poems will fit into several of these slots at once, and no amount of long-distance squinting can accurately reduce them to one or the other.

Local/Foreign Form/Content in Modernist and Postcolonial Poems

I've mentioned many poems in passing, but now let's look closely at two works, one modernist, the other contemporary, one American, the other postcolonial British, to see how these questions of local and foreign, form and content, play out in specific examples. As suggested by its title, Marianne Moore's "England" (1920) is a poem that slyly poses as monolocational in subject but quickly turns out otherwise. After two and a half lines about England, a coordinating conjunction abruptly swivels elsewhere:

> and Italy with its equal
> shores—contriving an epicureanism from which the grossness
> has been
>
> extracted: and Greece with its goats and its gourds, the nest of
> modified illusions:
> and France. . . .[37]

Of this poem that deploys and subverts cultural stereotypes, we might say its syntactic form is American—paratactic, even egalitarian in straddling one culture and another—that its metrical structure (unrhymed quatrains of 20, 15, 22, and 18 syllables) Americanizes classical syllabics, that its occasional use of a colloquial register "in plain American which cats and dogs can read" is American, albeit mixed with words and phrases like "epicureanism," "continents of misapprehension," and "cataclysmic torrent," all spilling forward in the headlong rush of heavily enjambed lines. So what at first seemed to be "local content" may instead look "foreign" on further reading, in a poem of localized form, or LFFC. But the jump from the national to the regional or hemispheric calls into question the kinds of cultural groupings that the poem, like taxonomic criticism, makes use of:

> and the East with its snails,
> its emotional
>
> shorthand and jade cockroaches, its rock crystal and its
> imperturbability,
> all of museum quality. . . .

We are asked to recognize the familiar East Asian animals and objects that might be housed in a museum, but as for the putative psychological

characteristics of "the East"—"emotional // shorthand" and "imperturb-
ability"—how are these "of museum quality"? Clearly something has gone
awry in the poem's syntactic straddling of discrepant cultures and locations. America is affectionately yet wryly described in skewed stereotypes: supposedly "there are no proof readers" and "no digressions,"
and no language even (a "language-less country"), but this presumably
"American" poem, which we thought was going to be about "England"
but turns out to be globally comparative and closes with a meditation
on America in its global relationality, vigorously demonstrates both
digression and precision in language. If responding defensively to views
of America as culturally deficient, Moore bespeaks a nationalism that
shades into transnationalism. By poem's end, she may have convinced
some readers that she is making a case for American exceptionalism—
America as the only place where the best qualities of China, Egypt, Pales-
tine, and elsewhere are to be found. But she pulls the rug out when she
says of such "superi- / ority," not accidentally one of only two words split
violently in the poem by an enjambment (the other, no less wittily, "con- //
clusions"): "It has never been confined to one locality." Although Moore
speaks from America (local content), she reveals that her national culture can only be conceptualized comparatively (foreign content). Indeed,
given that enjambment, syllabics, and zeugma go back to the ancients, we
could also see the form as having global bearings. Like many a modernist
poem, Moore's can be seen as FFLC, LFFC, LFLC, or FFFC, but is more
accurately understood as a complex amalgam of all at once.

What if we looked at a poem that represents itself as steadfastly
joined to one specific locale, instead of peregrinating across the world
like Moore's trickily named "England"? Rhyming this chapter with the
last by concluding with another poem by Indian British poet Daljit
Nagra, "The Punjab" (2011), let's consider how it represents the speaker's
relation to his familial homeland:

> Not 'The'—just 'Púnjab'!
> Was there once upon before partition a Púnjab
> whole? A Pan-jab of Hindu, Sikh, Muslim, anything?[38]

In the assertive first line, the speaker-as-native informant demands omission of the British definite article. But his Indian British pronunciation
places him at a diasporic remove from the homeland he claims: the Punjabi stress, as the poem later emphasizes, is on the second syllable ("Punjaaab"). Further eroding the appearance of locally anchored authority,

the assured tone dissolves in questions and uncertainties about Punjabi history and identity. An integral facet of its form, the quick tonal modulations position the poem's voice both within (the) Punjab and outside it, both locally and extrinsically. As in Eliot's relation to Prufrock, Nagra's to his speaker is one of both proximity and ironic distance. Although the talismanic place-name Punjab seems to confer local authenticity, it spirals beyond the local in interlingual wordplay, extravagant punning (and jabbing)—"Pan-jab," "Punjamentalist," "Punjaaab," "Punglanders"— that recalls Joyce's *Finnegans Wake*. When the speaker's questions about Punjabi identity twist into a Peter Piper–like alliterative tongue-twister, the poem ridicules claims to authentic representativeness and at the same time stereotypes of Punjabis as lascivious and fanatical:

> To play the pipes of a Punjamentalist—
> must I pin a badge, must I drop my pants—
> must I join a junta and jab-jab-jab for my Púnjab!?

Where is the poem's form-content amalgam now? It's in (the) Punjab, in an Asian British account of it, and in a field of translingual puns and sonic play that includes Spanish. The poem is both locally fixed on (the) Punjab and self-mockingly hyperbolic and extrinsic in its performance of that locality.

The toponym fastens the poem to a specific location with five rivers ("If it's five for the 'punj' and it's 'jaaab' for a river," in a cross-cultural riff on Elvis's "Blue Suede Shoes"), but a language of homage to rivers is hardly exclusive to this site, as emphasized by the refrain:

> *That old man river calls you loud and long*
> *from a land that you loved in a lullaby*

The refrain both bespeaks nativist longing and mocks it in a pseudo-negro-spiritual. The love of the land is displaced into a song that, echoing an African American source, shows that nostalgia to be stranded in foreign forms that mediate the speaker's relation to his homeland (so too the references to the English nursery rhyme "Row, Row, Row Your Boat," the American minstrel song "Swanee River," and "Over the Rainbow" in *The Wizard of Oz*). In subsequent iterations of the refrain, the land is rosily idealized ("*the rainbow glows*") yet sternly withheld ("*but you'll never know the land or the song*"). Through its insider knowledge, place-names, Punjabi words, and comic persona, which implicitly voices South

Asian robustness over against English restraint (even while sending up such stereotypes), the poem lays claim to Punjabi rootedness in form, tone, language, and content. At the same time, its interlingual punning, its alliteration and internal rhyme, its code-switching among Standard English and Punglish and Punjabi, its intergeneric melding of American musical ballad and soi-disant African American spiritual with literary poem, and its riotous allusions to Western literary texts ("jump aboard / for your unplucked jut-land, your bee-glade Indusfree!") situate even this regionally focused poem within a global matrix of forms, words, sounds, and places. To say that its humor is "Punjabi" or "Anglo-Punjabi," that its hetero- and polyglot mixing of discourses or its ironized speaker is "modernist," either to localize or to globalize it exclusively, would be to oversimplify the complexly translocal intermixing of language, place, and identity that drives the poem. Poems such as Nagra's and Moore's, outstripping "foreign form and local content," demand a more supple and nuanced critical vocabulary for the relations of foreign to local and form to content.

*   *   *

We may well be unable to forsake entirely the foreign form/local content paradigm in mapping the transnational migrations of literary techniques and strategies, amid the intensified globalization of the twentieth and twenty-first centuries. But in tracing literary flows, we should at least decenter it by multiplying the configurations of local and foreign, form and content. For to reduce world literary transmission to a single pattern is to occlude the mutually transformative nature of intercultural literary dialogue. It is also to limit "form" to one scale, when it ranges from the minute twists of enjambment and tone to the larger patterns of genre and argument. Although the foreign form/local content model may seem to have taken "dominion everywhere" in studies of literary globalization, it looks, like Stevens's jar, "gray and bare," when held up against the richly chromatic prism of individual poems. As we turn a poem over and over, it is likely to reveal a kaleidoscopic range of local-foreign configurations, no matter how firmly situated within the local or how foreign its form or content may at first appear. In their intricacy and complexity, poems vividly illustrate the interdependence of form and content, and of local and foreign. Instead of abstracting world literary evolution as a one-dimensional and one-directional model or scientific law, our form-content analysis should—taking its cues from poems—aspire to be polyphonic and multilayered, moving nimbly back and forth between micro and macro, local and global. Another way to enrich our vocabulary for exploring global literary migration is to reenergize the formal discourse of poetics: it can help make visible the many-sidedness of imaginative works—a multiplicity that may disappear if viewed from too great a distance, yet that helps poems live in and beyond their moment and their places of origin. As Pound showed in adapting an ancient Chinese inscription for the modernist imperative, sometimes an especially old vocabulary serves to "make it new."

CHAPTER 6

YEATS'S ASIAS: MODERNISM, ORIENTALISM, ANTI-ORIENTALISM

As literary and cultural studies have been transnationalizing themselves, a persistent question has been how to view the West's imaginative extensions elsewhere—artists like Matisse and Kandinsky, composers like Stravinsky and Stockhausen, novelists like Forster and Woolf, poets like Yeats, Eliot, and Pound.[1] Given the asymmetries of power and wealth, should we see these as acts of imperial theft, akin to the pilfering of antiquities from poorer or colonized parts of the world for display in homes and museums? Or do they exemplify humane, if touristic, engagements with non-Western cultures? Are they more like the brazen appropriation of Native names and mascots by US football teams, or are they respectful exercises in self-education that defy age-old demeaning stereotypes? Now that identitarian conceptions of cultural property are being vigorously debated, it may be time to reopen these questions.[2] Of all world regions that the modernists engaged, Asia had, as Christopher Bush indicates, the broadest impact on the development of literary modernism—South Asia on Eliot, East Asia on Pound, and so forth.[3] Among his contemporaries, Yeats was the only major poet who developed a multifaceted interest in East, South, and West Asian cultures; as such, he deserves a prominent role in reconsiderations of Euromodernism's non-Western engagements. Scholarship on Yeats and Asia has usually focused on either his Indian or his Japanese investments—understandably so, given their longevity and depth—but what about the West Asian coordinates that have received less attention? What happens if we pluralize Yeats's Asias and consider them together—South, East, and West? Is his Asian-facing poetry orientalist, anti-orientalist, or both? And how can his poetry help us rethink the paradigm of orientalism?[4]

"Asiatic Vague Immensities"

The only place where the word "Asiatic" appears in Yeats's poetry is the second stanza of his late poem "The Statues" (1939). I begin here, with what may be the most troubling representation of the East in his poetry. Having credited the mathematical calculations of Pythagoras with helping to shape the desires embodied in Greek art, this poem sculpted in *ottava rima* grants still more significance to ancient Greek artists than to philosopher-mathematicians:

> No! Greater than Pythagoras, for the men
> That with a mallet or a chisel modelled these
> Calculations that look but casual flesh, put down
> All Asiatic vague immensities,
> And not the banks of oars that swam upon
> The many-headed foam at Salamis.
> Europe put off that foam when Phidias
> Gave women dreams and dreams their looking-glass.[5]

In the phrase "All Asiatic vague immensities," Yeats not only recalls the vastness of the Persian fleet vanquished by a smaller Greek force but also imputes to Iranian culture an amorphous grandiosity. He sees the soft power of Greek philosophy and the arts as even more fundamental than the Greek city-states' naval victories over the Persians. As he puts it in *On the Boiler*, Europe was born "when the Doric studios sent out those broad-backed marble statues against the multiform, vague, expressive Asiatic sea."[6] In the poem, more important than arrows and spears but no less sharp are artistic instruments—mallets and chisels—that carve stone into human form.

As someone whose parentage is mostly Persian, I've long felt uncomfortable about this stanza, since it aligns with and updates the notion that my ancestors were the original "barbarians"—their unintelligible speech sounding to the ancient Greeks like an echoic and nonsensical *barbarbar* that marked them as the uncivilized other, especially after the Greco-Persian wars. If I may be forgiven a personal point of reference, while Yeats was writing this poem, his nearly exact contemporary in Iran, my maternal great-grandfather, Keikhosrow Shahrokh (1864–1939), who served in parliament as the elected representative of Zoroastrians, had recently completed the mausoleum for Iran's tenth-century epic poet Ferdowsi in ancient Iranian architectural style. Having been inspired by an Achaemenid architectural vocabulary, he would likely have rejected Yeats's contrast between ancient Greek sculptural precision and its supposed Persian opposite. For those who have seen the meticulously carved stonework and formal patterning still visible at Persepolis after two and a half millennia, the contrast between Greek precision and a "vague" Persia may well seem distortive. Moreover, as those carvings and the intricate metalwork of the time also indicate, ancient Persian and Greek art also had strong mutual influences, despite the stanza's harsh dichotomies. Yeats's enjambment of the phrase "put down" emphasizes Greek form's heroic defeat of Persian formlessness. His figurative language metonymically associates Persia with the "many-headed foam" of the sea. When that word is repeated—"Europe put off that foam"—it suggests the inferior, shapeless, nondurable qualities of Iranian culture.

Such views are hardly unique to Yeats. The Persians have been receiving bad press in the West ever since the ancient Greeks wrote the victors' history, not long after the battle at Salamis. To understand this broad cultural "put down," the almost inevitable framework, if one that Yeats's work can help us reconsider, is Edward Said's orientalist critique. According to Said, orientalism produces and reinforces a series of oppositions by which the West defines itself: orientals "are always symmetrical to, and yet diametrically inferior to, a European equivalent."[7] Yeats dichotomizes the heroic, individualized, antithetical West and the Asiatic, formless, many-headed, primary East. He doesn't go so far as to call the Persians, in Said's words for orientalist stereotyping, "backward, degenerate, uncivilized, and retarded," but their defeat confirms their weakness and cultural inferiority, while the Greeks are artistically, militarily, and philosophically superior.[8] Moreover, as Said writes, orientalism tends "to wipe out any traces of individual" persons or "narratable life histories."[9] The Persians here are an undifferentiated, formless mass ("the Persian hordes at Salamis," he calls them in *On the Boiler*), the Greeks possessed of form and individuality (Pythagoras, Phidias, dreaming women).[10]

Having begun with the hardest case, seen through Said's telling but homogenizing model, I want to show that it's relatively atypical of Yeats and inconsistent with many of his Asian-facing poems, which more sympathetically perform their relation to various Asian cultures. Witness Yeats's comments across his career about Asia: although he often associates the West with materialism, individualism, and realism, the East with spirituality, spontaneous religion, and immateriality, he nevertheless also frequently suggests (a) that Ireland and Asia have a common ancestry;

(b) that East and West have influenced one another over thousands of years; and (c) that, whether they came about through shared ancestry or influences, the resemblances between Ireland and Asia are profound. He remarks, for example: "We have borrowed directly from the East and selected for admiration or repetition everything in our own past that is least European, as though groping backward towards our common mother."[11] He later adds:

> It pleases me to fancy that when we turn towards the East, in or out of church, we are turning not less to the ancient west and north; the one fragment of pagan Irish philosophy come down, 'the Song of Amergin', seems Asiatic; that a system of thought like that of these books, though perhaps less perfectly organised, once overspread the world, as ours today; that our genuflections discover in that East something ancestral in ourselves. . . .[12]

Such claims build on what Joseph Lennon shows was a long-lived discourse linking Ireland to "the Orient"; for modern Irish intellectuals like Yeats, these Celtic-Oriental connections had usefully "subversive, antimodern, and (often) anticolonial resonances."[13] Even though some such ideas have been debunked as opportunistic or self-exoticizing pseudohistory, Yeats's general view finds support in subsequent research. Scholars have explored the contacts between Asians and migrant Celts living as far east as Asia Minor, poetic techniques shared across Indo-European languages, and "orientalizing" elements in Celtic art that may result from Persian, Scythian, or, perhaps most likely, intermediary Greco-Etruscan influences.[14] In typically orientalist fashion, Yeats is projecting the reality of the East backward in time, freezing it in the distant past; but in this, the East vitally resembles Celticism in his imagination. Asia and ancient Ireland represent twin alternatives to the degradations of modernity. As John Rickard argues, Yeats saw them both as repositories of the visionary mindset—antiscientific, antimaterialistic, spiritual—that he wanted to revive in Ireland.[15]

Even "The Statues" puts its orientalism into play with contrary views. Whereas orientalism—both the ideology and Said's account of it—tends to dichotomize, Yeats crams into the poem's third stanza hundreds of years of art history in which East and West cross and even fuse. As a result of the Greek Empire's extension into West and South Asia, Hellenistic sculptural forms "crossed" into a "tropic" region and were indigenized there in sculptures and other depictions of the Buddha (610). Yeats recalls Greco-Buddhist sculptures that are both idealist and realist, precise and patterned, such as those of the Gandharan style in Central Asia and the northern areas of the subcontinent. The orientalist oppositions may still be at work—the Western individuality and interiority of Hamlet-like figures set against "Buddha's emptiness" (611). But even if the fusion involves a slackening of Greek individuation, it reveals an important truth that reaches its full expression in the East:

> Empty eyeballs knew
> That knowledge increases unreality, that
> Mirror on mirror mirrored is all the show. (610)

Here the Buddhist embrace of the fundamental reality of emptiness represents an alternative to the Western knowledge system celebrated earlier in the poem, based on calculation, measure, and character. Yeats counterbalances his Euro-classicist idealization. The Buddha's empty eyeballs, even if traceable back to Greece, are more akin to those of the meditating Hindu ascetics on Mount Meru, who strip away all illusions and see into "the desolation of reality" ("Meru," 563).[16] In the final stanza of "The Statues," Patrick Pearse's revolutionary heroism recalls Attic Greece, but this Western individuality is paradoxically thrown up out of the depths of a "formless," Asiatic modernity (611). "We Irish," the poem declares, but were it not for the iambic pentameter, it might just as well have said "We Asiatic Europeans," or "We Greco-Indian-Persian Irish," or "We Eastern Westerners." The poem is, as Helen Vendler shows, Yeats's most agitated and unbalanced use of the graceful *ottava rima* stanza—witness the irregularities and asymmetries, the imperfect rhymes and heterogeneous proper names.[17] As such, a poem that hails the importance of "plummet-measured" form is itself exemplary of the disruptions of formlessness within form, of the "Asiatic vague immensities" overbrimming a well-wrought urn. Understood within its own terms, the poem's distorted form and its conceptual torsions and self-disruptions ironically seem party at least as much to the "many-headed" East as to a measured, calculating West. Although the poem begins with an opposition between inferior Persian vagueness and salvific Greek form that seems to validate Said's model of orientalism, it puts counterdiscursive pressure on it in its form-disrupting form, its endorsement of an Asian conception of reality's vacancy, and its art-historical understanding of the blurred cultural lines between East and West.

Persia, Byzantium, and Form

In *A Vision* and affiliated poems, far from consigning the East in general and Persians in particular to many-headed formlessness, Yeats credits the seeming enemies of form in "The Statues" with being the creators of form, above all the formal vocabularies that are central to Byzantium. Yeats follows William Morris in seeing Byzantine art as synthesizing Eastern (including Persian) design and mystery with Western classicism and, as noted by Elizabeth Bergmann Loizeaux, in being "especially attracted by the Persian-influenced use of continuous line," or what Yeats calls in *A Vision* "that decoration which seems to undermine our self-control, and is, it seems, of Persian origin, and has for its appropriate symbol a vine whose tendrils climb everywhere and display among their leaves all those strange images of bird and beast, those forms that represent no creature eye has ever seen, yet are begotten one upon the other as if they were themselves living creatures."[18] As in "The Statues," Persian form may press against the limits of form—"decoration which seems to undermine our self-control"—but at the same time the vines delineate space. In keeping with the work of the Austrian art historian he repeatedly cites in *A Vision*, Josef Strzygowski, Yeats understands the nonrepresentational lines, patterns, and creatures in Byzantine art to be of Persian origin.[19] The passage's self-replicating, nonmimetic forms ("forms . . . begotten one upon the other") anticipate the lines in "Byzantium" about self-generative forms, "flames begotten of flame" (498). Independent of the natural world, they require no fuel ("no faggot feeds"), are unaffected by meteorological events ("Nor storm disturbs"), and in their glorious self-sufficiency have no direct effect outside the imaginative or spiritual realm ("An agony of flame that cannot singe a sleeve") (498). The multiply and ecstatically echoic diction and sounds in "Byzantium" evoke a patterning that surpasses nature. Pace "The Statues," Yeats's Byzantium poems build on the idea of nonrepresentational, vitalizing, self-replicating Persian forms as embedded in Byzantine art and as reflected in their own intricate stanzaic patterning.

Nor is this fusion of Greco-Roman with Persian art visible to Yeats only in Byzantium at the middle or end of the first millennium. Despite the civilizational dichotomy in "The Statues," he discovers a cross-cultural blend even in Attic Greece itself: "With Callimachus pure Ionic revives again, as [Adolf] Furtwängler has proved, and upon the only example of his work known to us, a marble chair, a Persian is represented, and may one not discover a Persian symbol in that bronze lamp, shaped like a palm, known to us by a description in Pausanias?"[20] Callimachus's lamp fashioned for the Acropolis is indeed known to us from Pausanias, but neither the geographer nor Furtwängler describes a Persian carved on a marble chair: Yeats learned of this elsewhere and sees the palm-like shape—which the Greek account says is meant to draw away the lamp's smoke—as Persian.[21] Callimachus's Ionic art exemplifies for Yeats a melding of Persian and Greek, East and West. When he returns to Callimachus in "Lapis Lazuli," he again praises the lamp-and-palm chimney assembly, but more specifically, under Furtwängler's influence, he says the marble is as fluid as metalwork:[22]

> No handiwork of Callimachus,
> Who handled marble as if it were bronze,
> Made draperies that seemed to rise
> When sea-wind swept the corner, stands;
> His long lamp-chimney shaped like the stem
> Of a slender palm, stood but a day;
> All things fall and are built again,
> And those that build them again are gay. (566)

In this poem's five-part structure, Callimachus is the geocultural hinge between West and East. Between two stanzas set in Europe and two in China, Yeats places the Persianized Greek art of Callimachus. The poem's eastward transition is fully legible only if we're aware of the putative Persianness of Callimachus's art.

Returning to Byzantium, we can flesh out the story of its nonmimetic forms "of Persian origin," with "a vine whose tendrils climb everywhere and display among their leaves all those strange images of bird and beast." Yeats saw Byzantine mosaics with such designs in his visits to Ravenna in 1907 and Sicily in 1925.[23] Although his vision of Byzantium as a site of the blending of East and West is frequently acknowledged, less fully embraced is the idea of a specifically Persian influence. Indeed, at least one critic is exasperated by the idea, saying that "Yeats is too dependent on Strzygowski's obsession with the supposed Persian origin of Byzantine art."[24] Strzygowski knew that a claim for Iranian and Mesopotamian influences on the Byzantine Empire was sure to meet resistance, because of "the deplorable narrowness with which students concentrate their gaze upon Rome and the Mediterranean. They do not think it worth their while to search the East for traces of Christian art, and indeed meet my pioneer work with a hostility which is the measure of their prejudice."[25]

But he sought to "call attention, in the representational art of Italian mosaics, to an older influence which, in my opinion, must be connected with Iran, and more particularly with Mazdean [that is, Zoroastrian] ideas" (172). Yeats's embrace of Strzygowski's Iran-centered analysis of early Christian art makes this art historian's account particularly worthy of attention, as we explore a perhaps surprising Asian undercurrent in Yeats's work. Although Strzygowski's eccentrically morphological work may have exaggerated some Persian elements in Byzantine art, recent scholarship has begun to recognize that despite his appallingly racist political sympathies, Strzygowski helped lead the way to a newly globalized kind of art history. As the historian Suzanne Marchand puts it, he challenged "Eurocentrism" and attacked the "classicizing elitism" of the art-historical establishment, which "failed to give the Orient sufficient credit for its independent inventions."[26]

Yeats indicates that he is well aware of the Iranian conceptual basis that Strzygowski identifies in semi-abstract forms, suggesting of his "copy of an old Persian carpet that its winding and wandering vine had once that philosophical meaning, which has made it very interesting to Josef Stryzgowsky [*sic*] and was part of the religion of Zoroaster."[27] In Strzygowski's view, pre-Islamic Iran affords Byzantine art what he calls its "anti-representational" forms that are rooted in the Zoroastrian idea of *hvarenah* or "glory" in ancient Iran (also transliterated *khvarenah* or *khwarnah*, and in Middle Persian *khvarrah* or *xwarrah*), the propulsive force of life associated with the creator god, Ahura Mazda (118). As indicated by a hymn in the Avesta, it represents, according to Strzygowski, "the might and majesty of departed spirits," akin to the generative power of departed spirits arriving from across the sea in Yeats's "Byzantium." Further, *hvarenah* "is the power that makes running waters gush from springs" and even "governs the courses of sun, moon, and stars" (118). But how is *hvarenah* visually depicted? Its landscapes are "based upon significance and form, not . . . upon natural objects exactly reproduced" (119). Here again we recall the self-sufficiency of the nonmimetic forms in "Byzantium," self-begotten and self-begetting, as well as Yeats's lifelong symbolist adherence to a theory of art that refused subordination to nature ("Art is art because it is not nature," Yeats repeatedly quoted Goethe).[28]

And what form specifically does this Iranian death-derived lifesource take in art? A miraculous bird is prominent among these unnatural beasts. "The bird Varegan" (or *vareghna*), writes Strzygowski, "is the vehicle of Hvarenah" (121): "The glory flew forth in the likeness of a bird," he quotes from an ancient text (121), supernatural fowl that resembles other magical Iranian birds such as Simorgh and the *senmurv*. Just as Yeats conceives the continuous vine as Persian, he would also have known from Strzygowski that a bird made by Grecian goldsmiths in sixth-century Byzantium to "keep a drowsy Emperor awake" ("Sailing to Byzantium," 408) may have borne "Persian" traces—the element in Byzantine art, as quoted above, that includes "all those strange images of bird and beast, those forms that represent no creature eye has ever seen, yet are begotten one upon the other as if they were themselves living creatures." So too the emphatically nonnaturalistic bird of "Byzantium" may recall the Persian prototype that Strzygowski emphasizes:

> Miracle, bird or golden handiwork,
> More miracle than bird or handiwork,
> Planted on the star-lit golden bough,
> Can like the cocks of Hades crow,
> Or, by the moon embittered, scorn aloud
> In glory of changeless metal
> Common bird or petal
> And all complexities of mire or blood. (497–98)

Yeats famously conjures this magic bird partly in rebuttal to Sturge Moore's complaint that the bird of "Sailing to Byzantium" hardly escaped natural form. But when we tell the story of the second Byzantium poem's origins, perhaps we should also remember Strzygowski's concept of the nonmimeticism of Persian art. How to square the circle of the seeming contradiction of birdlike natural forms that are somehow beyond nature? This is at the heart of Strzygowski's discussion. Gibbon's *Decline and Fall of the Roman Empire*, which Yeats bought with his Nobel money, reinforces the at least partly Persian derivation of Yeats's metallic birds. Exemplifying how the Abbasid caliphs "aspired to emulate the magnificence of the Persian kings," Gibbon quotes a Syrian account of the splendors of the Baghdadi court—a model in turn for the Byzantine court—including "a tree of gold and silver . . . on which, and on the lesser boughs, sat a variety of birds, made of the same precious metals," while the mechanical "birds warbled their natural harmony."[29]

As we've seen, Yeats found in Strzygowski's analysis of Persian influences on early Christian art Zoroastrian symbols such as the vine, "free from the familiar realism of Roman work" (Strzygowski, 122), and an "Iranian decorative style" that lacks a "representational element" (133). In his description of Byzantine mosaics such as those Yeats visited in Ravenna and Sicily, Strzygowski attributes the "general scheme" to Iranian influences, "Hvarenah motives in the form of a vase between birds, or of whole landscapes with sheep or stags by the side of a shepherd and flanked by palms," or, as at the tomb of Galla Placidia in Ravenna, a cross with a starry background, features that "seem to indicate an Eastern origin, and the supposition is confirmed by the decoration of the adjacent barrel-vaults" and "apses" (134), with vine-scrolls, "acanthus scrolls and figures of stags at watersprings" and "colours suggested by bird's plumage" (135). Similarly, the Church of San Vitale in Ravenna also has *hvarenah* symbols in the roof mosaic's converging tree designs forming a circle, "the intermediate spaces being filled with continuous scrolls enclosing a large number of birds and animals" (136). For Strzygowski, other non-representational elements, such as interlaced geometric patterns and scrollwork in capitals, are "distinctively Iranian" (147).[30] Although not all of Strzygowski's claims can be substantiated, recent art historians such as Matthew P. Canepa have traced the influence of Persian ornamental art especially through silk textiles on Byzantine edifices of the sixth and seventh centuries such as Hagia Sophia and San Vitale (key models for the Byzantium poems), including features such as medallions, lozenges, ovals with wings, the *senmurv*, birds in roundels, vegetal and geometric motifs and patterns, and the pomegranate and palmette and spiky acanthus in symmetrical and semivegetal arrangements, all covering the architectural surface in Persian fashion.[31] In Yeats scholarship, it is often noted that Yeats's Byzantium may well recall sites in Ravenna, Sicily, and Constantinople (Istanbul), and as we've noted, it is a commonplace that Byzantium for Yeats represents a fusion of East and West. But to specify an important aspect of that Easternness as Iranian is to give the generality more precise intercultural force.

Arabian Multiculturalism

Except for the Byzantium poems, the place-name *Byzantium* appears in only one other of Yeats's poems, "The Gift of Harun Al-Rashid" (1924). Although I've been focusing on the pre-Islamic, Zoroastrian elements of Persian culture believed to be manifest in Byzantine art, Persian culture is also known to have been a central influence on Arab Muslim culture, particularly during what is often called the Golden Age of Islam, which reached its apex in the Arabian peninsula under the rule of Abbasid caliph Harun Al-Rashid (786–809). (Harun closely followed, for example, the Sasanian royal precedent when he presented dazzling gifts to Charlemagne.)[32] Yeats's poem is a dramatic monologue, spoken by the doctor and translator Kusta ben Luka (or Qusta ibn Luqa al Ba'lbakki), which enfolds an epistolary poem, recounting a letter he has written to the caliph's treasurer, which includes a dialogue poem, a "colloquy" between Harun and Kusta.[33] These frames within frames, genres within genres, recall the layering of the Persian queen Scheherazade's recitations in the poem's prototype, *A Thousand and One Nights*, the amalgam of largely West and South Asian narratives that Yeats said most moved him after Shakespeare.[34]

Harun's caliphate in the long eighth century was a time of relatively peaceful coexistence between Byzantium and the Muslim world. Accordingly, Yeats's semihistorical narrative refers to the intercultural exchange between Baghdad and Byzantium, as Kusta instructs an unnamed messenger to carry "this letter" past the caliphs' dark banners inscribed with calligraphy:

> Pass books of learning from Byzantium
> Written in gold upon a purple stain,
> And pause at last, I was about to say,
> At the great book of Sappho's song; but no, (461)

he corrects himself, out of fear that a love-obsessed young reader of Sappho might drop the letter on the floor. Instead,

> Pause at the Treatise of Parmenides
> And hide it there, for Caliphs to world's end
> Must keep that perfect, as they keep her song,
> So great its fame. (461)

Early foundational Greek works that are later known only in fragments are still whole in the caliph's eighth-century library. In a note originally accompanying the poem, Yeats wrote, "I do not think it too great a poetical licence to describe Kusta as hesitating between the Poems of Sappho and the Treatise of Parmenides as hiding places. Gibbon says the poems of Sappho were extant in the twelfth century, and it does not seem impossible that a great philosophical work, of which we possess only fragments, may have found its way into an Arab library of the eighth century" (829). Although it may be a stretch to locate these two particular works there, they are synecdochic of the abundance of ancient Greek works in medieval Muslim libraries.

Islamic learning was crucial to the preservation and transmission of ancient Greek texts—an "Eastern" detour that Yeats foregrounds but that is sometimes forgotten in narratives of the seemingly unbroken line of transmission of the Western heritage. The Golden Age of Islam saw the development of institutions of scientific, medical, philosophical, and cultural learning such as the House of Wisdom, founded in Baghdad by Harun Al-Rashid, which brought together Muslim, Christian, and Jewish scholars. In both the poem and his note to it, Yeats refers to the historical execution of Harun's vizier Jaffar (or Jaffer), in 803, saying he had been "head of the family of the Barmecides" (or Barmakids), an important family of advisors now thought to have been of Persian Buddhist origin in the caliph's court (828). Add to this cross-cultural mix Kusta's reference in the poem to the "great Harun Al-Rashid," born in Rey, Iran, near Tehran, as sometimes being "occupied / With Persian embassy or Grecian war" (462). And in the poem's first printing, the letter's addressee, later fictionalized as Abd Al-Rabban, meaning the rabbi, was Faristah, a Persian name meaning angel, the equivalent of Angelo.[35] Arab, Persian, Greek, Jewish, Muslim, Buddhist, Byzantine—this is a world of cross-cultural intersections. As if to mark his difference while imaginatively entering a world under Muslim rule, Yeats speaks through the mask of the Christian narrator Kusta, someone who has "accepted the Byzantine faith" (464). In these cross-cultural references, and in the poem's central dialogue between Christian and Muslim, Yeats conveys something of the spirit of a medieval Muslim world in which peoples of different faiths (Muslim, Jewish, Christian), working across different languages (Arabic, Persian, Greek), collected and advanced world thought and culture. Like Byzantium, Yeats's Baghdad exemplifies an East-West cosmopolitanism that is far from an Orient presumed "backward, degenerate, uncivilized, and retarded."[36] As in Byzantium, Gandharan Asia, Callimachus's Greece, and medieval Ireland, Yeats sees in Harun Al-Rashid's Golden Age Arabia an East-West dialogue of civilizations.

No doubt Yeats is engaged in a kind of orientalist projection, as evident in what both Jon Stallworthy and Roy Foster call the "fancy dress" he bestows on himself and his automatic-writing wife.[37] The supposed dialogue is creakily artificial. He gets some facts and dates wrong, as he later acknowledged: it might have been difficult for two men alive at different times, Harun Al-Rashid (766–809) and Kusta ben Luka (820–912), to converse in the flesh, let alone for Harun to find Kusta a wife.[38] And in this poem, as in his two poems written in the voice of specifically Muslim versions of biblical figures, "Solomon to Sheba" and "Solomon and the Witch," the newly married Yeats goes to Muslim Asia in part because it provides an opening to relatively free and frank references to sexual relations—in his case, between husband and wife.[39] Elsewhere he adapts Scheherazade's remark in Powys Mathers's *Arabian Nights*: "it is not shameful to talk of the things that lie beneath our belts."[40] Yeats activates linkages of the Muslim East with sexuality and sensuality that are, Said shows, intrinsic to orientalism. By reimagining himself as the Arab Solomon—a prophet who can speak with animals and control djinns and the wind—and his new wife as a "dusky" "Arab lady" who lies with him "under the wild moon" (332, 387), he reinforces associations of a racialized East with magic and nonrational communication.

At the same time, in "Solomon and the Witch," Solomon's philosophical disquisition on the painful difference between one's "imagined image" and the "real image" of the beloved, and on the extraordinary blessing of unifying these two images when Choice merges with Chance, suggests a robust conception of the intellectual capacities of Muslim Asia (388). Moreover, this poem ends with a remarkable assertion of female sexual desire and agency: "O! Solomon! let us try again" (389). Later, in the poem "His Bargain," Yeats echoes the Persian poet Hafez's variation on the Sufi idea of erotic love as also mystical love of the divine, specifically in the form of a covenant with the beloved's tresses, or what Yeats calls "A bargain with that hair / And all the windings there" (520).[41] In the Arabian poems, despite the received image of Solomon and Sheba in the West as Judeo-Christian icons, Yeats embraces the Islamicization of them. And despite the popular image of Yeats's poetry as focused almost entirely on Ireland, one of the longest poems he wrote in maturity—"The Gift of Harun Al-Rashid"—reimagines the intellectual learning and cultural splendor of the Abbasid era as a context within which to dramatize the beginnings of his marriage. Ireland is understood not in isolation but in a series of parallels and connections with the Byzantine Empire, Abbasid Arabia, India, Japan, and other Asian civilizations.

Perspectivist India

Albeit written largely within English, Irish, and Euro-classical traditions, Yeats's poetry also engages, as we've been seeing, a variety of Asian cultural spheres. "I have always sought to bring my mind close to the mind

of Indian and Japanese poets," he declares in *Per Amica Silentia Lunae*.[42]
The donning of "fancy dress" in his Arab poems, written in middle age,
harkens back to the staginess and costuming of some of Yeats's earliest
published poems, dramatic monologues and dialogues set in India: "Anashuya and Vijaya" (earlier titled "Jealousy"), "The Indian upon God"
(earlier "From the Book of Kauri the Indian— / Section V. On the Nature
of God," then "Kanva, the Indian, on God"), and "The Indian to His
Love" (earlier "An Indian Song"). The latter two were published in the
Dublin University Review in 1886, when Yeats was only twenty-one years
old, not long after he met and fell under the spell of the Bengali Brahmin
Theosophist Mohini Chatterjee in Dublin—a figure who reminds us of
the crucial role of Theosophy and the occult in making possible Yeats's
cross-cultural vision, particularly Theosophy's absorption and adaptation of aspects of Indian philosophy.[43] These early "Indian" poems,
though often dismissed as apprentice work, can be seen as important
stepping stones in Yeats's poetic development. To consider that three of
the first eight poems Yeats published were meant to be South Asian in
setting, voice, and thought is to become aware of India's foundational
significance for his lifework.

Take "The Indian upon God," a poem spoken in the voice of an Indian
named Kauri in the original version, a name Yeats took from Kalidasa's
Sanskrit play *Shakuntala*. Scholars have differed over the extent to which
the poem sets forth specifically Indian religious tenets, suggesting that
Yeats may have drawn on a passage in the Bhagavad Gita about the limit-
lessness of the divine's manifestations or on a creation story in the Bri-
hadaranyaka Upanishad—the same Upanishad that inspired a key part of
the last section of Eliot's *Waste Land*.[44] Perhaps more simply, the poem
tries out a concept of the multiplicity of gods—each made in the image
of the believer—an idea that can be seen as closer to the so-called poly-
theisms of South Asia than to Christian monotheism. Walking along the
water in a state between sleep and waking, the Indian speaker listens to
what various creatures profess about their deities. A moorfowl imagines
that an eternal moorfowl created the world and holds it in its bill. A lotus
projects God in its own image and sees the water as but "*a sliding drop of
rain between His petals wide*." And a roebuck conceives of God as "The
Stamper of the Skies": "*how else, I pray, could He / Conceive a thing so sad
and soft, a gentle thing like me?*" (76–77). Last comes the peacock. Figures
of repetition—polysyndeton ("*and...and*") and conduplicatio ("*made the
...made the...made my*")—thrum in a heptameter that builds toward the
splendor of the ending:

Who made the grass and made the worms and made my feathers gay,
He is a monstrous peacock, and He waveth all the night
His languid tail above us, lit with myriad spots of light. (77)

Like the others, this culminating image shifts in scale between small and vast, minute and cosmic. Albeit the great peacock is a fourth example of religious projection, it is also a meta-example, in that his many colors and "*myriad spots of light*," like this poem, evoke the beauty and multi-dimensionality of creation within which all these living things conceive distinct worlds.

The poem dramatizes perspectivism, or *Perspektivismus*, as Nietzsche called it—the idea that all conceptualizations come from particular perspectives. But it's Yeats's encounter with Asia, long before he became a deep reader of Nietzsche, that helps instill his perspectivism. After all, the imaginative extension of a young Anglo-Irish poet into South Asian thought is itself an exercise in cultural perspectivism. Hence the poem's meditation on the plurality of images of divine creation can be seen as corresponding to Yeats's willingness to don "fancy dress," to ventriloquize the East through an Indian persona, to try out a foreign perspective.[45] As Richard Ellmann observed, although the poem can be read as either debunking or affirming the multiplicity of religious projections, it does neither but rather keeps both possibilities in play.[46] If, as I'm trying to suggest, the early engagement with the East is foundational for what will emerge as Yeats's celebrated multiperspectivism, then it becomes harder to consign him to a derogatory orientalism. Yeats learned how to be multiple, how to fashion an art that holds discrepant perspectives in play, in part because of his divided allegiances as an Anglo-Irish writer to both English and Irish culture, akin to many other postcolonial writers with split affiliations.[47] But he also learned how to be multiple in part because of his self-reflections through non-Western cultures, and if there has ever been a culture of multiplicity, of syncretism, it is surely to be found in multireligious, multicultural, multilingual India. Too often we think of Eliot and Pound as the leading syncretists, comparativists, or perspectivists and see Yeats as the nationalist, even though his poetic eye is also—to quote an Indian poet he influenced, A. K. Ramanujan—"a rainbow bubble."[48]

Reflecting East Asia

Often what that poetic eye beholds is its mirror reflection. In his forays into the East, Yeats signals a self-consciousness about his cross-cultural self-extension, in contradistinction to a blindly appropriative orientalism. In addition to Persia, Arabia, Byzantium, and India, East Asia was, of course, a fertile site for his imaginative development, perhaps especially in his much-discussed adaptations of the formal vocabulary of noh drama.[49] In his lyric poems as well, there are sporadic Chinese and Japanese engagements. Elsewhere I argue that the use of the verb "imagine" and the enjambment of "I" as a pivot in "Lapis Lazuli" ("and I / Delight to imagine them seated there") signal the poem's awareness that its Western imagination is playing with and projecting onto a Chinese carving.[50] Similarly, in "A Dialogue of Self and Soul," Self describes the magnificent Japanese sword not so much as a weapon ready to do violence but as a mirror, and this conjunction of the image of self-reflexivity with deliberate projection and fabrication ("I set" the sword and other images, he declares) suggests the poem's self-consciousness about its cultural crossing:

> The consecrated blade upon my knees
> Is Sato's ancient blade, still as it was,
> Still razor-keen, still like a looking-glass
> Unspotted by the centuries;
> That flowering, silken, old embroidery, torn
> From some court-lady's dress and round
> The wooden scabbard bound and wound,
> Can, tattered, still protect, faded adorn. (477)

"My Self" is looking into the looking glass of a Japanese artifact, and in this regard the poet sees himself making it into a symbol—of enduring secular life, of the conjunction of masculine and feminine, and so forth. In the description of the cloth wound around the scabbard, moreover, the winding of an additional internal rhyme into the octave's double envelope rhymes ("torn," "round," "bound and wound," "adorn") is a sonic correlative to the mirror effects earlier attributed to the Japanese sword.[51]

"Visuality is central to Japanism," according to Christopher Reed, and "must be crucial to intersections of cultures that do not share a written or spoken language."[52] Hence, it seems, the importance of Sato's sword. But similar effects can be seen in a textually mediated poem that Yeats wrote in December 1936 and placed immediately after "Lapis Lazuli" in *New Poems* (1938). In "Imitated from the Japanese," as Edward Marx has shown, Yeats adapts three haiku by the beloved Japanese haiku grand-master Kobayashi Issa (1763–1827) as translated by Yeats's friend Yone Noguchi, who helped introduce haiku into English-language poetry.[53] Yeats's three-stanza poem implicitly contrasts the poet's chronological aging with spring's endless and joyous (if melancholy-inducing) recurrence, echoing haiku's frequent seasonal setting in a transient nature (*kigo*) and aesthetic principles such as compression, comparison, alternation, and contrast (*kireji*). Topoi recognizable from haiku tradition include loneliness (*sabi*), lightness (*karumi*), poetic eccentricity (*fukyo*), ascetic freedom (*wabi*), and deep, mysterious beauty (*yugen*).[54] Whereas in modern Japan and the West, the haiku has often been treated as a stand-alone poem, it was traditionally linked with other haiku, almost as if each haiku were, as Adam L. Kern puts it, "one instalment—or 'stanza.'"[55] Yeats's linked verses might look odd to those of us habituated to the isolated three-line poem, but their verbal, formal, and thematic linkage brings them closer to traditional haiku, in which, as Kern says, "the link (*tsukeai*) is the thing."[56] Premodern haiku sequences were collaboratively produced, each poet writing in response to preceding haiku. Yeats's poem is collaborative in a different sense, written in close association with Noguchi ("Imitated from . . ."), who in turn drew together and translated three of Issa's haiku from different sources.

In homage to the minimalism of haiku, Yeats restricts his lexical palette to a bare handful of repeated words. But in so doing, he makes the tripartite poem even more heavily recursive than either Issa's three haiku or Noguchi's rendering of them, in ways that may suggest the self-consciousness and heightened formality seen in "A Dialogue of Self and Soul." Four of the poem's nine lines begin with the anaphora "Seventy years," three with a swinging trisyllabic rhythm: "Seventy years have I lived" (567).[57] In the middle stanza "Spring" occurs at the end of one line and again near the beginning of the next: "(Hurrah for the flowers of Spring, / For Spring is here again.)" Except for the half-rhyme of "again" and "man," the rest of the rhyme scheme resounds with sonic and lexical replication (*ab ac bcbdd*). Even within a line like "No ragged beggar man" ("Seventy years have I lived / No ragged beggar man"), we can see repetition: the middle words are nearly mirrorlike anagrams of each other. At midline, even the letters *d* and *b* mirror each other. This poetic reflexivity doesn't exempt Yeats from orientalism, but it seems at a considerable remove from the kind of unselfconsciously appropriative logic that Said ascribes to orientalism. In potentially awkward traversals of the East/

West divide, it harnesses and makes fruitful use of lyric's capacities for rich self-awareness.

Here again it's worth attending even more specifically to the way the East—though Yeats sometimes dismisses it as "formless," at other times celebrates it as rich in form—informs his forms. Although Yeats doesn't follow the syllabic patterning of haiku (only loosely followed in premodern Japan), he plays on haiku's syllabic alternations and stays close to its middle, seven-syllable line. His accentual equivalent for the brevity of the haiku line is trimeter lines that trade off iambs and anapests. Whereas Noguchi's translations of Issa appear as three three-line haiku, Yeats rearranges the sequence as two couplets followed by a quintet (or quintain). The first couplet is in lines of seven syllables, followed by a stanza with lines of eight and six syllables. These first two stanzas might well look like violations of what is taken in the West to be the three-line, 5-7-5 norm, but each is in fourteen syllables—as it happens, exactly like the less-well-known, premodern haiku form known as *tanku*.[58] Yeats follows these two *tanku*-like couplets with a five-line stanza in lines of 7, 6, 7, 7, and 8 syllables. This stanzaic structure—again far from the three-line Western haiku norm—resembles another related form, the *tanka*, the dominant form of Japanese poetry or *waka* for over a millennium. The *tanka* is a "short verse" of thirty-one syllables in five measures (5-7-5-7-7), with allowances for additional syllables—a form that Noguchi and the Imagists had helped bring into English.[59] Often *tanka* pivots between its haiku-like, 5-7-5 upper part and its 7-7 lower part. By virtue of rhyme and repetition, Yeats's stanza also bifurcates: the first and third lines of his thirty-five-syllable stanza are identical, forming a haiku-like upper part (rhymed *bcb*), before closing with a couplet (*dd*). The Japanese form's structure has been seen as arising from "a complex interplay between the classical East Asian ideal of symmetry on the one hand and a desire for its complementary opposite in the form of an asymmetric (and therefore indigenous) structure on the other."[60] Even if Yeats isn't deliberately engaging the Japanese *tanka* or *tanku*, he develops parallel forms that balance symmetric with asymmetric structures, setting two stanzas of two lines against one of five, and in the final quintet, three lines against a couplet. This structural mixture helps accentuate the poem's tonal mixture of joy ("Hurrah") with regret ("never have I danced"), triumph ("Seventy years") with melancholy (also "Seventy years"). The septuagenarian poet may never have danced with joy, but in lamenting this lack, he sets his verse forms dancing.

Orientalist, Anti-orientalist, or . . . ?

After this reconsideration of some Eastward-reaching moments in Yeats's poetry, where are we on the questions of the extent to which his poetry is and isn't orientalist and of whether we should see his Eastern excursions as appropriative theft or productive cross-cultural engagement? More broadly, can we glean any insight from his example that could be useful for the future development of transnational literary studies? One way to approach these questions is to place Yeats's work between the divergent disciplinary frameworks of orientalist critique and world literature.[61] In Said's model of orientalism, Western forays into the East are often seen as inherently prejudicial and deprecating, because Westerners can't see the East except through the skewing imbalances of power and wealth. In the world literature model, these political and historical differences are less prominent, because of the emphasis on transit, translation, and circulation from one culture to another. In my view, a challenge for transnational literary studies is to navigate a path between the sensitivity to power and historical injustice in orientalist critique and the neutral tracking of cultural dissemination and reproduction in "world literature." My hope is that the foregoing analysis demonstrates one way of negotiating the differences between these models, which usefully correct for each other's excesses. As Stefan Helgesson writes, we should take advantage of "the potential for a mutually enriching exchange" between the two approaches.[62]

Although I've been trying to counterbalance the one-sidedness of Said's model, in *Orientalism* Said himself briefly anticipates a nuanced approach by carving out an exception for two writers, Gérard de Nerval and Gustave Flaubert. According to Said, "they produced work that is connected to and depends upon the kind of Orientalism we have so far discussed, yet remains independent from it."[63] The same could be said of Yeats, who, like these writers, reimagined the Orient as a space of possibility. As in Said's end-of-career work on what the Palestinian scholar called "late style," in which idiosyncrasy and unresolved tensions are crucial to artistic creation, he says of these two French writers: "What mattered to them was the structure of their work as an independent, aesthetic, and personal fact, and not the ways by which, if one wanted to, one could effectively dominate or set down the Orient graphically. Their egos never absorbed the Orient, nor totally identified the Orient with documentary and textual knowledge of it (with official Orientalism, in short)."⁶⁴ Although Yeats's representations of the Orient have little of the corporeality, decrepitude, and experiential immediacy that Said sees in the work of these French writers, he too engages various Asias through an emphatically personal prism without seeking domination or documentation. Just as Said differentiates these French writers from most of the Englishmen who write ultimately in the service of strengthening the British Empire, so too Yeats's Anglo-Irishness, even with his living much of his life in the imperial center of London, places him on a different footing in relation to the so-called East from that of many British orientalists. Said famously argues in "Yeats and Decolonization" that Yeats is a "poet who during a period of anti-imperialist resistance articulates the experiences, the aspirations, and the restorative vision" of a colonized people.⁶⁵ To the extent that Yeats's identifications are at least semi-anticolonial, they connect him with parts of the world that have been on the receiving end of empires.

Bearing this exception in mind, let's take a last look at Yeats in relation to the standard features of orientalism. As we saw in a stanza in "The Statues," Yeats is complicit in the orientalist othering of the East as formless, many-headed, weak, sensual, and unintellectual, as opposed to the West's individualism, formalism, and antithetical strength. But even though he sometimes thought "East and West seem each other's contraries," his poetry also complicates and even confutes these oppositions and the very strategy of dichotomizing.⁶⁶ It's hard to view Yeats's work as merely making, in Said's terms, "more rigid the sense of difference between the European and Asiatic parts of the world."⁶⁷ As we've seen, Yeats foregrounds cross-cultural blending and interplay in his Asian-oriented poetry, as in the Irish-Asiatic and Greco-Indian fusions in "The Statues," the mingling of Persian and Western forms in the Byzantium poems, of Greek and Persian, Christian and Muslim learning and culture in the Arabian poems. The East may be different, alien, "other" in various ways, but it's also an important dimension of the West—Asiatic ancient Greece, Asiatic early Christianity, Asiatic ancient and modern Ireland, and so forth. Poetry's capacity for syncretic layering provides a particularly useful structure by which to embody these convergences.

What of the orientalist idea of the East as formless? Various parts of Asia also provide strong formal vocabularies that figure in Yeats's work: the Persian nonmimetic line, vine, patterning, color, and nonnaturalistic beasts in his Byzantium; the Arab interest in measurement, mathematics, and geometry that are a recurrent theme in his Arabian poems (as well as his semi-imaginary Arab tribe of the Judwalis, meaning diagrammatists);[68] the South Asian structures of multifacetedness and plurality that are presupposed in some of Yeats's earliest poems; the East Asian compression and alternations that he loosely adapts from haiku and related forms. Also, even though there is some overlap among Yeats's Asias—as is perhaps fitting, given the amount of trade, migration, and artistic and religious circulation across the continent—these regions are also each reimagined with some distinctness as well, in contrast to the view that, in Said's words, "Orientals were almost everywhere nearly the same."[69] Even when Yeats claims that meditative practices of East Asia and India have largely similar aims, he is alert to the differences in "technique" they employ.[70]

What of the idea of orientalism as negatively prejudicial? In Yeats's poetry, Eastern worlds are often intellectually, sensually, culturally robust sites of wisdom and insight and cross-cultural integration: witness the empty-eyed Buddhism and *contemptus mundi* Hinduism of north India in poems such as "The Statues" and "Meru"; the vitalizing Zoroastrian forms integrated with Christian and classical elements in Yeats's Byzantium; the multicultural libraries and Solomonic-and-Sheban wisdom of the Arabian poems; the prismatic refractions of divinity in the multitheistic Indian poems; and the cultural stability, social hierarchy, asymmetric symmetry, and renunciatory ethos in poems that invoke East Asia.

Finally, what of orientalism's de-individualizing of the East, reducing it and its people, as Said says, to "'attitudes,' 'trends,' statistics," leaving it "dehumanized"?[71] As we've seen, Yeats repeatedly speaks through named Arab, Indian, and other masks, and while we can surely see stereotyping in these poetic performances, he is also demonstrating that literature can, as Said puts it, speak "more or less directly of a living reality," instead of just absorbing these different cultures into blanket abstractions.[72] Hence Yeats's avoidance of what Said calls the orientalist's substitution of texts "for any actual encounter with the real Orient."[73] I've been focusing on Yeats's poetry, but it's worth remembering that even though his desires to travel to Japan and India were never fulfilled, Yeats befriended and collaborated with a number of Asians—Mohini Chatterjee, Rabindranath Tagore, Shri Purohit Swami, Yone Noguchi, Junzo Sato, Michio Ito, Shotara Oshima, and others whose relationships with him have been extensively discussed in Yeats scholarship.[74] We all know that friendships can coexist with prejudices, but on the evidence of his letters, essays, poems, and collaborative projects, it's clear that Yeats was intellectually open to these Asian friends and that, in some cases, he made important contributions to their careers as well as their texts, just as they did to his. More significant than Yeats's partly distortive pre-suppositions about "other" cultures—and it bears repeating that we all have them, however unconscious—is that he took Asian cultures seri-ously: he engaged them, performed them, learned from them, and made poetry and theater enmeshed with them—reasons to keep him at the center of discussions of modernism's global bearings.

CHAPTER 7

POETRY, THE PLANET, AND THE ECOLOGICAL THOUGHT: WALLACE STEVENS AND BEYOND

Is Wallace Stevens a global poet in any sense of the term? At least some of his poems, such as "O, Florida, Venereal Soil," would seem an obstacle to such a designation:

> The dreadful sundry of this world,
> The Cuban, Polodowsky,
> The Mexican women,
> The negro undertaker. . . .[1]

Far from commending Stevens as a prospective resource for a Benetton ad or a UNESCO campaign, these lines show him retreating from the world's ethnographic heterogeneity. As Helen Vendler observes, "when he is faced with the gross heterogeneity of the world he recoils"; when he is faced with the world's "multiple reality," "the revulsion shows."[2] Critics, poets, and other commentators diverge on whether such portraits in Stevens should be characterized as "extraordinary racism," commonplace Euro-American "exoticism," or otherwise.[3] But in any case, it's hard to see them as meeting at least the second of ecocritic Ursula Heise's dual criteria for literary globalism: that the forms "do justice both to the sense that places are inexorably connected to the planet as a whole and to the perception that this wholeness encompasses vast heterogeneities."[4] As Vendler says of Stevens, "His preferred view of totality is not the heterogeneous but a great One—the Celestial Sun—which is, needless to say, still far away."[5] Counterintuitive though it might seem, is it possible to understand a poet of totality rather than heterogeneity as a world, global, or planetary poet? If so, another kind of case would have to

be made than for anglophone modernists now read in such terms, since
Stevens's work doesn't have the robust welcoming of South, East, and
West Asian cultural resources in Yeats's lyrics and verse dramas, the overt
engagement with South Asian philosophy in Eliot's *Waste Land* and *Four
Quartets*, the encyclopedic cultural reach of Pound's *Cantos*, the jaggedly
mongrelizing cultural collage in Mina Loy's *Anglo-Mongrels and the Rose*,
the syncretic religious embrace of H.D.'s *Trilogy*, the tensile hybridization of cultural perspectives from the global South and North in Claude
McKay's lyrics, or comparable features in the work of Marianne Moore,
Gertrude Stein, Melvin Tolson, and others. What grounds remain for
seeing Stevens as a poet with strong transnational bearings?

For starters, however much he may recoil from globalizing processes, his poetry is marked and energized by them. His youth and early
development coincide with the period, roughly 1870 to 1914, said to be
"notable for the increased extensity and intensity of international flows
of trade, people, finance and capital investment."[6] Although Stevens
wryly said, "I hope that I am American" (800) and has long been treated
by some as a uniquely American writer, critics such as Bart Eeckhout
and Stephen Matterson have been reglobalizing his work.[7] While it is
true that American history, high culture, language, race relations, politics, and economics all shape Stevens's poetry, we distort it if we con-
fine our horizon of understanding to the nation's borders. Despite a
declaration in the *New Yorker* that "he is certainly the quintessentially
American poet of the twentieth century,"[8] Stevens himself rejected "fac-
titious Americanism" (805) and refused an identity that was "flagrantly
American" (800), claiming to forget about his nationality "except as a
quality, a savor" (805). Notwithstanding efforts to nationalize his work,
we can distinguish a number of different if overlapping layers of transnational extensity that cut across it. Globalization, Paul Hopper summarizes, is "a plural rather than unitary phenomenon," such that there
are "multiple dimensions to globalization"—"different histories, processes and forms of interconnectedness" characterized by "complexity,
plurality and multidimensionality."[9] As Arjun Appadurai writes of the
various flows of globalization, they are not always isomorphic, and so it
is worth separating them out for purposes of analysis.[10] Although each
of these layers in Stevens deserves substantive and separate treatment,
I briefly enumerate them, before focusing on what may be the most distinctive form of globality in his poetry.

The most obvious layer is the ethnographic, the various peoples who
populate his purportedly place- rather than people-centered work—the

Cubans, Poles, Mexicans, and African Americans already noted in the lines of "O, Florida, Venereal Soil," to which we could add the Chinese, Irish, Arabs, Dutch, Jews, Native Americans, Germans, Swedes, and so forth, often represented exotically. The mere presence of such a range of human cultures evidences an awareness of the world's ethnographic plurality, as enhanced by migration, trade, and communication, even if the typing of peoples seems meant to simplify and control that heterogeneity. A second, related layer is technology. Experiencing modernity's space-time compression as a devoted radio listener, Stevens noted, with a mixture of wonder and ambivalence, a newfound human intimacy with peoples elsewhere: "We are close together in every way. We lie in bed and listen to a broadcast from Cairo, and so on. There is no distance. We are intimate with people we have never seen and unhappily, they are intimate with us."[11] Such communications include the news of global warfare from "Europe, Asia and Africa all at one time" that shapes modern consciousness.[12] The poetic imagination is dialectically produced as a counterforce against this global pressure, "a violence from within that protects us from a violence without" (665). Third is the transnational movement of goods and capital—cigars, pineapples, bananas, and so forth. Stevens repeatedly writes, for example, to a contact in Ceylon (now Sri Lanka), asking that he procure necklaces, boxes, tea, and other commodities, initially for Christmas presents.[13] That his correspondent was a "descendant of the early Dutch settlers of Ceylon" indicates the extent to which such trade, if expanded, continued to move in part along the well-worn tracks laid by colonialism.[14] A fourth layer is the influence of international thought and the visual and literary arts. Even though Stevens never traveled to Europe, Asia, or South America, critics have been increasingly attentive to the influence on his work of East Asian philosophies like Buddhism (e.g., "The Snow Man") and literary forms like haiku ("Thirteen Ways of Looking at a Blackbird"), as well as of French, Dutch, East Asian, and other kinds of painting ("Six Significant Landscapes"), let alone his direct literary exchanges with people in France, Ireland, Latin America, and elsewhere.[15] A fifth layer is geographic—the accumulation of topographical traces in his poetry, whether sites he actually visited, such as the Canadian Rockies, the Florida Keys, and Cuba, or places of imaginative or indirect contact, such as the Cliffs of Moher, China, and Arabia.

In these various dimensions, Stevens seems to have wanted people, commodities, artistic forms, and places to be true to stable cultural identities—a poet, as Matterson surmises from the letters, "who believed very much in the need for the nation's things to represent that nation, who wanted Cuba to be 'full of Cuban things' (L 495), the gods of China to be Chinese (OP 263), and was surprised that sausages were sold in Ireland because they seemed insufficiently Celtic (L 616)."[16] As Jonathan Culler notes of tourist desire, Stevens wished for foreign people, things, arts, and places to signify themselves.[17] Despite this apparent aversion to intercultural hybridization, his poetry gleefully gathers—while holding distinct—peoples, commodities, artistic influences, and topographies from around the world. In yet another stratum, language—a stratum more fully under his control—his poetry more boldly mixes diverse ingredients. Asserting that "French and English constitute a single language," Stevens intensifies the creolization of English not only with French but also with Dutch, Latin, Spanish, German, and other languages.[18] As a linguistic field, his poetry is unusually vibrant with polyglossia. Cannibalizing a range of languages, it also reveals and rejoices in the linguistic heterogeneity embedded in English.

In short, Stevens's poetry richly evidences, even when in revulsion, the impact of various long-term and more recent processes of globalization, which reverberate across his poetry and contribute to the apperception of the worldhood of the world, or what sociologist Roland Robertson terms "globality," "the circumstance of extensive awareness of the world as a whole."[19] After deconstruction, after poststructuralism, claims to wholeness may seem suspect. A great deal of humanities scholarship has argued against what is disparaged as "totalization," as ecotheorist Timothy Morton observes. But as Morton writes, that consciousness of "totality" is key to strong ecological thinking.[20] Although Stevens may fall short as a multiculturalist or visionary pluralist, he seeks ways to think, envision, and formally represent the wholeness of the earth and indeed of the environmental cosmos, including the human imagination that helps conceive and construct the worldhood of the world. Like the supreme fiction, this planetary wholeness is never fully graspable, an ever-receding horizon, an always-morphing impossible possibility. Stevens's imagination oscillates between part and prospective whole, the local and the all-encompassing global. His poems enact the process of trying to envision reality on a planetary scale. This planetary aspiration may be his signal contribution to a global poetics, as I attempt to show by closely examining a few poems in the light of a cosmopolitan ecotheory drawn from works by Morton, Heise, Bruno Latour, Lawrence Buell, Dana Phillips, and Rob Nixon. The global ecopoetic reconceptualization of place and scale that Lynn Keller usefully traces in twenty-first-century North American experimental poetry is, I hope to show, already emergent in Stevens's work.[21] Since until recently, ecocriticism and globalization theory have been, despite their mutual attention to the traversal of various boundaries, largely separate from one another, I also hope to suggest how poets from Stevens to A. K. Ramanujan, Juliana Spahr, and Jorie Graham can help further knit them together.

The Giant in the Window

Perhaps Stevens's most striking early evocation of the wholeness and vastness of planet Earth is a 1904 journal entry. After describing a walk through the awe-inspiring landscape along the Hudson River at Stony Point and Tomkins Cove, Stevens writes:

> I thought, on the train, how utterly we have forsaken the Earth, in the sense of excluding it from our thoughts. There are but few who consider its physical hugeness, its rough enormity. It is still a disparate monstrosity, full of solitudes & barrens & wilds. It still dwarfs & terrifies & crushes. The rivers still roar, the mountains still crash, the winds still shatter. Man is an affair of cities. His gardens & orchards & fields are mere scrapings. Somehow, however, he has managed to shut out the face of the giant from his windows. But the giant is there, nevertheless.[22]

What Stevens has seen on his walk and can contemplate on his train ride by the Hudson instills in him an apprehension of the earth's gigantic scale and power. Long before space travel in the 1960s and 1970s made it possible literally to see the earth in its entirety in images such as "Earthrise" and "The Blue Marble," the vehicular technology of the train, if less rapid and distancing than a rocket, helps stimulate Stevens's aspiration toward an imaginative visioning of the earth as a whole. So too Langston Hughes's train ride across the Mississippi River inspired the vast spatiotemporal palimpsest of "I've Known Rivers," although Hughes's emphasis is the layering of deep time in human history, while Stevens's is spatial dimensionality. Even if Stevens's revelation comes out of an experience of the nonhuman natural world, it's also entangled in the technologies and urbanization of modernity. As Robertson writes of the "rapidly spreading consciousness of the global world as such," particularly in the period of 1870 to 1925, it was "greatly facilitated by recently developed rapid means of travel and communication."[23]

The seeds of many prototypically Stevensian preoccupations are here—the devotion to the earth, the fascination with immense scale, the

evocation of a nonhuman world that is active, powerful, sometimes violent, the vision of the giant, and the desire to remove habits of thought
that shutter the cosmos. Toward these ends, Stevens doesn't deploy, even
in a journal entry, an aesthetically depleted or self-subordinating micro-
referential realism. For him, an ecological vision freed of mental encrus-
tations demands an aesthetic heightening—as later, when "casual flocks
of pigeons make / Ambiguous undulations as they sink, / Downward to
darkness, on extended wings" (56), or much later, when another "bird's
fire-fangled feathers dangle down" (477). Stevens's prose is so cadenced
and rhetorically shaped, even shadowed by iambic pentameter, that it
could be lineated as poetry, like Yeats's anthologized version of Walter
Pater's "Mona Lisa."[24] As if to embed the earth's rough enormity in
syntax, Stevens's tricolonic sentences are knit with polysyndetic multiplicity ("solitudes & barrens & wilds," "dwarfs & terrifies & crushes"),
and these are framed in turn by asyndetic sentences, one of them also
tricolonic ("The rivers still roar, the mountains still crash, the winds still
shatter"). The passage vivifies the earth's manifold agency and ceaseless
energy by shifting from nouns to triads of active verbs. Its evocation of
the earth's vast scale, terrifying power, and ecological variety, all rendered
as persisting despite modern neglect and urbanization ("still," "still,"
"still," "still"), is indebted to the Romantic sublime, possibly including
its pictorial adaptation by the Hudson River School. A commentator
aptly compares this passage's scene to the remote, nonhuman otherness
in Shelley's "Mont Blanc" but less persuasively argues that Stevens sternly
resists anthropomorphic projection;[25] instead, as Scott Knickerbocker
surmises of Stevens's journal entry, "his use of figurative language and literary conventions implicates humans in nature."[26] After all, here Stevens
figures the earth's "monstrosity" in a Gulliver-like giant whose face has
been shuttered. Stevens doesn't conform to the distinction later codified
in deep ecology between anthropocentric and biocentric apprehensions
of nonhuman nature, a distinction criticized by Ramachandra Guha,
among other ecotheorists.[27] Even a poem like "The Snow Man," which
zeroes out consciousness to apprehend the nonhuman other, cannot do
so without building on a long anthropomorphic association between the
negation of the human and the snow-and-ice-encrusted, dead-leaved
barrenness of winter.[28] The journal passage intimates what Stevens will
later declare as a kind of raison d'être for his oeuvre, more central to his
art than it is to Eliot's, Yeats's, Pound's, H.D.'s, Loy's, McKay's, Moore's,
or Stein's: "the great poems of heaven and hell have been written and the
great poem of the earth remains to be written."[29]

Although Stevens's poetics of the earth made a poor fit with mimetic, bioregionalist, nature-as-other varieties of ecocriticism, more recent ecological approaches are better suited to illuminating his work. Philosopher-anthropologist Bruno Latour has influentially fostered ecological attention to globality, not just locality; to interconnectedness, not just discrete places or times; and to the interwovenness of the human and the nonhuman. "The smallest AIDS virus," in his example, "takes you from sex to the unconscious, then to Africa, tissue cultures, DNA and San Francisco," even though we may be tempted to slice these networks into discrete disciplinary and geographical compartments.[30] Such perspectives make it easier to grasp the reach of Stevens's ecopoetics. Since the global is networked by the "continuously local," as Latour states, we should refrain from overdichotomizing the local and global.[31] In Stevens's journal entry, after all, the earth is not a featureless, placeless sphere, of the kind that Gayatri Chakravorty Spivak disparages as "global": it teems with rivers, mountains, and winds.[32] Stevens evokes wholeness through an accretion of earthly elements—"solitudes & barrens & wilds." As in Kant's mathematical sublime, the apprehension of not empirically graspable, planetary vastness arises out of an "on and on" accumulation that extends through and beyond locality.[33] The scalar juxtaposition of the eye of one blackbird with twenty snowy mountains vivifies both the small and the large. Each of Stevens's globally expansive poems, moreover, lives partly in its exquisitely local phrases and textures and techniques.

Still, a planetary perspective can help correct for an overly localist ecocriticism that overlooks Stevens's eco-cosmopolitanism. In two recent ecocritical discussions, Knickerbocker and Matthew Griffiths recognize the connection between Latour's and Stevens's hybrid view of nature as both real and constructed, objective and subjective—an understanding of the globality of this hybrid planetary vision that I seek to develop further.[34] Timothy Morton, a key figure in elaborating such ecocritical tenets, recalls the slogans of the environmental movement of the late 1960s—"Small is beautiful. Diet for a small planet. The local is better than the global"—and polemically turns them on their head, declaring their opposite: "the best environmental thinking is thinking big."[35] If we embrace such ways of thinking, he avers, "Our perspective becomes very vast."[36] As we've seen in the prose rhapsody on the rough enormity of the earth, we needn't give up the small or local for the global: that entry is built on microparticulars of observation, rhetoric, and language, even as Stevens is indeed thinking big.

Stevens famously proposes that life is for him "an affair of places,"[37] and it's fascinating to map his poems, as Stephanie Burt has shown, onto the specific places he names directly or indirectly evokes, especially those he lived in or visited, but also perhaps those he knew from correspondence, commodities, or literary contact: "to see Stevens as a poet of place-attachment," Burt avers, "is to see his relevance to ecocriticism."[38] In a similar vein, Eeckhout pins "Earthy Anecdote" to the experiential Oklahoma that Stevens visited. But interestingly, he then shows this place also to be an imaginative and cosmopolitan construct.[39] If so, then it may be that a loco-materialist reading of place in Stevens's poetry takes you only so far. Although I've criticized certain uses of distant reading in a previous chapter, I've also suggested that its strategies can be useful in combination with close reading; here, it's worth observing the sheer number of times Stevens's poems mention specific place-names. Each of the multitude of place-names in his poetry appears relatively infrequently. Only twice does he name Pennsylvania, Haddam, Tennessee, Athens, Mexico, Oklahoma, and New York, and only once Appalachia, Arkansaw (sic), Denmark, Egypt, Esthonia (sic), Florence, Iceland, Moscow, Norway, Tallapoosa, the Yangtse, and Zurich.[40] The most frequently mentioned place-names appear only a handful of times: Yucatan (7 mentions); America, Ceylon, and Hartford (5); China, Spain, and Connecticut (4). The variety of such places is more impressive in Stevens than is any effort at the literary re-creation of Pennsylvania or Hartford, Mexico or Egypt. Compare Stevens's place-names with Pound's in *The Cantos*, in which the density of specified reference contributes to the poetic substantiation of topographies, including France at 52 mentions, America 36, London 35, Venice 32, Paris 31, Spain 23, Boston 19, Taishan 18, and China 16.[41] Far more abundant than individual place-names in Stevens's diction are abstractive, totalizing words that appear more often in his poetry than in that of even a fellow Romantic modernist like Yeats: *earth* (120 vs. 53), *world* (219 vs. 174), and *whole* (69 vs. 37).[42] Granted, Stevens often differentiates among places and regions in broad strokes, as reflected in the importance of the geographical trajectory of "The Comedian as the Letter C" and the repeated contrast between a cold, ascetic, intellectual North and a lush, fecund, erotic South. Even so, many specifically named places in Stevens are more emblematic of our locatedness on Earth than they are detailed evocations of a discrete microlocation. His poetry delights in imaginative leaps from one part of the globe to another. And for Stevens, who said that "words, above everything else, are, in poetry, sounds," it's often as much the sound of the place-name as the place that is its passport into a poem.[43]

Here again, as we consider the place of place in Stevens's poetry, it's worth pausing over some developments in ecocriticism. "Fixation on place," Morton writes, "impedes a truly ecological view,"[44] and "a localist poetics . . . is in greater measure part of the problem than part of the solution. Our notions of place are retroactive fantasy constructs determined precisely by the corrosive effects of modernity."[45] Even Lawrence Buell, though indebted to an earlier paradigm, welcomes the cosmopolitan turn in ecocritical studies and suggests "place-attachment" can be a problem when it "falls into a sentimental environmental determinism."[46] So too Heise criticizes the "excessive investment in the local," warns that it can block an understanding of larger patterns that require "abstract" thinking, and hails the movement in environmentalism from "ecolocalism" to "a global environmental perspective."[47] The challenge for environmental thinking, she writes, is to shift from a "sense of place to a less territorial and more systemic sense of planet."[48] Protesting bioregionalism's "unselfconscious parochialism" and its "moral imperative of the local," Rob Nixon urges environmentalism to be "more, not less, transnational than other fields of literary inquiry."[49] And in a cri de coeur for a new ecopoetics, Morton asks, "Could we have a progressive ecology that was big, not small; spacious, not place-ist; global, not local (if not universal); not embodied but displaced, spaced, outer spaced?"[50] Such an ecocosmopolitan framework, if accentuating the localities that thread across it, may be better attuned to Stevens's poetic practice and can help disrupt lingering assumptions that the more locally referential and literal the literary text, the more ecologically minded it is. His example can also help right the genre balance in ecocriticism, which even in its cosmopolitan orientation has devoted more attention to narrative prose than to poetry.[51]

An Orb

"Seeing the Earth from space," argues Morton, "is the beginning of ecological thinking," and Stevens is among the poets who—even before technology could physically achieve this distance—aspire through imaginative abstraction to see Earth as a whole.[52] Ayesha Ramachandran traces to early modern poets, mapmakers, and thinkers "the desire to see the world whole, a desire that culminates in 'Earthrise' "—the desire to "comprehend the world, to organize and capture its variety in a single harmonious frame," "the relentless intellectual and cultural drive to uncover a comprehensive vision of the whole" by "envisioning an abstract totality."[53] That capacity isn't autonomous in the early modern or in the modernist era: it depends to some extent on the reach of techno-logical developments and other globalizing processes, as already hinted by Stevens's train-induced journal entry. Walt Whitman, hymning "the vast terraqueous globe," invokes the time-space compression afforded by the new Suez Canal, the first transcontinental railroad, the laying of a transatlantic cable, and the journeys of explorers.[54] "O, vast Rondure, swimming in space, / Cover'd all over with visible power and beauty," he exclaims, "Now first it seems my thought begins to span thee"—a power and beauty that includes "the manifold grass and waters, animals, moun-tains, trees."[55] Whitman's poetic effort to "span" the earth is an imagina-tive act, but it is fueled by the globe's having been "spann'd, connected by network."[56] Indebted to Whitman, Stevens's vision of the earth's totality emerges at a later stage in globalizing technologies. But it also requires what Ramachandran calls "the synoptic energies of the imagi-nation" to realize "the totalizing concept of the 'world,'" the "poiesis—artful making—" of the world.[57] It depends on the poet's power, as Stevens argues, "to abstract himself and also to abstract reality, which he does by placing it in his imagination."[58]

The giant of Stevens's journal entry reappears in various guises in his poems, extensively in "A Primitive like an Orb," an underread late poem, which was published separately in a 1948 pamphlet with two illustrations of the giant by the surrealist Kurt Seligmann. In addition to its publi-cation history, another indication of this highly abstract poem's impor-tance for Stevens is his use of the word *poem* in it more often than in any other poem, including much longer poem-thematizing sequences that also incorporate ars poetica like "Notes toward a Supreme Fiction" or "An Ordinary Evening in New Haven." In "A Primitive like an Orb"—an "orb" that descends from Whitman's "Rondure" and the Latin for "the world," *orbis terrarum* (circle of lands)—Stevens tries out various ways of conceiving the totality of reality and the totality of human creation, "the world" and "the central poem," which ideally mirror and even fuse with one another, "each one the mate / Of the other," "both one" (379). As throughout his work, he has multiple models for the relation of mind to reality, human to nonhuman, and they continually shift throughout the poem.

At first, the giant, or primitive, appears almost as a sunlike celes-tial orb: "A giant, on the horizon, glistening," "crested" with "fire" (379). Emphasizing immensity, Stevens calls the giant "an abstraction given head," "A massive body and long legs," "a large among the smalls / Of it, a close, parental magnitude" (379). In Gyorgyi Voros's ecocritical reading, the giant is the "combined sun and earth—which is to say, . . . the physical universe."[59] In J. Hillis Miller's deconstructionist reading, it is the unnameable sun, the absent center around which the poem weaves an "astonishing diversity" and even "bewildering proliferation" of metaphors that cancel each other out.[60] These include arias, gorging good, essential gold, being, a feast in the woods, the blue of thunder, the joy of language, the fulfillment of fulfillments, summer's mate, a secular light, a force, a principle, a meditation of a principle, an inherent order, a beneficent being, a repose, and, in closest proximity to the giant's first appearance, "the muscles of a magnet" (379). Both Voros's and Miller's interpretations are valuable, but this giant seems more than a personification of either the physical universe or its ineffability.

Before I turn to *how* Stevens evokes environmental and creative totality in this challenging poem, let me venture a condensed synopsis of the poem's *what*. The poem's giant emerges out of a long, restlessly self-revising search for metaphors and terms for what Stevens calls the "central" or "essential poem at the center of things" (377). Suggestive both of an imaginative totality and of a physical totality, the central poem has the vastness of a "huge, high harmony"—"the largest, bulging still with more" (378). As ever in Stevens, the world is truly apprehended only with the removal of cliché and habit—"the used-to earth and sky, and the tree / And cloud, the used-to tree and used-to cloud" (378). In particular, creative forms, "arias that spiritual fiddlings make" (377), enable this freshness of vision. A modified Shakespearean trio of imaginative makers, "The lover, the believer and the poet" (378), exemplifies desire-flushed creative efforts to unshutter the ground of everything.[61] Although the existence of the central poem, which these efforts manifest and contribute to, is unprovable and elusive ("It is and it / Is not and, therefore, is"), we apprehend it in "lesser poems" (378). It includes not only literary works like this poem but "the total / Of letters, prophecies, perceptions, clods / Of color" (380). Stevens attributes wholeness without fixed or determinate borders to the environmental cosmos, to all imaginative work, and to an individual literary work like this twelve-part poem.

But *how* does Stevens evoke this cosmic totality? Appropriately at the center of "A Primitive like an Orb" is an octave about the "central poem" as "the poem of the whole," which describes both all creation as a totality and all poetry as a totality, linked by the etymological sense of poem as *poiema*, or made thing (with a possible buried pun in the enjambed phrase "poem of"):

> The central **poem** is the **poem of the whole**,
> **The poem of the** composition **of the whole**,
> The composition *of blue* sea *and of green*,
> *Of blue* light *and of green*, as *lesser poems*,
> And the miraculous multiplex of *lesser poems*,
> Not merely into a **whole**, but a **poem** of
> The **whole**, the essential compact of the parts,
> The roundness that pulls tight the final ring (379; highlights added)

To an extent that's notable even in Stevens's resoundingly echoic verse, each of the stanza's first seven lines repeats diction in the preceding line, like sonic stitches that are meant to bind the textual fabric into an emblem of wholeness. After a series of insistently repeated end-words, the octave ends with the final *ring* that almost anagrammatically recalls the earlier *green* as it pulls the stanza tight—a sonic interlacing that may distantly recall the recursiveness of the Petrarchan octave. The regular iambic pentameter also pulls the verse tightly together, as if in an orb-like five-beat-by-eight-line shape. If the aesthetic is "mirror" and "mate" to the globe (379), then the sonic plaiting within this stanza and the rest of the poem, along with the extraordinary amount of self-echoing within and across Stevens's oeuvre, is suggestive of the world's enmeshment. Sound, rhythm, and syntax hold together the poem's kaleidoscopic multiplicity of tropes. If we are looking for an ecopoet who will naturalistically describe for us a locale, such a poem will not suit. But its abstract and self-echoing artifice evokes the world's interconnectedness, vastness, and roundness, encompassing sea, light, and land. Even Stevens's poems that don't touch on questions of earthly wholeness contribute to the effect of a whole harmonium. "The ecological thought" is what Morton calls "the thinking of interconnectedness," "a vast, sprawling mesh of interconnection without a definite center or edge."[62] As indicated by this poem and more familiar ones like "The Idea of Order at Key West," "Notes toward a Supreme Fiction," and "The Auroras of Autumn," there may be no stronger example in modernist poetry of the thinking of interconnectedness than Stevens. In a *pensée* that both demonstrates and undoes the aphoristic drive toward self-containment, Stevens writes, "Nothing is itself taken alone. Things are because of interrelations or interactions."[63]

Although it is in spatializing language of part and whole, small and large that Stevens evokes the worldhood of the world and its imaginative co-creation, this is not a static unity: as human arts, expressions, and perceptions change, the giant is "ever changing, living in change" (380). Displaying this ever-changingness is the poem's quicksilver movement of thought and trope, its shifts and adjustments of appositions and figures and syntax as it searches for ways to conceptualize the totality of the world and of poetry. At one moment this wholeness can seem silly, "whirroos / And scintillant sizzlings such as children like," the next recast in language grave and regal, "Vested in the serious folds of majesty," but always "Moving around and behind," as this poem moves among such metaphors (380). The wholeness of the cosmos is continually being remade as it's reimagined, receding as each trope refigures it. Even the stanza about "the central poem," for all its "roundness" and "ring"-edness, is but the first of three stanzas threaded through by a magniloquent, ever-unspooling, twenty-four-line sentence. This sentence ends with a synesthetic celebration of *opsis* and *melos*, the dovetailing visual and sonic dimensions of both the sun-and-earth world and the poem-as-world: "A source of trumpeting seraphs in the eye, / A source of pleasant outbursts on the ear" (380).

Merely Circulating

The temporality of the world's enmeshment is still more prominent in other Stevens poems, where repetition, revolution, and circulation are dominant tropes. Such a poem is "The Pleasures of Merely Circulating," which revolves in rhythmic loops that anapestically evoke waltz time, imagistic loops that double back on themselves, and syntactic loops that interlink different realms:

> The garden flew round with the angel,
> The angel flew round with the clouds,
> And the clouds flew round and the clouds flew round
> And the clouds flew round with the clouds. (120)

Stevens's syntax giddily inter-involves the human, the natural, and the divine in its looping motion. Grounded in "the interconnectedness of all living and non-living things," "ecological awareness," Morton writes, "takes the form of a loop," and our time is "a loop within a much larger loop": "One finds oneself on the insides of much bigger *places* than those constituted by humans."[64] So too locations in Stevens are absorbed in much bigger places. In his late "The River of Rivers in Connecticut," for example, Farmington and Haddam are dwarfed by the river's "Flashing and flashing in the sun" (451).

Morton describes a tragic, melancholic realization of our "inextricable coexistence with a host of entities that surround and penetrate us," but which give us also an "anarchic, comedic sense of coexistence" and an awareness of "ourselves as a species."[65] A poem such as "Domination of Black," which Stevens told a reader is supposed to fill the mind with "heavens full of the colors and full of sounds,"[66] is bound by the darker, fearful realization of the loops within loops in which we find ourselves:

> At night, by the fire,
> The colors of the bushes
> And of the fallen leaves,
> Repeating themselves,
> Turned in the room,
> Like the leaves themselves
> Turning in the wind. (7)

Inside and outside, human and nonhuman are looped together in cycles that turn ever more tightly and ferociously, until the speaker comes face to face with an interplanetary spectacle of doom: "I saw how the planets gathered / Like the leaves themselves / Turning in the wind" (7).

But the dissolution of distinctions in the interlooping cycles of earthly motion seems vertiginously delightful in "The Pleasures of Merely Circulating." It may be particularly odd for the subject "garden" to take "flew" as its verb, but also enmeshed in this circulation are an imagined or statuary angel and the clouds. In a poem at the end of *The Auroras of Autumn*, a later angel speaks in words that will provide the title for Stevens's collection of essays: "Yet I am the necessary angel of earth, / Since, in my sight, you see the earth again, // Cleared of its stiff and stubborn, man-locked set" ("Angel Surrounded by Paysans," 423). Unbound to the earth, an angel—not unlike the abstractive poet—paradoxically reveals the earth-hood of the earth. In "The Pleasures of Merely Circulating," the threefold repetition of one syntactic unit in two waltzlike lines—"And the clouds flew round"—dizzily enacts the pleasure of earthly circulation, humorously completing the preposition with an object that mirrors the subject—"And the clouds flew round with the clouds."

In an abrupt shift of rhythm and tone, the middle stanza weakens the anapestic patterning in a dark reflection on death and ritual:

Is there any secret in skulls,
The cattle skulls in the woods?
Do the drummers in black hoods
Rumble anything out of their drums? (120)

After the giddy circulation of the first stanza, the second counterposes the finality of empty cattle skulls. Evoking sound in a remote wooded environment, the stanza distantly recalls the famous question attributed to Bishop Berkeley, "If a tree falls in the forest and no one is around to hear it, does it make a sound?"[67] Do cattle skulls in the woods have any meaning if no one is there to bestow it? Do drummers in the woods create sheer sound, or is there anything else to it? The drummers seem to want, by imposing ritualistic repetition, to order experience and perhaps override death's nothingness. In keeping with the association of lyric poetry with ritual by critics like Andrew Welsh and Jonathan Culler, the poem, even after its departure from round-like circulation, evokes ritual in its sonic repetitions and strong cadences.[68] It recalls *abba* envelope rhyme in this middle quatrain by rhyming "woods" with "hoods" and coupling in assonance "skulls" with "drums." But ritualistic though it may sound, the poem also questions, interrupts, and impedes ritual. Stevens plays on the resemblances and differences between the repetitions in ritual and the ur-repetition in the rotations, revolutions, and circulations of the earth.

The last line of the middle stanza resumes the rollicking anapestic rhythms of the beginning, rhythms that return more humorously in the final quatrain:

Mrs. Anderson's Swedish baby
Might well have been German or Spanish,
Yet that things go round and again go round
Has rather a classical sound. (120)

Here fictions of separate national lineage and continuity seem slightly ridiculous, parodies of earthly circulation. Although we share the vast majority of our DNA with other humans and other great apes, nationalisms insist on our separateness. "The ecological thought," declares Morton, "cannot abide national boundaries."[69] Stevens, albeit sometimes lending support to the idea of the distinctiveness of peoples, here pokes fun at it. Ultimately, all such distinctions are less significant than our enmeshment with each other and with the turning world. In contrast to the ludic pleasure the first stanza takes in the ever-circulating earthly mesh, this stanza takes a wry look at national efforts to slice and dice it with ideological difference. As in "A Primitive like an Orb," Stevens's planetary poetics calls into question the retreat into nationalism, localism, or regionalism.

Makings of Self and Sun

Stevens's most overt linkage between the planetary and the poetic is his late poem "The Planet on the Table." Having explored it and other of Stevens's late poems as self-elegies elsewhere, I focus here on its implications for Stevens's poetics of eco-enmeshment at the level of the planet and the poem.[70] The title conjoins two massively discrepant scales. But even at the level of orthography, they are entangled, since the noun *table* shares four of its five letters with *planet*—and nearly a fifth in the allophones *b* and *p*. The planet is to some extent, as many critics remark, Stevens's recently completed *Collected Poems* (1954), but as seen in "A Primitive like an Orb," the poetic and the planetary often figure one another in Stevens.

The table is, perhaps, a humdrum table on which those pages of poetry lie. But in the context of a meditation on poetry and reality, the word *table* also evokes a long history of philosophical debate over what Plato in the *Republic* offered as an example of the forms or ideas. In Benjamin Jowett's translation that Stevens read at Harvard and kept thereafter,[71] Socrates tries to prove that the artist or the poet is a mere imitator, not a creator, copying reality at three removes: a "maker . . . makes a bed or he makes a table for our use, in accordance with the idea—that is our way of speaking in this and similar instances—but no artificer makes the ideas themselves."[72] The artist or poet merely copies the specific, earthly table or bed, which is in turn a copy of the idea of the table or bed. In his implied ars poetica, Stevens mounts an entirely different theory of poetic "making"—a gerund that is central to this poem's defense of poetry:

> His self and the sun were one
> And his poems, although makings of his self,
> Were no less makings of the sun. (450)

Long before Latour, before Morton, before the new ecopoetics, Stevens plainly asserts the enmeshment of the human and the nonhuman—"His self and the sun were one." This enmeshment helps account for ambiguities as to which is acting upon which. In a characteristic genitive play on the preposition *of*, Stevens suggests that his poems have been made by himself and made by the sun, and that his poems have made himself and have made the sun, and moreover have been made out of self and sun alike. So much for the Platonic view of art's tertiary imitativeness, if poems are actively made by or out of self and sun, and actively make self and sun. The sun, as it were, plays a starring role here, as in "A Primitive like an Orb"—an image that appears with great frequency in Stevens's poetry (he uses the word more than twice as often, for example, as Yeats).[73]

But as in "A Primitive like an Orb," the world that co-creates and is co-created by his poems is also the earth:

> It was not important that they survive.
> What mattered was that they should bear
> Some lineament or character,
>
> Some affluence, if only half-perceived,
> In the poverty of their words,
> Of the planet of which they were part. (450)

In the context of a meditation on the co-creative work of the poem and the world, the adjective "half-perceived" echoes a canonical earlier moment in lyric meditation on this theme: Wordsworth's suggestion in "Tintern Abbey" that nature is partly made, partly received by the poet's eye and ear, "both what they half create, / And what perceive."[74] But Stevens goes further in dissolving distinctions between creating and perceiving, subject and object, passive and active, human and nonhuman. The words "lineament" (what has been drawn) and "character" (what has been impressed, engraved, inscribed) both suggest something distinctive. In view of the previous stanza, it's ambiguous whether the poet or the sun or a combination of them is writing itself into the poetry and revealing something distinctive about the planet, as well as, presumably, its human or solar author.

One of the most significant developments in ecocriticism has been resistance to what's been termed "ecomimesis"—a naive realism based in a strong subject/object distinction that casts nature as independent, solid, and susceptible to being experienced directly by the reader.[75] "Ecocriticism," observes Buell, has traditionally privileged "literature's capacity for mimesis and referentiality" and "has tended to favor literary texts oriented toward comparatively local or regional levels of place-attachment."[76] In that critical context, Stevens could be no more than a minor player; realist mimesis, determinate referentiality, and place

attachment are not his game. Favoring a cosmopolitan and comparative perspective that recognizes the "formality" of even seemingly trans-
parent nature writing, Dana Phillips has sharply criticized ecocriticism
for its "fundamentalist fixation on literal representation," its "realism-
cum-positivism," its view of poets as "bards of the neighborhood and the
microclimate."[77] For similar reasons, Heise champions the global reach
of allegorical forms of representation.[78] As is often the case, the poetry
has been well ahead of the criticism. Because lyric poems by a writer like
Stevens accentuate artifice and their own work of both fashioning and
being fashioned by the world, they can perhaps help ecocriticism turn
even more sharply away from mimeticist, literalist assumptions about
the arts. Foregrounding its sonic patterning, self-referentiality, and allusiveness, Stevens's "The Planet on the Table" suggests that the planet of
the collected poems, for all its abstraction and formality, is no less made
by and made of the earth and the sun. In the planet of Stevens's poetry,
"The rivers still roar, the mountains still crash, the winds still shatter."

After Stevens

Conceiving and writing about the earth as a whole has become all the
more important since Stevens. If he is unusual among the high modernists in writing such poems, more poets since the 1960s have been
writing poems of the earth—poems, that is, of earthly enmeshment and
totality. The further development of technologies of communication
and transportation, the worldwide migrations of peoples, the circulation of scientific knowledge, the spread of ecological devastation, and
other globalizing processes have contributed to this turn. To indicate
some developments in the poetics of "the environmental thought" after
Stevens, I offer a brief look at a handful of poems that ought to figure
prominently in ecocriticism.

Few poems more effectively capture the mutual interfusion of the
human and the nonhuman than W. H. Auden's "A New Year Greeting," in
which the poet, drawing on a 1969 article in *Scientific American*, exuber-
antly welcomes the microorganisms on his skin, while opening the skin
of his lyric to scientific discourse:

> On this day tradition allots
>   to taking stock of our lives,
> my greetings to all of you, Yeasts,
>   Bacteria, Viruses,

Aerobics and Anaerobics:
   A Very Happy New Year
to all for whom my ectoderm
   is as Middle-Earth to me.[79]

Seeing his body from the perspective of its inhabitants, the poet details the variety of its environments. If Stevens sought to disclose the giant-like earth to the human mind, here the human is the Gulliver-like earth to everything that lives on its surfaces:

For creatures your size I offer
   a free choice of habitat,
so settle yourselves in the zone
   that suits you best, in the pools
of my pores or the tropical
   forests of arm-pit and crotch,
in the deserts of my fore-arms,
   or the cool woods of my scalp.[80]

Upending otherizing conventions of pastoral, Auden transposes landscape onto himself, its various habitats fusing the human and the non-human in thoroughly enmeshed ecosystems. The playful tone and conversational idiom help disguise the poem's patterning—seven octaves of almost imperceptibly but strictly alternating three-beat lines of eight and seven syllables. Its unobtrusive sonic structure parallels the quiet ordering of the natural world.

Also drawing on science, as well as Hindu metaphysics, A. K. Ramanujan, in "Elements of Composition" (1986), sees himself not only as lyrically composing an outside natural world but also as thoroughly composed of that world:

Composed as I am, like others,
   of elements on certain well-known lists,
father's seed and mother's egg

gathering earth, air, fire, mostly
   water, into a mulberry mass,
moulding calcium,

carbon, even gold, magnesium and such
   into a chattering self. . . .[81]

If human and nonhuman are so thoroughly enmeshed, then even the act of composing a lyric poem like this one has to be seen, as Stevens suggests, as a making of the self and of the sun. If so, to recompose the self is also to devolve it into the world that has made it: "even as I add, / I lose, decompose / into my elements."[82] Linking various elements of the self into a multifaceted whole that is linked in turn to the wholeness of the environment, the poem interlaces its two hundred and fifty words in the twisting syntactic chain of a single sentence.

The interconnections between poetic and natural composition and decomposition—indeed, the inextricability of poem, person, and earth—also helped fuel A. R. Ammons's poetry. His book-length poem *Garbage* (1993), which recalls Stevens's "Man on the Dump," was also inspired by a Florida landfill off highway I-95:

> we are natural: nature, not
>
> we, gave rise to us: we are not, though, though
> natural, divorced from higher, finer configurations:
>
> tissues and holograms of energy circulate in
> us and seek and find representations of themselves
>
> outside us. . . .[83]

Because of this constant circulation, enacted in the Möbius-strip syntax that twists sentences across enjambments and across thoughts, Ammons sees his poetry, as did Stevens, as the embodiment of these processes that traverse any supposed human/nonhuman divide. The composition and decomposition of a landfill is a fit emblem of poetic making: "there is a mound, // too, in the poet's mind dead language is hauled / off to and burned down on."[84]

"Poetry should be able to comprehend the earth," writes Robert Hass in his ten-sectioned poem "State of the Planet" (1999), playing on *comprehend* to suggest that "to understand" is "to encompass."[85] Although we often stress poetry's tactile immediacy and local detail, a poetry of planetary scope has become increasingly visible, even in poems without a direct environmental bearing, as the state of the earth has become ever more precarious. In Lucille Clifton's unrhymed sonnet "the mississippi river empties into the gulf" (1996), the title spills into the first line, "and the gulf enters the sea and so forth." The poem enacts in its syntax, enjambments, and repetitions "the great circulation / of the earth's body," in which "every water / is the same water coming round."[86] For Clifton, as for Stevens, on the earth, "things go round and again go round."

In longer lyrics across several volumes, Jorie Graham has wrestled with climate change and the challenge of engaging both the micro-world of local experience and the macro-world of systemic change. In her book *Place* (2012), she directly echoes Stevens, and it's hard not to see in a poem titled "Earth" a Stevensian subject and ambition. Experiencing dawn less as sunrise than as Earth's rotation on its axis, she writes, "I see you my planet, I see your exact rotation now," in the changes of the sunlight on the floor.[87] Continuing to apostrophize Earth, she echoes the insistent planetary turning of "Domination of Black," as the turning of lines and the turning of the earth become inextricable, as emphasized by chiasmus: she wants "to lie here arms / spread / on your almost eternal / turn / and on the matter the turn takes-on as it is turned by that / matter—Earth."[88] As she reflects on Earth's rotation, the poet also wants to reach out with her fingers and grasp its planetary movement, "as we / orbit the / oval hoop and / the silence in here is staggering— / how huge you / carrying / me are."[89] Graham crafts a poetic style that would dip its fingers into the sensually immediate and yet also imagine, as Stevens sought to do, the immensity of the earth, as it carries rivers and, as in "The Pleasures of Merely Circulating," "the clouds one looks up to / to see / as they too / turn—."[90]

Juliana Spahr also tries to formally comprehend the totality of the earth, but she does so by developing a Steinian poetics of parataxis and accretive repetition. Although the collage, fragmentation, and pro-ceduralism of post-Language poetics would seem to be antithetical to totalities of any kind, her eco-poetry demonstrates the contrary. In a poem in *This Connection of Everyone with Lungs* (2005), she repeats a sentence that begins, "as everyone with lungs breathes the space," gradually expanding that human/nonhuman connective space to include the space within and around the hand, the room, the building, neighborhoods, and cities, all the way across continents and oceans and the mesosphere.[91] In *Well Then There Now* (2011), she repeatedly echoes Robert Frost's chiastic declaration in "The Gift Outright," "The land was ours before we were the land's," repudiating what she sees as the colonizing, nationalist ethos of such nature poetry, at the same time that her verbal enmeshment with Frost indicates the difficulty of ever fully extricating poetry from this inheritance.[92] In a poem in the collection that scrambles and upends Frost's statement, she recombines words and phrases to assert the mutual interpenetration of the human and the nonhuman: "Some of we and the land that was never ours while we were the land's."[93] In another poem that also plays on Frost's line, she writes:

> We came into the world at the edge of a stream.
> The stream had no name but it began from a spring and flowed
> down a hill into the Scioto that then flowed into the Ohio that then
> flowed into the Mississippi that then flowed into the Gulf of Mexico.
> The stream was part of us and we were part of the stream and we
> were thus part of the rivers and thus part of the gulfs and the oceans.[94]

As we learn later in the poem, these bodies of water bear not only an astonishing variety of flora and fauna—catalogued in great detail—but also what Rob Nixon terms the "slow violence" of pollutants: "animal wastes, oil, grease, dioxins, heavy metals and lead go / through our skin and into our tissues."[95] As in Stevens's "The Pleasures of Merely Circulating," the things that go round and again go round intermix the human and the nonhuman, but as in "Domination of Black," this circulation takes on apocalyptic rather than joyous overtones. Toward the end of that poem, Stevens writes in a surprisingly naked line, "I felt afraid." As we humans continue to ravage and imperil the planet, we can expect this grimmer aspect of "the mesh" to figure all the more prominently in poetry, as in our lives.

CHAPTER 8

SEAMUS HEANEY'S GLOBE

In "Alphabets," one of Seamus Heaney's most ambitious mid-career poems, written for Harvard's 1984 Phi Beta Kappa Exercises, this arch-poet of the local, the ground, and Irishness prominently uses the word *globe* twice. "A globe in the window tilts like a coloured O," he writes at the end of the first section, and at the beginning of the last he adds, "The globe has spun. He stands in a wooden O."[1] Deferring close consideration of these lines, I cite them at the outset because they raise several questions about Heaney's poetry—questions of a sort that haven't yet been engaged fully. As we asked of Stevens in the previous chapter, Is Heaney in any way a poet of the global? What is the relation between the evidently local qualities of his poetry and any global dimensions we might identify? And is there anything to be learned about his poetry from the global, and about the global from his poetry? At the same time that such questions should be broached, there is a risk and possibly even violence in putting together the nuances of poems by Heaney—as by Yeats, Stevens, Goodison, Nagra, and others who figure prominently in this book—with such a large and bland abstraction as the word *global*. Originating largely in the social sciences, global studies can't be smoothly assimilated to the qualitative reflections of the humanities. We should bring a word like *global* into contact with poems like Heaney's only if we're willing to see how the poems test, challenge, and revise assumptions about it—and only if it enhances rather than damages attention to the poetry as poetry, its language, technique, and self-reflection.

What might the student majoring in global studies notice in Heaney? Maybe that his extensive travels, as a celebrity writer in demand across much of the world especially after the Nobel Prize, generate an ever-wider range of geographic and cultural reference in his poetry. Maybe that his reading in the classics (say, Horace and Virgil) and in poetry from England (Hughes and Larkin), the United States (Frost and Robert Lowell), Eastern Europe (Milosz and Mandelstam), and elsewhere extends his understanding of the formal possibilities and ethical significance of poetry.[2] Obviously that his public image and his poetry were globally disseminated, the subject of heavy media interest, his words on the lips of pundits and politicians and poets, and translated into many languages. Maybe, too, that his academic perches at global institutions of higher education such as Queen's, Berkeley, Harvard, Oxford, and Emory brought him into contact with writers and academics from around the world. Poems directly inspired by global matters would seem to invite global studies: climate change in the poem "Höfn"; the September 11 attacks in New York in "Anything Can Happen" and the July 7 attacks in London in "District and Circle"; and human rights, such as his Amnesty International–requested poem "From the Republic of Conscience" and the Art for Amnesty book publication of "Anything Can Happen" with translations into twenty-three languages.[3]

But somewhat similar things could be said of other Nobel laureates and celebrity writers of our time, such as Derek Walcott and Salman Rushdie. To delve meaningfully into these questions, we need to turn from global studies positivism to interpretation, from extrinsic to intrinsic analysis. The complexity and specificity of Heaney's engagement with the global are hidden, I think, unless it is teased out of the formal and conceptual intricacies of his poems. The poems I mention regarding climate change, terror attacks, and human rights would reward such close examination. But I focus on two others that might be overlooked in such discussions because they are less obviously "global" in their purview, starting with "Alphabets," a kind of proem to his 1987 volume *The Haw Lantern*. Like the other of these two focal poems, "Electric Light," "Alphabets" tells a story about Heaney's emergence as a poet, in this case through the experience of learning different languages— English, Latin, Irish, and Greek. In a poem that repeatedly points to the globe, he has, in a way, already posed the question: what is the relation between the globe and the act of writing, especially the writing of poems?

The Lucent O

In the first of the three parts of "Alphabets," a boy learning his alphabet and numbers at primary school sees them in comparison to familiar shapes—a Y looks like a forked stick, a 2 like a "swan's neck and swan's back" (1). Like the poet he will become, he sees signs not just as stand-ins for meanings but as sensual, material things in their own right. Populating pages of the poem's earliest drafts are groups of block and cursive letters and of checkmarks ("a little leaning hoe") written out as if to retrieve a child's fascination with their visual shapes.[4] This early attention to the graphic dimension of language, its differential sounds ("the letter some call *ah*, some call *ay*") (1), and its metaphoric resemblances lays the ground for this poet's extraordinary alertness to the riches and resonances of words. But the section's last line suddenly reverses the direction of figuration—reverses, that is, tenor and vehicle: "A globe in the window tilts like a coloured O." Now instead of the written character being compared to a thing in the world, the thing in the world is compared to the letter O. Except that the globe isn't just a thing in the world, of course: it is itself a representation, a spherical map, a vehicle for the tenor of the world, and not just of any random thing in the world but of the world itself. Even at this early moment in the personal development traced by the poem, when the simple diction and rhythms ("he can see now as well as say"), when the repetitions, linking verbs, and declaratives ("There are charts, there are headlines") convey a child's perceptions, among them is the complex idea of a global totality as the construct of the mind, of language—the roundness of the letter O encountered more directly than the roundness of the world (1). The globe, as Wallace Stevens might have put it, had to be imagined—another poet, as we've seen, of planetary scope and interconnectedness. As Ayesha Ramachandran writes of other "worldmakers," "synthesis into a global whole required an act of imagination, a leap of theoretical speculation that left the precision of the example for the abstraction of totality."[5] The globe is an imaginative totality different from the materiality of written characters and of the worldly things they evoke, but it is partly projected out of its resemblances to them. Like ever-expanding smoke rings, the capital letter O in the poem evokes the "coloured O" the child drew, which evokes the O in the window, which evokes the O of the world. Highlighted at the end of the line, the letter O already hints at both the astonishment of glimpsing global totality and the connection between poetry and the globe—O as the empty cipher of poetic apostrophe. The globe, like poetic language, is simultaneously a form of representation that signifies something beyond itself and an object of representation, a made thing, a result of *poiesis* ("making"). Maybe it's not preposterous after all to see an intimacy between poetry and the globe, both belonging to the imagination, wonder, making.

In the poem's second section, the child learns Latin at secondary school, a language compared to military conquest ("column after strati-fied column," in appropriately Latinate diction with a buried pun on St. Columb's College, the name of Heaney's school) (1). Heaney remarked that, as with Borges, whose "immersion in several languages in early childhood" was formative for his sense of being a writer, his "own fasci-nation with words was keenly related to . . . learning Latin as a young boy. And the way words travelled and changed between languages, the Latin roots, the etymological drama."[6] The initiation into poetry comes with the dislocations of cross-cultural and interlingual travel, a small-scale encounter with the global, and Heaney's mature poetry indeed moves noticeably among words of different origins, as in this Anglo-Latinate-Irish-Greek poem. He thus hints at a macaronic and interlingual poetics, already glimpsed in poets like Hardy and Stevens, and explored in more depth in subsequent chapters. But at the poem's structural center—the middle stanzas of the middle section—it is especially when the boy learns Irish script that he is visited by the muse, as evoked in the wordplay on "feet" and the self-consciously poetic diction:[7]

> Here in her snooded garment and bare feet,
> All ringleted in assonance and woodnotes,
> The poet's dream stole over him like sunlight
> And passed into the tenebrous thickets. (2)

Drawing on the *aisling* tradition in which Ireland appears in a dream vision to the poet, Heaney's verse becomes assonantal, as one might expect given his association of Irish with vowels (*poet's*, *stole*, *over*).[8] This system of writing is special and distinctive, a welcoming habitation (it "felt like *home*") yet with an acknowledgment of a remove (it "felt *like* home") (2). This calligraphy, like the written English characters, is under-stood in comparison to things in the world—the letters as trees and capi-tals as blooming orchards—although for Irish, there is a long tradition of association of specific letters with particular trees, an almost magical way of thinking about trees that anticipates the allusion to Robert Graves's *White Goddess*.

But in the poem's third and final section, when Greek is the new lan-guage, the direction of figuration is again reversed, with the linguistic world primary and the natural world seen through a screen of signifiers, parts of a (now vanished) cultivated field looking like lambdas and deltas. "The globe has spun. He stands in a wooden O," self-mockingly begins this section, in a direct echo of the previous line about the globe. The university lecture hall is the poet's stage—as is all the world, in the *theatrum mundi* topos beloved by the bard of the Globe Theatre. Now the globe has still more meanings: it is Earth, spinning as the years pass; a model of Earth, as earlier in the poem; Shakespeare's theater, the Globe, and the "wooden O" of the prologue to *Henry V*; the literal space of the round theater in which the lecturer speaks; and even the world of the poem in which the lyric speaker speaks. The poet's education has made language and literature primary, a literary globe that he inhabits and from which he evokes that secondary, real world. The poet is like a necromancer, who hangs from his ceiling

> A figure of the world with colours in it
> So that the figure of the universe
> And 'not just single things' would meet his sight
>
> When he walked abroad. (3)

Drawing on Frances Yates's account of the Neoplatonist Marsilio Ficino,[9] Heaney joins that first schoolroom globe, the second—the globe of literary language and imagination—together with this third, the magician's globe meant to reinforce a sense of the interconnectedness of things. Heaney frequently refers to poetry's special power as lying in, to quote from several different essays, "The secret between the words, the binding element," "that binding secret between words in poetry," "a religious, a binding force"—well aware that in doing so he is attributing to poetry "a religious force, especially if we think of the root of the word in *religare*, to bind fast."[10] It is that binding force in poetry—phonological, semantic, etymological, mythic, psychological—that is linked to an ability to imagine and figure the totality of the globe, "not just single things" in their scattered nonrelation. Early modern Neoplatonism is the avatar of a contemporary global vision—the concept of the world, as globalization theorists put it, as a "'single place,' a 'singular system,' a 'global ecumene.'"[11]

   The poem is both about the globe and itself a globe. Formally exemplifying this binding force, its verbal architecture holds it together not only with the parallelism between the lines about the globe at the end of part 1 and those at the beginning of part 3, and with the Irish muse's visitation at the center, but also with the parallelism between the first stanza's fall into representation under the sign of the father (as if in fulfillment of Lacan's linguistic retheorization of the oedipal fall) and the last stanza's inscription of the father's name on the house, anticipating Heaney's signature on this poetic structure. The early drafts of the poem spell out even more clearly another embracing parallel, between the A-like gable or gable-like A in the opening and the closing sections. At the sonic level, too, the poem englobes its heterogeneity through heroic quatrains of rhyme and slant rhyme and much-varied iambic pentameter, and above all an insistent echoing of the "O" at the end of lines at the close of the first and beginning of the last sections, first rhyming *hoe/O* (1), then *O/window* (2), and then again *window/O* (3), as well as "IN HOC SIGNO" rhymed slant with "good luck horse-shoe" (3), let alone line endings like "Mer*o*vingian" and "*o*vum" (2, 3), as well as the word "gl*o*be" itself. Fatherly frame joins with motherly center, or ovum-like O, to produce the poet. The binding force of the poem's sonic and structural form represents the globe in uniquely poetic fashion—neither as an economic system of equivalence nor as an imperial domain but as an auditory and visual artifact, an imaginative structure, that binds together and sets free meanings, resonances, analogies, languages, and patterns. For the global studies major, used to exploring the "global" through an economic development paradigm, it might well be surprising to learn that there's something poetic about the global in its interlacings across discrepant spaces and scales, a sublime congeries of connections that exceeds measurement and calculation, even as the MFA student, likely to prefer the local in food and in action, might be surprised to hear that the binding force of the global has something poetic about it.

Another way of seeing the world whole is to leave it, a possibility that the necromancer could only dream of and that the child in the poem has experienced through writerly and linguistic defamiliarization, but that modern space travel has made even more fully possible. When the letter O appears for the third time by itself at the end of a line (3), it signifies again the globe, this time literally Earth and not only a model of it, as seen by an astronaut from afar, his vision of this "singular" whole akin to the necromancer's seeing "not just single things," in lines that sound trisyllabic substitutions: "The risen, aqueous, singular, lucent O / Like a magnified and buoyant ovum" (3). The roundness of the globe is mirrored in an expression of wonder at seeing it, the utterance of an apostrophic O, like the child's "wide pre-reflective stare / All agog" at the sight of his family name written on his home's gable (3). Heaney implicitly rhymes the O of poetry with the O of the globe. He explicitly compares the wonder felt by a child perceiving his earthly and linguistic origins (his name written "letter by strange letter") to the wonder of an astronaut peering down on the world, "all that he has sprung from" (3), just as the poet in this poem gazes down on the languages he and indeed this poem have sprung from. The global is often conceived of not only as the spatial but also as the temporal opposite of the local, in the sense of development beyond the local toward the global (say, from rural back-water to world metropolis). But Heaney holds the global and local in balance: his poetry's origin in exposure to multiple languages, with Irish at the center; the boy gazing uncomprehendingly at the patrilineal family name from which he has sprung; the astronaut looking down on mother Earth and seeing it as a location, in keeping with what sociologist Mike Featherstone calls, in another context, "the localization of globality, the perception of the finite and limited nature of our world."[12] So too, written characters, multiple languages, and literary texts have both dis-located the poet and revealed him in locality. Globalization has often been described as an intensified interconnectedness across the world's surface, and if poetry is for Heaney above all a binding force, as exempli-fied in this poem's multiply nested verbal, aural, and analogical design, then perhaps it shouldn't surprise us that one of his major poems about coming into being as a poet is also a globe-like poem about the globe. But where the globe is sometimes thought to be a preexisting order of reality, Heaney's emphasis is on the imaginative apprehension, the lit-erary and linguistic construction, the binding *poiesis* of the globe. And where the globe is often opposed to locality, parish, province, region, or nation, Heaney enfolds within the global his locatedness in a name and a culture, his education in particular languages and literatures that shape how he sees the world, his wonder toward "all that he has sprung from." A vision of the global intensifies rather than diminishes a consciousness of the contingencies of local origins.

Glocating Heaney

But Heaney as a global poet? Surely that's a stretch, for all his worldwide fame. There are few poets more firmly located in place than this rural County Derry–born poet, author of a book titled *Opened Ground* and a poem called "Digging," of poems filled with a rural Ulster childhood's peat and bogs, frogs and cows, plows and pumps. A crude mapping of his poetry's geography along the lines of the *New Yorker*'s *View of the World from 9ᵗʰ Avenue* by Saul Steinberg would give us one version of Heaney's globe, particularly if it ignored the formal complexities and just went with toponyms: County Derry would be at the center, with Ireland occupying most of the space, some of the remainder devoted to other parts of the British Isles and Northern Europe, especially Denmark or ancient Jutland, and lesser space devoted to Spain, Greece, and Italy, with distant outcroppings of peripheries like Massachusetts, Iowa, and California to the west, and China and Japan to the east. Heaney's poetry has often been distinguished, as in a standard anthology, from exilic and less obviously "Irish" Irish poetry,[13] or what a poetry encyclopedia calls "cosmopolitan" poetry by the "European-Ir. poets" affiliated with Beckett and by Ulster Protestants such as Louis MacNeice and Derek Mahon, because it is firmly grounded in a sense of Irish "cultural identity" and "of history, place, lang., and religion."[14] Similarly, in *Irish Poetry after Joyce*, Dillon Johnston separates Heaney and other poets who write "about areas of Irish life" from poets who "thoroughly avoid Irish modes and write in a more European, even Eastern European mode."[15] While this is a neutral distinction for some critics, for others it is to Heaney's detriment. In a transnationally sophisticated study, Cheryl Herr differentiates the laudably "cross-regional" or "dislocational" poetry of Paul Durcan from Heaney's verse, which she associates with "a reclaimed, centered, historicized, and wholly indigenous viewpoint."[16] More severely, David Lloyd castigates Heaney for his "reified . . . bourgeois ideology": "his work relocates an individual and racial identity through the reterritorialization of language and culture"; his metaphors and language "promise a healing of division simply by returning the subject to place, in an innocent yet possessive relation to his objects."[17] Nor, in Lloyd's view, is there anything plural, transnational, or heterogeneous in this forced Romantic equation of poetry with the land: Heaney's writing is said to allow the culture "to be envisaged as retaining a continuity with an homogeneous, undifferentiated ground."[18]

But if Heaney has been condemned for his rooting of poetry in the Irish ground, he has also been applauded for it. In *Local Attachments: The Province of Poetry*, Fiona Stafford sets up her argument about Romanticism with a discussion of Heaney's "celebration of local truth," as "a poet who not only celebrates local connection, but makes it central to the existence of true poetry."[19] Heaney is credited with "elevating the idea of the 'local' as the touchstone for the best kind of art."[20] Far from seeing Heaney's work as being in concert with the global, Stafford speculates that it is formed in reaction against it: "His very recognition of the value of the local, the particular, and the distinct may have been heightened by a growing awareness of globalization, which has facilitated both easy international communication and the growth of a somewhat homogenized consumer culture."[21] She repeatedly returns to Heaney's Nobel lecture, "Crediting Poetry," which affirms "local setting" and "local work" in the arts.[22]

But while Heaney considers the local and the indigenous to be crucial as "bearers of value" in art,[23] and while scholars such as Stafford are right that, as we've seen in "Alphabets," his poetry is deeply responsive to his rural Irish origins, a localist account is insufficient to the complexities of his work. In the Nobel lecture, he is leery, as he puts it, of "being sentimental or simply fetishizing—as we have learnt to say—the local."[24] He begins the lecture with the formative experience of growing up on a farm in County Derry, but this local site is always traversed by spaces elsewhere. There is "the voice of a BBC newsreader speaking out of the unexpected like a *deus ex machina*," a voice that mingles with the local voices and with the sounds of Morse code.[25] By virtue of modern technologies and media that have accelerated globalization—what the anthropologist Arjun Appadurai calls technoscapes and mediascapes[26]—the "here" is layered with the "elsewhere," even in this seemingly isolated spot: along with "the names of neighbours being spoken in the local accents of our parents," there were "in the resonant English tones of the newsreader the names of bombers and of cities bombed, of war fronts and army divisions, the numbers of planes lost and of prisoners taken, of casualties suffered and advances made."[27] Like the languages he learns in "Alphabets," these alien voices and names both dislocate the boy, defamiliarizing his local experience, and relocate him, contrastively illuminating the specificities of his cultural experience. As he grew older, Heaney says, "my listening became more deliberate," and "I had to get close to the actual radio set in order to concentrate my hearing, and in that proximity to the dial I grew familiar with the names of foreign stations, with Leipzig and Oslo and Stuttgart and Warsaw and, of course, with Stockholm."[28] As he heard "short bursts of foreign languages," he listened to the dial sweep, he writes, "from the intonations of London to those of Dublin, and even though I did not understand what was being said in those first encounters with the gutturals and sibilants of European speech, I had already begun a journey into the wideness of the world. This in turn became a journey into the wideness of language."[29] It is that interrelationship of an initiation into the wideness of the world and into the wideness of language that Heaney explores in "Alphabets," and that he associates with poetic consciousness.

It might seem unfair to rely too heavily on his Nobel address, written after all to be delivered in Continental Europe, to support my argument for a more expansive view of his poetry than "redemptive localism," in Ian Baucom's terms, based wholly in the "identity-endowing properties of place."[30] But even if we return to the essay "Mossbawn," Heaney's first in his inaugural collection of essays, in which he describes in intimate detail the specifics of the childhood farm that shaped him, he similarly notes in the oft-quoted first paragraph the groaning of American bombers and the sight of American troops maneuvering in the field.[31] The Northern Irish ground isn't sealed off from the wider world, the movements of people, aircraft, and weapons. Moreover, at the start of that inaugural essay his most emphatic affirmation of his rootedness is a ritualistic incantation of "the Greek word, *omphalos*, meaning the navel, and hence the stone that marked the centre of the world," which he compares to the sound of someone manually pumping water.[32] In Joyce's *Ulysses*, Stephen Dedalus famously thinks of an *omphalos* as interconnecting all humans, like a telephone line going all the way back to Eve. In Heaney, the *omphalos* is emphatically Irish, emblematic of rural Derry's primordial rhythms and reminiscent of Joyce, but it is also emphatically cosmopolitan, a foreign word, after all, that ultimately connects Heaney with Homer through Joyce, and that figures a shared humanity and writerly tradition across divisions of time, culture, and language. "I would begin with the Greek word, *omphalos*," writes Heaney, opening with a split signifier of both rootedness and travel, indigeneity and the cross-cultural. It's through a detour to Delphi that he affirms his relation to the Irish ground. "I began as a poet," he declares, "when my roots were crossed with my reading," as encapsulated in his Greek trope for his umbilical connection to the land.[33]

Roaming the Stations of the World

The title poem of Heaney's 2001 collection *Electric Light*, placed last in the book as a kind of summa and so occupying a special place like "Alphabets," echoes many of these motifs.[34] Like the Nobel lecture, it traces poetry to the crossing of the local with the foreign, Heaney's deep rural roots with cultural sites elsewhere. Like "Alphabets," this similarly ambitious three-part lyric—the first and last parts in five unrhymed tercets, the middle part in four, all alluding to terza rima—is again about the poet's origins and genesis, but whereas polyglossia is a primary site of the global and of poetic emergence in "Alphabets," this poem's emphasis is on travel and technology. The first house where he saw electric light is also, ironically, where the poet recalls his grandmother as an almost primeval and immobile figure. By means of the ancient transcultural technique of allusion, she is made to resemble the Cumaean Sibyl (with wordplay on "sibilant" and "sybilline" [96, 97]). Her strange language—the word "ails" nearly rhyming with her fearsome "nail" (96)—initiates a childhood journey into poetry, like Aeneas's into the underworld, and indeed the poet comes out of the London tube in the next section after his kata-basis. Although the grandmother is unmoving, light and radio cut across the space over which she reigns:

> If I stood on the bow-backed chair, I could reach
> The light switch. They let me and they watched me.
> A touch of the little pip would work the magic.
>
> A turn of their wireless knob and light came on
> In the dial. They let me and they watched me
> As I roamed at will the stations of the world. (98)

Both electric light and radio give the child an experience of freedom, albeit contained by (grand)parental will: "They let me and they watched me" sounds as an incantation in the same stanzaic position, casting the two magical acts in perfect parallel. In these moments, the verbs endow the child with more agency than he has elsewhere in the poem: "I could reach," "I roamed at will." The language suggests a kinship, too, between these acts and the making of poetry: "A touch," "A turn" gives the power and freedom to "work the magic" and to roam "at will the stations of the world" (as distinct from the less freewheeling Stations of Station Island or the Stations of the Cross). To create light, to fly across space—these aren't just the textbook's global flows of technoscapes and mediascapes but imaginatively charged acts filled with wonder.

The poem also closely associates poetry with travel, albeit from one deeply known place to another, from literal to literary origins. Its middle section recalls, as Heaney wrote elsewhere, his "first trips to London, by ferry and train, but is also meant to suggest a journey into poetic voca-tion,"[35] or as he puts it in the poem,

> ferries churned and turned down Belfast Lough
> Towards the brow-to-glass transport of a morning train,
> The very "there-you-are-and-where-are-you?"
>
> Of poetry itself. (97)

For a world-famous poet to plant in a poem the phrase "Of poetry itself" is to make a strong claim, and the claim is for poetry as founded not in rootedness, locality, or unchanging place, but in travel and disorienta-

tion: "The very 'there-you-are-and-where-are-you?' // Of poetry itself."
In Heaney's case, there are multiple dimensions to this dislocation, as he
indicated years earlier to a reporter: "Everybody's in exile to start with,
everybody who writes. Especially if you're in the minority, you're in two
places at once at the very beginning. . . . I never had a feeling of comfort-
able consonance between myself and a place. The travel reinforces a condition that would be there anyway."[36] And as Richard Kearney writes,
in a philosophical rebuttal of the idea of Heaney as statically insular,
"Heaney's poems are not in fact primarily about place at all; they are about
transit, that is, about transitions from one place to another."[37] The reso-
nance of this poem's word "transport'" with *metaphor*—etymologically, to
transfer or carry across—strengthens the idea that poetry is intimately
allied with travel, and that travel is a kind of poetry. The image of a young
man with his brow pressed against the glass of a train encapsulates something of the simultaneous distance and movement, stilled contemplation
and mobility that the poem suggests is endemic in poetry.

It's not that this travel is placeless wandering in an empty nowhere.
In another context, Heaney attributes the expression "there-you-are-
and-where-are-you?" to the rural area around Bellaghy where he grew
up, and so it bespeaks displacement with a peculiarly local twist.[38] The
travel in the poem is highly specific and translocal, a straddling of Ulster
and London, taking the young poet not accidentally to the seat of the
empire and of English-language poetry. It is the journey to the metropolitan center that so many young colonials have made, once again a
recovery of localized (in this case literary) origins at the same time as a
venture across space. On his way he sees

> fields of grain like the Field of the Cloth of Gold.
> To Southwark too I came, from tube-mouth into sunlight,
> Moyola-breath by Thames's "straunge stronde." (97)

If the evocations of Shakespeare's *Henry VIII* and Eliot's *The Waste
Land* weren't clear enough, the young poet arrives at Southwark on the
Thames, site of both the Globe Theatre, where certain plays began their
global travel, and the Tabard Inn, where Chaucer's pilgrims begin their
travel (the quote from the General Prologue concerns the goal of way-
faring "palmers," or professional pilgrims).[39] The young poet superim-
poses his originating Moyola River on the Thames's Strand. The breath
or spiritus of his poetry combines metropolitan Englishness ("from
tube-mouth") and rural Irishness ("Moyola-breath"), like the verbal

fabric of this London poetry-soaked stanza. His poetry is born in the travel between, and the confluence of, these spaces, these histories, these discrepant Englishes. Albeit a limited, archipelagic piece of it, the global here is lived not in the transcendence of places but in the specific interconnections among them, which in turn retrace and partly reverse patterns of movement in trade, colonization, and demography—what Appadurai calls the "ethnoscape" of the global.[40]

Netted Routes

What does Heaney's poetry indicate about the nature of the global, and the global about the nature of his poetry? Surely Heaney isn't "global" in the same way as Yeats, Eliot, and Pound in their Asian excursions, let alone contemporary writers whose poetry seems to log frequent flyer miles.[41] Even so, his poetry articulates global flows at all five of Appadurai's different levels:[42] the technoscape of electric light, Morse code, airplanes, weapons, diesel, "combines and chemicals";[43] the mediascape of radio-transmitted voices from London, Europe, and the "wideness of the world"; the ethnoscape of peoples moving from country to city, rural underdevelopment to global metropolis, let alone the ancient traces in Ireland of Vikings, Romans, Phoenicians, and Anglo-Saxons; the financescape in the trade enacted by these and other peoples; and finally the ideoscape of political and cultural ideas exported abroad and imported from elsewhere, from ritually significant if fearsome Viking violence to modern human rights. Heaney's poetry acknowledges that modern and contemporary technology, media, and travel have sped up globalization, as theorists such as Appadurai emphasize, but in the debate over *when* was globalization, he also gives the nod, like the sociologist Roland Robertson, to a much longer, older history of the global.[44] As he writes in "Viking Dublin: Trial Pieces," about the Viking settlement of, and remains in, Dublin, the artistry on a piece of bone leaves

> foliage, bestiaries,
>
> interlacings elaborate
> as the netted routes
> of ancestry and trade.[45]

The pun on "routes" and "roots"—well before it was developed by scholars like James Clifford and Paul Gilroy—calls attention to how even the most deeply planted Irish roots are entwined with peoples and trade patterns from elsewhere, like the inwardly netted roots and outwardly networked routes of his poetry. Examining the intricate Viking design, Heaney uses a vocabulary that points toward both the literary—textlike "interlacings"—and the global—what theorists have emphasized as the ever greater enmeshment of globalization. And here we might add a sixth "scape" to Appadurai's—"poetryscape," the binding force of poetic language and form within a poem and among poems of different times and places. The stretch, the enmeshment, the connectiveness of the global—these aren't just objective forces; they are also imaginative experiences, embedded in and made visible by the binding texture of the parallels, allusions, figurations, architectonics, etymologies, and resonances of Heaney's poetry.

Rather than merely reacting against various globalizing forces, from the tenth to the twenty-first century, Heaney's poetry participates in and illuminates them. He shows globalization to enter individual lives even in remote rural sites, introduced by radio, electric light, mobile populations, war, travel, poems, and different languages. He reveals that the global is not only a social-scientific datum but also an imaginative projection, a difference-spanning construct, as mirrored within the intrinsic binding structures that hold together a poem's teeming patterns. Heaney's poetry's attention to itself as medium, as globe-like microcosm of complexly homologous sounds, sights, and meanings, helps remind us that the global is partly given, partly made. In these poems that are keenly attentive to their own and the poet's genesis out of locality, poetry becomes a space in which the local isn't simply opposed to or contrasted with the global—a last holdout against the brutal and indifferent and homogenizing forces of globalization—but rather reveals and revels in the interpenetrating vortices of localization and globalization. Heaney's is a poetry thickly textured with the impasto of local history and experience that also shifts among places, registers, and identities; that travels between figure and frame, the literal and the metaphoric, origins and ends; and that retraces a transnationally sedimented and fluid history in Ireland, in the North Atlantic, and in the English language—all within the binding euphonies and parallels of his richly patterned lyricism.

Finally, there is also an ethical dimension to the global in Heaney's poetry. As we saw in an earlier chapter, his poems owe partly to Wilfred Owen and other poets of the first global war an emphasis on compassion toward a common humanity amid what Heaney called, with reference to Owen, "the shock of the new century's barbarism."[46] The structure of feeling Isaac Rosenberg named "cosmopolitan sympathies" is another thread in the "binding force" of the poetic that Heaney brings to our often positivistic understanding of the global.[47] His poetry always registers an awareness that he comes from a place, a community; yet he tries to think with and through it to forge human connections, to rhyme his experience with that of others. Examples include his empathic poem about a Protestant neighbor, "The Other Side"; his dramatic monologue "Bog Queen," written from the vantage point of a woman long preserved in, and reborn from, a bog; and his multiperspectival poem "Punishment" that performs identifications with the executioner ("I can feel the tug / of the halter"), the adulteress (the same words, with the opposite construal of which end of the rope the speaker is on), the adulterer ("I almost love you"), the stone-throwing crowd ("would have cast, I know, / the stones of silence"), the outraged witness ("civilized outrage"), and combinations of these viewpoints.[48]

Heaney's work also demonstrates what I termed, in an earlier chapter, an etymological cosmopolitanism, and it, too, has an ethical dimension. When translating *Beowulf*, Heaney discovered a cross-cultural connection in the word *thole* as straddling his local Ulster speech and a supremely canonical Anglo-Saxon text, just as he had also found it in John Crowe Ransom's Scots Irish–inflected diction of the American South:

> The far-flungness of the word, the phenomenological pleasure of finding it variously transformed by Ransom's modernity and *Beowulf*'s venerability made me feel vaguely something for which again I only found the words years later. What I was experiencing as I kept meeting up with *thole* on its multicultural odyssey was the feeling which Osip Mandelstam once defined as a "nostalgia for world culture." And this was a nostalgia I didn't even know I suffered until I experienced its fulfillment in this little epiphany.[49]

It is easy to dismiss the connective force of such cross-cultural, cross-temporal sympathies as sentimental, and indeed the word "nostalgia" hints at Heaney's wariness of going too far in that direction. Elsewhere he warns against poetry that "rampages so permissively in the history of other people's sorrows that it simply overdraws its rights to our sympathy."[50] But for all such ethically astute hesitations about the excesses of nostalgia and sympathy, his etymological engagement with a world-traveling word affirms the interconnectedness of widely scattered cultures—the expansive ethical sensibility that "Alphabets," "Electric Light," the bog poems, and other works are built on.

Heaney's poems exemplify a post-Enlightenment cosmopolitanism that, as Bruce Robbins writes, isn't neutral or detached but "plural and particular," including "(re)attachment, multiple attachment, or attachment at a distance."[51] His is a poetry of engagement with the complexly apprehended, layered, and imagined space of Irish locality and of cosmopolitan openness to wide-ranging traversals and translocations of language, culture, and geography. No wonder, as Paul Muldoon said in eulogizing him, that Heaney "was recognized worldwide as having moral as well as literary authority and, as such, may be the last major poet to even entertain such a possibility."[52] That moral authority derives in part from his poetic affirmation and interlacing of both local fidelities and cosmopolitan sympathies. Reprising a favorite metaphor for poetry, Heaney said in his Nobel lecture that "poetry can make an order as true to the impact of external reality and as sensitive to the inner laws of the poet's being as the ripples that rippled in and rippled out across the water in [a] scullery bucket."[53] The singular, minutely local O of his poetry ripples outward by means of large-hearted sympathies and verbal magic to the multitudinous O of the globe and back again, "letter by strange letter."

CHAPTER 9

CODE-SWITCHING, CODE-STITCHING: A MACARONIC POETICS?

"*Daahaa, taarof nakon!*," or "Darn it, stop being so self-denyingly polite!," my parents chided me affectionately in our largely English-speaking household. They would code-switch to Persian for expressions of irrita-tion, anger, love, and culturally specific social norms, such as *taarof* (تعارف), or the Persian system of etiquette in which you deny your own will, as in the elaborate negotiations when you're offered food or you approach a doorway or you attempt to pay a restaurant bill. Despite having been born and raised in the United States, I've often been accused of being more prone to *taarof* than is our Iranian-born family. Like Persian in my family, Yiddish in my wife's Ashkenazi family often functions as what John J. Gumperz terms a "we code," the ethnically specific speech of an insider group, as opposed to a "they code."[1] Having gradually been partly assimilated into the "we" of a Jewish "we code," I find myself saying "*Oy gevalt!*" on a daily basis in our blended household, and *farblondzhet* (פֿאַרבלאָנדזשעט) now seems to me the indispensable term for states of befuddlement. Like everyone else, I code-switch according to social con-text and the "we codes" I inhabit.

Except for the particular languages involved, none of this is unique to me: in a world in which plurilingual outnumber monolingual speakers, code-switching occurs with great frequency, especially in the wake of the intensified globalization of the past century or so, with multitudes on the move, whether as elective or forced migrants. As a code-switching student of poetry and of the globalization of culture, I wonder: What kind of home has poetry provided for code-switching over the course of the past hundred years? Given that speech and literary writing overlap but are distinct from one another, how should we think about the code-switching that's particular to poetry? Is there something about code-switching as a language practice that we could think of as especially poetic? What can we learn from the analysis of poetry about code-switching, and from the analysis of code-switching about poetry? These are among the impossibly large questions I broach, exploring an under-studied aspect of poetry's transnationalism, with a focus on mixed anglophone examples.[2] English functions in these instances as what linguist Carol Myers-Scotton terms the Matrix Language Frame, the primary grammatical frame of these interlingual poems, if often modified by the Embedded Language(s).[3]

Code-switching is a term in linguistics for the alternation between two or more languages. The term comes from communications technology, originally referring to the electronic transference of signals, as noted by Penelope Gardner-Chloros.[4] As such, it is a metaphor that both illuminates and distorts: illuminates, in that it suggests sudden shifts between discrepant systems, but distorts, in that it hypostasizes the different languages as discrete. But languages are vastly more porous than "code-switching" may suggest: languages such as the English you are reading creolizes German, French, and many other languages (including, as my two sets of relatives often remind me, Persian-derived words like *paradise*, *khaki*, and *cummerbund*, and Yiddish words like *schlep*, *shtick*, and *kvetch*). As Roman Jakobson observed in 1952, wryly glancing at Cold War divisions, languages in contact with one another do not exist "in segregation. If there is an iron curtain, we know how easily such a curtain is penetrated by various forms of verbal communication."[5] And as Steven G. Kellman writes, "Linguistic purity is of course a chimera; English, Korean, and Arabic are each already mongrel, and creolization among existing languages proceeds wherever cultures touch and collide, which is to say virtually everywhere."[6] Alert to the origins of words and the routes they've traveled, poets often make visible the permeability of languages. Linguists have been redefining code-switching as a more dynamic, blurred process to avoid the appearance of "citadels of rigid structures," in Myers-Scotton's words.[7] Or they have supplemented it with terms like "translanguaging" to emphasize interlingual process and practice—what Li Wei calls "multilinguals' creativity—their abilities to push and break boundaries between named language[s] and between language varieties."[8] Even though code-switching mainly designates, as in this chapter, switching between what are conventionally understood to be languages, the distinction between interlingual and intralingual code-switching isn't hard and fast. Switching sociolects—say, between formal and dialect or pidgin varieties of a language—can be as significant in plurilingual settings as interlingual code-switching.[9] Creoles are often held to be distinct languages, and so switching from Standard English to Jamaican Creole can be counted as either inter- or intralingual code-switching. But code-switching has often been deprecated as a corruption or as ill-mannered behavior, even by those who practice it, especially where linguistic purity is an ideal,[10] and one reason poets bring code-switching into the culturally prestigious discourse of poetry is to legitimize such interlingual speech practices.

Code-Switching in Poetry: For and Against

Is code-switching a liability for or a benefit to poetry? On the one side, it has been seen as detrimental. Exemplifying this position with clarity and force, Helen Vendler wrote, in a review of the poetry collection *The Fortunate Traveller* (1981), that Derek Walcott, though admirable in many ways, had not established a "conclusive and satisfying aesthetic relation" between his formal diction and his Saint Lucian patois:

> A macaronic aesthetic, using two or more languages at once, has never yet been sustained in poetry at any length. There are Hispano-American poets now writing in a mixture of Spanish and English, where neither language gains mastery; once again, such work may accurately reflect their linguistic predicament, but the mixed diction has yet to validate itself as a literary resource with aesthetic power. These macaronic strategies at least break up the expected; and anyone can understand Walcott's impulse to wreck his stately and ceremonious rhythms.[11]

Walcott's defenders have argued for the validity of his code-switching primarily on mimetic grounds: that the poet is being faithful to the texture of everyday speech in Saint Lucia, where people switch regularly among French Creole, English Creole, and Standard English—a legacy of alternating French and British colonial rule. Scholars of code-switching in English-Spanish poetry, Arabic-French rap, and Japanese-English popular songs often make analogous arguments. Although I agree with these scholars about the social contexts of code-switching and have made similar claims, when it comes to poetry in particular such sociolinguistic arguments aren't exhaustive. As Gary D. Keller writes in relation to Chicanx writers, "there *must be* significant differences between literary code-switching and real life code-switching."[12] Many poets living in interlingual societies have eschewed literary code-switching, writing instead in one or another language, often the more reputable one but occasionally the more humble. Although I am more sanguine than Vendler is about the possibilities of a "macaronic aesthetic," she raises a question not fully answered by the mimetic defense—whether a given poet has established a "satisfying aesthetic relation" between the languages straddled in a poem. Like any other linguistic or poetic resource—parataxis and hypotaxis, rhyme and enjambment, alliteration and assonance—code-switching can be used poorly or deftly, in a way that is tired or fresh, hackneyed or vivifying.

Although not responding directly to Vendler, a critic on the other side of this issue, also writing about Walcott, makes the opposite general claim. Citing a heavily code-switching poem of 1976, "Sainte Lucie," J. Edward Chamberlin argues, "Both for Walcott and for West Indian poetry, this poem marks a turning point, bringing together a mature poet's confidence in his literary inheritance with a corresponding—and newly found—confidence in his West Indian heritage," listing names of places, flora, and fauna of his island, such as "Laborie, Choiseul, Vieux-fort, Dennery," or

> Pomme arac,
> otaheite apple,
> pomme cythère,
> pomme granate,
> moubain,
> z'ananas
> the pineapple's
> Aztec helmet,
> . . . .
> Come back to me
> my language.[13]

Chamberlin concludes: "This is where contemporary West Indian poetry begins, not so much with this poem alone as with the distinctive ambitions it represents."[14] The stark differences between these claims for and against code-switching poetry can help frame our investigation. Bearing them in mind, let's consider poems from a small sampling of worldwide communities to help develop and refine our understanding of both the aesthetics and the social mimesis of a macaronic poetics.

The Aesthetics and Social Mimesis of Code-Switching

Published in the same year as Walcott's *Fortunate Traveller*, "Poema para los Californios Muertos" in the book *Emplumada* by Lorna Dee Cervantes exemplifies the abundant Spanish-English code-switching in Latinx poetry to which Vendler refers (and indeed, for all her misgivings about the macaronic, Vendler included the poem in one of her anthologies).[15] What light does this poem shed on either the social mimetic or the aesthetic template for poetic code-switching? It meditates on a plaque outside a restaurant in Los Altos, California, that marks the site as a refuge for Californios, the Mexican Latinx population largely dispossessed of their lands during the mid-nineteenth-century Gold Rush by Euro-American settlers. Written mostly in English, the poem switches frequently into Spanish, in keeping with Gloria Anzaldúa's mestiza manifesto, published a few years later with her own code-switching poems: "The switching of 'codes' in this book from English to Castilian Spanish to the North Mexican dialect to Tex-Mex to a sprinkling of Nahuatl to a mixture of all of these, reflects my language, a new language—the language of the Borderlands."[16] Cervantes turns to Spanish particularly for words that function as markers of identity, or a "we code," as we might expect in Chicanx poetry, such as words for the earth ("la tierra"), mother ("la madre"), blood ("la sangre fértil"), each noun ritualistically repeated, as well as curses on white people that might read less well in English.[17] Linguists identify this as "metaphorical" or "emblematic" code-switching, the turn to a language for the cultural world it evokes.[18] Work on Latinx code-switching often emphasizes its affirmation of cultural identity and resistance. In Cervantes's case, such emblematic code-switching is particularly intriguing since, even though we might assume she is returning to her "native" language, she grew up speaking primarily English because Spanish was forbidden to her. Reclaiming her ancestral and cultural language in the poem is itself a performative act. So the poem both meets and complicates the social context paradigm: a poem's code-switching may not merely reflect participation in a borderland or contact zone or mixed society but stage, enact, even will it.

Coming after four lines of Spanish, the poem ends with a code-switching strophe:

> In this place I see nothing but strangers.
> On the shelves there are bitter antiques,

yanqui remnants
y estos no de los Californios.
A blue jay shrieks
above the pungent odor of crushed
eucalyptus and the pure scent
of rage.[19]

Amid the harsh mix of sound, smell, and sight, the pugnacious bird that sings (or rather "shrieks") at the end of this commemorative elegy isn't soothingly redemptive; the blue jay sounds an ongoing melancholic woundedness and angry resistance like the poet who imagines it. Although the poem closes on a note of combative rage, and although most of the poem pits Chicanx against white culture ("white, high-class houses" and "fantasmas blancas")[20] and sees in the landscape a record of rape, exploitation, and violence perpetrated against the Californios, the ending sonically and orthographically knits together the English and Spanish it has been playing against one another. In three successive words, Spanish in the middle, the sounds /an/ and /k/ and the letters *qu* cross the linguistic and cultural divide: "*an*ti*qu*es, / *yanqui* remn*a*nts." Three lines also begin with a /y/ sound, albeit varied: "yanqui," "y estos," and "eucalyptus." The eucalyptus, an alien species that, like the white settlers who imported it, took dominion over California, sonically recalls not only "yanqui" but also the apostrophe earlier to "you," the ghosts of the Californios, to whom the speaker pledges herself. Whereas prose fiction, TV, movies, and other genres also deploy code-switching to represent the sociolinguistic context of Chicanx experience, cross-lingual chiming is more marked in poetry. It's in poetry that code-switching often becomes code-stitching. Almost against the grain of the poet's apparent desire to pit Latinx and English cultures against one another, the poetic impetus toward sonic and conceptual coupling interbraids the two tongues, conceding their seemingly irreversible if still vexed mixture.

To return briefly to Walcott, we recall that his *Omeros* frequently switches from formal literary English into French and English creoles:

"Mais qui ça qui rivait-'ous, Philoctete?"

"Moin blessé."

"But what is wrong wif you, Philoctete?"

"I am blest
wif this wound, Ma Kilman, *qui pas ka guérir pièce.*

Which will never heal."[21]

Walcott is playing here on a convention of literary code-switching in which the "foreign" language is translated, except that here it is punningly mistranslated, when the French and French Creole for "wounded," *blessé*, becomes "blest." The rest of Walcott's long poem will explore how the wounds inflicted by colonialism, including the imposition of European languages on enslaved Africans and their descendants, can sometimes be turned into blessings.[22] Subversive mistranslation can also be found in Latinx poems, such as the hilariously mischievous alternating English and Spanish in Urayoán Noel's exuberant double *décima* "ode to coffee / oda al café." Its rhyme-rich lines toggle between English and Spanish, in what at first seems a straightforward self-translation. But soon we realize Noel is playfully subverting such expectations by juxtaposing lines that often lead in different directions, such as the rhyming pairs "return us to our tribe that grew dark beans / devuélvenos al semillero isleño" ("tribe that grew dark beans" as "semillero isleño," i.e., island seedbed?) and "where luckless lovers stare at tiny screens / haz que el amante no muera de sueño" ("stare at tiny screens" as "no muera de sueño," i.e., not die of sleep?).[23] Rubbing Spanish and English against one another, the translingual poem teasingly proliferates differences that are flattened by the often racist insistence on "English only."

Noel, Walcott, and Cervantes are being true to the social worlds that formed them, but they are also being true to the medium of poetry. As in Cervantes's "antiques, / yanqui remnants," Walcott's "*blessé*" and "blest," and Noel's interlaced rhymes, the campaign slogan "I like Ike" performs an insistent sonic repetition that, for Roman Jakobson, is fundamental to "poeticity" or "the poetic function of language."[24] "The poetic function," he famously claimed, "projects the principle of equivalence from the axis of selection into the axis of combination."[25] Poetry draws on the repeated sonic patterns in everyday language and intensifies them, amplifying this poeticity to the point where its artifice is inescapable. Poetry "is the form that most clearly asserts the specificity of literature, its difference from ordinary discourse," according to Jonathan Culler; "the specific features of poetry have the function of differentiating it from speech and altering the circuit of communication within which it is inscribed."[26] The idea might well seem bizarre in this context, since code-switching is usually seen as bringing a literary text closer to speech, to the actual exchanges of daily life, as opposed to the monologic formality of high literary writing. Nineteenth-century novelists like Charles Dickens enhanced prose fiction's speechlike social mimesis by code-switching into different sociolects, a heteroglossia that was, as Bakhtin famously argued, less common in poetry.[27] But code-switching in poetry often points in two opposite directions at once: by virtue of breaking with monologic literariness, it heightens poetry's speech-effect, its seeming orality; and yet by virtue of its pattern-rich code-stitching, it also signals poetry's literariness, its bending back of reference onto itself, its insistence on the verbal materiality and sonic textures that resonate even across languages.

There are, of course, precedents for the code-switching in contemporary poetry, such as multilingual medieval lyrics and Renaissance poems like Tifi Odasi's satiric "Macaroneae," which may be the source of the word "macaronic,"[28] and later poems like Byron's *Don Juan* that embed learned foreign tags. The modernists Ezra Pound and T. S. Eliot, as well as Mina Loy, Louis Zukofsky, and Melvin Tolson, among others, dramatically break poetry open again to polyglossia. In the modernist era, poetry may lag behind fiction in its heteroglossia (intralingual code-switching), but it may leap ahead of fiction in its experiments in polyglossia (interlingual code-switching), partly because of poetry's relative freedom from the constraints of realist mimesis. In *Hugh Selwyn Mauberley* Pound switches between English and multiple languages, both dead and alive, including ancient Greek:

> O bright Apollo,
> τίν' ἄνδρα, τίν' ἥρωα, τίνα θεὸν,
> What god, man, or hero
> Shall I place a tin wreath upon![29]

Here, the standard defense of code-switching as socially mimetic falls short—what sociologists Paul Drew and John Heritage term "the 'bucket' theory of context in which some preestablished social framework is viewed as 'containing' [and thus fully explaining] the participants' actions."[30] It would be hard to argue that, just as Cervantes and Walcott are imitating the speech of their social worlds, so too is Ezra Pound in adopting Attic Greek, or Eliot in switching to Sanskrit in *The Waste Land*. We would have to reconceptualize the argument at a higher level of abstraction, seeing their code-switching as belonging to a moment in the history of globalization, which brought poets and their elite readership into contact with multiple literary and cultural traditions, including those of East Asia for Pound, who script-switches into Chinese in *The Cantos*. As for the aesthetics of code-switching, Pound is alert to the cross-lingual chimes, puns, and rhymes we've seen in other poems: he ironically enacts in this sonic coupling the degeneration from the Greek Olympians eulogized by Pindar (the "tin" sound as an exclamation of wonder) to the "tawdry cheapness" of their modern replacements ("tin" now as a base metal). Such interlingual punning is to be found not only in such markedly scribal poetry but also in oral forms like rap and rai, with their cross-lingual play on homophones such as the French *là* (there) and the Arabic ﻻ or *la* (no).[31] Code-switching in everyday speech is often focused on the addressee, whether a speaker changes languages to signify cultural commonality or to resist the expectations of linguistic code and adopt an alternative affiliation. Though implicated in such efforts, poets partly short-circuit the path of direct communication and turn the emphasis back on the linguistic medium itself, as evidenced in such cross-lingual sonic play that couples phonemes across languages in surprising ways.

Code-Skipping

But is interlingual chiming the only aesthetic function of code-switching in poetry? Two contemporary poets who may seem Pound's diametric opposite but who, like him, switch into ancient classical and other languages illustrate other possibilities. The Black British poet of English and Nigerian descent Bernardine Evaristo, whose novel-in-verse *The Emperor's Babe* is set in third-century Roman London, switches at remarkable speed between languages and registers. Her Afro-Roman heroine Zuleika recalls the value of her elocution lessons, having learned not "How now brown cow" but *"How nunc brown vacca,"* imperiously confronting her Scottish slaves and "sounding like every magniloqua // matrona I'd ever had the misfortune to meet."[32] The mishmash of English with Latin, Italian, Scots, and Black British vernacular, of high literary registers with racily colloquial street slang—"these macaronic strategies," as Vendler conceded of Walcott, "break up the expected." Evaristo's code-switching functions partly as social mimesis, although complexly indexed both to today's postcolonial, multiethnic London and to the classical Londinium that surprisingly anticipated it. And it functions aesthetically, heightening the humor of the anachronistic paralleling of ancient past and present (*"How nunc brown vacca"*) and energizing the verse's texture by shifting language gears to propel the verse forward. Along with code-stitching, code-skipping, as we might term such contrastive code-switching, is part of what a macaronic poetics can do for a poem. Perhaps this combination of stitching and skipping shouldn't surprise us, since various aspects of the aesthetics of poetry centrally involve the play of resemblances that both lump and split, both yoke and contrast—whether figures of thought, such as metaphor and metonymy, or figures of speech, such as rhyme, anaphora, and assonance.

In Korean American poet Cathy Park Hong's *Dance Dance Revolution*, a desert city tour guide even more hectically switches between English and other languages, including Latin, Spanish, West Indian English, and East Asian pidgins, as in her *invocatio* of a neon billboard ad:

> . . . Opal o opus,
> behole, neon hibiscus bloom beacons!
> "Tan Lotion Tanya" billboard . . . she
> your lucent Virgil, den I's taka ova
> as talky Virgil . . . want some tea? Some pelehuu?
> . . . .
> I speak sum Han-guk y Finnish, good bit o Latin
> y Spanish . . . sum toto Desert Creole en evachanging dipdong
> 'pendable on mine mood . . . ibid . . .[33]

In contemporary poetry studies, neither the avant-garde collage and pastiche paradigm nor the lyric, unitary-voice paradigm is adequate to a "translanguaging" poem like this. No less than Walcott, Cervantes, and Evaristo, Hong has it both ways. She twins polyglot collage with integrative harmonic voicing: her poetry playfully compresses multilingual heterogeneity within the awareness of her Dantean tour guide, a survivor of the 1980 Kwangju uprising. Instead of seeing code-switching and creolization as the degeneration of English, its corruption by the forces of globalization, all these poets revel in the linguistic vitality made available by intercultural contact. As such, they don't fully conform to the view that, in Juliana Spahr's words, the motives behind multilingual poetry are often "a form of realism or a pointed resistance to globalizing English."[34] In Hong's case, along with the vividly macaronic aesthetics of code-stitching and code-skipping, the poetry has a "realist" (social and contextual) function. But it is far in excess of our usual accounts of creolization as reflective of communication patterns of sociolinguistic groups brought into contact. Instead, just as Evaristo's code-switching evokes not only the present but also the ancient past and layers temporalities in surprising ways, so too Hong's forges a made-up creole that corresponds to no currently extant hybrid society but one that might

come about some day.[35] Both poets make use of poetry's relative temporal freedom by layering mimesis of today's speech practices with those
of other times, whether the ancient past or the emergent future. Over-
flowing the "bucket" of contemporary social context, the exuberant play
and sonic excess of such macaronic poetics recall much older histories
and project new futures of interlingual experience.

Postcolonial Code-Switching

As is well known, postcolonial writers often code-switch into a local language to reclaim, as Chamberlin suggested of Walcott, lost or subordinate or denigrated areas of cultural experience ("Come back to me / my
language"). They lace Standard English with the untranslatable names of
local flora, fauna, or divinities, as in Okot p'Bitek's Acholi; with robustly
humorous expressions and translingual puns, as in Daljit Nagra's Punjabi;
and with introspective self-address or implied address to a local audience, as in Lorna Goodison's Jamaican Creole. But in these and other
examples, as in Cervantes, code-switching often complicates even as
it fulfills paradigms of cultural affirmation, resistance, and indigenization. Consider Barbadian Kamau Brathwaite's epic trilogy *The Arrivants*,
often seen as a poetic landmark of cultural decolonization. In the middle
section, *Masks*, the poet delves into Akan, linguistically replicating the
poem's narrative and ideological return to the mother continent from
which Brathwaite's African ancestors were sold into slavery. But when
the speaker travels to Ghana, where Brathwaite worked from 1955 to
1962, his welcome in Akan typifies his crisis of understanding who he is
and where he is from:

> *Akwaaba* they smiled
> meaning welcome
>
> *akwaaba* they called
> *aye kooo*
>
> well have you walked
> have you journeyed
>
> welcome
>
> you who have come
> back a stranger
> after three hundred years[36]

The welcome is warm, as echoed in self-translation, but the poet falters when asked, "do / you remember?"[37] As Stuart Hall writes, and as Brathwaite's code-switching from exuberant Akan to melancholy English suggests, "cultural identity is not a fixed essence at all, lying outside history and culture. . . . It is not a fixed origin to which we can make some final and absolute Return."[38] The poet's effort to reconnect with his African origins yields questions and uncertainties:

> I tossed my net
> but the net caught
> no fish
>
> I dipped a wish
> but the well
> was dry[39]

In this passage the sonic stitching (*I/I/dry, net/net/caught, fish/wish, wish/well/was*) evokes sad introspection and futile repetition. Elsewhere in the book, Brathwaite incorporates Akan drum words and prayers that, as rhythms and sonorities seemingly echoing from the ancestral past, reaffirm Black Atlantic continuities and connections. But sometimes the switch into Akan figures both longing and alienation, both the desire to rejoin and the estrangement from ancestral origins. In poems like Brathwaite's, a macaronic aesthetic proves compatible both with the recuperative quest and with the ambiguities and ambivalences of that quest.

Another poet who code-switches partly to signify cultural identity and resistance, Craig Santos Perez, from the Pacific island of Guam, sometimes switches into Chamoru, the territory's indigenous language, embattled under American occupation. The native words are like islands of cultural continuity, history, and identity in a sea of English. (Indeed, Myers-Scotton uses the term "Embedded Language islands" for phrases in code-switching practice that are grammatically distinct from the Matrix Language.)[40] But Perez shows such words to be not only anchors of native rootedness going back thousands of years but also arrivals in a history of routing, travel, and movement. In his first book, the prickly *achiote* plant signifies for Perez the indigenous culture of his grandparents, even as he also traces it back through trade routes to Mayan Central America and the Caribbean where it originated.[41] In his second book, the word *saina*, used for parents or ancestors, is also the name given in 2007 to a *sakman*, or outrigger canoe, built on Guam—the first such large *sakman* constructed there for centuries.[42] As such, *saina* in the book of poems by that name figures both indigenous ancestry and oceanic mobility. As in Brathwaite's poetry, code-switching supports a strongly indigenist perspective, but one that is flexible enough to open out onto cross-cultural horizons, including in this case transnational affiliations with the code-switching writers Perez cites, such as Charles Olson, Theresa Hak Kyung Cha, Nathaniel Mackey, and Myung Mi Kim.

A paragraph of Perez's prose poetry reflects directly on the code-switching it is enacting, noting the traditional power relations between the languages:

> i say "saina" and i know i am not between two languages—not between fluency and fluency—not a simple switch—i say "saina"—heat along converging diverging linguistic boundaries—i write "saina"—seamount, island—within torrents of English—i am not between two languages—one language controls me and the other is a lost ocean—wavelength, wavebreak—not code, but compositions of history, story, genealogy, sound, change, meaning, practices—i say "saina" and it weaves the air i write 'saina' and it roots i read "saina" envelops—[43]

More than most everyday code-switching for the purposes of communication among bi- or multilinguals, Perez's chanting of his relation to the Chamoru word—exhibiting poetry's frequent recursiveness and reflexivity—meditates on the significance of moving between the languages. Bringing Chamoru words like *saina* into powerful "torrents of English" isn't as simple as "switching," because of the historical inequities between users of these languages; and the politically subordinate language isn't a mere "code," because it evokes a whole cultural history. Perez's poem enacts both code-switching and meta-code-switching. It straddles the charged divide between the languages and reflects on what it means to do so. It makes use of the gaps between the two languages it presses together to reflect on each in light of the other. The Chamoru word *saina* both "weaves the air" and "roots," both transnationalizes and indigenizes. Albeit drawing on the poet's intimate experience of Pacific Island code-switching, the poem's theorization of itself, its metaphorization of the subordinate language (at once "seamount, island" and "a lost ocean"), and its chant-like craftedness make of it more than a mere drop in the "bucket" of contextual speech.

Intralingual Code-Switching

If we extend the sense of code-switching beyond alternation between languages to alternation between discourses in a single language, the range of poems to consider widens, including poems that switch between speech and song. Whether we refer to "speech" or "song" in literary poetry, we are in either case being metaphorical, since a printed poem cannot literally speak or sing. But code-skipping between seeming-speech and seeming-song in poems highlights the overlap and distinction between them, whether in Eliot's adaptation of popular and operatic "songs" in *The Waste Land* or the incorporation of calypso, limbo, ska, reggae, or nursery rhyme in poems by Kamau Brathwaite, Linton Kwesi Johnson, and Jean Binta Breeze.[44] In experimental poems by writers like Rae Armantrout and Charles Bernstein, song helps intensify code-skipping to disrupt any appearance of lyric closure.[45] After ironic meta-commentary on providing "services" such as alliteration, rhyme, and unusual vocabulary, Bernstein writes in one of his long poems,

> *These are the sounds of science (whoosh, blat,*
> *flipahineyhoo), brought to*
> *you by DuPont, a broadly diversified company dedicated to*
> *exploitation through science and industry.*
>
> Take this harrow off
>
> my chest, I don't feel it anymore
>
> it's getting stark, too stark
>
> to see, feel I'm barking at Hell's spores.
>
> The new sentience.[46]

Ars poetica gives way to a humorous riff on Simon and Garfunkel's folk rock song "The Sound of Silence," which runs into a chemical company's advertising lingo (comically interrupted by onomatopoeia and punning word substitutions), followed by play on Bob Dylan's song "Knockin' on Heaven's Door," before a return to poetics in Bernstein's pun on Ron Silliman's "the new sentence." Concepts such as "the new sentence" underscore the disjunctiveness of such writing, one facet of which is intralingual code-switching—as in these intermedial jump-cuts among advertising, onomatopoeia, almost-song, and poetics. The poem delights in threading a jagged syntactic weave through these discourses, while parodying each of the discourses it disjunctively conjoins.

Whereas the intercode seams are usually less visible in modern and contemporary lyric poetry, the conspicuously interlingual and interdiscursive code-switching we've been exploring can help disclose its presence even where we might not think to look for it. Despite his image as the quintessentially English monologist, Philip Larkin mixes codes in poems like "Sunny Prestatyn," which, as we've seen, combines high-register diction ("tautened white satin") with vulgarity ("A tuberous cock and balls"). Whether by virtue of class, ethnicity, or region, poets who grew up code-switching between a vernacular or pidgin and Standard English have often evinced the interplay and friction between these codes in places like Hawaii, Black America, South Africa, India, the Caribbean—as well as in northern England. In his long poem *v.*, Tony Harrison, who was a scholarship boy uprooted from his origins in the working class, yokes its belittled language with the high literary discourse he learned in grammar school. Musing in the tradition of Gray's "Elegy Written in a Country Churchyard" on tombstones—but these sprayed with graffiti including ethnic slurs for Pakistani and Black Britons and Jews—he wonders,

> What is it that these crude words are revealing?
> What is it that this aggro act implies?
> Giving the dead their xenophobic feeling
> or just a *cri-de-coeur* because Man dies.
>
> *So what's a cri-de-coeur, cunt? Can't yer speak*
> *the language that yer mam spoke? Think of 'er!*
> *Can yer only get yer tongue round fucking Greek?*
> *Go and fuck yerself with* cri-de-coeur![47]

When the voice of the skinhead graffiti artist—later revealed to be the poet's alter ego—suddenly erupts, infuriated by the poet's upward-register code-switching, it transforms the poem. But the obscenity-spewing skinhead's "voice" is ironically framed, like the literary speaker's, in the alternating rhyme and iambic pentameter of the heroic quatrain. Here, as in some of our earlier examples, poetic code-switching looks both outward on the contemporary social world and backward through time, mediating the explosive class tensions of Thatcher-era northern England through the long history of allusive and formal memory, and so complicating the usual window-onto-society accounts of code-switching. Inhabiting both past and present, deploying both the stitch and the skip capacities of code-switching, the poem plays on the soccer team's name United and at the same time on "v" for verse and versus; figures the splenetic skinhead as both opposite and mirror-image (a quasi-poet literally writing *in* a churchyard); and knits together and tensely plays against one another the oral and literary, tradition and the revolt against it, northern British working-class and southern British upper-class sociolects.

Another "lyric" poet, Seamus Heaney, builds on the example of Harrison's *School of Eloquence* near-sonnets, which shove forsaken working-class speech up against intricate literary writing. Heaney's elegiac sonnet sequence "Clearances," written for his mother, code-switches between his family's Northern Irish dialect and the literary speech of his education:

> With more challenge than pride, she'd tell me, 'You
> Know all them things.' So I governed my tongue
> In front of her, a genuinely well-
> Adjusted adequate betrayal
> Of what I knew better. I'd *naw* and *aye*
> And decently relapse into the wrong
> Grammar which kept us allied and at bay.[48]

The poet returns to working-class Northern Irish grammar and pronunciation, which sounds "wrong" to the Standard English–attuned ear, to ally himself with his mother, and yet the poem itself both honors and betrays her by encasing her nonliterary speech and his in sonnet form. It epitomizes a code-switching aesthetics of dissonance-in-harmony, encapsulated in the final rhyme that joins and splits the dialect "*naw* and *aye*" and the standard "and at bay." As distant as poets like Heaney, Harrison, and Larkin may seem from more obviously macaronic poets like Walcott and Brathwaite, Cervantes, Evaristo, and Hong, Bernstein and Armantrout, they too intermix codes to striking effect.

* * *

Whether lyric or experimental, intralingual or interlingual, the poetic uses of code-switching include those I've encapsulated as code-stitching, code-skipping, and self-reflexivity; humor, localized address, and self-address;

the performance of cultural and cross-cultural identities in the present and of interlingualism in past and future histories; the reclamation of indigeneity and the marking of social alienation; the affirmation of rootedness and the enactment of geographic mobility. Sometimes the aesthetic and social mimetic functions of code-switching work together, as in Evaristo's and Hong's macaronic evocations of macaronic societies of the past, present, and future; at other times they work against one another, as when Cervantes sets English and Spanish against one another as social metonyms but aesthetically intertwines them, or when Brathwaite integrates Akan into his English but marks his distance from the African social world it figures. This complexity suggests caution in applying speech models to code-switching poetry, since poems have their own imperatives toward recursiveness, play, chiming, contrastive juxtaposition, multiple temporalities, ambiguity, and self-reflexivity, which tend to figure less prominently—though they also occur—in everyday exchanges.

Because code-switching in poetry often seems to hover between speech and writing, we might look to it to resolve ongoing debates over whether to emphasize the scribal or the oral dimensions of poetry, its textuality or its performativity.[49] If we do, we are likely to be disappointed, since such positions are inevitably bound by the hermeneutic circle. Whether you find the literary or the oral dimension of specific poems to be paramount likely depends on whether you come to poetry thinking about it primarily in terms of its written, textual, on-page or on-screen inscription, or primarily in terms of its vocal, performative embodiment and reception. Of course, some poems bear their own emphases on the scribal-oral spectrum, from concrete poems at one end to slam, rap, dub, and sound poetry at the other. But even a heavily "scribal" poem can be examined for its oral/auditory textures and resonances (e.g., high modernism or Language writing), and even a seemingly "oral" poem can be explored through a literary lens (e.g., rap or dub poetry).

Code-switching poetry would seem to tip the scales in the direction of orality, often foregrounding the speech-effect of even highly literary poetry. When a poet of highly stylized verse like James Merrill suddenly slips into African American Vernacular English in the middle of a long meditative poem, the text assumes a more speechlike quality:

A yellow plastic Walkman at my hip
Sends shiny yellow tendrils to either ear.
All us street people got our types on tape,
Turn ourselves on with a sly fingertip.[50]

Even so, some code-switching reinforces the literariness of the literary text. To evoke his downwardly mobile father, who lost one job after another, Robert Lowell quotes Mallarmé:

Night after night,
à la clarté déserte de sa lampe,
he slid his ivory Annapolis slide rule
across a pad of graphs—
piker speculations![51]

As Lowell affiliates himself with a literary rather than real father, the effect is more bookish allusion than hip-hop sampling, albeit leavened by a slang term for cautious gambler, "piker." Similarly, when Adrienne Rich sprinkles "Snapshots of a Daughter-in-Law" with the Latin "*tempora* and *mores*" and the "argument *ad feminam*" and the French "*ma semblable, ma soeur!*" and "*fertilisante douleur*," she intensifies—much to her chagrin years later—the literariness of her partly high-modernist, partly confessional poem.[52] If we approach code-switching poetry within a literary framework, its visual materiality becomes significant. "The page doesn't interest me that much," claimed Amiri Baraka.[53] Yet, despite the strong oral emphasis of his poetry, often dramatically shifting registers and discourses, intertwining chants and rants and jazz, Baraka makes extensive use of the graphic spacing of the poem on the page, often in excess of any function as stage direction for oral performance, and the homonymic play of the punning title of a sequence like *Wise, Why's, Y's*, for example, must be visualized or spelled out. As we saw in Evaristo's code-switching into Latin and Italian, a macaronic aesthetic can heighten a text's speech-likeness, but in other moments, as when her novel-in-verse quotes Ovid or Cicero, the effect can be decidedly bookish. Code-switching can serve either the oralist or the writerly paradigm for poetry. Or in cases such as Walcott's pun on *blessé* and *blest*, Pound's on "τίν'" and "tin," or Cervantes's cross-lingual patterning, it can serve both at the same time.

A macaronic poetics foregrounds the always-already dialogic nature of even the supposedly unitary poetic voice. All thought, all discourse, argued Bakhtin, is dialogic—formed in linguistic give-and-take with others—but with code-switching, it becomes all the more overtly so.[54] Even in lyric poems, though considered by Bakhtin and others to be expressions of a closed inner self, code-switching contravenes the notion of a subjectivity sealed off from linguistic impurities and delivering an inner essence on the page or in performance. Because poetry foregrounds the languageness of language—its verbal weight, texture, and history—code-switching poetry, creating an image of how different languages intersect, interact, and jostle, helps fine-tune our alertness to the congeries of languages, sociolects, and dialects even in seemingly monologic and monolingual speech. In a global age of increased human mobility and cross-cultural contact, code-switching is one of poetry's most visible and audible ways of giving shape and meaning to the convergences of peoples, texts, and cultures across sometimes-large cultural and social distances. Poets intercept, reshape, and torque our multilects and in doing so help bring new interlingual forms into the world.

CHAPTER 10

POETRY, (UN)TRANSLATABILITY, AND WORLD LITERATURE

Questions of translatability have figured prominently in recent debates over world literature. In David Damrosch's pithy formulation, "World literature is writing that gains in translation."[1] This influential model usefully foregrounds how literary texts multiply meanings and readers as they circulate beyond their sites of origin. But Damrosch's definition, as in a previous chapter I argued of Franco Moretti's distant reading of literary waves, may have unfortunate if unintended consequences for poetry. It is based on a distinction between works of world literature and those that "are so inextricably connected to their original language and moment that they really cannot be effectively translated at all"; they "are not translatable without substantial loss, and so they remain largely within their local or national context, never achieving an effective life as world literature."[2] Although world literature is conceived by Moretti, Damrosch, Pascale Casanova, and others as an expansive and multilingual category, a great deal of poetry would by this definition languish outside its precincts. "Translation can never really succeed," writes Damrosch, "if a work's meaning is taken to reside essentially in the local verbal texture of its original phrasing."[3] For poetry, more than perhaps any other literary genre, "the local verbal texture" is often meaningful, even indispensable.

Granted, this isn't so for all poetry, some kinds of which are readily translated, such as narrative, epic, dramatic, balladic, and some other long-form varieties, and even some lyric poems—at least features such as their visual metaphors, tonal modulations, and shifting poetic address. According to Justin Quinn, some Cold War–era Eastern European poems, free of dense sonic effects or wordplay, were meant to be as translatable as science, such that for Miroslav Holub, "the work of translation had already begun when he was writing the Czech originals," akin to the contemporary Chinese poems that Stephen Owen criticizes for seeming to "translate themselves," or the novels Rebecca Walkowitz characterizes as "born translated."[4] But are these the only kinds of poems that should qualify as world literature—a field that now gives prominence to the novel, mainly in English translation? And what of the special impediments to translating many other kinds of poetry?[5] The Greek translator David Connolly summarizes the view that "poetry translation is a special case within literary translation and involves far greater difficulties than the translation of prose" because unlike "ordinary language," its language is often "elaborate," "compact," "condensed," "heightened," and "connotational"; in it, "content and form are inseparably linked."[6] According to Paul Ricoeur, too, poetry presents "the serious difficulty of the inseparable combination of sense and sonority, of the signified and the signifier."[7] As we think about the place of poetry in world literature, it may be time to revisit such views, now that they are increasingly in dispute. At an MLA Convention roundtable on translation in January of 2017, for example, two speakers ridiculed the idea that it may be harder to translate a lyric poem than an instruction manual.[8] In accord with a tendency in cultural studies to downplay genre distinctions, a recent book on poetry and translation asserts, "Poetry is not a special case of language; it is the ordinary case of language."[9] Frost's dictum that "poetry is what is lost in translation" is now said to reflect "an essentialist definition of poetry" and "purist views of literary language."[10] Admittedly, Frost's aphorism, like any aphorism, oversimplifies; as we'll see, some aspects of poetry translate. Even so, the translation of the poetry of poetry is often especially complex. As Matthew Reynolds notes, in prose fiction, "the most salient formal elements (paragraphs, chapters) can readily be matched without damage to descriptive meaning";[11] not so the rhythms, rhymes, assonances, alliterations, compressed wordplay, certain syntactic and rhetorical patterns, and other meaning-bearing features of form-dense poems, such as lyrics in English by Hopkins, Yeats, and Hart Crane, Louise Bennett and Kamau Brathwaite, Geoffrey Hill and Seamus Heaney.[12] Although for some years I've been tracing such anglophone poetry's travel and transnationalism, even I would concede that lyric poetry, to the extent that it is embedded in the language of its articulation, is less mobile than, say, emojis, pop songs, novels, or instruction manuals. The language of lyric is in some ways a bridge, in others a wall.

At the same time that the model of literature-that-gains-in-translation may need to be reconsidered because it generically skews against a great deal of poetry, polemical arguments "against world literature" (Emily Apter's phrase) that are predicated on untranslatability may also need to be recalibrated, since some aspects of even dense lyric poems circulate in translation.[13] These arguments, moreover, have centered on "untranslatables," fascinating philosophical terms with no equivalents in other languages,[14] but the questions surrounding the (un)translatability of poetry—its phonemic, syntactic, rhythmic, and other specificities in different languages—extend into complexities well beyond the lexical, as we'll see. Building on the recent resurgence of interest in poetry and translation, as signaled by works by Quinn, Reynolds, Peter Robinson, Jean Boase-Beier, and others, I attempt to help bring poetry studies into conversation with "world literature."[15] Since this vast subject is impossible to treat comprehensively, and since poetry lives in intricacies that demand close analysis, I examine a handful of lyrics in different languages and test the "gains-in-translation" and the "untranslatability" models against poetry's language-specific and language-crossing affordances. In doing so, I hope to develop a more nuanced position that allows for both losses and gains—and for losses that are potential gains, for gains predicated on losses. And I explore what the implications of this cross-hatched understanding might be for the study of world poetry, widening the book's temporal, geographic, and linguistic scope.

Disaggregating Poetry's (Un)Translatability

I begin with distinctions still valuable even after decades of translation theory, made nearly a century ago by a poet-translator of poetry in Chinese, Anglo-Saxon, Occitan, French, Italian, Latin, and other languages. Complicating both the "gains-in-translation" and the "untranslatability" theses, Ezra Pound and other global modernists can help tease apart different strands of literary (un)translatability. He writes: "That part of your poetry which strikes upon the imaginative eye of the reader will lose nothing by translation into a foreign tongue; that which appeals to the ear can reach only those who take it in the original."[16] In his famous tripartite division, Pound demurs from hard untranslatability, arguing that *phanopœia*, "the casting of images upon the visual imagination," "can ... be translated almost, or wholly, intact."[17] But Pound's two other categories encapsulate poetry's stiff challenge to the "gains" model of world literature. "*Melopœia*," in which words are charged in meaningful ways with music, can be appreciated in an unknown, foreign language, but, with small exceptions, "It is practically impossible to transfer or translate it from one language to another."[18] W. H. Auden concurs that the poetic "imagery of similes and metaphors" is translatable (it's from shared "sensory experiences" and "not from local verbal habits") but that when the "'meaning'... is inseparable from the sound and the rhythmical values of the words," the poetry is "rarely, if ever translatable."[19] Similarly, Pound's third category, "*logopœia*," or wordplay on connotations and associations, "does not translate."[20] Pound's triad can help begin to disaggregate facets that are too often lumped together as the blanket translatability or untranslatability of poetry. No doubt his distinctions need to be qualified. Even visual images, for example, can be tricky—take the symbolic associations of what Pound thought were "natural images" in Chinese poetry, or the sometimes missed mystical implications of wine drinking in Sufi poetry. Pound's distinctions could also be supplemented by other schemata, whether Northrop Frye's Aristotelian triad of *lexis*, *melos*, and *opsis* (the latter two rendered babble and doodle), the classical Perso-Arabic distinction between *lafz* (form, articulation, phonetic effects) and *ma'na* (idea, topic, semantic content), or more variegated models such as William Frawley's quartering of a poem's phonological, syntactic, semantic, and allusive layers.[21] Still, Pound's translational trinity, rendered by Louis Zukofsky as "sight, sound, and intellection," is a useful point of departure.[22]

Consider briefly an example discussed in translation studies that illustrates the split between Pound's *phanopœia* and *melopœia*, the start of early twentieth-century poet Christian Morgenstern's playful "Das aesthetische Wiesel":

Ein Wiesel   *A weasel*

sass auf einem Kiesel   *sat on a pebble*

inmitten Bachgeriesel.   *amidst brook ripples.*[23]

Any semantic translation that conveys the poem's key images will be obviously inadequate since the poem lives mainly in its comically rhyming form. Is a *melopœic* adaptation to be preferred to a *phanopœic* image-by-image translation, even if that requires radically changing the content, as in Max Knight's wonderful renderings, "a mink sipping a drink in the kitchen sink," or "a lizard shaking its gizzard in a blizzard"?[24] Or should it be translated stereoscopically, in *phanopœic* and *melopœic* renderings? For such sound-centered poetry, the model of unitary translation falls short. As argued by Pound and another of his and Morgenstern's contemporaries, T. S. Eliot, although "we dream of an ideal translation" that does everything, we need both "literal" and "free" varieties.[25] Indeed, we may begin to wonder whether, for lyric poetry, multilayered translation should replace the one-to-one translational norm, what Ricoeur calls the "fantasy" or "ideal of the perfect translation," especially as electronic tools like hypertext can make available a menu of translational options—sonic and semantic, source and target, literal and creative.[26] Since lyric tends to be less linear and more synchronous than genres like realist fiction or newswriting, it may be especially suited to layered, interactive forms of translation.[27]

No less challenging for the translator is the *logopœia* of homophonic wordplay, also abundant in Morgenstern's lyrics. As Auden writes, "any association of ideas created by homophones is restricted to the language in which these homophones occur. Only in German does *Welt* rhyme with *Geld*, and only in English is Hilaire Belloc's pun possible.

When I am dead, I hope it may be said:
'His sins were scarlet, but his books were read.'"[28]

In *Jokes and Their Relation to the Unconscious*, published like Morgenstern's *Galgenlieder* in 1905, Freud defends the witty condensation of *Kalauer*, or punning wordplay, denying that it is the lowest form of humor.[29] As Julia Kristeva would go on to suggest, poetry can be seen as giving us rationally sanctioned access to the repressed, pre-referential childhood play with words as material objects.[30] *Melopœia* and *logopœia* can be understood as two aspects of Jakobson's "poetic function," in which the message is foregrounded for its own sake. Long before the current debate over world literature and untranslatability, Jakobson, like Pound and Auden, confounded the polarity. He refused what he called "the dogma of untranslatability," arguing that many different kinds of messages can be recoded from one language to another.[31] But he also set poetry apart by virtue of how in it, "phonemic similarity," such as punning, among other "verbal equations," "is sensed as a semantic relationship," to the extent that "poetry by definition is untranslatable" and only "creative transposition is possible."[32]

Sounding Rumi

Let's bring Pound's distinctions into play with a more complex lyric by a poet who would seem to be an outstanding example of "world literature" understood as "writing that gains in translation"—in this case, that gains in market share and readers eight hundred years after his birth. Jalal al-Din Rumi, or Mowlana (our master) or Mowlavi (my master) as he's known in the Persian-speaking world, is a best-selling poet in English, despite being a thirteenth-century Muslim claimed by modern-day Turkey, Iran, Afghanistan, and Tajikistan. Indeed, his transnationalism illustrates the heterogeneous body of work composed in Persian for centuries in West, Central, and South Asia, from the Balkans to Bangladesh, the Ottoman Empire to the Mughal Empire. In the second millennium, Persian poetry's cartography and influence were vast. Ironically, even though it helped lay the groundwork for Goethe's early formulation of the idea of *Weltliteratur*, it scarcely appears in the influential academic studies of world literature by Damrosch, Moretti, and Casanova.[33]

Local detective work in my university library turned up material indications of what Rumi has gained in translation. In one of the more than two million copies of Coleman Barks's Rumi translations, someone has drawn a box in ink around these lines:

This is how I would die
into the love I have for you:

as pieces of cloud
dissolve in sunlight.[34]

On the facing page, where translated excerpts continue on the theme of love, understood in secular rather than sacred terms, someone has pressed a flower to leave its impression on the page. Such readers have been so moved that they have wanted to leave their own affect-bearing marks next to lines like "Love is the mother. / We are her children."[35] In one poem we read, "Bitter goes sweet in the mouth"; in another, "Essence is emptiness. / Everything else, accidental."[36] Purveying wise sayings and memorable figurative language, such lines, circulating through greeting cards, email signature lines, t-shirts, popular songs, and other media, are consonant with the epideictic or broadly truth-telling strand Jonathan Culler has recently affirmed in lyric.[37] Although Barks has many scholarly detractors, Ahmad Karimi-Hakkak defends him for capturing something of Rumi's "mystical thrust" and largeness of mind, even if he betrays the letter of the original to do so, as did William Jones to give expression to "the sumptuous lyricism of Hafez," and Edward FitzGerald "the rebellious spirit of Khayyam."[38] Arguably Barks, like Rumi's other translators, conveys something of Rumi's sagacity, parables, stories, themes, values, images, and affective energy. Although Barks's translations have had little discernible impact on the development of English-language poetry, another poet's earlier translations of poetry from "the East," Pound's profoundly influential free-verse renditions of *Cathay* (1915) (an effort in Hugh Kenner's words "to rethink the nature of an English poem"), similarly convey something of Li Bai's visual images, narratives, tonal shifts, and meaning, even as they abandon his intensely rhymed and tightly measured form.[39]

But this translational conveyance can come at a cost. In assimilating Rumi, popular translators like Barks often "de-Islamize" him, in Annemarie Schimmel's verb, combing out his Muslim-specific content, such as terms like Allah and *houri*: "I avoid God-words," Barks avows, "because they seem to take away the freshness of experience."[40] As Pound's example reminds us, Barks is hardly alone in freely, if flagrantly, adapting poetry to a target culture. As Lawrence Venuti concedes, "Translations . . . inevitably perform a work of domestication."[41] But domesticating translations go too far, Venuti states, if "suppressing the linguistic and cultural differences of the foreign text, assimilating it to dominant values in the target-language culture."[42] Similarly, Gayatri Chakravorty Spivak criticizes the translation of "Third World" texts "into a sort of with-it translationese" that seems fully accessible, warning of "a species of neo-colonialist construction."[43] According to the orientalist critique that highlights asymmetries of power, Barks's de-Islamized Rumi is a colonized Rumi.

But while Barks may be an easy target, even scholarly translators such as Jawid Mojaddedi who are true to Rumi's Muslim *phanopœia* can only hint at his *logopœia* or his *melopœia*, the latter including varieties of *tajnis* (تجنيس, literally, "making homogeneous," as in wordplay, paronomasia, and alliteration) and other kinds of *lafz* (لفظ) in Perso-Arabic poetics.[44] Where discussions of the translation of poetry nitpick omissions and other flaws or focus mainly on ideological distortion, they often fail to address the constraints of language differences on even the most skilled and respectful translators. Take the facing-page, bilingual *Say Nothing* (2008), Rumi's poems knowledgeably translated by Iraj Anvar and Anne Twitty. Their volume includes one of the first classical poems I fell in love with when studying Persian literature, a ghazal on the theme of *fanâ* (فنا), the Sufi concept of annihilation, from the *Divan-e Shams-e Tabriz*. We can already hear in the strong opening *matla*, or form-setting couplet, how richly patterned and musically recursive is the Persian of Rumi's eleven-syllable hemistichs in *khafif* meter, including the repetitions and allitera-tions I've highlighted:[45]

وه چه بی رنگ و بی نشان که منم   کی ببینم مرا چنانکه منم

*k*ay bebinam <u>m</u>ar*â* <u>ch</u>on*â*n*ke*   vah <u>ch</u>e **bi** rang o **bi** nesh*â*n

<u>m</u>*a*n*a*<u>m</u>?   *ke* <u>m</u>*a*n*a*<u>m</u>

When will I see myself as I   Oh how nameless, how

really am?[46]   light I am!

Although the magisterial scholarly books on Rumi by Annemarie Schim-mel and Franklin Lewis provide indispensable insight into the poetry's thematic, imagistic, and theological dimensions, they devote much less attention to Rumi's unique poetic sound.[47] But given that how a lyric says what it says is often at least as important as what it says, the sonic texture is crucial to the distinctive poetry of a poem like this. Take its intensive repetition of a handful of vowel sounds in a pattern that partly repeats across the opening hemistich (مصراع, *mesrâ'*), which I attempt to delineate visually in a phonetic transliteration:

a e i a o i e â e a a
e e i a a â e â e a a

To some extent, these assonances shouldn't be surprising, since modern Persian has six to eight vowel sounds, close to Spanish and Arabic, but unlike English and German, which have more than twice as many. Rumi's poem intensifies the vowel repetitions in Persian to set up a resonant echo and variation across the hemistichs—an instance of the "reverbera-tion" Fatemeh Keshavarz finds throughout Rumi.[48] As Amin Banani puts it, Rumi displays "the strong vowel music of the Persian language," and as Christoph Bürgel remarks, Rumi's poetry is "pervaded" with internal rhyme, "more so than Persian poetry in general."[49] Like other poets who have stitched their verbal patterning to the sonic structure of the specific language in which they write, Rumi creates a sound texture that is unique to Persian and irreproducible in English.

Monorhyme, assonance, and sonic repetition come more easily in Persian and seem less contrived, since the language employs three dif-ferent types of syllables (consonant-vowel, consonant-vowel-consonant, and consonant-vowel-consonant-consonant), whereas English has about seventeen.[50] Witness the *bayt* (loosely, "couplet") about the key term *fanâ*, in which that word's terminal open vowel echoes, almost enacting a *fanâ*-like dissolution, in the swirling cadences and the paradoxical word-play and internal rhyme on *pâ* (foot or leg):

اینت بی پای پا دوان که منم	می‌شدم در فنا چو مه بی پا
mishodam dar fanâ cho mah bi pâ	eent bi pâ-ye pâ davân ke manam
Annihilated, I'm foot-free, leg-free, like the moon.	Here I am, your racing, fleet-footed, foot-free runner![51]

Faced with the original's irreproducible sonority, I've ventured in trans-lation, as do others, an inadequate sonic stand-in, alliteration. As Twitty writes in introducing her and Anvar's translation, listening to Anvar's recital of Rumi's ghazals reminded her that, as translators,

> we were entering the realm of impossibility. The richness of Rumi's sound is woven from a language that repeats its sounds and words with infinite subtle variations and glories in that; English just doesn't bend that way. It does not possess these beautifully detachable prefixes and suffixes, those rounded, open sounds that permit each word to spill over into the next, interweaving in an endless repetition. The laws and regularities of English are irremediably different, no matter how or how far they are stretched. . . .[52]

The challenges of translation are partly contextual: translating Rumi into a related language like Urdu or one with similar vowel structures, like Spanish or Arabic, might entail fewer *melopœic* losses. But as A. K. Rama-nujan puts it, "it is impossible to translate the phonology of one language into that of another—even in a related, culturally neighbouring language. . . . If we try and even partially succeed in mimicking the sounds, we may lose everything else, the syntax, the meanings, the poem itself."[53] Despite the West's embrace of Rumi, it's hard to see how the language-specific *melopœia* of his ghazals, as of much other sonically resonant poetry, could be thought to gain in English or German or French translation.

The connotative wordplay of *logopœia*, roughly akin to *ihâm* (ايهام) in Persian poetics,[54] also infuses this ghazal and many others like it, though again, it is largely un-re-creatable in English. Let's look at one last *bayt*, maybe the hardest in this ghazal to render in English, which deploys both *tajnis* and *ihâm* in playing on عین (*ayn*), a loan-word from Arabic that should qualify for a truly globalized dictionary of untranslatables:

in Persian, it means eye, same, spring, source, the best part of anything, essence, and as nominalized adjective (عیان, *aayân*), the visible, obvious, manifest:

عین چه بود درین عیان که منم   گفت ای جان تو عین مایی گفتم

goftam a jân to ayn-e mâ i,   ayn chebvad darin aayân ke manam[55]
goft

Note the huge differences between two excellent translations: Anvar and Twitty's reads, "I said: My Soul, you're the light of my eyes. / Where I am, he said, no need for eyes"; Franklin Lewis's reads, "I said / Friend, you are just like me! / He said / How can you speak of likeness to / the obviousness I am?"[56] Are these even recognizable as translations of the same text? In the first hemistich, *ayn* means "eyes" but also "likeness," "source," or "essence" (that is, "Soul, you are my eyes" but also "you are the same as me" or "you are my essence" or "source"). The second hemistich playfully counters meanings of the first *ayn*, asking, "What would eyes be [*ayn*], in this visibility everywhere [*aayân*] that manifests me?" or "What's a hidden essence [*ayn*], when the essence that I am hides in plain sight [*aayân*]?" It's the kind of paradoxical wordplay that is frequent in Rumi and that virtually dissolves in explanation—so many different connotations prance in what Pound calls *logopœia*'s "dance of the intellect among words."[57] Rumi is both more easily translated than many poets because of the homey soulfulness and affective accessibility of his reflections, yet harder as well, because of the symphonic layering of wordplay, sonic textures, and semantic content. As such, he both frustrates and fulfills key arguments for and against "world literature." Yes, you can make world literature of his poetry, but no, if that means literature in translation, much of the world will not receive what he gives readers in Persian. To calibrate what he gains and loses in translation, you can begin by comparing divergent translations—a frequent strategy in world literature criticism; but you also have to engage "the local verbal texture" of the originals.[58] If "world literature" is to give lyric-centered literatures their due—Persian, Arabic, Vietnamese, etc.—it needs a post-Eurocentric, language-attuned comparative poetics.

What Lives in Translation

Having drawn attention to what's lost in lyric translation even in a case like Rumi where so much is gained, I turn to a ghazal by a more recent

master of the form, because it instances how even with these losses, the
bridge of translation can provide vitally important glimpses into certain aspects of the poetic, social, and historical imagination in other
languages. Partly in response to Persian ghazals by Hafez, Rumi, Saʻdi,
and others, Goethe wrote that translation, even when techniques like
monorhyme may not be suited to the target language, can give us access
to "the history, the legends, the ethics in general" (*Geschichtlichen, Fabel-
haften, Ethischen im allgemeinen*), "the characteristic opinions and ways of
thinking" (*den Gesinnungen und Denkweisen*), of another culture or time.[59]
Despite the marginalization of Persian poetry in contemporary world
literary theory, Goethe's many Hafez-enthralled poems and his essays
and notes on Persian poetry in his *West-östlicher Divan*, a capacious tome
that relied on Joseph von Hammer-Purgstall's recent translations, exemplify such cross-temporal, cross-cultural, cross-lingual transport. The
contemporary Iranian poet Simin Behbahani might not seem promising
for an affirmative approach to translation, since an English rendering of
her lyrics, *A Cup of Sin*, concludes with a rigorous forty-four-page afterword that explains, ironically, what the poems lose in translation:[60] the
"original music and rhythms" and "geometry" (134), generic extension and
"innovation" in the ghazal (135), allusiveness and intertextual "friction"
(136, 141, 144–45), "crunchiness" or "granularity" of texture (142), shifting
registers of diction (143), syntactic "manipulations" (144), revisions of
Iran-specific symbolism (146–64)—in short, "the linguistic, musical, literary, cultural, social, and historical embeddedness of any poem" (168).
As with Rumi, this is much more than the untranslatability of certain
philosophical keywords. Such candor about translation's "inescapable
losses and mutilations" (174) paradoxically provides the best foundation
for valorizing the impossibly possible work of translation, for it illuminates the specificities of a writer's poetics and of the resources of both
the source and target languages. It can help us grasp the "work" and "dia-
logicality" that Ricoeur highlights in translation, as we "get beyond these
theoretical alternatives, translatable *versus* untranslatable."[61]

Is Behbahani's poem about the world, "The World Is Shaped like a
Sphere," or "Zamin Koravi Shekl Ast, زمین کروی شکل است", an example
of world literature? What's the ratio of losses to gains here? Recasting
the poem in English free verse, Farzaneh Milani and Kaveh Safa have
left aside refrain, rhyme, couplet structure, and internal chiming. But
perhaps because Behbahani's *melopœia* is more austere than Rumi's, her
Englished ghazal seems more adequate—suffused with Behbahani's wit,
vivid imagery, defiant boldness of address, and ironic turns of thought.[62]

Published in 1995 but written in 1981, when revolutionary Iran's hard-ening resistance to *gharbzadegi*, or westoxification, was resulting in the execution of thousands of leftists, including a beloved first cousin of mine, Farshad Miraftab, the poem allegorizes the violence that can come of simplistic East-West dichotomies, whether emanating from East or West. As Milani writes, Behbahani, who was "disillusioned by the revo-lution she had initially supported" and was horrified by "the reign of terror," had "always resisted binary modes of thinking."[63]

Addressing the listener as her collaborator, the speaker wittily decon-structs in the ghazal's first part the artificial directions and meanings we impose on the globe. A sphere has no left or right; like a toy, it can be made to turn one way or another:

It was our agreement to call this the East,
though we could push it westward, with ease

قرار تو شد با من که شرق بخوانیمش
اگرچه توان راندش به غرب، به آسانی

qarar-e to shod bâ man ke sharq bekhânimash
agar che tavân rândash be qarb, be âsâni[64]

The poem builds on the Qur'anic aversion to divisions of East and West (Qur'an 2:115) and warnings against exclusive adherence to East or West (Qur'an 2:177). Yet, within this broadly Muslim context, one of the words Behbahani uses for "globe" is the emphatically Greek term *atlas-e geog-râphie* (اطلس جغرافی), from the ancient god Atlas and the science of geog-raphy: implicitly, those in Iran and elsewhere who harshly divide East from West ironically rely on a Western paradigm to do so. At the same time, the West eludes those intoxicated with it, represented as chasing after a never-reachable setting sun.

Having playfully subverted the hard-and-fast distinctions that sustain both orientalism and occidentalism, the poem turns darker midway—a poem about binary division that itself divides in half, unlike the vast majority of Behbahani's poems in this volume. Now the world is seen as a corpse that is being devoured: "The world [*jahân*, جهان] divided by a line [*xat*, خط] is a dead body [*mordâr*, مردار] cut in two / on which the vulture and hyena are feasting." In Persian, the word for "feasting," *mehmâni*, مهمانی, is a form of the everyday word for invited guests, which in a culture built around rituals of hospitality and cuisine makes the spectacle of predatory beasts feeding on carrion all the more repulsive. Despite the difficulty of conveying such culturally specific resonances in translation, perceptively outlined by Dick Davis,[65] much else lives in Milani and Safa's rendition—Behbahani's dual vision of the globe as free-spinning sphere or as split, moldering corpse, her literalizing the idea of the division of the world as destruction, her grotesque images of hyena, vulture, and flies gleefully sating themselves, her taunting of the addressee for complicity in murder and in death-fed celebration, her tonal shift from collaborative engagement to defiance, from playfully toying with the world as directionless globe to fiercely witnessing the world's demise as carrion. Contrary to the untranslatability thesis, these aspects of this world poem are remarkably vivid in English translation.

Translation, Phonetics, and Language Difference

That said, many lyric poems that, as we saw in Rumi, intensify a language's sonic properties and refract its connotative potential impede their rearticulation in another language, even as these impediments can paradoxically generate yet more poetry. A recent poem that codeswitches between English and Hmong plays on the mutual sonic opacities between languages. In her homage to a mid-twentieth-century Hmong who was inspired by night visions to create an idiosyncratic script, Mai Der Vang plays on tonal differentiations among words, their rising or falling pitch (technically, "contour"), that are inaudible to the untrained Western ear. Her italicized Hmong words may sound phonetically the same to the outsider but have entirely different meanings:

> *Paj* is not *pam* is not *pab.*
> Blossom is not blanket is not help.
>
> *Ntug* is not *ntuj* is not *ntub.*
> Edge is not sky is not wet.
>
> On sheet of bamboo
> with indigo branch.
>
> To *txiav* is not the *txias.*
> To scissor is not the cold.[66]

Without the poem's guidance, the reader unfamiliar with Hmong would not know that the words spelled with the same initial letters sound virtually the same, and an audio recording reveals that *ntub* rhymes with "bamboo."[67]

Various East and Southeast Asian fixed forms weave such tonal contours into the fabric of long-lived poetic forms. They prescribe a tonal pattern in addition to their rhyme and syllabic requirements, making them only partly re-creatable in English. Sailing en route to Vietnam and Burma (Myanmar) on Semester at Sea in 2016, I had my students write English-language poems that followed the metrical and rhyming patterns of these countries' poetic forms. But I soon realized that even if an English-language poem replicates the complex, staircase-like end- and internal-rhyme pattern of forms such as the Vietnamese *lục bát* (six-eight) and its hybrid with the Chinese regulated poem (*lü-shi*), the *song thất lục bát* (double-seven six-eight), schematized below, it would be impossible to reproduce in English the prescribed alternation of flat (*bằng*) and sharp (*trắc*) syllables:[68]

	1	2	3	4	5	6	7	8
1		S			F		S A rhyme	
2			F		S A rhyme		F B rhyme	
3		F		S		F B rhyme		
4		F		S		F B rhyme		F C rhyme
5			S		F C rhyme		S D rhyme	
6			F		S D rhyme		F E rhyme	
7		F		S		F E rhyme		
8		F		S		F E rhyme		F

TABLE I Diagram of the *song thất lục bát* (double-seven six-eight), with its flat (*bằng*) [F] and sharp (*trắc*) [S] syllables.

That said, as Vang's code-switching poem and my Persian examples demonstrate, we become aware of the special qualities of one language only when we cross over into another. While Robert J. C. Young is right to remind us that the borders among languages are porous, he draws the surprising inference that "the whole point of translation is to keep languages apart," "to confirm the presumption of differences between them."[69] Although we've noted Arabic and Greek words in Persian, among innumerable examples of translingual enmeshment, we've also seen that, at least where poetry is concerned, phonetic differences between English and languages like Persian, Hmong, and Vietnamese matter. The act of translation crystallizes the capacities and limitations of our own and other languages by forcing us to grapple with linguistic and cultural difference. "Through the labor of the translator," as Naoki Sakai puts it, "the incommensurability as difference that calls for the service of the translator in the first place is negotiated and worked on."[70] The untranslatable elements of poetry can turn from a wall into a bridge if, instead of overlooking them, we examine the cultural and linguistic specificities they render visible on either side, though without letting those specificities become reified for nationalist purposes. As Rebecca Ruth Gould writes in relation to Persian poetry, "When negotiating the dialectic of translation and untranslatability, we should cherish felicitous disjunctures."[71] By virtue of heightening and stretching the sonic, syntactic, rhetorical, allusive, and other features of languages, lyric poetry, in an enlarged model of world literature that engaged both its translatable and its untranslatable facets, might provide a sharper lens for cross-cultural and interlingual understanding.

Translating Syntax

In addition to phonology, poets can make vigorous use of the syntactic and grammatical features of the languages they write in, often reworking, stretching, or bending them.[72] Nor is this the case only in non-Western languages. When I first learned to read classical Roman poets like Horace and Virgil, I was dazzled by the syntactic flexibility that a highly inflected language makes possible, with case endings—rather than word order—indicating function in a sentence, thus affording inversion, bracketing, and suspension. In one variety of hyperbaton, or syntactic transposition, a noun can be widely separated from its modifying adjective. The chiastic form of double hyperbaton—what classicist Stanley Hoffer calls "adjective interlacing" and "double suspension"—emerged into prominence in first-century Roman poetry, probably as a Hellenistic imitation.[73] The beginning of Horace's fifth ode exemplifies its remarkable effects. When the speaker addresses the fickle Pyrrha, the "you" or "*te*" that denotes her is doubly enclosed, in a double-garland-like word picture. In Latin, "you" can appear sandwiched in the middle of the first line between the adjective "*gracilis*" and the noun "*puer*," sandwiched in turn by the adjective "*multa*" and the noun "*rosa*":[74]

Quis multa *gracilis* **te** *puer* in rosa
perfusus liquidis urget odoribus
grato, **Pyrrha**, *sub antro*?[75]

What slender boy soaked in liquid perfumes
presses upon you amid many roses,
Pyrrha, in a pleasant cave?

Word by word, the first line would read "What, many, slender, you, boy, in, roses" (literally, "rose"). The concentric syntax accentuates Pyrrha's being pressed upon by the boy amid his roses, squeezing the pronoun within what encompasses it. In the third line, Pyrrha's name similarly appears toward the middle of the line to suggest her being enclosed within a cave and within the boy's amorous and odiferous attention. Because English lacks case endings, it doesn't afford the interlacing of double hyperbaton, which appears ninety-two times in Horace's odes.[76] Not that anglophone poets haven't tried. An editor of *Horace in English* singles out Milton's version of the fifth ode, saying it's the only Horace translation that, as Goethe recommended, creates, beyond paraphrase or domestication, "something new, an amalgam of the foreign or alien and the native."[77] Claiming to render the poem "almost word for word … as near as the language will permit," Milton, who replicates something like one ring of the verbal garland, begins, "What slender youth bedewed with liquid odours."[78] But while Milton's translation has been said to come "close to achieving the impossible" and exemplifies the nourishment of one literary language by another in translation, English syntax cannot "allow for the mosaic effects of Horatian hyperbaton."[79] Pound complained that Milton failed to recognize that "the genius of English is not the genius of Latin, and that one can NOT write an uninflected language in the same way, using the same word-order that serves in an inflected language."[80] As R. G. M. Nisbet says of Horace: "The words interact as in a miniature physical system," and unlike the syntax of what he calls "the triteness and triviality of the usual English translations," "the interlocking produced by hyperbata helps to bolt the monument together."[81] Modern and contemporary poets in English, from Frost to Heaney, have absorbed the translatable judiciousness, balance, and terse wit of Horace's poetry, but there are some qualities of his verse that can't shine in English as in Latin.

T. S. Eliot, French, and (Un)Translatability

Because poetry is often wound around the intricacies of the language in which it is written, poets like Milton and Pound have paradoxically been inspired to create forms analogous to those of the source language they're translating, thereby creolizing and hybridizing the target language's poetics. As Pound's early collaborator, T. S. Eliot, put it in essays on translations of Greek, Latin, Chinese, French, and other literatures, which elaborate a subtle understanding of poetry translation, the interlingual engagements of translation can provide "enrichment" and "substantial nourishment to our language," "the transformation of language and sensibility," "the invention of a new form of verse," and "a criticism of one language by another, a fertilisation."[82] His own translation of Saint-John Perse's *Anabase*, or, as he indicates, H.D.'s translations from the Greek, can be seen as exemplifying such translational gains for the target language. But like Pound and Jakobson, Eliot both embraces the translator's art and warns that ultimately "there is no substitute, no *adequate* translation."[83] Although an effective translator may make us believe that we can "really at last get the original," that a poet "has been 'translated,'" such a thing is merely an "illusion" of "translucence"; "we *think* we are closer to the Chinese" or French or Greek, but this is an effect of the creative translator's skill.[84] Translations like *Cathay* successfully render a foreign poem in "the idiom of our own language and our own time," but translation is an ever-moving target: Pound created a free-verse translational idiom for his own age, but in each age poets must re-create the literature of the past for the present.[85]

As a poet whose work was translated into many different languages in his lifetime, Eliot was especially alert to these issues. Of course some features of his poetry must have proved translatable; otherwise, it couldn't have had such an enormous impact on poetry in many different languages—features such as its striking figurative language, sharp tonal shifts, multiple registers, embedded quotations, sordid urban landscapes, apocalypticism, religious comparativism, polyglossia, and alternations of free with rhymed and metered verse. Yet in an unpublished 1952 letter to one of his translators, he cannily remarks:

> I must say that the poems you have chosen strike me as the most untranslatable of all my verse, since they are the most purely lyrical and the effect and meaning depend so very much upon the particular arrangement of syllables which is found in the English. You have, on the whole, made a fairly close literal translation, although it seems to me, especially in the case of the first two, that the value of the poems evaporates completely, and must evaporate completely in any translation.[86]

By his own reckoning, Eliot's "lyrical" poems and passages embed meaning in, and create crucial effects by, their syllabic arrangements. To the extent that they yoke meaning and effect to specific verbal textures, the poetry of such poetry is untranslatable.

Given Eliot's skepticism toward the "illusion" of translation, his

musical use of language, and his sensitivity to the different literary sensibilities embedded in different languages, it's fitting that he quotes significant chunks of untranslated text in his code-switching poems. The
implication of his poetry's polyglossia, as of Pound's, is that there are
some aspects of the originals in German, French, Greek, Latin, Italian,
Sanskrit, and other languages that would be lost if they were translated into English. Macaronic and creolized texts, writes Haun Saussy,
"do not translate, but 'migrate,' their source languages to a new target
language; they cite, echo, cut, paste, recombine."[87] Even more remarkably, Eliot goes further and adopts a nonnative language of composition
for its peculiar resources and proclivities. Of poems by predominantly
English-language writers who make this leap, Milton's Latin poems are
among the most accomplished, and in the twentieth century, Eliot's
poems in French among the most interesting—poems Eliot regarded
well enough that he included them in his slender selected canon and left
them untranslated. We're used to asking whether Eliot should be considered a British or an American poet, but what of Eliot as a French poet?—
a notion that warps the geography of francophony and anglophony. And
what light might this example of writing in an adopted language shed on
questions of poetry, world literature, and (un)translatability? After publishing his first collection, *Prufrock and Other Observations*, Eliot felt he
had "dried up completely" as a poet.[88] Writing poems in French released
the blockage, enabling him to tap into his emotions because, as he wrote
to Paul Valéry, "votre langue me donne une certaine liberté d'esprit et
de sentiments que la langue anglaise me réfuse" (your language gives me
a certain freedom of mind and feeling that the English language denies
me).[89] Explaining why he lived in Paris in 1910–11, Eliot said, "Depuis plusieurs années, la France représentait surtout, à mes yeux, la *poésie*" (For
many years, France represented above all, in my eyes, *poetry*).[90] While the
French influence on Eliot's English poetry has often been examined—
Laforgue, Baudelaire, et al.—less attention has been paid to how Eliot's
own poems in French embrace French traditions and techniques built
up in the language over hundreds of years. One of his self-consciously
cosmopolitan but linguistically anchored poems allows us to consider
how language-specific literary practices afford another way of being
global that is missed by the gains-in-translation paradigm: the gains in
nontranslation.

In "Mélange Adultère de Tout" (1917), Eliot polymorphously assumes
various global identities:

En Amérique, professeur;	*In America, a professor;*
En Angleterre, journaliste. . . .[91]	*In England, a journalist. . . .*

In this self-mocking autobiography—more directly autobiographical than usual for the poet of impersonality—Eliot humorously catalogues the various roles he has assumed as a world-trotting cosmopolite, changing like a chameleon in response to each new environment:

En Yorkshire, conférencier;	*In Yorkshire, a lecturer;*
A Londres, un peu banquier. . . .	*In London, a bit of a banker. . . .*

Even as Eliot playfully enumerates his global identities, the poem's literary techniques enact his metamorphosis into a French poet. Long a resource in French poetry, the line-splitting hemistich structure of the medial caesura (even stronger in the *alexandrin*) helps Eliot mark structurally the turn from place to role with effects of suspension, humor, and symmetry. He follows French prosody in counting the silent or mute *e* before the caesura as a syllable (e.g., both "Amérique" and "Angleterre" are counted as four syllables) but not counting the final *e* at the end of the line ("journaliste" as only three syllables). Repeatedly eliding both subject and verb, Eliot may take advantage of what a book-length comparative linguistic analysis shows to be the lesser proclivity in French than in English for explicit verbals and for determinate relations among syntactic elements.[92]

Octosyllabic verse has also long been prominent in French poetry—a tradition influentially taken up by Théophile Gautier's *vers de société* in *Emaux et Camées*, a volume that enabled Pound and Eliot to shift from free verse to rhyming quatrains in the late nineteen teens. A theorist of French versification, Benoît de Cornulier, has even postulated what he calls "la loi des huit syllabes"—that in the French syllabic line, we can remember the duration and acoustic patterning of a maximum of eight syllables.[93] Eliot accentuates his poem's octosyllabics through enclosed, triplet, and Gautier-like alternating rhyme. The tighter, more replicative syllabic structure of French verse, as against the looser accentual structure of English poetry, works well for Eliot's wryly snappy catalogue of his diverse occupations.

These job descriptors take a sportive turn in the middle of the poem, when Eliot names his French identity:

| C'est à Paris que je me coiffe | It's in Paris that I sport |
| Casque noir de jemenfoutiste. | The black beret of an I-don't-give-a-damn guy. |

"Jemenfoutiste"—a vulgarity compounded of four words—is obviously not an occupation in the same way as is a professor, a journalist, or a banker. Because it names Eliot's French self, it implicitly comes closest to the poem's adopted French mask. Indeed, in the poem, the poet takes on and off various masks, hats, or berets, if you will, but this activity is itself troped as not-giving-a-damn French insouciance. Elsewhere, Eliot suggests that a cosmopolite's mobile identity can be corrupt and potentially dangerous, as in the anti-Semitic portrait of a Jewish landlord, "Spawned in some estaminet of Antwerp, / Blistered in Brussels, patched and peeled in London," or of Bleistein, "Chicago Semite Viennese," in two poems that bizarrely coexist in the same volume with the French poems.[94] As Mark Jeffreys puts it, "Eliot's horror of the composite self coexisted with a keen desire to make of it, for himself at least, something that transcended ordinary, unified personality."[95]

Despite this fear, Eliot's French mask enables him to romp through a zanily arrayed series of easily adopted and abandoned selves. The contrast is sharp, for example, between the poet as French *jemenfoutiste* and his ponderous German self:

En Allemagne, philosophe	In Germany, a philosopher
Surexcité par Emporheben	Overcome by Exaltation,
Au grand air de Bergsteigleben. . . .	With the air of a mountaineer. . . .

Unlike in its likeness to the French compound *jemenfoutiste*, the intrusively German polysyllabic word *Emporheben* is wittily made to rhyme with *Bergsteigleben*, as if doing Hegelian philosophy were like scaling craggy abstractions. The Germanness of the German compound words, emphasized by a hypermetrical extension to nine syllables ("Surexcité par Emporheben"), seems jocular within the light swift rhythms and dandyish *jemenfoutisme* of the poem's octosyllabic French.[96] The tone is even more frolicsome in the ensuing triple rhyme and nonsense syllables:

J'erre toujours de-ci de-là	I wander always from here to there
A divers coups de tra là là	With diverse breaks for tra la la
De Damas jusqu' à Omaha.	From Damascus to Omaha.

Here, instead of a single location, the poeticity-riding versifier extends across continents. But from this peak of levity, the poem turns somber as it ventures to Africa, and from present tense to future, imagining the speaker's cenotaph displayed on the hot coasts of Mozambique, a place that promises the ultimate evacuation of identity, as the final line deliquesces to ten syllables (counting the mute *e*'s):

On montrera mon cénotaph	*They will display my cenotaph*
Aux côtes brûlantes de	*On the burning coasts of*
Mozambique.	* Mozambique.*

As Michael North puts it, "wayward and free, the speaker gravitates toward Africa, which is in this sense the place of placelessness."[97] Eliot distills and reactivates a primitivist cultural stereotype, far grimmer than French drollery or German ponderousness. Although he skids lightly among localized identities in Europe and America, to follow Rimbaud into Africa is to risk the ultimate dissolution of the Western subject. Jewish cosmopolitanism and African subjectivity mark the outer limits to Eliot's costume-shuffling globalism—limits that enable the rapid-fire circulation they help make imaginable and yet threaten. Even so, it is notable that it is in writing in a nonnative language with its specific literary techniques and possibilities that Eliot most boisterously performs his globally intersecting identities. In its carnivalesque play amid multiple selves, this is a world poem; but it's the specific formal possibilities of French poetry that enable Eliot to spin his lyric globe. Our models of world poetry should be as attentive as poets are to the distinctive literary conventions encoded in different language traditions, even when poets are consciously adopting and not more directly inheriting them.

To Domesticate, to Foreignize, or . . . ?

Although I've been skirting the normative questions that dominate discussions of poetry translation, maybe the implications of such an approach are worth spelling out briefly. Is a target-oriented or source-oriented translation of poetry to be preferred? Should a poetry translation be domesticating or defamiliarizing? Such polarities, as we've seen, oversimplify. Excessively domesticating translations can bleach a poem of its particularities, but excessively foreignizing translations can rob it of pleasure. Overly domesticating Western translations of Rumi miss out on the opportunity to disrupt widespread assumptions about

Islamic zealotry and intolerance, but overly foreignizing translations might risk consigning Rumi to exotic unfamiliarity. As Mark Polizzotti indicates, the production of "even less approachable translations" would only exacerbate the low interest in translated books in North America.[98] So too in African contexts Evan Maina Mwangi observes that, pace much postcolonial theory, fluent translations aren't necessarily colonialist, and "foreignizing translations might entrench oppressive practices and thought."[99] It seems unwise to try to resolve this question a priori, since the range of difficulties and opportunities in poetry translation varies widely, depending on the texts, languages, and power asymmetries involved. With a poet like Behbahani, who is little known in the West, a sensitive target-oriented translation practice that focuses on imagery, tone, and rhetorical strategy might be most effective in conveying something of her poetry to readers in translation. Or it may be, as Eliot argued, that in "introducing a poem to the English-speaking public," as he did Perse's *Anabase*, greater "liberties" might be warranted to engage the reader, while later, "a more literal translation" could be appropriate.[100]

Hybrid foreignizing-domesticating strategies, moreover, are possible. In the *West-östlicher Divan*, Goethe was already proposing a kind of translation that would amalgamate features of both the translating and the translated text.[101] Even a target-oriented translation can, without overdoing the foreignness of the foreign poem, occasionally remind readers of the "remainders" of translation—a word, a technique, a sonority that doesn't carry across—or of the embeddedness of the translator in a particular cultural context.[102] Such is the effect in Heaney's *Beowulf* of "a bleeper" like the previously cited Northern Irish word *thole*: the etymological linkage to Old English reminds the reader of the translator's (and also the reader's) cultural locatedness.[103] Interlingual code-switching can also function as such a bleeper, as in Ugandan Okot p'Bitek's embedding of Acholi and semitranslated words in his code-switching English self-translation of *Song of Lawino*.[104] Venuti highlights a translation's capacity to "cultivate a heterogeneous discourse, opening up the standard dialect and literary canons to what is foreign to themselves, to the substandard and the marginal."[105] A recent carnivalesque example is Daljit Nagra's heteroglot retelling of the *Ramayana* (2013), which draws on a dizzying variety of South and Southeast Asian versions of the epic poem and, in leaps from low to high, slang to magisterial English, as well as typographical play with shifting fonts, breaks open the heterogeneity of the narratives and of the overlapping and colliding Englishes of the English language.[106] Translations like Heaney's, Okot's, and Nagra's confound the debate over whether it's more important to be true to the original's meanings or to the target culture's literary values, whether to produce a crib or a poem in its own right. As Karimi-Hakkak writes, we need to get beyond the "scholarly-versus-creative binary."[107] Both kinds of translations, and variations in between, have their uses and should more often be produced side by side.

According to Kwame Anthony Appiah, "what counts as a fine translation of a literary text—which is to say a taught text—is that it should preserve for us the features that make it worth teaching."[108] By this criterion, lyric poems would seldom qualify without comparative attention to the original, at least for those of us who think that to teach lyric poetry as poetry, you must attend to its intricacies. The exception might be works like FitzGerald's *Rubáiyát* (Appiah's example), Pound's *Cathay*, Eliot's *Anabasis*, Heaney's "Anything Can Happen," and others by Elizabeth Bishop, Robert Lowell, Kenneth Rexroth, Okot p'Bitek, A. K. Ramanujan, John Ashbery, and Anne Carson—the kind of translation that, in Appiah's words, "aims itself to be a literary work, a work worth teaching."[109]

Translational Poems on Translation: Agha Shahid Ali

To conclude this preliminary effort to nudge the discussion beyond the current polarization between world literature's advocates and detractors, between supporters and opponents of the untranslatability thesis, let's turn once more to what lyric poetry itself has to say on the subject of translation. Yet another ghazal speaks to issues of translatability, poetry, and world literature. Written by a Kashmir-born poet who was the leading proponent of the form in English and who wrote his dissertation on Eliot, Agha Shahid Ali's loosely patterned "Arabic" begins with a couplet that can be spun in either direction of the debate:

> The only language of loss left in the world is Arabic—
> These words were said to me in a language not Arabic.[110]

Against those supposing that languages are neutral technologies, the first line stakes a claim for the untranslatability of the grief in Arabic. It would seem to support the idea that some aspects of poetry, such as the *melopœia*, *logopœia*, syntax, and literary techniques peculiar to poems in German, Persian, Hmong, Vietnamese, Latin, French, and other languages, are lost in English translation. After all, more than a millennium before Frost, Eliot, Pound, or Jakobson, the Abbasid polymath al-Jahiz wrote:

> Excellence with regard to the art of poetry is limited to the Arabs and those who speak the Arabic language. Poetry cannot be translated and does not render itself to transmission. And whenever it is converted into another language its concinnity [*nazm*, harmony of elements] is broken, its meter is rendered defunct, its beauty evaporates, and that something that inspires wonder and admiration simply absents itself.[111]

Already in the early 800s, a literary critic was warning about what poetry loses in translation.

That said, like Pound, Eliot, and Jakobson, al-Jahiz, who praised the wisdom and eloquence of Persian literature, acknowledged that "some of these works have increased in excellence" in translation.[112] Indeed, the second line of Ali's ghazal sides with those who would emphasize interlingual transmissibility, since it wryly suggests that the speaker has learned something about Arabic's uniqueness in a language other than Arabic. As we've seen, some features of poetry can survive and even thrive in translation—*phanopœia*, narrative, poetic address, tonal shifts, epideixis, affectivity, not to mention fixed forms like the ghazal, haiku, *lục bát*, and octosyllabic line, all of which can be studied and taught in secondary languages. Ali rewrote "Arabic" as "In Arabic," a ghazal that now maintains the form's penultimate rhyme, or *qafia*—here, on *business/pitiless*. "In Arabic" mocks the poet's protestations on behalf of a language in a language other than itself:

> This much fuss about a language I don't know? So one day
> perfume from a dress may let you digress in Arabic.[113]

While the internal rhyme on "digress" may fulfill the *qafia*, it also echoes Eliot's "The Love Song of J. Alfred Prufrock" ("Is it perfume from a dress / That makes me so digress?") and so wryly stitches this particular expression of longing for Arabic even more tightly into English.[114]

"Arabic" and "In Arabic" champion the specificities and powers of Arabic: the language of Qur'anic prophecy, of Muslim prayers in many different countries, of literary traditions that range from the medieval *Laila and Majnoon* to the contemporary Darwish, and of poetic forms such as the ghazal and the *qasida*. Ali also praises the "delicate calligraphy" in Arabic that may ironically temper the anti-iconographic tradition it is supposed to foster, as in miniatures where it looks like "Kashmiri pais-leys tied into the golden hair of Arabic" (24). At the same time, Ali glances at how Arabic travels beyond Arabic, as we've seen in Rumi and Beh-bahani's poetic play on Arabic loan words, their allusions to the Qur'an and the hadith, and in their ghazals refashioned in the Persian tradition, which added to the ghazal's canonical form key features such as the *matla*, *takhallos*, and discrete *bayt*.[115] Displaying the profound stimulus to cre-ativity that is translation, Ali's poems on Arabic stray from a narrow focus on Arabic:

> When Lorca died, they left the balcony open and saw:
> his *qasidas* braided, on the horizon, into knots of Arabic. (24)

Along with the Spanish poet, the poem "Arabic" enlists an international and multilingual array of names, including Anton Shammas, the Pal-estinian poet, novelist, and translator who writes in Arabic but also in Hebrew, and the Israeli writer Yehuda Amichai, who pioneered collo-quial Hebrew in poetry. While centered on Arabic, this ghazal written in English by a poet who grew up in Kashmir, hearing Persian and Urdu poetry often quoted in his family home and speaking Arabic-peppered and Persian-infused Urdu, displays the transnational convergences enacted by "world" lyrics even when they live in their "local verbal tex-tures," themselves often translocated.[116] For all the differences between the languages in which poetry is written, these differences don't result in monadic isolation: it's ironically because of them that poets are drawn to mixing, bridging, re-creating, and translating them. Persian lyrics that resound with Arabic, Hmong tones in an English-language poem, English syntax stretched to mimic Latin, French adopted by an Anglo-American modernist for its peculiar freedoms, strictures, and techniques—these are among the interlingual braidings by which poetry verbally enacts the worldhood of the world.

Having named a variety of writers from other cultures, Ali ends "Arabic" with a *takhallos*, or poetic signature, that splits the poet's own name across two languages:

> They ask me to tell them what Shahid means—
> Listen: it means "The Beloved" in Persian, "witness" in Arabic. (25)

Although the concluding signature couplet would seem an opportu-nity for locating one's uniqueness in a unitary name, here a Kashmiri

American poet translates his name into English, only to cleave that supposed self-identity in two different languages, mediated by a third. It is as if he were himself the refractions of translation. With apologies for debasing a hallowed poetic convention in critical prose, perhaps I could conclude in the spirit of the ghazal's signature line. As someone whose given name, Jahan, is also a commonplace word in Persian for the "world," yet in English becomes a proper name only, I think we would do well to follow "Shahid," glorying in the untranslatable peculiarities and affordances of languages as illuminated by poetry, and at the same time embracing his suggestion that a language's signature capacities are often revealed in the interlingual junctures of translation. If we want a model of world literature that will be adequate to lyric poetry, it needs to incorporate the translingual emphasis on linguistic specificity in poems by Ali and other writers. With the help of a language-sensitive comparative poetics, perhaps the world of world literature can be made large enough to encompass and render visible both the translatables and the untranslatables of lyric poetry.

LYRIC POETRY: INTERGENERIC, TRANSNATIONAL, TRANSLINGUAL?

This book hasn't concerned only lyric poems; ballads, epics, long poems, found poems, antilyrics, and other kinds have also found a place. But from the Great War and modernism to postcolonial and contemporary, lyrics have been its mainstay. I conclude by drawing out some implications of my work—this book and, if I may, earlier ones—for thinking about lyric. As I mentioned in the introduction, the question of how to understand lyric's historical, generic, and cultural coordinates has been central to recent debates about poetry, and an epilogue seems an appropriate place for a synthesis and some fresh departures. I venture a series of postulates meant not to exhaust a large and complex subject but to open it up for further inquiry.

Is This a Lyric?

What is a lyric? Is it possible that you're reading a lyric right now? After all, I'm addressing "you," and such address has often been taken to be a key feature of lyric poetry. So too has apostrophe, and even though you're unlikely to be a tree or conceptual abstraction or dead person, for me you're not a real but a prospective reader. The potentially embarrassing artificiality of apostrophe and the intimacy of direct address have been seen as qualities that help distinguish lyric from other discourses.[1] You're not yet convinced?

What if I focus instead on the pronoun "I" that I've been using? Are you encountering a "lyric 'I'"? Like apostrophe and address, the use of the first person has long been seen as an integral feature of lyric.[2] Utterance of the feelings and thoughts of the lyric "I," unmediated by a narrator, is said to distinguish lyric from prose fiction. Still unpersuaded?

What if I told you that it's a rain-glittering spring morning, that as I rise I see the sun firing valley-folded ripples of fog? To the "you" and the "I," I've added some expressive language of thinking and feeling. I've also thrown in metaphor and alliteration, and both figures of thought and figures of sound are said to be key aspects of lyric. Not yet ready to refer this text to *Poetry* or the *New Yorker*?

> What if I broke
> my syntax into lines?—
> (that last one in pentameter, if the pieces make a line,
> or is that a mimetic enjambment with "broke,"
> the syntax swiveling from one line to the next . . . ?).
> Lineation is often seen as what makes poetry,
> or what poetry makes [*poiein*],
> though I could also list the groceries I'll buy
> after picking my son up from track practice:
> tomatoes
> cucumbers
> potatoes
> fish
> Is that lyric poetry, too?

Let's not forget brevity! Is this epilogue already too long to qualify as lyric? How short is short? How long is long? Should I end this reflection quickly, before it's too long to fit into an anthology?[3] And what of this text's self-reflexivity (did you note the mirrorlike reflection in the chiasmus "makes poetry / [. . .] poetry makes"?), its awareness of its own procedures and its rhetorical artifice, even if I can't claim with Horace, *exegi monumentum aere perennius*?[4]

Apostrophic "you," lyric "I," expressive language, figurative and sonic density, lineation, rhythmic patterning, brevity, self-reflexivity—aren't these the characteristics most frequently ascribed to lyric poetry? Perhaps, but as I've dramatized, no feature or features can define lyric, since they are not exclusive to it but are shared in varying degrees by other discourses. Hence Roman Jakobson coined the term "poetic function" for the verbal and formal weighting of medium over message—a function not limited to poetry though especially strong in it—and wryly compared poetry's boundaries with those of the Chinese empire.[5]

Does this mean there is no genre of lyric poetry? Is this exercise fodder for the varieties of genre skepticism, from Benedetto Croce's nominalism and Paul de Man's deconstruction to cultural studies' absorption of the literary into the nonliterary, and the historicist critique of "lyric" as an anachronistic projection? Perhaps, but in my view, poetics since Aristotle has usefully clarified how elements of genres work. I'd want to defend the idea that lyric has "affordances" or "tendencies," including those I've enumerated above.[6] But these characteristics don't simply inhere within texts; they can be seen as a shorthand for a formal-phenomenological matrix that includes the shaping presuppositions that cluster around them. A poetics of lyric is crucial but insufficient: it needs to be joined to a hermeneutics. Not a fixed constellation in the literary firmament, lyric is a changing set of conventions, schemata, and practices that writers and audiences bring to works, sometimes unconsciously—works that summon, resist, remix, defy, and remake those encoded presuppositions, or what we might call, after Hans Robert Jauss, horizons of lyric expectation.[7]

But if this is true of all genres, including film and the novel, painting and opera, then why is it lyric that so often comes in for especially corrosive critique? As a literary practice and as a critical paradigm, lyric has found itself on the defensive and even an object of shame.[8] After the waning of the New Criticism, some academics felt the well-wrought urn was too polished, too tightly sealed—an attitude personified in Gerald Graff's figure of the young, theoretically savvy professor who dismisses both lyric and what Virginia Jackson later terms "lyric reading" as elitist, undertheorized, and ahistorical.[9] Tumbling from the pinnacle it had enjoyed not only in the New Criticism but also in deconstruction (recall Shelley's centrality to the book *Deconstruction and Criticism*), lyric also endured opprobrium from some antilyric Language writers and conceptualists as politically repressive and ethically suspect.[10] Never mind that volumes from Lyn Hejinian's *My Life* (1980, 1987, 2002) to Susan Howe's *The Midnight* (2003) and Charles Bernstein's *Recalculating* (2013) are imbued with the personal and elegiac expressivity often attributed to lyric, and that even Kenneth Goldsmith hails the "moments of unanticipated beauty" in rhythmic, reframing, defamiliarizing poetry that obliquely "delivers emotion."[11] "Lyric" came to be seen as the name for the mystified poetic expression of personal feeiing in complicity with the privatist ideology of modern capitalism.

Theorizing Lyric

But in recent years, Anglo-American "new formalists" have been championing lyric to renovate literary aesthetics; "new lyric studies" critics have been applying historical methods to lyric meters and communities of reception; and European critics have been systematizing the theory of lyric. Perhaps the most far-reaching and ambitious recent effort to restore the category of lyric is Jonathan Culler's *Theory of the Lyric* (2015). Turning to Culler's landmark tome for preliminary help, I attempt to distill a handful of my ideas on the subject in dialogue with Culler's, while perhaps opening up fresh areas for exploration.

I welcome the transhistorical and comparative scope of Culler's capacious book, as well as his emphasis on lyric's apostrophic voicing, rhythmic patterning, extravagance, and irreducibility to mimesis. His theory represents an alternative to the New Critical model of lyric and to the new materialist models that have been supplanting it in the American academy. As I argued in the introduction, chapter 2, and elsewhere, because of lyric's thickness in mediating the world—its frequent compression, sonic richness, self-reflexive artifice, dense metaphoricity, long formal memory, and allusive layering—it has a highly complex relation to factual places and times, even when, as with loco-descriptive poetry, it may seem firmly grounded in a specific location at a particular moment.

Two main tendencies in lyric criticism come under fire in Culler's book. First, he resists the historicist discrediting of lyric, the idea that it's a mystified abstraction, showing that writers and their readers reactivate for their own time the lyric structures of the past. As Stephanie Burt puts it, there are "reasons to keep on using 'lyric' as a frame for a large, important and chronologically extended set of poems," even though conceptions of lyric have obviously changed over time.[12] Similarly, Eric Hayot criticizes what he calls "historicist fundamentalism," whether "produced in the name of cultural recognition and sensitivity" or "in the name of rigor and respect for historical difference"; "lyric" provides a useful comparative category, even though in certain times and languages there may be no exact equivalent to it.[13] Despite grounding and delimiting my readings historically, I agree with Culler, Burt, and Hayot, as someone who has traced how lyric subgenres such as elegy can survive in being severely remade: my first two books, *Yeats and the Poetry of Death* (1990) and *Poetry of Mourning* (1994), explore how modern and contemporary poets reanimate the elegy by making it less consolatory, more fiercely ambivalent.[14] My subsequent books, though limited to anglophony, also attempt to help widen the compass of lyric studies beyond the global North.

Second, developing ideas of Hegel's and Käte Hamburger's, Culler also shows that lyric is neither the merely personal gush of the author's feelings nor the dramatic soliloquy of a fictive persona—the latter presented by Culler as the predominant model of lyric articulation since the

New Criticism. I think Yeats put it cogently: a poet speaks not as "the bundle of accident and incoherence that sits down to breakfast"; "there is always a phantasmagoria."[15] Hence, a lyric is an iterable enunciation that readers or hearers can assume for themselves. Critics of various stripes have been converging on similar ideas, including Helen Vendler (lyric as abstracting the social so readers can adopt its "I"), Kendall Walton ("thoughtwriting" by analogy with ghostwriting), and Peter Hühn (the reader "can take over and imaginatively live through" the lyric "I").[16] Lyric becomes a script that readers or listeners performatively apply to themselves.

As indicated by this performance-centered model, one of Culler's strategies is to illuminate the qualities of lyric, paradoxically, by drawing connections between it and other genres and practices. After all, as we've seen, there are no lyric-exclusive characteristics. In Culler's book, as in other poetry criticism, lyric is often compared to ritual, song, riddles, charm, promises, and other genres and speech-acts. But as I argue in *Poetry and Its Others* (2014), we need to attend not only to the affinities but also to the differences and tensions between lyric and other closely related genres and discourses.[17] Within the ever-changing ecology of genres, lyric should be seen in terms of both its collaboration and its competition with its generic kin.

Take Culler's frequent claims that lyric is ritualistic.[18] Rebutting the novelization of lyric theory, Culler is right to emphasize lyric's iterability, rhythmic intensity, and memorability. But it is also important to consider the ways in which lyric poetry is not ritual (from the Latin *ritualis*, relating to religious ceremonies).[19] Although lyric may have roots in ritual and at times has performed ritual service, often it doesn't function as a prescribed practice, observance, or act subsumed to doctrine or collective belief. Rather, in much of its history it veers toward the idiosyncratic and strange, even when it's religiously inspired. And it tends to foreground its signifying function, its artifice and inventiveness, as Culler observes in *Structuralist Poetics*.[20] Lyric's frequent refusal to subordinate its verbal and imaginative energies to prescribed actions in the service of religious doctrine or cultural system has at times made it an object of suspicion: Too much self-reflexive play. Too much revelry in the materiality of the signifier. Too much delight in imaginative energy for its own sake. On the evidence of the sometimes contentious relationship I've traced between poetry and prayer especially but not exclusively under modernity, I infer that lyric is both ritualistic and anti- or at least metaritualistic, with examples sometimes tipping in one direction or the other.[21]

Similarly, Culler proposes song as a "model for thinking about this literary form," a link embedded in the word's etymology and in our current use of the word "lyrics" for words vocally performed to music.[22] But while lyric poetry more nearly resembles song, as well as ritual, than it does more mimetic genres like realist fiction, it has also diverged from song in various ways at various times, especially since the Renaissance. Across the twentieth century and now in the twenty-first, poetry has often competed with its musical counterpart, especially as recording technologies have made it easier to commodify and circulate song almost everywhere.[23] Many lyric poems aspire to the sonic qualities of song and what Culler calls its "memorability, ceremoniousness, harmony, charm,"[24] but others, such as concrete or heavily enjambed poems, emphasize their visuality on the page, or twist, like dense modernist texts, through complex involutions unconducive to song, or, like some avant-garde writing, deliberately interrupt or impede sonic fluency. Although Culler compares lyric to "the catchiness, the memorability" of song,[25] many poets struggle against the lodged-in-your-brain mnemonics of the pop song or the advertising jingle, seeking subtler forms of cognitive endurance. At least in modern and contemporary writing, poetry is both like and unlike song—a sister genre but also a rival and even antagonist.

For Culler, poetry also isn't mere pseudostatement, as emphasized by its epideictic roots, but a form of truth telling, and lyrics typically focus on the present.[26] But this position, while usefully resisting the fictionalization of lyric, may also be worthy of reexamination. Consider that, ever since the Industrial Revolution, maybe the most present-centered discourse of truth telling has been journalism. If we explore the fractious dialogue between lyric poems and the news, we discover that lyrics often enlist the present moment in patterns of recurrence, also insisting upon their artifice, materiality, and mediation, while undoing claims to objectivity. Even when they report on current events like the Easter Rising, the world wars, or 9/11, their allusive texture and long formal memory place the present in wider time horizons than those favored by quickly obsolescent newswriting.[27] It's only by virtue of their indirection, self-reflexivity, and dense artifice that lyrics tell the "news that STAYS news," to recall Ezra Pound.[28]

Thus far, I've hazarded the first handful of a dozen general claims about lyric: (1) *it can't be defined by one or even many formal features that are exclusive to it;* (2) *it can be described as a range of nonexclusive formal strategies encoded in texts and the communities that produce and receive them;* (3) *thus, if we understand "genre" in a way that fuses poetics with hermeneutics, lyric is a*

*genre; (4) lyric and affiliated subgenres and modes live historically but survive
transhistorically, albeit often dramatically refashioned; (5) lyric is neither merely
personal nor entirely impersonal, making it readily appropriable; (6) lyric differs
from more empirical and mimetic genres by virtue of the density of its verbal
and formal mediation of the world; (7) lyric is intergeneric, best understood in
its dialogue with its others.* In claiming that lyric is intergeneric, I depart
from Bakhtin's view of lyric poetry as monologic even as I endorse his
method for tracing literature's dialogic echoes, its compressed heteroglossia.[29] If we look closely enough, we can discern lyric's absorption
and refashioning of shards of alien discourses, albeit often transformed
almost beyond recognition. The dialogic poetics I've proposed has two
axes: along the vertical axis of poetics, we study lyric in relation to itself
and its literary genealogy, exploring how its specific (if shared) structures
work, including its deep memory of forms and words; at the same time,
along the horizontal axis of dialogic analysis, we trace how lyric often
implicitly defines itself in its affiliative and contentious relation to the
genres and discourses it both draws on and resists, such as news, obituaries, philosophy, the novel, the law, prayer, song, science, and—as seen
above—tourism.[30]

Transnational Lyric

Rethinking lyric as open to other discursive worlds by virtue of being
actively intergeneric, we should also conceptualize it as open to worlds
beyond nation, locality, region, or hemisphere. In brief, *(8) lyric is transnational.* Contrary to the long-held view of lyric as especially national or provincial, I argue in *The Hybrid Muse* (2001), *A Transnational Poetics* (2009),
and this book that lyric poetry is often a genre of transnational affiliation
and migration, of travel and hybridization.[31] Transnational approaches
to poetry can highlight what we might call both contacts and commonalities—that is, both literary flows and resistances across national borders (as in the diffusionist and "writes back" models examined in chapters 4 and 5), and global historical convergences and affinities across
discrepant spaces (as in the singular modernity model in chapter 4).
Tracking the migration of literary tropes, forms, subgenres, techniques,
and cultural ideas, we can explore how they are translocally redirected,
remade to address proximate circumstances. And even when there is no
direct influence, we can uncover connections that arise from shared historical experiences across national and even hemispheric lines—tourism,
for example, as a global practice. Under modernity, all writers swim in

global currents, even when imagining themselves as exclusively regional or national. With attention to the intricate intercultural melding and friction at the level of trope, stanza, rhyme, idiom, and sonic texture, a dialogically transnationalized, transregionalized, and translocalized lyric studies can thus help move us beyond (a) local and national models, in foregrounding how the local or national is traversed by translocalities, how nationalisms and nativisms are often reaction-formations to global flows; (b) civilizational models that hypostatize the "clash" of monolithic cultural blocs, as in Samuel Huntington's work;[32] (c) one-way models of globalization as westernization, such as Fredric Jameson's and Franco Moretti's;[33] (d) closed models of cross-cultural interaction, such as Edward Said's orientalist critique, according to which the West is seen as monolithically producing and managing the East, and the East is stripped of counterdiscourses and cultural agency—a paradigm meant to be complicated by this book's discussion of Yeats, Press, Goodison, and Nagra, as of other poets in *A Transnational Poetics*.[34]

This doesn't mean that the flows of lyric transnationalism are friction free. Indeed, unlike dance, the novel, architecture, music, painting, and many other art forms, lyric, as we've seen especially in the preceding chapter's discussion of translation, tends to be so tightly wound around the sonic, allusive, and formal structures of the language in which it's written as to impede its movement across languages, even as its relative brevity, vividness, and nonmimetic freedom enable transfers. Holding to the view that lyrics frequently remember other works written in the same language, I've focused much of this and my other books on anglophone poetry of the North Atlantic, Africa, India, the Caribbean, and the Pacific Islands. In so doing, I emphasize that (9) *lyric needs to be studied at both the micro and macro levels—both its language-specific intricacies and textures, and its participation in broader patterns of genre, history, and cultural migration.* As I've argued above and as this book's variegated methodology, zooming in and out, has attempted to demonstrate, distant reading in poetry studies benefits from combination with close, language-sensitive analysis.

Lyric across Languages

Even so, despite lyric's language specificities, (10) *the strategies of a transnational poetics can be extended across languages.* As we saw in the previous two chapters, far from being monolingual, as is commonly assumed, lyric has sometimes prospered in macaronic combinations, code-switching among languages it stitches together and skips between; the languages crossed and fused are far from being hermetically discrete; and the labor of translation and of writing in secondary languages has often been a prime stimulus to poetic creativity. Even when not overtly code-switching, poems are often shadowed and nourished, as we've seen, by other languages—Rumi by Arabic, Milton by Latin, Stevens and Eliot by French, Okot p'Bitek by Acholi, Heaney by Irish and Old English, and Ali by Urdu.[35]

In addition to micro-interlingualism within and across lyrics, at the macro level, an entire prosodic system is sometimes grafted from one language onto another. Writers and critics have perennially struggled to fit English accentual rhythms to the ill-suited model of feet in short and long syllables, the quantitative meters of classical antiquity. Such trans-lingual prosodic hybridization has also occurred outside the West. In the aftermath of the Muslim conquest in the seventh century, for example, Persian poetry adapted Arabic meters. Although it was long assumed that Persian-language poets copied the Arabic metrical system, scholars have shown that Persian poetry prosodically diverged from Arabic early on, at least partly because of phonetic differences and an indigenous literary history. Whereas the number of syllables in most Arabic meters is constant, for example, it varies significantly in Persian, and despite the overlapping prosodic taxonomy, some of the most widely used meters in Persian are rare or nonexistent in Arabic.[36]

Such differences reinforce the following tenet: (11) *a transnational poetics should be attentive to cross-cultural hybridization, creolization, and vernacularization.* To restrict the study of Persian poetry to the nation-state, despite its being written in a region extending from Turkey and Iran to Afghanistan and India, makes no more sense than to draw hard national boundaries around anglophone, sinophone, or hispanophone poetry. A Persian poet like Rumi, who was born in either modern-day Tajikistan or Afghanistan and traveled across much of the Muslim world before his death and burial in modern-day Turkey, is claimed, as we've seen, by several different countries in West and Central Asia, and is even a best-selling poet in the United States. Prenational long before it became national or postnational, what we now call lyric is much older than the nation-state, and its aesthetic forms have often outlasted the political forms they have been made to serve.

Like Persian, Chinese was a prestige language that spread widely: for hundreds of years, it was the language of administration and culture in Korea, Vietnam, and (to a lesser extent) Japan, with poetry, as in Per-

sianate cultures, seen as the highest form of expression, to the extent
that prospective civil servants were sometimes tested on their ability to
write poems that met strict formal requirements, as in China during the
Tang, Song, and Qing dynasties.[37] Chinese poetic forms diffused, but
they were also indigenized. The Vietnamese *song thất lục bát* that was formally diagrammed in the previous chapter—one of several lyric forms
(*oli, haiku, tanka, lüshi, ya-du, than-bauk, ghazal*, etc.) that I taught students
on a semester-long journey mostly along coastal Asia and Africa—is a
splendid example of this hybridization, in that it combines the indigenous Vietnamese *lục bát* ("six-eight" because of its alternation between
lines of six and eight syllables) with a Tang dynasty "double-seven" couplet, or *song thất*, drawn from the Chinese *lüshi*. In the intricately inter-
braided rhyme scheme of this Sino-Vietnamese quatrain, the last syllable
of alternating lines rhymes with the penultimate stressed syllable in the
following line. Although the uniform six-eight alternation of the *lục bát*
worked well for long narrative poems, it was, as Huỳnh Sanh Thông puts
it, "less desirable to poets who wanted to convey a welter of feelings and
emotions . . . , psychological moods and nuances."[38] The "asymmetrical
but regular configuration" of six-eight with double seven, the "tense yet
happy marriage between euphony and dissonance," helped make *song thất
lục bát* "one of the most expressive vehicles for poetry in the world," especially "the rendering of feelings and emotions in all their complexity, in
long lyrics."[39] Although Vietnamese poetry has often been a vehicle for
nationalist resistance and pride—witness the lyrics of Ho Chi Minh, or
"Uncle Ho," that Vietnamese schoolchildren can recite today (much of
it originally composed in Chinese)—its complex formal history, like that
of other kinds of lyric, tells a story of cross-cultural enmeshment across
boundaries of the nation.

In the West, where we frequently hear either critiques of lyric as ideological mystification, or laments for lyric as a dead and overinstitution-
alized art, a transnational perspective reveals that, on a global scale, (12)
lyric isn't dead, and it isn't only an elite form. However you may assess its
fortunes in the West (and the increasing interest in recent years suggests
that its death is greatly exaggerated), consider its central cultural role in
other parts of the world, such as those I've been discussing, as indicated
by samplings from *The Princeton Encyclopedia of Poetry and Poetics.* "Poetry
permeates all aspects of Vietnamese life and became the most important
medium of expression in Vietnamese society," begins one entry.[40] During
the Vietnam War, John Balaban wandered through the Vietnamese
countryside gathering *ca dao* that he would translate and anthologize—

"short lyric poems, passed down by word of mouth and sung without instrumental accompaniment by ordinary individuals."[41] As in Southeast and East Asia, so too in West Asia. "As the most prestigious form of verbal discourse and artistic expression in Persian culture," states another entry, "Poetry is traditionally the privileged form of verbal discourse and the preferred vehicle for the transmission of wisdom and knowledge."[42] (When I lived for a year in Iran as a schoolboy, I was astonished that even relatives of humble means could finish one another's quotations of medieval lyric poems.) Even with television and the electronic media, the tradition still lives. On a Persian poetry TV game show, you can watch a first-grader named Raha performing brilliantly as a contestant in a popular poetry game, *mosha'ereh* (مشاعره), in which a player takes the last letter of the previous person's quotation and begins another quotation with the same letter.[43] In another such game, she instantly responds to the prompts of the Persian words for "flame," "poppy," "wind," "orchard," "trust," "desert," "mirror," "apple," "realm," and "tree" with a classic *bayt* (بیت), loosely a couplet, that includes them.

As Alexander Beecroft notes, "for much of the early modern period, Persian was in fact the prestige language for literary composition in much of the Arabophone world."[44] Notwithstanding current political tensions between Iran and states across the Persian Gulf, there, too, as in the rest of the Arab world, lyric poetry has long prospered. "Until relatively recently," according to yet another entry in *The Princeton Encyclopedia of Poetry and Poetics*, "poetry has served as the predominant mode of literary expression among those who speak and write in Arabic . . . ; poets had and continue to have a particular status in their own community."[45] Like poetry elsewhere, Arabic lyric poetry may have recently suffered some decline in status. But if TV is again any indication, it has hardly slipped into insignificance. A show taped in Abu Dhabi since 2006, *Million's Poet* has had an audience of up to 70 million.[46] Poet participants recite lyrics they've written in an Arab dialect to compete for a prize worth more than a million dollars. So much for the idea that lyric poetry is dead, or is an illusory construct of the West. Indeed, with an incentive like that, maybe it's worth reopening the question of which texts we write could be considered lyric poems.

"The global" as it has been used in this book hasn't aspired to and would obviously fall short of anything like an all-encompassing perspective on lyric and other kinds of poetry, of the sort that critics such as Jonathan Culler and Earl Miner have propounded.[47] Yet neither should poetry studies, even if historically and linguistically centered, be overly restrictive in its scope. Even as it stays attuned to local histories and specific languages, the field also needs to draw inspiration from, and contribute to, world literary studies, global studies, transnational studies, world anglophone studies, and postcolonial studies, if it's to prosper in the coming decades. I have attempted to read lyric and other kinds of poetry in relation to differently located and historically situated varieties of globality—the compassionate, cross-national solidarities in First World War poetry, the radial extensions of the glocal poem, the meta-touristic imaginative travel in lyrics and poetic sequences, the post-colonization of specific modernist inheritances, the modern transplantation of local and global forms, Yeats's orientalist and anti-orientalist excursions, Stevens's eco-cosmopolitanism, the globe-sprung reach of Heaney's translocal imaginings, the code-switching and -skipping techniques from modernist to contemporary poetry, and lyric's (un)translatable permeabilities and impermeabilities. As I hope these assorted expeditions into a vast terrain have suggested, poetry's polyspatiality and polytemporality have enabled it to thrive amid the challenges of our global age.

ACKNOWLEDGMENTS

Many people contributed to the making of this book. I have continually learned from my spirited and inspiring students at the University of Virginia. My colleagues have provided me with an open, nourishing, and stimulating intellectual community. I could not have wished for a more sharp-eyed, poetry-attentive reader than Herbert Tucker, who scrupulously combed through the manuscript and made brilliant suggestions. Peter Miller and Jordan Burke provided superb research assistance; I feel lucky to have benefited from their quick and rigorous labors. Sam Walker carefully checked notes at the eleventh hour. Michael Suarez shared astute pointers on book history, Mary Kuhn on ecocriticism, Carmen Lamas on Latinx terms, Eric Ramírez-Weaver on Byzantine art history, and John Miller on Latin poetry. Valuable insights into Persian poetry and poetics came from Farzaneh Milani, Shankar Nair, Jane Mikkelson, Ahmad Karimi-Hakkak, Houchang Chehabi, Abbas Milani, Mojtaba Rouhandeh, Sajedeh Hosseini, and Marie Ostby. The stimulus of two teaching journeys around the world on Semester at Sea, happily made possible by deans Bob Chapel and Victor Luftig, has proved abiding. Over years of writing, Cynthia Wall, Stephen Arata, and John O'Brien have been terrifically supportive department chairs. My dean, Ian Baucom, and my president, Jim Ryan, exemplify the best in academic administration; I thank them both, as well as Jim's predecessor, Terry Sullivan, for their leadership and all they have done to sustain my work. Two anonymous readers provided excellent guidance for strengthening and refining the book: I am grateful for the time, energy, and wisdom they brought to the task. Alan Thomas is a dream editor—shrewd, tough minded, yet kindly cheering—and Randy Petilos expertly oversaw the metamorphosis of the manuscript into a book.

I also feel enormous gratitude for my family's emotional and intellectual sustenance. Generously reading chapter drafts, Caroline Rody has unstintingly encouraged me and, with welcome candor, has lit up pathways for developing and enriching my work in more ways than I can say. She and our beloved boys, Cyrus and Gabriel, have been my constant companions in living, loving, and thinking, year after year. My mother, Nesta, and my late father, Ruhi, immigrants from Iran who exposed me to global politics, culture, and languages, provided vast reserves of support. And my brother Vaheed drew on his deep knowledge of French literature to edify and reassure me on several points.

Generous hosts gave me the opportunity to test-drive and fine-tune parts of this book in lectures and seminars. I thank them for the abundantly stimulating occasions they made possible: Jernej Habjan for the conference "Globalizing Literary Genres" at LMU Munich; Youngmin Kim for the conference of the English Language and Literature Association of Korea at Sookmyung Women's University, Seoul; Fran Brearton for the Seamus Heaney Commemoration and Conference at Queen's University, Belfast; Lucy Alford, Caroline Egan, Julia Noble, and Roland Greene for the Poetics Workshop at Stanford University; Ali Behdad for the Mellon symposium "Teaching Poetry in a Global Age" at the University of California, Los Angeles; Stefan Helgesson for The Higher Literary Seminar at Stockholm University; Allan Hepburn, Maggie Kilgour, and Derek Nystrom at McGill University; Eric Hayot for the Comparative Literature series at Pennsylvania State University; Santanu Das and Kate McLoughlin for the British Academy conference "The First World War: Literature, Culture, Modernity" in London; Mark Byron for the Transnational Modernisms conference, organized by the Australasian Modernist Studies Network and the Transnationalism and Literature Project at the University of Sydney; Priya Joshi for the roundtable "English, British, Anglophone: What's in a Name?" at the Modern Language Association Convention; Vered Karti Shemtov, Anat Weisman, Amir Eshel, and Giddon Ticotsky for the conference "Spoken Word, Written Word: Rethinking the Representation of Speech in Literature" at Stanford University; Justin Quinn at the Charles University in Prague; Pavlína Flajšarová and Jiří Flajšar for the EU Project on Interdisciplinary Innovation in Culture Studies at Palacky University, Olomouc, Czech Republic; John McAuliffe for the John Edward Taylor Lecture at the University of Manchester, England; Matthew Campbell for the Derek Attridge conference at the University of York, England; Diederik Oostdijk for the symposium "Studying Transnational Poetics: Practices and Methods" at VU

University, Amsterdam; Francesca Fiorani and Raffaele Laudani for the Summer School in Global Studies and Critical Theory at the University of Bologna; Lee Jenkins for the "Irish-Caribbean Connections" conference at the University College Cork; Claire Connolly for the conference of the International Association for the Study of Irish Literatures at University College Cork; Christine Gerhardt and Judith Rauscher for the conference "The Environment and Human Migration: Rethinking the Politics of Poetry" at the University of Bamberg; Seán Golden for the conference "Yeats and Asia" of the International Yeats Society at the Autonomous University of Barcelona; Carrie Bramen and Chris Gair for the Symbiosis conference at the State University of New York at Buffalo and Daemen College; Andrew Goldstone and Anjali Nerlekar for the Modernism and Globalization Research Group of Rutgers University and the New York–New Jersey Modernism Seminar of Rutgers University and Columbia University; Akshya Saxena for the Trans-Area Literature Collective at Vanderbilt University; Martin Hägglund for Comparative Literature and Brandon Menke and Langdon Hammer for the 20th- and 21st-Century Studies Colloquium at Yale University; Abbas Milani for the Moghadam Program in Iranian Studies at Stanford University; Peter Kalliney for the roundtable "Literary History after the Nation?" at the MLA Convention; Dominique Jullien and Dustin Lovett for the Graduate Center for Literary Research's Comparative Literature conference "Borderlines" at the University of California, Santa Barbara; Will Waters for the Literary Translation Seminar Lecture Series in Romance Languages and for the conference "Situating Lyric" of the International Network for the Study of Lyric, both at Boston University; Srikanth Reddy, Michael Rutherglen, and Lucy Alford for the History and Forms of Lyric Series and the Poetry and Poetics Workshop at the University of Chicago; Henghameh Saroukhani and Mariam Pirbhai for the Congress of the Canadian Association for Commonwealth Literature and Language Studies in Regina, Canada; Bart Eeckhout and Gül Bilge Han for the conference "Wallace Stevens as World Literature" at Stockholm University; Frances Dickey for the T. S. Eliot Society conference in Rapallo; Lauren Arrington, Matthew Campbell, and Geraldine Higgins at the W. B. Yeats International Summer School; Anthony Cuda, Ronald Schuchard, and Gail McDonald at the T. S. Eliot International Summer School; Zach Ludington and Margo Lukens for the McGillicuddy Humanities Center Annual Symposium at the University of Maine; Joe Fritsch, Tesla Cariani, and Nathan Suhr-Sytsma for the Kemp Malone Lecture at Emory University; Zoey Dorman, Talin Tahajian, Yopie Prins, and Gillian White for the Poetry and Poetics Workshop at the University of Michigan; Antonio Rodriguez and Rachel Falconer for the conference "The Between-ness of Lyric / L'entre-deux lyrique" of the International Network for the Study of Lyric at the University of Lausanne; Andrew McGowan for the W. B. Yeats Society of New York; and David Hobbs for the Modern and Contemporary Colloquium at New York University with respondents Alliya Dagman, Kristin Grogan (Rutgers), and Tiana Reid (Columbia). At conferences at the University of Virginia, Debjani Ganguly, Farzaneh Milani, Annie Galvin, Jesse Bordwin, Cherrie Kwok, and Andrew Stauffer also gave me opportunities to try out and receive feedback on my work.

In addition, I wish to express my thanks to editors and publishers for their invitations to compose—and for their helpful responses to—essays that they published in earlier form, all of which were written with this book in mind: chapter 6 in Lauren Arrington and Matthew Campbell, eds., *The Oxford Handbook of W. B. Yeats* (Oxford: Oxford University Press, forthcoming), and in Seán Golden, ed., *Yeats and Asia* (Cork: Cork University Press, forthcoming); chapter 10 in Debjani Ganguly, ed., *The Cambridge History of World Literature* (Cambridge: Cambridge University Press, forthcoming), with parts of it in Jonathan Hart and Ming Xie, eds., "World Poetics, Comparative Poetics," special issue, *University of Toronto Quarterly* 88, no. 2 (2019): 210–28; the epilogue in "Lyric: Words and Worlds," special issue, *Journal of Literary Theory* 11, no. 1 (2017): 97–107; chapter 2 in *Critical Inquiry* 43, no. 3 (Spring 2017): 670–96, © 2017 by The University of Chicago, all rights reserved; chapter 5 in Eric Hayot and Rebecca Walkowitz, eds., *A New Vocabulary for Global Modernism* (New York: Columbia University Press, 2016), 114–29; a few pages of the introduction in "Lines and Circles: Transnationalizing American Poetry Studies," *American Literary History* 28, no. 2 (2016): 308–14, published by Oxford University Press; chapter 9 in *Dibur Literary Journal*, issue 1 (Fall 2015): 29–42, with a few sentences in *New Literary History* 50, no. 4 (Fall 2019): vii–xxxviii, Copyright © 2019 The Johns Hopkins University Press; chapter 4 in Alex Davis and Lee M. Jenkins, eds., *A History of Modernist Poetry* (Cambridge: Cambridge University Press, 2015), 459–78; chapter 8 in the *Irish Review* 49–50 (2015): 38–53, and subsequently in *Irish Pages* 9, no. 1 (2015): 90–106; chapter 1 in *Modernism/modernity* 23, no. 4 (November 2016): 855–74, Copyright © 2016 The Johns Hopkins University Press, and in a different version in Santanu Das and Kate McLoughlin, eds., *The First World War: Literature, Culture, Modernity* (Oxford: Oxford University Press/British Academy, 2018), 175–96, by permission of the British Academy; and chapter 3 in *New Literary History* 46, no. 3 (Summer 2015): 459–83, Copyright © 2015 The Johns Hopkins University Press. I am also grateful for permission to quote from T. S. Eliot's unpublished letter to R. P. Jean Mambrino, SJ, copyright © the Estate of T. S. Eliot.

NOTES

Introduction

1. Leonard E. Read, "I, Pencil: My Family Tree as Told to Leonard E. Read" (1958), Library of Economics and Liberty (1999), http://www.econlib.org/library/Essays/rdPncl1.html.

2. Stevie Smith, "The Frog Prince," in *New Selected Poems of Stevie Smith* (New York: New Directions, 1988), 95; Frances Cornford, "She Warns Him," in *Selected Poems* (London: Enitharmon Press, 1996), 15; and John Banister Tabb, "The Lake," in *Poems by John B Tabb* (Boston: Copeland and Day, 1894), 38.

3. Karl Marx and Friedrich Engels, *The Communist Manifesto*, ed. Jeffrey C. Isaac, trans. Samuel Moore [1888] (New Haven: Yale University Press, 2012), 77; *Das Kommunistische Manifest* (Leipzig: Verlag der Expedition des "Volksstaat," 1872), 7–8.

4. Eric Nelson, "Global Supply Chains Explained ... in One Graphic," US Chamber of Commerce, May 2, 2016, https://www.uschamber.com/series/above-the-fold/global-supply-chains-explained-one-graphic.

5. Arjun Appadurai, *Modernity at Large: Cultural Dimensions of Globalization* (Minneapolis: University of Minnesota Press, 1996), 42, 34.

6. William Carlos Williams, introduction to *The Wedge*, in *Collected Poems*, ed. Christopher MacGowan (New York: New Directions, 1988), 2:54.

7. Bruno Latour, *We Have Never Been Modern*, trans. Catherine Porter (Cambridge, MA: Harvard University Press, 1993), 75. In place of this translation's "DIY expert," I have substituted the original's *bricoleur*; see Bruno Latour, *Nous n'avons jamais été modernes: Essai d'anthropologie symétrique* (Paris: Éditions La Découverte, 1991), 102.

8. Bruno Latour, *Reassembling the Social: An Introduction to Actor-Network-Theory* (Oxford: Oxford University Press, 2005), 222, 223.

9. Jonathan Culler, *Theory of the Lyric* (Cambridge, MA: Harvard University Press, 2015); Virginia Jackson, *Dickinson's Misery: A Theory of Lyric Reading* (Princeton, NJ: Princeton University Press, 2005).

10. Latour, *We Have Never Been Modern*, 74.

11. Bruno Latour, "Morality and Technology: The End of the Means," trans. Couze Venn, *Theory, Culture & Society* 19, nos. 5–6 (2002): 249; "La fin des moyens," *Réseaux* 18, no. 100 (2000): 43.

12. Also pertinent here is global or transnational book history; see, e.g., *The Book: A Global History*, ed. Michael F. Suarez and H. R. Woudhuysen (Oxford: Oxford University Press, 2013), and *New World Order: Transnational Themes in Book History*, ed. Swapan Chakravorty and Abhijit Gupta (Delhi: Worldview, 2011).

13. Latour, "Morality and Technology, 249; "La fin des moyens," 43.

14. In this instance, Latour is describing a lecture hall; see his *Reassembling the Social*, 200.

15. Matt Rasmussen, "Reverse Suicide," in *Black Aperture* (Baton Rouge, LA: Louisiana State University Press, 2013), 61; ensuing quotes are from this page.

16. Gerard Manley Hopkins, "Spring and Fall," in *The Poetical Works of Gerard Manley Hopkins*, ed. Norman H. MacKenzie (Oxford: Clarendon-Oxford University Press, 1990), 166. For the Hardy examples, see C. H. Salter, "Unusual Words Beginning with 'Un, En, Out, Up' and 'On' in Thomas Hardy's Verse," *Victorian Poetry* 11, no. 3 (1973): 257.

17. See Jahan Ramazani, *Poetry and Its Others: News, Prayer, Song, and the Dialogue of Genres* (Chicago: University of Chicago Press, 2014).

18. See Jahan Ramazani, *Poetry of Mourning: The Modern Elegy from Hardy to Heaney* (Chicago: University of Chicago Press, 1994).

19. See the recent discussion of poetic diction in James Longenbach, *How Poems Get Made* (New York: W. W. Norton, 2018), chap. 2, 15–26.

20. After a dearth of attention, postcolonial poetry has recently been the subject of a number of valuable studies, including Robert Stilling, *Beginning at the End: Decadence, Modernism, and Postcolonial Poetry* (Cambridge, MA: Harvard University Press, 2018); Nathan Suhr-Sytsma, *Poetry, Print, and the Making of Postcolonial Literature* (Cambridge: Cambridge University Press, 2017); and Omaar Hena, *Global Anglophone Poetry: Literary Form and Social Critique in Walcott, Muldoon, de Kok, and Nagra* (New York: Palgrave Macmillan, 2015). It is also the subject, including two examples cited below, of my book *The Hybrid Muse: Postcolonial Poetry in English* (Chicago: University of Chicago Press, 2001) and the essays I gathered in *A Cambridge Companion to Postcolonial Poetry* (Cambridge: Cambridge University Press, 2017).

21. Vahni Capildeo, "Heirloom Rose, for Maya," in *Venus as a Bear* (Manchester, UK: Carcanet, 2018), 77–78.

22. Federal Trade Commission, "Complying with the Made in USA Standard," accessed February 8, 2020, https://www.ftc.gov/tips-advice/business-center/guidance/complying-made-usa-standard. The National Book Foundation considers exceptions for those living in the United States and aspiring to American citizenship; see National Book Foundation, "Deadlines and Guidelines," accessed February 8, 2020, https://www.nationalbook.org/national-book-awards/submissions/.

23. Terrance Hayes, *American Sonnets for My Past and Future Assassin* (New York: Penguin, 2018).

24. Wendell V. Harris, "What Is Literary History?" *College English* 56, no. 4 (1994): 444, 445. On postnational literary history, see the special issue "Literary History after the Nation?," ed. Peter Kalliney, *MLQ* 80, no. 4 (2019).

25. See the note above for recent books on postcolonial poetry. Recent examples of

transnational poetics focused on modern and contemporary poetry include Eric Falci, *The Value of Poetry* (Cambridge: Cambridge University Press, 2020); Lucy Alford, *Forms of Poetic Attention* (New York: Columbia University Press, 2020); Jacob Edmond, *Make It the Same: Poetry in the Age of Global Media* (New York: Columbia University Press, 2019); Walt Hunter, *Forms of a World: Contemporary Poetry and the Making of Globalization* (New York: Fordham University Press, 2019); Rachel Galvin, *News of War: Civilian Poetry 1936–1945* (Oxford: Oxford University Press, 2018); Harris Feinsod, *The Poetry of the Americas: From Good Neighbors to Countercultures* (Oxford: Oxford University Press, 2017); Janet Neigh, *Recalling Recitation in the Americas: Borderless Curriculum, Performance Poetry, and Reading* (Toronto: University of Toronto Press, 2017); and Sonya Posmentier, *Cultivation and Catastrophe: The Lyric Ecology of Modern Black Literature* (Baltimore: Johns Hopkins University Press, 2017).

26. See Juliana Spahr, *Du Bois's Telegram: Literary Resistance and State Containment* (Cambridge, MA: Harvard University Press, 2018), 10, 25.

27. Latour, *Reassembling the Social*, 219.

28. Terrance Hayes, "How to Draw a Perfect Circle," in *How to Be Drawn* (New York: Penguin, 2015), 90.

29. See Cara Buckley, "Transit Officer Is Stabbed in Queens," *New York Times*, July 12, 2012, http://cityroom.blogs.nytimes.com/2012/07/04/officer-is-stabbed-in-queens/?_r=0.

30. Hayes, *How to Be Drawn*, 91.

31. Hayes, *How to Be Drawn*, 90.

32. Hayes, *How to Be Drawn*, 93.

33. See Appadurai, *Modernity at Large*; I draw here on the definition of globalization by David Held et al., *Global Transformations: Politics, Economics, and Culture* (Stanford: Stanford University Press, 1999), 2. For a popular journalistic account, see Thomas Friedman, *The World Is Flat* (New York: Farrar, Straus and Giroux, 2005).

34. See Thomas Hylland Eriksen, *Globalization: The Key Concepts* (Oxford: Berg, 2007), 3–4, 10–11, and Manfred B. Steger, *The Rise of the Global Imaginary: Political Ideologies from the French Revolution to the Global War on Terror* (Oxford: Oxford University Press, 2008), 180. On time-space compression, see David Harvey, *The Condition of Postmodernity* (Oxford: Blackwell, 1989), 260–307.

35. Digital poems would also include computer-generated sonnets and haiku, multimedia and hypertext poems, and visual and kinetic poems, thus far mainly in the so-called First World. For a taxonomy of digital forms, see Leonardo Flores, "Digital Poetry," in *The Johns Hopkins Guide to Digital Media*, ed. Marie-Laure Ryan, Lori Emerson, and Benjamin J. Robertson (Baltimore: Johns Hopkins University Press, 2014), 155–61. Perhaps the most famous example of visual and kinetic poetry is Brian Kim Stefans's swirling abecedarius, *the dreamlife of letters*, accessed February 8, 2020, http://collection.eliterature.org/1/works/stefans__the_dreamlife_of_letters/dreamlife_index.html, discussed in Marjorie Perloff, "Screening the Page/Paging the Screen: Digital Poetics and the Differential Text," in *New Media Poetics: Contexts, Technotexts, and Theories*, ed. Adalaide Morris and Thomas Swiss (Cambridge, MA: MIT Press, 2006): 143–64.

36. See Marjorie Perloff, "Screening the Page/Paging the Screen," and her *Unoriginal Genius: Poetry by Other Means in the New Century* (Chicago: University of Chicago Press, 2010), xi, and Jessica Pressman, *Digital Modernism: Making It New in New Media* (New York: Oxford University Press, 2014).

37. Kenneth Goldsmith, "Post-Internet Poetry Comes of Age," *New Yorker*, March 10, 2015 https://www.newyorker.com/books/page-turner/post-internet-poetry-comes-of-age.

38. While celebrating the "renaissance" afforded by digital publishing, the founder of the Nigerian digital magazine *Saraba*, Dami Ajayi, remarked in 2017, when he announced the journal's first print issue, "we are moving, as it were, into the international space—upping our game, so to speak," as if print were paradoxically conceived as more global than digital platforms. See Kọ́lá Túbọ̀sún, "Each Collection Dictates Its Own Process: Conversation with Dami Ajayi," October 12, 2017, in *This is Africa*, accessed February 7, 2019, https://thisisafrica.me/lifestyle/each-collection-dictates-its-own-process-conversation-with-dami-ajayi/. On the Swahili remediation of older poetic forms in a digital social network, see Meg Arenberg, "The Digital *Ukumbi*: New Terrains in Swahili Identity and Poetic Dialogue," *PMLA* 131, no. 5 (2016): 1344–60.

39. Gayatri Chakravorty Spivak, *Death of a Discipline* (New York: Columbia University Press, 2003), 72.

40. Spivak, *Death of a Discipline* 72.

41. See, e.g., Lynn Hunt, *Writing History in the Global Era* (New York: W. W. Norton, 2014), 129; Lui Hebron and John F. Stack Jr., *Globalization: Debunking the Myths*, 3rd ed. (Lanham, MD: Rowman & Littlefield, 2017), 2; Adam McKeown, "Periodizing Globalization," *History Workshop Journal*, no. 63 (2007): 224; and A. G. Hopkins, "The History of Globalization—and the Globalization of History?" in *Globalization in World History*, ed. A. G. Hopkins (New York: W. W. Norton, 2002), 19.

42. Sebastian Conrad, *What Is Global History?* (Princeton: Princeton University Press, 2016), 100, 108. Similarly, Hebron and Stack say globalization should be defined as a "multitiered, multidimensional, and multinational set of processes" (*Globalization*, 25).

43. Gayatri Chakravorty Spivak, *An Aesthetic Education in the Era of Globalization* (Cambridge, MA: Harvard University Press, 2012), 1, 105.

44. Spivak, *Aesthetic Education*, 2.

45. Agha Shahid Ali, "Lenox Hill," in *Rooms Are Never Finished* (New York: W. W. Norton, 2002), 17.

46. Lorna Goodison, "Where the Flora of Our Village Came From," in *Collected Poems* (Manchester, UK: Carcanet, 2017), 389.

47. Spivak, *Death of a Discipline*, 108; *Aesthetic Education*, 443.

48. Seamus Heaney, "Alphabets," in *The Haw Lantern* (New York: Farrar, Straus and Giroux, 1987), 2.

49. In addition to the "wooden O" of *Henry V* (Prologue, *Henry V*, in *The Riverside Shakespeare*, ed. G. Blakemore Evans et al. [Boston: Houghton Mifflin, 1974], line 13), see *A Midsummer Night's Dream* 4.1.97; *The Tempest* 4.1.153, 154; and *Othello* 5.2.100.

50. Roland Robertson, *Globalization* (London: Sage, 1992), 8, 183-84; see also Steger, *Rise of the Global Imaginary*, 179, 183-84.

51. Ayesha Ramachandran, *The Worldmakers: Global Imagining in Early Modern Europe* (Chicago: University of Chicago Press, 2015), 14-15.

52. Conrad, *What Is Global History?*, 97.

53. Michael Lang, "Globalization and Its History," *Journal of Modern History* 789 (2006): 901.

54. Hebron and Stack, *Globalization*, 2.

55. See Hunt, *Writing History in the Global Era*, 129. On "archaic" and "modern" globalization, see C. A. Bayley, "'Archaic' and 'Modern' Globalization in the Eurasian and African Arena, ca. 1750-1850," in A. G. Hopkins, *Globalization in World History*, 45-72.

56. Jürgen Osterhammel and Niels P. Petersson, *Globalization: A Short History*, trans. Dona Geyer (Princeton: Princeton University Press, 2005), 146.

57. Justin Jennings, *Globalizations in the Ancient World* (Cambridge: Cambridge University Press, 2011); Janet Abu-Lughod, *Before European Hegemony: The World System A.D. 1250-1350* (Oxford: Oxford University Press, 1989). Other examples of large-scale integration include the consolidation of political units within empires, as after the Mongol invasion; the development of Christian, Muslim, and Buddhist ecumenes across political borders; long-distance trade along shipping routes around the Indian Ocean and between the Mediterranean and China along the Silk Road; and the mass migration of peoples, such as Bantu-speakers to various parts of Africa; see Osterhammel and Petersson, *Globalization*, 31-37.

58. See Susan Stanford Friedman, *Planetary Modernisms: Provocations on Modernity across Time* (New York: Columbia University Press, 2015); Wai Chee Dimock, *Through Other Continents: American Literature across Deep Time* (Princeton: Princeton University Press, 2006); and Paul Jay, *Global Matters: The Transnational Turn in Literary Studies* (Ithaca, NY: Cornell University Press, 2010), chap. 2, 33-52. Regarding the periodization of cultural modernism in relation to the global, see Richard Begam and Michael Valdez Moses, introduction to *Modernism, Postcolonialism, and Globalism: Anglophone Literature, 1950 to the Present* (Oxford: Oxford University Press, 2019), 10-14.

59. Kwame Anthony Appiah, *The Politics of Culture, the Politics of Identity* (Toronto: Royal Ontario Museum, 2008), 39; *Cosmopolitanism: Ethics in a World of Strangers* (New York: W. W. Norton, 2006), 5; *The Lies That Bind: Rethinking Identity; Creed, Country, Color, Class, Culture* (New York: W. W. Norton, 2018), 208.

60. Kwame Anthony Appiah, *The Ethics of Identity* (Princeton: Princeton University Press, 2005), 216, and *Cosmopolitanism*, 107; see also Jahan Ramazani, "Appiah's Identities: An Introduction," *New Literary History* 49, no. 2 (2018): v–xxxiv.

61. See Hamid Dabashi, *The World of Persian Literary Humanism* (Cambridge, MA: Harvard University Press, 2012).

62. "Zarif Narrates Story of Iranian Carpet Hung up on UN's Wall," *Iran Front Page*, April 19, 2017, https://ifpnews.com/exclusive/zarif-narrates-story-iranian-carpet -hung-uns-wall/; Moṣleḥ b. ʿAbdollāh Saʿdī, *Golestān*, in *Kolleyāt-e Saʿdī*, ed. Moḥammad ʿAlī Forūghī (Tehrān: Enteshārāt-e Hermes, 1385 [2006]), 31.

63. Osterhammel and Petersson, *Globalization*, 42–49; Conrad, *What Is Global History?*, 97, 111; Michael Lang, "Histories of Globalization(s)," in *A Companion to Global Historical Thought*, ed. Prasenjit Duara, Viren Murthy, and Andrew Satori (Oxford: Wiley-Blackwell, 2014), 402–3.

64. The phrase and part of the list are from Nayan Chanda, *Bound Together: How Traders, Preachers, Adventurers, and Warriors Shaped Globalization* (New Haven: Yale University Press, 2007); see also Conrad, *What Is Global History?*, 126, and Hunt, *Writing History in the Global Era*, 69.

65. Anthony Giddens, *The Consequences of Modernity* (Cambridge, UK: Polity, 1990), 64.

66. Robertson, *Globalization*, 54.

67. Robertson, *Globalization*, 170, 58.

68. Manfred B. Steger, *Globalization: A Very Short Introduction*, 4th ed. (Oxford: Oxford University Press, 2017), xvi.

69. Jernej Habjan, introduction to *Globalizing Literary Genres*, ed. Jernej Habjan and Fabienne Imlinger (New York: Routledge, 2016), 3.

70. Robertson, *Globalization*, 59; Chanda, *Bound Together*, xiv; Benedict Anderson, *Under Three Flags: Anarchism and the Anti-colonial Imagination* (London: Verso, 2005); Osterhammel and Petersson, *Globalization*, 81; Steger, *Globalization*, 130.

71. See C. A. Bayly, *The Birth of the Modern World, 1780–1914: Global Connections and Comparisons* (Malden, MA: Blackwell, 2004), and C. A. Bayly, *Remaking the Modern World, 1900–2015: Global Connections and Comparisons* (Hoboken, NJ: Wiley-Blackwell, 2018).

72. Osterhammel and Petersson, *Globalization*, 83.

73. Osterhammel and Petersson, *Globalization*, 86; Robertson, *Globalization*, 179.

74. Time still wasn't standardized universally as late as the 1940s; see Vanessa Ogle, *The Global Transformation of Time, 1870–1950* (Cambridge, MA: Harvard University Press, 2015).

75. "Population Facts," United Nations Department of Economic and Social Affairs, Population Division, December 2017, no. 2017/5, https://www.un.org/en/development/desa/population/publications/pdf/popfacts/PopFacts_2017-5.pdf; Daniel Cohen, *Globalization and Its Enemies* (Boston: MIT Press, 2006), 27.

76. A. G. Hopkins, "History of Globalization," 34.

77. Lang, "Globalization and Its History," 908; Osterhammel and Petersson, *Globalization*, 146; A. G. Hopkins, "History of Globalization," 35.

78. These remarks preface a racist study of Japanese immigration: see Robert E. Park, introduction to Jesse Frederick Steiner, *The Japanese Invasion: A Study in the Psychology of Inter-racial Contacts* (Chicago: A. C. McClurg, 1917), 8–10; partly (and inaccurately) cited in McKeown, "Periodizing Globalization," 218–19.

79. Osterhammel and Petersson, *Globalization*, 97.

80. Osterhammel and Petersson, *Globalization*, 88–89.

81. C. A. Bayly sees the nineteenth century's increasing homogeneity—the nation-state, religion, political ideologies, and economic life—as global connections that ironically heighten the sense of difference; see his *Birth of the Modern World*. Hunt

sees nationalism as both fostering and hindering globalization (*Writing History in the Global Era*, 74–75). Steger argues that as nation-states come to matter, they are forced into transnational relationships that in turn undermine the claims of national governance and noninterference (*Globalization*, 72). Lang believes that the "deepening internationalization of the economy intensified political tensions between European states" ("Globalization and Its History," 927). McKeown observes that global interactions have grown in tandem with the proliferation of borders, nations, racialization, and bureaucracies ("Periodizing Globalization," 220), and that national units and boundaries are "a relatively recent product of the globalization of political forms" (224).

On the "modular" character of the nation, see Benedict Anderson, *Imagined Communities: Reflections on the Origin and Spread of Nationalism*, rev. ed. (London: Verso, 1991), 4, 135.

82. McKeown, "Periodizing Globalization," 221.

83. Lisa Lowe, "Metaphors of Globalization," in *Interdisciplinarity and Social Justice*, ed. Ranu Samantrai, Joe Parker, and Mary Romero (Albany, NY: State University of New York Press, 2010), 46. For the historians, see Conrad, *What Is Global History?*, 95, 227–28, and Osterhammel and Petersson, *Globalization*, 86–87. See also anthropologist James Ferguson's observation that "flow is a particularly poor metaphor for the point-to-point connectivity and networking of enclaves"; instead, the global "hops . . . the spaces that lie between the points." See his *Global Shadows: Africa in the Neoliberal World Order* (Durham, NC: Duke University Press, 2006), 47.

84. W. B. Yeats, *A Vision* (London: Macmillan, 1937), 68.

85. W. H. Auden, "Ode to Terminus," in *Selected Poems of W. H. Auden: New Edition*, ed. Edward Mendelson (New York: Random House, 1979), 291, 290.

86. Kenneth Burke, *Language as Symbolic Action: Essays on Life, Literature, and Method* (Berkeley: University of California Press, 1966), 45.

87. Ramazani, *Poetry and Its Others*, 1.

88. Alastair Fowler, *Kinds of Literature* (Cambridge, MA: Harvard University Press, 1982); Virginia Jackson, "Who Reads Poetry?" *PMLA* 123, no. 1 (2008): 183.

89. Spivak, *Death of a Discipline* 73.

90. Eric Hayot, "Against Periodization; or, On Institutional Time," *New Literary History* 42, no. 4 (2011): 739. For discussions of the terms "world poetry" and "global poetics," see Harris Feinsod, "World Poetry: Commonplaces of an Idea," in "Literary History after the Nation?," ed. Peter Kalliney, special issue, *MLQ* 80, no. 4 (2019): 427–52, and Romana Huk, "'A New Global Poetics?' Revisited, Ten Years On: Coming to Terms," in "World Poetics, Comparative Poetics," ed. Jonathan Hart and Ming Xie, special issue, *University of Toronto Quarterly* 88, no. 2 (2019): 292–306.

Chapter 1

1. See Sigmund Freud, *Civilization and Its Discontents*, in *The Standard Edition of the Complete Psychological Works of Sigmund Freud*, ed. and trans. James Strachey (New York: W. W. Norton, 1961), 59.

2. Carol Ann Duffy, "The Christmas Truce," *The Guardian*, November 11, 2011; *The Christmas Truce* (London: Picador, 2011); rpt. in her *Collected Poems* (London: Picador-Macmillan, 2015), 542–45.

3. Duffy, "Christmas Truce," in *Collected Poems*, 543.

4. Duffy, "Christmas Truce," in *Collected Poems*, 543–44.

5. Seamus Heaney, "The Government of the Tongue," in *The Government of the Tongue: Selected Prose, 1978–1987* (New York: Farrar, Straus and Giroux, 1988), 107.

6. "Christmas 1914," Sainsbury's ad, accessed February 8, 2020, https://www.youtube.com/watch?v=NWF2JBb1bvM.

7. For an example of the negative press response, see Ally Fogg, "Sainsbury's Christmas Ad Is a Dangerous and Disrespectful Masterpiece," *The Guardian*, November 13, 2014. The Advertising Standards Authority received two hundred and forty complaints.

8. Duffy, "Christmas Truce," in *Collected Poems*, 544, 542, 543.

9. *Oxford English Dictionary Online*, s.v. "cosmopolitan" and "cosmopolite," accessed February 8, 2020, http://dictionary.oed.com/.

10. Isaac Rosenberg, "Break of Day in the Trenches," in *The Collected Works of Isaac Rosenberg*, ed. Ian Parsons (London: Chatto and Windus, 1979), 103–4; further references are to this text.

11. Paul Fussell, *The Great War and Modern Memory* (Oxford: Oxford University Press, 1975), 250.

12. "The wider aim," writes Santanu Das of his collection, "is to embed the experience and memory of the First World War in a more multiracial and international framework"; see his introduction to his *Race, Empire and First World War Writing* (Cambridge: Cambridge University Press, 2011), 1. See also his *India, Empire, and First World War Culture: Writings, Images, and Songs* (Cambridge: Cambridge University Press, 2018).

13. Bruce Robbins, "Actually Existing Cosmopolitanism," in *Cosmopolitics: Thinking and Feeling beyond the Nation*, ed. Pheng Cheah and Robbins (Minneapolis: University of Minnesota Press, 1998), 1, 2–3; Kwame Anthony Appiah, "Rooted Cosmopolitanism," *The Ethics of Identity* (Princeton: Princeton University Press, 2005), 213–75, and *Cosmopolitanism: Ethics in a World of Strangers* (New York: W. W. Norton, 2006).

14. Jürgen Osterhammel and Niels P. Petersson, *Globalization: A Short History*, trans. Dona Geyer (Princeton: Princeton University Press, 2005), 97.

15. Richard Rorty, *Contingency, Irony, and Solidarity* (Cambridge: Cambridge University Press, 1989), esp. chaps. 7 and 8, and Martha Nussbaum, *Cultivating Humanity* (Cambridge, MA: Harvard University Press, 1997), 85–112. Appiah also prizes "the narrative imagination" in *Ethics of Identity* (257), though his work on cosmopolitanism ranges across a variety of literary and artistic forms, including poetry.

16. Paul Gilroy, *Postcolonial Melancholia* (New York: Columbia University Press, 2005), 79, 63.

17. On the rat, the Jew, and modernism, see Daniel T. McGee, "Dada Da Da: Sounding the Jew in Modernism," *ELH* 68, no. 2 (2001): 501–27, and Maud Ellmann, "Writing like a Rat," *Critical Quarterly* 46, no. 4 (2004): 59–76.

18. *OED Online*, s.v. "rat," etym., February 8, 2020, http://dictionary.oed.com/.

19. Jean Moorcroft Wilson, *Isaac Rosenberg: The Making of a Great War Poet, A New Life* (Evanston, IL: Northwestern University Press, 2009), 11, 117–18.

20. See Santanu Das, *Touch and Intimacy in First World War Literature* (Cambridge: Cambridge University Press, 2005), which includes in its excellent reading of "Break of Day in the Trenches" insights into the poem's hand trope and Jewish background (96–98). For examples of critiques of war poetry when it isn't rooted in immediate facts, see the discussion of Thomas Hardy in Tim Kendall, *Modern English War Poetry* (Oxford: Oxford University Press, 2006), chap. 1, and of Eliot, Sitwell, and Dylan Thomas in Peter Robinson, "'Down in the Terraces Between the Targets': Civilians," in *The Oxford Handbook of British and Irish War Poetry*, ed. Tim Kendall (Oxford: Oxford University Press, 2007), 516–18.

21. Roland Robertson, *Globalization* (London: Sage, 1992), 166–77, and Bruno Latour, "Some Experiments in Art and Politics," *E-Flux*, no. 23 (March 2011), https://www.e-flux.com/journal/23/67790/some-experiments-in-art-and-politics/.

22. See the reproduction of the Imperial War Museum typescript in Jon Stallworthy, *Anthem for Doomed Youth: Twelve Soldier Poets of the First World War* (London: Constable & Robinson, 2002), 173.

23. *OED Online*, s.v. "rat," 3, accessed February 8, 2020, http://dictionary.oed.com/: "*allusively*. With reference to the notional killing or expulsion of rats in Ireland by incantation. . . . E. C. Brewer . . . states that it was popularly believed that rats could be eliminated by cursing them in rhyming verse, although does not explain the connection with Ireland"; see E. Cobham Brewer, *Dictionary of Phrase and Fable, Giving the Derivation, Source, or Origin of Common Phrases, Allusions, and Words That Have a Tale to Tell*, new ed. (Philadelphia: Henry Altemus, 1898), 1040. The *OED* entry cites Shakespeare, Jonson, Pope, and Yeats.

24. John McCrae, "In Flanders Fields" (1915), in *"In Flanders Fields" and Other Poems* (New York: Knickerbocker Press of G. P. Putnam's Sons, 1919), 3; Fussell, *Great War and Modern Memory*, 248.

25. Neil Corcoran, "Isaac Rosenberg," in *The Cambridge Companion to the Poetry of the First World War*, ed. Santanu Das (Cambridge: Cambridge University Press, 2013), 109.

26. The text of the poem as published in the magazine includes some completely different lines near the end.

27. Rorty, *Contingency*, xvi.

28. Rorty, *Contingency*, 94; Appiah, *Ethics of Identity*, 256–57, and *Cosmopolitanism*, 97.

29. Rosenberg to Edward Marsh, late December 1915, in *Collected Works*, 227.

30. See Stephen Barbour and Cathie Carmichael, ed., *Language and Nationalism in Europe* (Oxford: Oxford University Press, 2000).

31. Rosenberg, "The Jew," in *Collected Works*, 101.

32. That is, "you are," "he was," "I will," "he shall." Thomas Hardy, *The Complete Poems of Thomas Hardy*, ed. James Gibson (New York: Collier-Macmillan, 1976), 542. The title is from *Othello*, in *The Riverside Shakespeare*, ed. G. Blakemore Evans et al. (Boston: Houghton Mifflin, 1974), 4.1.195.

33. Hardy to Florence Henniker, March 23, 1915, in *The Collected Letters of Thomas*

Hardy, ed. Richard Little Purdy and Michael Millgate, 8 vols. (New York: Clarendon Press of Oxford University Press, 1978), 5:86.

34. Hardy to Florence Henniker, May 20, 1917, *Collected Letters*, 5:215.

35. Thomas Hardy, *The Personal Notebooks of Thomas Hardy*, ed. Richard H. Taylor (London: Macmillan, 1978), 291.

36. On the demise of this idea, see Peter Edgerly Firchow, *The Death of the German Cousin: Variations on a Literary Stereotype, 1890–1920* (Lewisburg, PA: Bucknell University Press, 1986), chap. 1.

37. Joanna Bourke, *An Intimate History of Killing: Face-to-Face Killing in Twentieth-Century Warfare* (New York: Basic Books, 1999), 129.

38. Rudyard Kipling, "For All We Have and Are," in *Rudyard Kipling's Verse: Definitive Edition* (New York: Doubleday, 1940), 328, and Rev. Abel Aaronson, "To the Kaiser," in *One Hundred of the Best Poems on the European War*, ed. Charles F. Forshaw (London: Elliot Stock, 1915), 1:11. On these and other poems that demonize the German other, as well as their German and French counterparts, see Elizabeth A. Marsland, *The Nation's Cause: French, English and German Poetry of the First World War* (London: Routledge, 1991), 62–69.

39. Hardy to Florence Henniker, March 4, 1917, in *Collected Letters*, 5:204.

40. Florence Emily Hardy, *The Later Years of Thomas Hardy, 1892–1928* (London: Macmillan, 1930), 173. Tim Kendall cites the remark and Hardy's discomfort with patriotic poems; see "Civilian War Poetry: Hardy and Kipling," in Das, *Cambridge Companion to Poetry of the First World War*, 202–3.

41. Hardy, "Men Who March Away," in *Complete Poems*, 538; Hardy to John Galsworthy, August 4, 1918, *Collected Letters*, 5:275.

42. Marsland, *Nation's Cause*, 158 (citing W. G. Hartmann's poem "Mein Bruder Feind").

43. Martha C. Nussbaum, *Upheavals of Thought: The Intelligence of Emotions* (Cambridge: Cambridge University Press, 2001), 431. Rorty also emphasizes detail-packed "genres such as ethnography, the journalist's report, the comic book, the docudrama, and, especially, the novel" (*Contingency*, xvi).

44. Gilroy, *Postcolonial Melancholia*, 79.

45. Hardy, "The Man He Killed," in *Complete Poems*, 287.

46. Edgar Allan Poe, "The Raven," line 2.

47. See, e.g., Sarah Cole, *Modernism, Male Friendship, and the First World War* (Cambridge: Cambridge University Press, 2003), chap. 3.

48. Robert W. Service, "A Song of the Sandbags," in *Rhymes of a Red Cross Man* (New York: Barse & Hopkins, 1916), 73; Duffy, "The Christmas Truce," in *Collected Poems*, 544.

49. Service, "Song of the Sandbags," 71.

50. Gilroy, *Postcolonial Melancholia*, 80, 67.

51. Homi K. Bhabha, "The Vernacular Cosmopolitan," in *Voices of the Crossing*, ed. Ferdinand Dennis and Naseem Khan (London: Serpent's Tail, 2000), 133–42; Service, "Song of the Sandbags," 72.

52. Service, "Song of the Sandbags," 70.

53. Appiah, *Ethics of Identity*, 254.

54. Gilroy, *Postcolonial Melancholia*, 8, 63.

55. Gilroy, *Postcolonial Melancholia*, 67.

56. Service, "Only a Boche," in *Rhymes*, 109. Further references appear in text.

57. Gilroy, *Postcolonial Melancholia*, 78.

58. Rorty, *Contingency*, 192.

59. Susan Sontag, *Regarding the Pain of Others* (New York: Farrar, Straus and Giroux, 2003), 79.

60. Gilroy, *Postcolonial Melancholia*, 67.

61. Desmond Graham, *The Truth of War: Owen, Blunden, Rosenberg* (Manchester, UK: Carcanet, 1984), 45.

62. Sigmund Freud, "The Uncanny," trans. Alix Strachey, in *On Creativity and the Unconscious: Papers on the Psychology of Art, Literature, Love, Religion*, ed. Benjamin Nelson (New York: Harper & Row, 1958), 141. For a Lévinasian reading of the encounter with the other in Owen's poem, see Kate McLoughlin, *Authoring War: The Literary Representation of War from the "Iliad" to Iraq* (Cambridge: Cambridge University Press, 2011), 192–94.

63. Wilfred Owen, "Strange Meeting," in *The Poems of Wilfred Owen*, ed. Jon Stallworthy (New York: W. W. Norton, 1986), 125–26; further references are to this text.

64. Richard Barber, *The Knight and Chivalry*, rev. ed. (Woodbridge, UK: Boydell Press of Boydell & Brewer, 1995), 245. On this and other examples of the love and symmetry between enemy combatants, see Barbara Ehrenreich, *Blood Rites: Origins and History of the Passions of War* (New York: Henry Holt, 1997), 137–41.

65. Owen to Susan Owen, May [16?], 1917, in *Selected Letters*, ed. John Bell (Oxford: Oxford University Press, 1985), 247.

66. Seamus Heaney, "The Grauballe Man," in *Poems, 1965–1975* (New York: Farrar, Straus and Giroux, 1980), 191.

67. Seamus Heaney, "Sounding Auden," in *Government of the Tongue*, 112–13.

68. Heaney, "Punishment," in *Poems*, 193.

69. Seamus Heaney, "In Memoriam Francis Ledwidge," in *Field Work* (London: Faber, 1979), 60. Further references are to this text (59–60). For a reading of the poem that sees in it a confusion of Catholic postpartition politics with the views of an earlier era, see Fran Brearton, "'All the strains / Criss-cross': Irish Memory and the First World War," *Anglophonia* 33 (2013): 105–22.

70. W. B. Yeats, *Letters on Poetry from W. B. Yeats to Dorothy Wellesley* (London: Oxford University Press, 1940), 113.

71. W. H. Auden, "In Memory of W. B. Yeats," in *Selected Poems of W. H. Auden: New Edition*, ed. Edward Mendelson (New York: Random House, 1979), 82, 83. Jahan Ramazani, *Poetry of Mourning: The Modern Elegy from Hardy to Heaney* (Chicago: University of Chicago Press, 1994), 189–90.

72. W. B. Yeats, "An Irish Airman Foresees His Death," in *The Variorum Edition of the Poems of W. B. Yeats*, ed. Peter Allt and Russell K. Alspach (New York: Macmillan, 1968), 328.

73. Yeats, "In Memory of Major Robert Gregory," in *Variorum Edition*, 327.

74. David Goldie, "Archipelagic Poetry of the First World War," in Das, *Cambridge Companion to the Poetry of the First World War*, 171.

75. Siegfried Sassoon, "Glory of Women," in *Collected Poems, 1908–1956* (London: Faber, 1961), 79.

76. Siegfried Sassoon, *Memoirs of an Infantry Officer* (London: Faber, 1930), 89.

77. Mary Borden-Turner, "The Song of the Mud," *English Review* 25, no. 2 (1917): 99. On the poem, see also Margaret Higonnet, "The Great War and the Female Elegy: Female Lamentation and Silence in Global Contexts," *Global South* 1, nos. 1–2 (2007): 131–32, and Peter Howarth, "Poetic Form and the First World War," in Das, *Cambridge Companion to the Poetry of the First World War*, 58.

78. Borden-Turner, "Song of the Mud," 100.

79. Mary Borden-Turner, "The Hill," *English Review*, 102.

80. See Bourke, *Intimate History of Killing*, 146.

81. On these developments and the Anthropocene, see Shital Pravinchandra, "One Species, Same Difference? Postcolonial Critique and the Concept of Life," *New Literary History* 47, no. 1 (2016): 27–48.

82. Das, introduction to *Race, Empire and First World War Writing*, 1.

83. Edna Longley, "The Great War, History, and the English Lyric," in *The Cambridge Companion to the Literature of the First World War*, ed. Vincent Sherry (Cambridge: Cambridge University Press, 2005), 73, 74–75.

84. Kipling, "Epitaphs of the War," in *Rudyard Kipling's Verse*, 385.

85. Gilroy, *Postcolonial Melancholia*, 67.

86. Appiah, *Cosmopolitanism*, 135.

87. Gilroy, *Postcolonial Melancholia*, 80.

88. Gilroy, *Postcolonial Melancholia*, 79.

Chapter 2

1. "About Poetry of Place," *Windfall: A Journal of Poetry of Place*, February 8, 2020, http://www.hevanet.com/windfall/poetryofplace.html.

2. "Afterword: Poetry of Place," *Windfall: A Journal of Poetry of Place* 1, no. 1 (Fall 2002), February 8, 2020, http://www.hevanet.com/windfall/wfl/wflafterword.pdf.

3. Bruce Robbins, "Comparative Cosmopolitanisms," in *Cosmopolitics: Thinking and Feeling beyond the Nation*, ed. Pheng Cheah and Bruce Robbins (Minneapolis: University of Minnesota Press, 1998), 251, 253.

4. Samuel Johnson, "Denham," in *The Works of Samuel Johnson* (Cambridge, MA: Harvard Coöperative Society, 1912), 4:7.

5. Robert Arnold Aubin, *Topographical Poetry in Eighteenth-Century England* (New York: Modern Language Association, 1936), vii.

6. Stephanie (published as Stephen) Burt, "Scenic, or Topographical, Poetry," in *A Companion to Poetic Genre*, ed. Erik Martiny (Oxford: Wiley-Blackwell, 2012), 602. See also the overview of the prospect poem, including an analysis of its late twentieth-century manipulation to explore global ecological damage, in Walt Hunter, "The No-Prospect Poem: Poetic Views of the Anthropocene," in *Forms of a World: Contem-*

porary Poetry and the Making of Globalization (New York: Fordham University Press, 2019), 90–117.

7. Burt, "Scenic," 611. Resisting the mimetic model of the topographical poem, John Barrell argues that, "far from suggesting any sense of locality," eighteenth-century poets treat landscape as "a theatre where the poet's own moral reflections are acted out"; see his *The Idea of Landscape and the Sense of Place, 1730–1840: An Approach to the Poetry of John Clare* (Cambridge: Cambridge University Press, 1972), 35. Bonnie Costello explores landscape poetry that "foregrounds our transitory manipulations and abstractions of the physical world as it is lived in and imagined"; see her *Shifting Ground: Reinventing Landscape in Modern American Poetry* (Cambridge, MA: Harvard University Press, 2003), 9.

8. See Robert Crawford, *Identifying Poets: Self and Territory in Twentieth-Century Poetry* (Edinburgh: Edinburgh University Press, 1994); Angus Fletcher, *A New Theory for American Poetry: Democracy, the Environment, and the Future of the Imagination* (Cambridge, MA: Harvard University Press, 2004); and Fiona Stafford, *Local Attachments: The Province of Poetry* (New York: Oxford University Press, 2010).

9. Alex Davis and Lee M. Jenkins, introduction to *Locations of Literary Modernism: Region and Nation in British and American Modernist Poetry*, ed. Davis and Jenkins (Cambridge: Cambridge University Press, 2000), 5, 4.

10. Marjorie Levinson, *Wordsworth's Great Period Poems* (Cambridge: Cambridge University Press, 1986), 15, 17.

11. Levinson, *Wordsworth's Great Period Poems*, 15, 25, 37, 56. In art history, too, similar arguments emerged in the 1980s, as in Fred Orton and Griselda Pollock's analysis of Paul Gauguin and Emile Bernard's paintings of Brittany: seen in the light of tourist guidebooks, the paintings were found to primitivize and exoticize the region, occluding actual economic and modernizing forces. See their essay "Les données bretonnantes: la prairie de représentation," *Art History* 3, no. 3 (1980): 314–44.

12. Marjorie Levinson, "What Is New Formalism?" *PMLA* 122, no. 2 (2007): 558–69.

13. Virginia Jackson, *Dickinson's Misery: A Theory of Lyric Reading* (Princeton: Princeton University Press, 2005), 100, 90. See also the cluster she introduced and edited on the new lyric studies in *PMLA* 123, no. 1 (2008).

14. Doreen Massey, *For Space* (London: Sage, 2005), 9.

15. Jonathan Culler, *Theory of the Lyric* (Cambridge, MA: Harvard University Press, 2015). Although quite different from Culler's book, Gillian White's *Lyric Shame: The "Lyric" Subject of Contemporary American Poetry* (Cambridge, MA: Harvard University Press, 2014) also seeks to renovate the category of lyric, finding more complexity and self-critical rigor in the genre than its detractors sometimes allow. For examples and overviews of a rejuvenated formalism in poetry studies, see Angela Leighton, *Hearing Things: The Work of Sound in Literature* (Cambridge, MA: Belknap Press of Harvard University Press, 2018); Herbert Tucker, "Unsettled Scores: Meter and Play in Two Music Poems by Robert Browning," *Critical Inquiry* 21 (2014): 24–52; Derek Attridge, *Moving Words: Forms of English Poetry* (Oxford: Oxford University Press, 2013), chap. 1; Verena Theile, "New Formalism(s): A Prologue," in *New Formalisms and Literary Theory*, ed. Theile and Linda Tredennick (New York: Palgrave Macmillan, 2013),

3–26; and Fredric V. Bogel, *New Formalist Criticism: Theory and Practice* (New York: Palgrave Macmillan, 2013).

16. Caroline Levine, *Forms: Whole, Rhythm, Hierarchy, Network* (Princeton: Princeton University Press, 2015), 6–11.

17. Ezra Pound, *Lustra* (1916; New York: Alfred A. Knopf, 1917), 50.

18. Ezra Pound, *Gaudier-Brzeska: A Memoir* (New York: New Directions, 1970), 89.

19. Pound, *Gaudier-Brzeska*, 86.

20. See William Logan, "Pound's Metro," *New Criterion* 33 (April 2015): 4+.

21. Ezra Pound, "A Retrospect," in *Literary Essays of Ezra Pound*, ed. T. S. Eliot (New York: New Directions, 1968), 3.

22. Doreen Massey, *Space, Place, and Gender* (Minneapolis: University of Minnesota Press, 1994), 155.

23. Bruno Latour, *Reassembling the Social: An Introduction to Actor-Network-Theory* (Oxford: Oxford University Press, 2005), 204.

24. Bruno Latour, "Some Experiments in Art and Politics," *E-Flux*, no. 23 (March 2011), https://www.e-flux.com/journal/23/67790/some-experiments-in-art-and-politics/.

25. Wright as quoted in an interview with Bruce Hendricksen, in *James Wright: A Profile*, ed. Frank Graziano and Peter Stitt (Durango, CO: Logbridge-Rhodes, 1988), 98, and in Dave Smith, "James Wright: From the Pure Clear Word, an Interview with Dave Smith," rpt. in *Written in Water, Written in Stone: Twenty Years of Poets on Poetry*, ed. Martin Lammon (Ann Arbor: University of Michigan Press, 1996), 76. See also Robert Bly, "Introduction: James Wright's Clarity and Extravagance," in James Wright, *Selected Poems*, ed. Robert Bly and Anne Wright (New York: Farrar, Straus, and Giroux, 2005), xx.

26. On the Ansari parallel, see the Wright interview with Hendricksen, in Graziano and Stitt, *James Wright*, 98. Alan Williamson notes the Rimbaud echo in *Introspection and Contemporary Poetry* (Cambridge, MA: Harvard University Press, 1984), 70.

27. Vidyan Ravinthiran, "How James Wright Wasted His Life," *Literary Imagination* 16, no. 1 (2014): 95–116.

28. "Poetry Atlas," accessed May 22, 2013, http://www.poetryatlas.com/. The introductory text has been revised to read, in part, "The world is mapped in poetry. We believe there is a poem about just about arywhere [*sic*] on earth. We map this iambic cartography—by great poets, or by you"; accessed February 8, 2020. For a more sophisticated digital geomapping of two poets' work, though tellingly focused on their prose notebooks rather than their poetry, see "Mapping the Lakes: A Literary GIS," http://www.lancaster.ac.uk/mappingthelakes/. We can hope that future scholars will develop digital tools for the palimpsestic and plural intermapping of poetry and place.

29. Stafford, *Local Attachments*.

30. Thomas Babington Macaulay, "Indian Education" (1835), in *Prose and Poetry*, ed. George M. Young (London: Hart-Davis, 1967), 722.

31. Thomas Hardy, "Geographical Knowledge," in *The Complete Poems of Thomas Hardy*, ed. James Gibson (New York: Collier-Macmillan, 1976), 288.

32. Anthony Giddens, *The Consequences of Modernity* (Cambridge, UK: Polity Press, 1990), 21.

33. Henri Lefebvre, *The Production of Space*, trans. Donald Nicholson-Smith (Oxford: Blackwell, 1991), 86.

34. "I had still the ambition, formed in Sligo in my teens, of living in imitation of Thoreau on Innisfree, a little island in Lough Gill"; see W. B. Yeats, *Autobiographies*, ed. William H. O'Donnell and Douglas N. Archibald, vol. 3 of *The Collected Works of W. B. Yeats*, ed. Richard J. Finneran and George Mills Harper (New York: Scribner, 1999), 139.

35. Yeats writes: "when walking through Fleet Street very homesick I heard a little tinkle of water and saw a fountain in a shop-window which balanced a little ball upon its jet, and began to remember lake water"; see his *Autobiographies*, 139. W. B. Yeats, "The Lake Isle of Innisfree," in *The Variorum Edition of the Poems of W. B. Yeats*, ed. Peter Allt and Russell K. Alspach (New York: Macmillan, 1968), 117, and Theodor Adorno, "On Lyric Poetry and Society," in *Notes to Literature*, vol. 1, trans. Shierry Weber Nicholson (New York: Columbia University Press, 1991), 37–54.

36. Yeats, *Variorum Edition*, 117.

37. R. F. Foster, *The Arch-Poet, 1915–1939*, vol. 2 of *W. B. Yeats: A Life* (Oxford: Oxford University Press, 2003), 131.

38. Claude McKay, "The Tropics in New York," in *Complete Poems*, ed. William J. Maxwell (Urbana: University of Illinois Press, 2004), 154. On other poetic afterlives, see Lee M. Jenkins, "Water Songs: 'The Lake Isle of Innisfree' and Jamaican Poetry," in *Caribbean Irish Connections: Interdisciplinary Perspectives*, ed. Alison Donnell, Maria McGarrity, and Evelyn O'Callaghan (Kingston, Jamaica: University of the West Indies Press, 2015), 189–202.

39. William Wordsworth, "The Reverie of Poor Susan," in *Selected Poems and Prefaces*, ed. Jack Stillinger (Boston: Houghton Mifflin, 1965), 13.

40. Latour, *Reassembling the Social*, 200.

41. Grace Nichols, "Island Man," in *The Fat Black Woman's Poems* (London: Virago, 1984), 29.

42. Arun Kolatkar, "Pi-dog," in *Collected Poems in English*, ed. Arvind Krishna Mehrotra (Highgreen, UK: Bloodaxe, 2010), 75.

43. Kolatkar, "Pi-dog," 75.

44. Kolatkar, "Pi-dog," 75.

45. Giddens, *Consequences of Modernity*, 18–19.

46. Latour, *Reassembling the Social*, 195.

47. Anjali Nerlekar, "The Cartography of the Local in Arun Kolatkar's Poetry," *Journal of Postcolonial Writing* 49, no. 5 (2013): 609, 618. See also her *Bombay Modern: Arun Kolatkar and Bilingual Literary Culture* (Evanston: Northwestern University Press, 2016); and "The City, Place, and Postcolonial Poetry," in *The Cambridge Companion to Postcolonial Poetry*, ed. Jahan Ramazani (Cambridge: Cambridge University Press, 2017), 195–208. See also Laetitia Zecchini, *Arun Kolatkar and Literary Modernism in India: Moving Lines* (London: Bloomsbury, 2014), 59–61, 100–102, 140.

48. Kolatkar, "Breakfast Time at Kala Ghoda," in *Collected Poems*, 125.

49. Lefebvre, *Production of Space*, 86 (emphasis in original).

50. Roland Robertson, "Glocalization: Time-Space and Homogeneity-Heterogeneity," in *Global Modernities*, ed. Mike Featherstone, Scott Lash, and Roland Robertson (London: Sage), 35.

51. Kolatkar, "Breakfast Time," in *Collected Poems*, 125.

52. Kolatkar, "Breakfast Time," 128.

53. Kolatkar, "Breakfast Time," 135.

54. Kolatkar, "Breakfast Time," 134.

55. A. K. Ramanujan, "Small-Scale Reflections on a Great House," in *The Collected Poems of A. K. Ramanujan* (Delhi: Oxford University Press, 1995), 96.

56. Ramanujan, "Small-Scale Reflections," 97.

57. Ramanujan, "Small-Scale Reflections," 97.

58. Lorna Goodison, "To Us, All Flowers Are Roses," in *Selected Poems* (Ann Arbor: University of Michigan Press, 1992), 1. See Kei Miller's similar list of Jamaican "places named / after places," "a palimpsest / of maps," in *The Cartographer Tries to Map a Way to Zion* (Manchester, UK: Carcanet, 2014), 25.

59. Massey, *For Space*, 4, 55.

60. A. R. Ammons, "Corsons Inlet," in *Collected Poems, 1951–1971* (New York: W. W. Norton, 1972), 148, 149.

61. Ammons, "Corsons Inlet," 150, 151.

62. On Williams's *Paterson*, the local, and the global, see Jahan Ramazani, *Poetry and Its Others: News, Prayer, Song, and the Dialogue of Genres* (Chicago: University of Chicago Press, 2014), 105–9.

63. J. E. Malpas, *Place and Experience: A Philosophical Topography* (Cambridge: Cambridge University Press, 14.

64. Charles Olson, *The Maximus Poems*, ed. George F. Butterick (Berkeley: University of California Press, 1983), 14, 631. Further references are cited in text.

65. Nigel Thrift, *Non-representational Theory: Space, Politics, Affect* (London: Routledge, 2008), 17.

66. See also the spiral holograph, 479.

67. Malpas, *Place and Experience*, 34, 172.

68. Michael Davidson, *The San Francisco Renaissance: Poetics and Community at Midcentury* (Cambridge: Cambridge University Press, 1991), 103.

69. Gary Snyder, *The Gary Snyder Reader* (Berkeley: Counterpoint, 1999), 401. Ensuing references are to this page.

70. See Lorine Niedecker to Cid Corman, July 12, 1966, in *Lake Superior: Lorine Niedecker's Poem and Journal along with Other Sources, Documents, and Readings* (Seattle, WA: Wave, 2013), 50. All further Niedecker references are cited in text. On the poem's composition, see Jenny Penberthy, "Writing 'Lake Superior,'" in *Radical Vernacular: Lorine Niedecker and the Poetics of Place*, ed. Elizabeth Willis (Iowa City: University of Iowa Press, 2008), 61–79.

71. Shakespeare, *The Tempest*, in *The Riverside Shakespeare*, ed. G. Blakemore Evans et al. (Boston: Houghton Mifflin, 1974), 1.2.398.

72. Jahan Ramazani, "Traveling Poetry," in *A Transnational Poetics* (Chicago: University of Chicago Press, 2009), chap. 3.

73. Aubin, *Topographical Poetry*, chaps. 2 and 7.

74. Agha Shahid Ali, "I See Chile in My Rearview Mirror," in *A Nostalgist's Map of America* (New York: W. W. Norton, 1991), 96. Ensuing references are in text. See also Judith Rauscher, "On Common Ground: Translocal Attachments and Transethnic Affiliations in Agha Shahid Ali's and Arthur Sze's Poetry of the Southwest," *European Journal of American Studies* 9, no. 3 (2014), https://ejas.revues.org/10434.

75. Jean Baudrillard, *America* (London: Verso, 1988), 6, and Carla Kaplan, *Questions of Travel* (Durham, NC: Duke University Press, 1996), 68–85.

Chapter 3

1. Elizabeth Bishop, "Arrival at Santos," in *The Complete Poems, 1927–1979* (New York: Farrar, Straus and Giroux, 1983), 89.

2. *OED Online*, s.v. "tourist," a, accessed February 8, 2020, http://www.oed.com/.

3. *OED Online*, s.v. "verse" and "tour," etym.

4. Dean MacCannell, *Ethics of Sightseeing* (Berkeley: University of California Press, 2011), 6, and *The Tourist: A New Theory of the Leisure Class* (Berkeley: University of California Press, 1999), 1.

5. Jahan Ramazani, *Poetry and Its Others: News, Prayer, Song, and the Dialogue of Genres* (Chicago: University of Chicago Press, 2014).

6. Robert von Hallberg, "Tourists," in *American Poetry and Culture, 1945–1980* (Cambridge, MA: Harvard University Press, 1985), 62–92; Jeffrey Gray, *Mastery's End: Travel and Postwar American Poetry* (Athens, GA: University of Georgia Press, 2005); and Anthony Carrigan, *Postcolonial Tourism: Literature, Culture, and Environment* (New York: Routledge, 2011).

7. David Held et al., *Global Transformations: Politics, Economics, and Culture* (Stanford: Stanford University Press, 1999), 360.

8. John Urry and Jonas Larsen, *The Tourist Gaze 3.0* (London: Sage, 2011), 28.

9. MacCannell, *Tourist*, 94, 104; Jonathan Culler, "The Semiotics of Tourism," in *Framing the Sign: Criticism and Its Institutions* (Oxford: Blackwell, 1988), 156.

10. MacCannell, *Tourist*, 10, 164.

11. MacCannell, *Tourist*, 9.

12. Urry and Larsen, *Tourist Gaze*, 97.

13. MacCannell, *Tourist*, 191.

14. MacCannell, *Ethics of Sightseeing*, 6.

15. Jamaica Kincaid, *A Small Place* (New York: Farrar, Straus and Giroux, 1988), 77. See Jorge Arango, "Antiguan Impressions," *Essence* 32, no. 1 (2001): 216.

16. See James Clifford, *Routes: Travel and Translation in the Late Twentieth Century* (Cambridge, MA: Harvard University Press, 1997), and Arjun Appadurai, *Modernity at Large: Cultural Dimensions of Globalization* (Minneapolis: University of Minnesota Press, 1996).

17. Graham Huggan, *The Postcolonial Exotic: Marketing the Margins* (London: Routledge, 2001), xi, xii, 56.

18. Jamaica Kincaid, *Among Flowers: A Walk in the Himalaya* (Washington, DC: National Geographic Society, 2005), 185–86.

19. See Sarah Brouillette, *Postcolonial Writers in the Global Literary Marketplace* (Basingstoke, UK: Palgrave, 2007), 33–40; Carrigan, *Postcolonial Tourism*, 41–49, 78, 87–88, 177–81, 183–89; and Natalie Melas, "Forgettable Vacations and Metaphor in Ruins: Walcott's *Omeros*," *Callaloo* 28, no. 1 (2005): 147–68.

20. Derek Walcott, "The Antilles: Fragments of Epic Memory," in *What the Twilight Says: Essays* (New York: Farrar, Straus and Giroux, 1998), 81.

21. Derek Walcott, *Omeros* (New York: Farrar, Straus and Giroux, 1990), 289.

22. Edward Hirsch, "The Art of Poetry" (interview with Derek Walcott), in *Critical Perspectives on Derek Walcott*, ed. Robert D. Hamner (Washington, DC: Three Continents Press, 1993), 78.

23. Walcott, *Omeros*, 3, 4. See Jahan Ramazani, "The Wound of Postcolonial History: Derek Walcott's *Omeros*," in *The Hybrid Muse: Postcolonial Poetry in English* (Chicago: University of Chicago Press, 2001), chap. 3.

24. Walcott, *Omeros*, 227, 228.

25. Robert Chi, "Toward a New Tourism: Albert Wendt and Becoming Attractions," *Cultural Critique*, no. 37 (1997): 95.

26. Ara Shirinyan, *Your Country Is Great: Afghanistan-Guyana* (New York: Futurepoem Books, 2008), 7. See Eric Rettberg, "Comic Poetics of Imaginative Travel in *Your Country Is Great*," *Comparative Literature Studies* 51, no. 1 (2014): 55–77.

27. These figures come from the World Tourism Organization; see Urry and Larsen, *Tourist Gaze*, 7, and Chris Ryan, *Recreational Tourism: Demand and Impacts* (Bristol: Channel View Publications, 2003), who states that "the period after the Second World War was to usher in the age of cheap air transport" (17).

28. Bishop, "Over 2,000 Illustrations and a Complete Concordance," in *Complete Poems*, 58; subsequent references appear in text.

29. Michael Harkin, "Modernist Anthropology and Tourism of the Authentic," *Annals of Tourism Research* 22, no. 3 (1995): 667. See Chi, "Toward a New Tourism," 91.

30. Bethany Hicok, "Becoming a Poet: From North to South," in *The Cambridge Companion to Elizabeth Bishop*, ed. Angus Cleghorn and Jonathan Ellis (New York: Cambridge University Press, 2014), 118. Among readings of the poem, see Thomas Travisano, *Elizabeth Bishop: Her Artistic Development* (Charlottesville: University Press of Virginia, 1988), 114–21; Bonnie Costello, *Elizabeth Bishop: Questions of Mastery* (Cambridge: Harvard University Press, 1991), 132–37; and Gray, *Mastery's End*, 31–36.

31. On the specific allusions, see Costello, *Elizabeth Bishop*, 135.

32. Bishop, "In the Waiting Room," in *Complete Poems*, 159; I explore this idea in my *Transnational Poetics*, 63–68.

33. Walter Pater, conclusion to *The Renaissance*, in *Selected Writings of Walter Pater*, ed. Harold Bloom (New York: Columbia University Press, 1974), 60.

34. John Ashbery, "Throughout Is This Quality of Thingness: Elizabeth Bishop," in *Selected Prose*, ed. Eugene Richie (Ann Arbor: University of Michigan Press, 2004), 122.

35. John Ashbery, "The Instruction Manual," in *Selected Poems* (New York: Viking Penguin, 1985), 7. Subsequent references appear in text. Readings include Marjorie Perloff, "'Fragments of a Buried Life': John Ashbery's Dream Songs," in *Beyond Amazement: New Essays on John Ashbery*, ed. David Lehman (Ithaca: Cornell University Press, 1980), 74–76; Mutlu Konuk Blasing, *Politics and Form in Postmodern Poetry: O'Hara, Bishop, Ashbery, and Merrill* (Cambridge: Cambridge University Press, 1995), 124–27; Gray, *Mastery's End*, 113–16; and Jasper Bernes, "John Ashbery's Free Indirect Labor," *MLQ* 74, no. 4 (2013): 517–20.

36. Culler, "Semiotics of Tourism," 155.

37. Urry and Larsen, *Tourist Gaze*, 18.

38. Kincaid, *Small Place*, 18.

39. MacCannell, *Tourist*, 98–102.

40. Samuel Richardson, preface to *The History of Sir Charles Grandison*, in vol. 3 of *The Novels of Samuel Richardson* (London: Hurst, Robinson, 1824), iv.

41. Maxine Feifer, *Going Places: The Ways of the Tourist from Imperial Rome to the Present Day* (London: Macmillan, 1985), 269–70.

42. Dennis Merrill, *Negotiating Paradise: U.S. Tourism and Empire in Twentieth-Century Latin America* (Chapel Hill: University of North Carolina Press, 2009), 30.

43. David A. Fennell, *Tourism Ethics* (Bristol: Channel View Publications, 2006), 1–2. See also Urry and Larsen, *Tourist Gaze*, 43, and Victor T. C. Middleton and Leonard John Lickorish, *British Tourism: The Remarkable Story of Growth* (London: Routledge, 2007), xx.

44. Philip Larkin, "Sunny Prestatyn," in *The Complete Poems*, ed. Archie Burnett (New York: Farrar, Straus and Giroux, 2012), 64. Subsequent references are to 64–65.

45. *Granger's Index to Poetry*, 6th ed., ed. William James Smith (New York: Columbia University Press, 1973), 215–24.

46. Roman Jakobson, "Linguistics and Poetics," in *Language in Literature*, ed. Krystyna Pomorska and Stephen Rudy (Cambridge: Belknap Press of Harvard University Press, 1987), 67–68.

47. Urry and Larsen, *Tourist Gaze*, 176.

48. Larkin as cited by Maeve Brennan, *The Philip Larkin I Knew* (Manchester: Manchester University Press, 2002), 60, and Larkin, *Further Requirements*, ed. Anthony Thwaite (London: Faber, 2001), 89.

49. Joseph Bristow, "The Obscenity of Philip Larkin," *Critical Inquiry* 21, no. 1 (1994): 178. On opposite sides of this issue, see Janice Rossen, *Philip Larkin: His Life's Work* (Iowa City: University of Iowa Press, 1989), 73–75, and Steve Clark, "'Get Out As Early As You Can': Larkin's Sexual Politics," in *Philip Larkin*, ed. Stephen Regan (New York: St. Martin's Press, 1997), 121–24.

50. Larkin, "Sad Steps," in *Complete Poems*, 89.

51. MacCannell, *Tourist*, 94.

52. Urry and Larsen, *Tourist Gaze*, 7, and Sharon Bohn Gmelch, "Why Tourism Matters," in *Tourists and Tourism*, ed. Gmelch, 2nd ed. (London Grove, IL: Waveland, 2010), 4. For an analysis of tourism that seeks in postcolonial writing ideas for sustainable forms of tourism, see Carrigan, *Postcolonial Tourism*.

53. Karen Press, *Echo Location: A Guide to Sea Point for Residents and Visitors* (Umbilo, Durban: Gekko, 1998). Subsequent references appear in text. For a reading of the book's vexed engagement with whiteness, see the thoughtful discussion in Mary West, *White Women Writing White: Identity and Representation in (Post-) Apartheid Literatures of South Africa* (Claremont, South Africa: David Philip, 2009), chap. 5.

54. Allen Garth and Frank Brennen, *Tourism in the New South Africa: Social Responsibility and the Tourist* (London: I. B. Taurus, 2004), 18–20.

55. Kincaid, *Small Place*, 18–19.

56. Vicki Bertram, "Karen Press in Conversation," *PN Review* 27, no. 1 (2000): 47.

57. Arun Kolatkar, *Jejuri* (1976), in *Collected Poems in English*, ed. Arvind Krishna Mehrotra (Highgreen, UK: Bloodaxe, 2010). All references appear in text. Commentaries include Anjali Nerlekar, *Bombay Modern: Arun Kolatkar and Bilingual Literary Culture* (Evanston, IL: Northwestern University Press, 2016), chaps. 5 and 6; Emma Bird, "Re-reading Postcolonial Poetry: Arun Kolatkar's *Jejuri*," *Journal of Commonwealth Literature* 47, no. 2 (2012): 229–43; Mehrotra, "Introduction: Death of a Poet," in Kolatkar, *Collected Poems*, 12–40; Amit Chaudhuri, introduction to *Jejuri* (New York: New York Review of Books, 2005), vii–xxvi; Shubhangi Raykar, *Jejuri: A Commentary and Critical Perspectives* (Pune: Prachet Publications, 1995).

58. See Laetitia Zecchini, "Contemporary *Bhakti* Recastings: Recovering a Demotic Tradition, Challenging Nativism, Fashioning Modernism in Indian Poetry," *Interventions: International Journal of Postcolonial Studies* 16, no. 2 (2014): 257–76. Zecchini develops these ideas in her *Arun Kolatkar and Literary Modernism in India: Moving Lines* (London: Bloomsbury, 2014).

59. MacCannell, *Tourist*, 110–11, and Culler, "Semiotics of Tourism," 159–60.

60. See Urry and Larsen, *Tourist Gaze*, 226, and MacCannell, *Tourist*.

61. MacCannell, *Tourist*, 111.

62. MacCannell, *Tourist*, 43–44.

63. Urry and Larsen, *Tourist Gaze*, 55.

Chapter 4

1. Though endlessly debated, "postcolonial" literature is typically ascribed to imaginative works written in the shadow and aftermath of Western colonialism, often in resistance to it, such as Chinua Achebe's *Things Fall Apart*, Salman Rushdie's *Midnight's Children*, and Derek Walcott's *Omeros*. "Modernist" or "Euromodernist" literature is usually understood as innovative writing developed in early-twentieth-century Europe and America, from Joseph Conrad, Gertrude Stein, and James Joyce to T. S. Eliot and W. H. Auden. With obvious exceptions such as Rabindranath Tagore and Claude McKay, and obvious complications such as semi-postcolonial Irish literature, the great efflorescence of postcolonial writing in English is generally seen as coming after World War II, whereas the heyday of modernism is usually seen as coming earlier.

2. Fredric Jameson, "Modernism and Imperialism," in Jameson et al., *Nationalism, Colonialism, and Literature* (Minneapolis: University of Minnesota Press, 1990), 64.

3. For the orientalist critique of modernism, see, e.g., Mariana Torgovnik, *Gone Primitive: Savage Intellects, Modern Lives* (Chicago: University of Chicago Press, 1990); see also the rebuttal in Ben Etherington, *Literary Primitivism* (Stanford: Stanford University Press, 2018), 13.

4. See Harish Trivedi, "'Ganga Was Sunken': T. S. Eliot's Use of India," in *The Fire and the Rose: New Essays on T. S. Eliot*, ed. Vinod Sena and Rajiva Verma (Delhi: Oxford University Press, 1992), 44–62.

5. Chinua Achebe, "An Image of Africa: Racism in Conrad's *Heart of Darkness*," *Massachusetts Review* 18 (1977): 782–94.

6. See, e.g., Robert Stilling, "Multicentric Modernism and Postcolonial Poetry," in *The Cambridge Companion to Postcolonial Poetry*, ed. Jahan Ramazani (Cambridge: Cambridge University Press, 2017), 127–38; Omaar Hena, "World Modernist Poetry," in *A Companion to Modernist Poetry*, ed. David E. Chinitz and Gail McDonald (Oxford: Blackwell, 2014), 296–309; and Jahan Ramazani, *A Transnational Poetics* (Chicago: University of Chicago Press, 2009), chaps. 5 and 6.

7. See, e.g., Susan Stanford Friedman, *Planetary Modernisms: Provocations on Modernity across Time* (New York: Columbia University Press, 2015), and her "World Modernisms, World Literature, and Comparativity," in *The Oxford Handbook of Global Modernisms*, ed. Mark Wollaeger with Matt Eatough (New York: Oxford University Press, 2012), chap. 21.

8. Charles W. Pollard, *New World Modernisms: T. S. Eliot, Derek Walcott, and Kamau Brathwaite* (Charlottesville: University of Virginia Press, 2004), and Peter J. Kalliney, *Commonwealth of Letters: British Literary Culture and the Emergence of Postcolonial Aesthetics* (Oxford: Oxford University Press, 2013).

9. Neil Lazarus, "Modernism and African Literature," in Wollaeger with Eatough, *Oxford Handbook of Global Modernisms*, 235, 236.

10. Karen Press, *Bird Heart Stoning the Sea* (Cape Town: Buchu Books, 1990), 21. Ensuing references are to this page.

11. On art's value in challenging bourgeois ideology, see René Magritte, *Selected Writings*, ed. Kathleen Roony and Eric Plattner, trans. Jo Levy (Minneapolis: University of Minnesota Press, 2016), 46, 63. On the importance of not confusing art with politics and of not prescribing political limits on the artist, see Magritte, *Selected Writings*, 102, 104, 133.

12. Kamau Brathwaite, *History of the Voice: The Development of Nation Language in Anglophone Caribbean Poetry* (1984), rpt. and rev. in *Roots* (Ann Arbor: University of Michigan Press, 1993), 286. For critical discussions of Brathwaite's statement, see Ramazani, *Transnational Poetics*, 199n7. Walcott cites recordings of Eliot's *Four Quartets* as a crucial early influence; see Walcott, "Leaving School," rpt. in *Critical Perspectives on Derek Walcott*, ed. Robert Hamner (Washington, DC: Three Continents Press, 1993), 31. On Eliot as global poet, see Elisabeth Däumer and Shyamal Bagchee, eds., *The International Reception of T. S. Eliot* (New York: Continuum, 2007).

13. Lorna Goodison, "Quest," in *Supplying Salt and Light* (Toronto: McClelland & Stewart–Random House, 2013), 55. Ensuing references are to this page.

14. T. S. Eliot, "Journey of the Magi," in *The Complete Poems and Plays* (London: Faber, 1969), 104.

15. Eliot's phrase is from his preface to Saint-John Perse, *Anabasis*, rev. and corr. ed., trans. Eliot (New York: Harcourt, Brace, 1949), 10. On Eliot and Perse, see Ronald Bush, *T. S. Eliot: A Study in Character and Style* (New York: Oxford University Press, 1983), 124–29, and Anita Patterson, *Race, American Literature and Transnational Modernisms* (Cambridge: Cambridge University Press, 2008), 32–42, 62–78.

16. T. S. Eliot, "Dante," *Selected Prose of T. S. Eliot*, ed. Frank Kermode (New York: Farrar, Straus and Giroux, 1975), 206.

17. Brathwaite, *History of the Voice*, 262–63.

18. Roman Jakobson, "What Is Poetry?," trans. Michael Heim, in *Language in Literature*, ed. Krystyna Pomorska and Stephen Rudy (Cambridge, MA: Belknap Press of Harvard University Press, 1987), 378.

19. See A. L. Kroeber, "Stimulus Diffusion," *American Anthropologist* 42, no. 1 (1940): 1–20.

20. See Susan Stanford Friedman, "World Modernisms," 502.

21. Laura Doyle, "Afterword," in Wollaeger with Eatough, *Oxford Handbook of Global Modernisms*, 675.

22. Gayatri Chakravorty Spivak, *Death of a Discipline* (New York: Columbia University Press, 2003), 6.

23. Anthony Giddens, *The Consequences of Modernity* (Stanford: Stanford University Press, 1990), 175.

24. Kwame Anthony Appiah, *In My Father's House: Africa in the Philosophy of Culture* (New York: Oxford University Press, 1992), 72; *Cosmopolitanism: Ethics in a World of Strangers* (New York: W. W. Norton, 2006), 111, 103.

25. Bill Ashcroft, Gareth Griffiths, and Helen Tiffin, *The Empire Writes Back: Theory and Practice in Post-colonial Literatures* (London: Routledge, 1989). The Rushdie quote is the book's epigraph.

26. Appiah, "Topologies of Nativism," *In My Father's House*, 47–72, and "Europe Upside Down: Fallacies of the New Afrocentrism," in *Perspectives on Africa*, ed. Roy Richard Grinker and Christopher B. Steiner (London: Blackwell, 1997), 728–31.

27. Arif Dirlik, "Modernity in Question? Culture and Religion in an Age of Global Modernity," *Diaspora* 12, no. 2 (2003): 152.

28. Fredric Jameson, *A Singular Modernity: Essay on the Ontology of the Present* (London: Verso, 2002), 12.

29. Lazarus, "Modernism and African Literature," 235. For a cogent critique, see Susan Stanford Friedman, "World Modernisms," 501–3.

30. Warwick Research Collective (Sharae Deckard et al.), *Combined and Uneven Development: Towards a New Theory of World-Literature* (Liverpool: Liverpool University Press, 2015), 50.

31. Lazarus, "Modernism and African Literature," 235. See also Dilip Parameshwar Gaonkar, ed., *Alternative Modernities* (Durham: Duke University Press, 2001).

32. Jameson, *Singular Modernity*, 12.

33. Lazarus, "Modernism and African Literature," 233.

34. Arjun Appadurai, *Modernity at Large: Cultural Dimensions of Globalization* (Minneapolis: University of Minnesota Press, 1996), 32.

35. Appadurai, *Modernity at Large*, 7.

36. Daljit Nagra, "A Black History of the English-Speaking Peoples," in *Tippoo Sultan's Incredible White-Man-Eating Tiger Toy-Machine!!!* (London: Faber, 2011), 50–53. Further references appear in text.

37. W. H. Auden, "Spain," in *Selected Poems of W. H. Auden: New Edition*, ed. Edward Mendelson (New York: Random House, 1979), 51.

38. W. J. Perry, *The Growth of Civilization* (London: Methuen, 1924), 1. On this influence, see John Fuller, *W. H. Auden: A Commentary* (Princeton: Princeton University Press, 1998), 284.

39. Auden, "Spain," 54.

40. *OED Online*, s.v. "bumf" or "bumph": 2, "toilet paper" (somewhat archaic); 3, useless printed or written paper materials; accessed February 8, 2020, http://dictionary.oed.com/.

41. Alfred Lord Tennyson, "The Defence of Lucknow," line 29.

Chapter 5

1. Wallace Stevens, "Anecdote of the Jar," in *Collected Poetry and Prose*, ed. Frank Kermode and Joan Richardson (New York: Library of America–Penguin Random House, 1997), 60–61. Subsequent quotations are from this text. See Kenneth Koch's famous poem "Variations on a Theme by William Carlos Williams."

2. Caroline Levine, *Forms: Whole, Rhythm, Hierarchy, Network* (Princeton, NJ: Princeton University Press, 2015), 7. According to Levine, all historical uses of the term "share a common definition: 'form' always indicates *an arrangement of elements— an ordering, patterning, or shaping*" (3). My use of the term is largely consonant with Levine's, though I see "form" and "genre" as intertwined rather than sharply distinct in their portability (13). Form is the subject of much recent scholarship; in addition to Levine, overviews and discussions include Susan Wolfson, "Form," in *The Princeton Encyclopedia of Poetry and Poetics*, 4th ed., ed. Roland Greene, Stephen Cushman, Clare Cavanagh, Jahan Ramazani, and Paul Rouzer (Princeton: Princeton University Press, 2012), 497–99; Derek Attridge, *Moving Words: Forms of English Poetry* (Oxford University Press, 2013), chap. 1; Verena Theile, "New Formalism(s): A Prologue," in *New Formalisms and Literary Theory*, ed. Theile and Linda Tredennick (New York: Palgrave Macmillan, 2013), 3–28; Fredric V. Bogel, *New Formalist Criticism: Theory and Practice* (New York: Palgrave Macmillan, 2013); and Angela Leighton, *On Form: Poetry, Aestheticism, and the Legacy of a Word* (Oxford: Oxford University Press, 2008).

3. See Jennifer Rae Greeson, *Our South: Geographic Fantasy and the Rise of National Literature* (Cambridge, MA: Harvard University Press, 2010).

4. See the cluster of essays responding to these scholars, edited by Dan Sinykin, "Cultural Analytics Now," *Post45* (May 2019), http://post45.research.yale.edu/2019/05/introduction-cultural-analytics-now/.

5. Franco Moretti, *Distant Reading* (London: Verso, 2013), 50.

6. Moretti, *Distant Reading*, 52, 57.

7. Moretti, *Distant Reading*, 57.

8. Moretti, *Distant Reading*, 60.

9. Moretti, *Distant Reading*, 110. Moretti cites and responds to previous critics in "More Conjectures," in *Distant Reading*, 107–19.

10. Jahan Ramazani, *A Transnational Poetics* (Chicago: University of Chicago Press, 2009), chap. 5.

11. Edwige Tamalet Talbayev, "Berber Poetry and the Issue of Derivation: Alternate Symbolist Trajectories," in *The Oxford Handbook of Global Modernisms*, ed. Mark Wollaeger with Matt Eatough (New York: Oxford University Press, 2012), 82; Neil Lazarus, "Modernism and African Literature," in Wollaeger with Eatough, *Global Modernisms*, 240–41; and Nergis Ertürk, "Modernism Disfigured: Turkish Literature and the 'Other West,'" in Wollaeger with Eatough, *Oxford Handbook of Global Modernisms*, 531.

12. Pascale Casanova, "Literature as a World," *New Left Review* 31 (2005): 80n14, 80.

13. Casanova, "Literature as a World," 88. On Darío, as well as a fuller presentation of her argument, see Casanova, *The World Republic of Letters*, trans. M. B. DeBevoise (Cambridge, MA: Harvard University Press, 2007), 19.

14. Moretti, *Distant Reading*, 57.

15. Moretti, *Distant Reading*, 49.

16. Alexander Beecroft, "World Literature without a Hyphen: Towards a Typology of Literary Systems," *New Left Review* 54 (2008): 88.

17. Moretti, *Distant Reading*, 59.

18. Susan Stanford Friedman, "World Modernisms, World Literature, and Comparativity," in Wollaeger with Eatough, *Global Modernisms*, 502.

19. Chinweizu, Onwuchekwa Jemie, Ihechukwu Madubuike, "Toward the Decolonization of African Literature," *Transition* 48 (1975): 37. They elaborated their argument against modernist influences in African poetry in *Toward the Decolonization of African Literature* (1980; Washington, DC: Howard University Press, 1983), chap. 3.

20. Chinweizu et al., "Toward the Decolonization," 30.

21. Kamau Brathwaite, *History of the Voice*, as rev. and rpt. in *Roots* (Ann Arbor: University of Michigan Press, 1993), 275n17, 275.

22. Brathwaite, *History of the Voice*, 265.

23. Derek Walcott, "Hurucan," in *Collected Poems, 1948–1984* (New York: Farrar, Straus, and Giroux, 1986), 423.

24. Derek Walcott, *Omeros* (New York: Farrar, Straus, and Giroux, 1990), 52.

25. Moretti, *Distant Reading*, 48.

26. Moretti, *Distant Reading*, 51n13.

27. Moretti, *Distant Reading*, 52n15.

28. Moretti, *Distant Reading*, 52n17.

29. Moretti, *Distant Reading*, 129–31.

30. Moretti, *Distant Reading*, 66.

31. Andrew Piper, *Enumerations* (Chicago: University of Chicago Press, 2018), 34.

32. Robert Creeley as quoted in Charles Olson, "Projective Verse," in *Collected Prose*,

ed. Donald Allen and Benjamin Friedlander (Berkeley: University of California Press, 1997), 240.

33. See, e.g., Sarah Allison et al., *Style at the Scale of the Sentence*, Pamphlet 5 of the Stanford Literary Lab, June 2013, http://litlab.stanford.edu/LiteraryLabPamphlet5 .pdf.

34. Moretti, *Distant Reading*, 86.

35. Allen Ginsberg, "Howl," in *Selected Poems, 1947–1995* (New York: HarperCollins, 1996), 49–51, 54.

36. Moretti, *Distant Reading*, 77.

37. Marianne Moore, "England," in *The Poems of Marianne Moore*, ed. Grace Schulman (New York: Viking-Penguin, 2003), 141–42. Ensuing quotations are from these pages.

38. Nagra, "The Punjab," *Tippoo Sultan's Incredible White-Man-Eating Tiger Toy-Machine!!!*, 34–35. Ensuing quotations are from these pages.

Chapter 6

1. I cite much of the pertinent scholarship on either side of the question in *A Transnational Poetics* (Chicago: University of Chicago Press, 2009), 184, 201–2.

2. See, e.g., Kwame Anthony Appiah, "Whose Culture Is It, Anyway?," *Cosmopolitanism: Ethics in a World of Strangers* (New York: W. W. Norton, 2006), 115–35.

3. Christopher Bush, "Modernism, Orientalism, and East Asia," in *A Handbook of Modernism Studies*, ed. Jean-Michel Rabaté (Chichester, West Sussex: Wiley-Blackwell, 2013), 193–208.

4. I write briefly about Yeats, Eliot, and Pound as orientalist and anti-orientalist in *A Transnational Poetics*, 109–14. See also Joseph Lennon, "W. B. Yeats's Celtic Orient," in *Irish Orientalism: A Literary and Intellectual History* (Syracuse: Syracuse University Press, 2004), 247–89.

5. W. B. Yeats, "The Statues," in *The Variorum Edition of the Poems of W. B. Yeats*, ed. Peter Allt and Russell K. Alspach (New York: Macmillan, 1968), 610. Subsequent references to Yeats's poetry appear parenthetically.

6. W. B. Yeats, *Later Essays*, ed. William H. O'Donnell, with Elizabeth Bergmann Loizeaux (New York: Scribner, 1994), vol. 5 in *The Collected Works of W. B. Yeats*, ed. Richard J. Finneran and George Mills Harper, 5:249.

7. Edward W. Said, *Orientalism* (New York: Random House, 1978), 72. On the West's often ambivalent fascination with Persian poetry and culture, see Hamid Dabashi, *Persophilia: Persian Culture on the Global Scene* (Cambridge, MA: Harvard University Press, 2015), and John D. Yohannan, *Persian Poetry in England and America: A 200-Year History* (Delmar, NY: Caravan Books, 1977).

8. Said, *Orientalism*, 207.

9. Said, *Orientalism*, 229.

10. Yeats, *Later Essays*, 249.

11. Yeats, *Later Essays*, 134.

12. Yeats, *Later Essays*, 173–74.

13. Lennon, *Irish Orientalism*, 250.

14. See, e.g., Calvert Watkins, *How to Kill a Dragon: Aspects of Indo-European Poetics* (Oxford: Oxford University Press, 1995); Anna June Pagé, "The Description of Dond Cúalnge in the LL 'Táin Bó Cúalnge' and Indo-European Catalogue Poetry," *Proceedings of the Harvard Celtic Colloquium* 32 (2012): 229–56; N. K. Sandars, "Orient and Orientalizing in Early Celtic Art," *Antiquity* 45 (1971): 103–12; and Ruth Megaw and Vincent Megaw, "The Nature and Function of Celtic Art," in *The Celtic World*, ed. Miranda J. Green (New York: Routledge, 1996), 347.

15. John Rickard, "Studying a New Science: Yeats, Irishness, and the East," in *Representing Ireland: Gender, Class, Nationality*, ed. Susan Shaw Sailer (Gainesville: University Press of Florida, 1997), 94–112.

16. For a source of the image in Diasetz Suzuki's *Essays in Zen Buddhism*, see Matthew Gibson, "'What Empty Eyeballs Knew': Zen Buddhism in 'The Statues' and the *Principles* of *A Vision*," *Yeats Annual* 11 (1995): 141–56.

17. Helen Vendler, *Our Secret Discipline: Yeats and Lyric Form* (Cambridge, MA: Belknap Press of Harvard University Press, 2007), 270–72.

18. T. McAlindon, "The Idea of Byzantium in William Morris and W. B. Yeats," *Modern Philology* 64, no. 4 (1967): 307–19; Elizabeth Bergmann Loizeaux, *Yeats and the Visual Arts* (New Brunswick, NJ: Rutgers University Press, 1986), 133; W. B. Yeats, *A Vision* (London: Macmillan, 1937), 281. The passage already appeared in the first edition: see Yeats, *A Vision (1925)*, ed. Catherine E. Paul and Margaret Mills Harper (New York: Scribner, 2008), in *The Collected Works of W. B. Yeats*, 13: 160. Loizeaux sees Yeats's assimilation of Byzantine to Pre-Raphaelite art as also drawing on John Ruskin, Arthur Symons, Oscar Wilde, and Edward Burne-Jones (133).

19. On Yeats and Strzygowski, see Russell Murphy, "Josef Strzygowski and Yeats' 'A Starlit or a Moonlit Dome,'" *College Literature* 13, no. 1 (1986): 106–11; Russell Elliott Murphy, "'Old Rocky Face, look forth': W. B. Yeats, the Christ Pantokrator, and the Soul's History (The Photographic Record)," *Yeats* 14 (1996): 69–117; and Daniel Albright, "Yeats, *A Vision*, and Art History," *Yeats Journal of Korea* 36 (2011): 5–29.

20. Yeats, *A Vision*, 270; *A Vision (1925)*, 152.

21. See *Pausanias's Description of Greece*, ed. and trans. James George Frazer (London: Macmillan, 1898), 1:39, 1.26.6–7 and 1.27.1. On Furtwängler, see Yeats, *A Vision* (1925), 295n23. But the Persian is mentioned, e.g., in Stanley Casson, *Catalogue of the Acropolis Museum* (Cambridge: Cambridge University Press, 1921), 2: 278.

22. See F. A. C. Wilson, "The Statues," in *Yeats: Last Poems, A Casebook*, ed. Jon Stallworthy (London: Macmillan, 1968), 170–72.

23. See Murphy, "'Old Rocky Face, look forth," and Giorgio Melchiori, "The Dome of Many-Coloured Glass," in *The Whole Mystery of Art: Pattern into Poetry in the Work of W. B. Yeats* (London: Routledge, 1960), chap. 6.

24. Brian Arkins, *Builders of My Soul: Greek and Roman Themes in Yeats* (Savage, MD: Barnes and Noble, 1990), 182.

25. Josef Strzygowski, *Origin of Christian Church Art*, trans. O. M. Dalton and H. J. Braunholtz (Oxford: Clarendon Press of Oxford University Press, 1923), 195. Ensuing references appear parenthetically. On Iran and Ireland, see *Erin and Iran: Cultural*

Encounters between the Irish and the Iranians, ed. H. E. Chehabi and Grace Neville (Boston: Ilex Foundation, 2015).

26. Suzanne L. Marchand, "The Rhetoric of Artifacts and the Decline of Classical Humanism: The Case of Josef Strzygowski," *History and Theory* 33.4 (1994): 111, 119. See also her "Appreciating the Art of Others: Josef Strzygowski and the Austrian Origins of Non-Western Art History," in *Von Biala nach Wien: Josef Strzygowski und die Kunstwissenschaften*, ed. Piotr Otto Scholz and Magdalena Anna Dlugosz (Vienna: European University Press Verlagsgesellschaft, 2015), 257–85, and *German Orientalism in the Age of Empire: Religion, Race, and Scholarship* (Cambridge: Cambridge University Press, 2009), 403–10.

27. W. B. Yeats, *The Variorum Edition of the Plays of W. B. Yeats*, ed. Russell K. Alspach and Catharine C. Alspach (New York: Macmillan, 1966), 805.

28. W. B. Yeats, *The Letters of W. B. Yeats*, ed. Allan Wade (London: Rupert Hart-Davis, 1954), 440; Yeats to F. J. Fay, August 28, 1904, in *The Collected Letters of W. B. Yeats, 1901–1904*, ed. John Kelly and Ronald Schuchard (Oxford: Clarendon Press; New York: Oxford University Press, 1994), 3:643.

29. Edward Gibbon, *The Decline and Fall of the Roman Empire* (London: Jones, 1828), chap. 52, 3:516. On the Baghdad-Byzantium connection, see A. Clare Brandabur, "Arabic Sources of Yeats' Byzantium Poems," *Time's Fool: Essays in Context* (Newcastle upon Tyne: Cambridge Scholars, 2016), 325–26. For a synopsis of possible sources of Yeats's Byzantine birds, see Archibald A. Hill, "Method in Source Study: Yeats' Golden Bird of Byzantium as a Test Case," *Texas Studies in Literature and Language* 17, no. 2 (1975): 525–38.

30. So too, when Yeats refers in *A Vision* to "a Romanesque stream perhaps of bird and beast images" (*A Vision*, 283; *A Vision [1925]*, 161), he recalls, as the editors of *A Vision* note (*A Vision [1925]*, 305n82), Strzygowski's discussion of Iranian influences on Romanesque art, such as "the vinescroll with enclosed animals": comparison "reveals that fusion of Iranian and Greek art which succeeded the displacement of the late Roman times, and led gradually to the development of Byzantine art on the Mediterranean, of 'Romanesque' in the West, and to the complete triumph of Iranian art in the world of Islam" (Strzygowski, *Origin of Christian Church Art*, 112–14).

31. See Matthew P. Canepa, *The Two Eyes of the Earth: Art and Ritual of Kingship between Rome and Sasanian Iran* (Berkeley: University of California Press, 2009), 205–23, and "Textiles and Elite Tastes between the Mediterranean, Iran and Asia at the End of Antiquity," in *Global Textile Encounters*, ed. M.-L. Nosch, Zhao Feng and L. Varadarajan (Oxford: Oxbow Books, 2014), 1–14. See also Matteo Compareti, "Evidence of Mutual Exchange between Byzantine and Sogdian Art," in *La Persia e Bisanzio*, ed. Antonio Carile et al. (Rome: Accademia Nazionale dei Lincei, 2004), 865–922; A. Shapur Shahbazi, "Byzantine-Iranian Relations" (1990), in *Encyclopædia Iranica*, http://www.iranicaonline.org/articles/byzantine-iranian-relations; and D. Talbot Rice, "Persia and Byzantium," in *The Legacy of Persia*, ed. A. J. Arberry (Oxford: Clarendon Press, 1953), 39–59. Rice sees Persian influences in decorative motifs such as the peacock feather, the sacred tree, the vase with symmetrical plants, horse trappings and riders' ribbons, a man struggling with beasts on either side, the winged gryphon in a circle,

even Justinian's high soft boots and Theodora's two-pointed crown in the Church of San Vitale, as well as the elliptical arch, adorning niches, and squinches for the transition from square base to dome (45–49).

32. Canepa, *Two Eyes of the Earth*, 225.

33. See Daniel A. Harris, "The 'Figured Page': Dramatic Epistle in Browning and Yeats," *Yeats Annual* 1 (1982): 133–94. For an overview of Yeats's interest in Arab lore and his Arab-related poems, see S. B. Bushrui, "Yeats's Arabic Interests," in *In Excited Reverie: A Centenary Tribute to William Butler Yeats, 1865–1939*, ed. A. Norman Jeffares and K. G. W. Cross (London: Macmillan, 1965), 280–314. The poem had prefaced book 2 of *A Vision (1925)* under the title "Desert Geometry or the Gift of Harun Al-Raschid" (97–102).

34. W. B. Yeats, *Essays and Introductions* (London: Palgrave Macmillan, 1961), 447. "Clearly derived from the Arabic source," Susan Bazargan notes, "are the references to marble fountains, 'goldfish in the pool,' 'slender bride[s],' 'jasmine bough,' 'the peacock and his mate,' and of course the Djinn"; see her "W. B. Yeats: Autobiography and Colonialism," *Yeats: An Annual of Critical and Textual Studies* 13 (1995): 209–10. She believes that Yeats's erasure of Scheherazade and idealist refashioning of Harun is "an act of colonial appropriation" (212).

35. See Jon Stallworthy, *Between the Lines: Yeats's Poetry in the Making* (Oxford: Clarendon Press of Oxford University Press, 1963), 80. Mazen Naous remarks on "the rabbi" in "The Turn of the Gyres: Alterity in 'The Gift of Harun Al-Rashid' and *A Thousand and One Nights*," in *The Ashgate Research Companion to Nineteenth-Century Spiritualism and the Occult*, ed. Tatiana Kontou and Sarah Willburn (Farnham, UK: Ashgate, 2012), 204.

36. On medieval Cordoba as a similar cross-cultural nexus, see Robert J. C. Young, "Postcolonial Remains," *New Literary History* 43, no. 1 (2012): 19–42.

37. Stallworthy, *Between the Lines*, 86; R. F. Foster, *The Arch-Poet, 1915–1939*, vol. 2 of *W. B. Yeats: A Life* (Oxford: Oxford University Press, 2003), 603.

38. He characteristically appeals to "poetic licence"; see Yeats, *A Vision*, 54.

39. On the Solomon and Sheba of the Arabs, see Bushrui, "Yeats's Arabic Interests," 308–11.

40. Yeats, *Letters*, 832; Yeats to Ethel Mannin, March 4, 1935, *The Collected Letters of W. B. Yeats, Electronic Edition, Unpublished Letters (1905–1939)*, ed. John Kelly, InteLex, 6194. http://crkn.nlx.com/xtf/view?docId=yeats_c/yeats_c.04.xml;chunk.id=div.el .yeats.unpublished.6502;toc.id=div.el.yeats.unpublished.6499;brand=default;query -prox=.

41. On the various incarnations of this image from Hafez in Yeats, see Oliver Scharbrodt, "'From Hafiz': Irish Orientalism, Persian Poetry, and W. B. Yeats," in Chehabi and Neville, *Erin and Iran*, 73–77.

42. Yeats, *Later Essays*, 16.

43. On the importance of Theosophy's boundary-crossing internationalism, including the role in Yeats's thinking of the Moroccan-born spirit Leo Africanus, see Gauri Viswanathan, "Spectrality's Secret Sharers: Occultism as (Post)colonial Affect," in *Beyond the Black Atlantic: Relocating Modernization and Technology*, ed. Walter Goebel

and Saskia Schabio (Abingdon, UK: Routledge, 2006), 135–45, and Bushrui, "Yeats's Arabic Interests," 280–85.

44. Sankaran Ravindran, *W. B. Yeats and Indian Tradition* (Delhi: Konark, 1990), 31–33.

45. On Yeats's self-consciousness about the poem's projection, see Lennon, *Irish Orientalism*, 261.

46. Richard Ellmann, *The Identity of Yeats*, 2nd ed. (New York: Oxford University Press, 1964), 54.

47. Jahan Ramazani, "W. B. Yeats: A Postcolonial Poet?," in *The Hybrid Muse: Postcolonial Poetry in English* (Chicago: University of Chicago Press, 2001), 21–48.

48. A. K. Ramanujan, "Mythologies 2," in *The Collected Poems of A. K. Ramanujan* (Delhi: Oxford University Press, 1995), 226. Helen Vendler states that Yeats attempted "to write as a European" and even "to write poetry as a citizen of the world"; "he brought Irish verse (as Joyce brought Irish prose) out of insularity and into European culture"; see her "Yeats as a European Poet: The Poetics of Cacophony," in *Yeats the European*, ed. A. Norman Jeffares (Gerrards Cross, UK: Colin Smythe, 1989), 33.

49. See, e.g., the recent discussion in Carrie Preston, *Learning to Kneel: Noh, Modernism, and Journeys in Teaching* (New York: Columbia University Press, 2016), 63–101.

50. Ramazani, *Transnational Poetics*, 112.

51. On Sato's sword and cross-cultural exchange, see Aoife Assumpta Hart, *Ancestral Recall: The Celtic Revival of Japanese Modernism* (Montreal: McGill-Queen's University Press, 2016), 263–72, 309–10, 379–80. See also the documents, some with a bearing on Sato's sword, collected in Shotara Oshima, *W. B. Yeats and Japan* (Tokyo: Hokuseido Press, 1965).

52. Christopher Reed, *Bachelor Japanists: Japanese Aesthetics and Western Masculinities* (New York: Columbia University Press, 2017), 26.

53. Edward Marx, "No Dancing: Yone Noguchi in Yeats's Japan," *Yeats Annual* 17 (2007): 83–86.

54. See Yoshinobu Hakutani, *Haiku and Modernist Poetics* (New York: Palgrave Macmillan, 2009), 1–16, and Adam L. Kern, introduction and glossary to *The Penguin Book of Haiku* (London: Penguin, 2018), xxiii–lxxi, 399–415.

55. Kern, *Penguin Book of Haiku*, lxxiv.

56. Kern, *Penguin Book of Haiku*, 3.

57. Ensuing references are to the same page.

58. Kern, *Penguin Book of Haiku*, 222, 412.

59. Gustav Heldt, "Waka," in *The Princeton Encyclopedia of Poetry and Poetics*, 4th ed., ed. Roland Greene, Stephen Cushman, Clare Cavanagh, Jahan Ramazani, and Paul Rouzer (Princeton: Princeton University Press, 2012), 1528. See also Mark Morris, "Waka and Form, Waka and History," *Harvard Journal of Asiatic Studies* 46, no. 2 (1986): 551–610, and Yoshinobu Hakutani, "Ezra Pound, Yone Noguchi, and Imagism," *Modern Philology* 90, no. 1 (1992): 46–69.

60. Heldt, "Waka," 1528.

61. See Barry Sheils, *W. B. Yeats and World Literature: The Subject of Poetry* (Farnham,

UK: Ashgate, 2015). Unlike world literary scholars such as David Damrosch and Pascale Casanova, Sheils emphasizes the material imbrication of Yeats's work in a world economic system.

62. Stefan Helgesson, "Postcolonialism and World Literature: Rethinking the Boundaries," *Interventions* 16, no. 4 (2014): 484.

63. Said, *Orientalism*, 181.

64. Said, *Orientalism*, 181. See also Said, *On Late Style: Music and Literature against the Grain* (New York: Pantheon Books, 2006).

65. Edward W. Said, "Yeats and Decolonization," *Culture and Imperialism* (New York: Knopf, 1993), 220; I develop and complicate the argument in "W. B. Yeats: A Postcolonial Poet?" and in "Poetry and Decolonization," chap. 7 of *A Transnational Poetics*, 141–62.

66. Yeats, *Later Essays*, 134.

67. Said, *Orientalism*, 204.

68. Bushrui, "Yeats's Arabic Interests," 295.

69. Said, *Orientalism*, 38.

70. Yeats, *Later Essays*, 177–78.

71. Said, *Orientalism*, 291.

72. Said, *Orientalism*, 291.

73. Said, *Orientalism*, 80.

74. An incomplete sampling of the scholarship would include Preston, *Learning to Kneel*; Hart, *Ancestral Recall*; Sheils, *W. B. Yeats and World Literature*; Sirshendu Majumdar, *Yeats and Tagore: A Comparative Study of Cross-cultural Poetry, Nationalist Politics, Hyphenated Margins and the Ascendancy of the Mind* (Bethesda, MD: Academica Press, 2013); Hakutani, *Haiku and Modernist Poetics*; R. F. Foster, *The Apprentice Mage, 1865–1914*, vol. 1 of *W. B. Yeats: A Life* (Oxford: Oxford University Press, 1998), and *Arch-Poet*; Ravindran, *W. B. Yeats and Indian Tradition*; Masaru Sekine and Christopher Murray, *Yeats and Noh: A Comparative Study* (Gerrards Cross, UK: Smythe, 1990); and Richard Taylor, *The Drama of W. B. Yeats: Irish Myth and the Japanese Nō* (New Haven: Yale University Press, 1976).

Chapter 7

1. Wallace Stevens, "O, Florida, Venereal Soil," in *Collected Poetry and Prose*, ed. Frank Kermode and Joan Richardson (New York: Library of America–Penguin Random House, 1997), 38. Subsequent references to this collection appear parenthetically in text.

2. Helen Hennessy Vendler, *On Extended Wings: Wallace Stevens' Longer Poems* (Cambridge: Harvard University Press, 1969), 50, 51.

3. On the charge of "extraordinary racism" by Geoffrey Jacques, see Rachel Galvin, "Race," in *Wallace Stevens in Context*, ed. Glen MacLeod (Cambridge: Cambridge University Press, 2016), 286–96, and on "the exotic," see Stephanie (published as Stephen) Burt, in MacLeod, *Wallace Stevens in Context*, 316–25.

4. Ursula K. Heise, *Sense of Place and Sense of Planet: The Environmental Imagination of the Global* (New York: Oxford University Press, 2008), 64.

5. Vendler, *On Extended Wings*, 50.

6. Paul Hopper, *Understanding Cultural Globalization* (Cambridge: Polity, 2007), 23.

7. See Bart Eeckhout, "Preface: (Re)Globalizing Stevens," *Wallace Stevens Journal* 25, no. 2 (2001): 107–10, and in the same special issue on international perspectives on Wallace Stevens, Stephen Matterson, "'The Whole Habit of the Mind': Stevens, Americanness, and the Use of Elsewhere," 111–21. See also the special issue's other essays, as well as Bart Eeckhout, "The Planet—or Just America?: On Helen Vendler's Claims about Stevens' Americanness," *Wallace Stevens Journal* 38, no. 2 (2014): 233–49.

8. Peter Schjeldahl, "Insurance Man," review of Paul Mariani's *The Whole Harmonium: The Life of Wallace Stevens*, *New Yorker*, May 2, 2016, 73.

9. Hopper, *Understanding Cultural Globalization*, 35, 2.

10. Arjun Appadurai, *Modernity at Large: Cultural Dimensions of Globalization* (Minneapolis: University of Minnesota Press, 1996), 33–37.

11. Wallace Stevens, "The Noble Rider and the Sound of Words," in *Collected Poetry and Prose*, 653.

12. Stevens, *Collected Poetry and Prose*, 655. See my chapter "Poetry and the News," in *Poetry and Its Others: News, Prayer, Song, and the Dialogue of Genres* (Chicago: University of Chicago Press, 2014), 63–125. See also Rachel Galvin, "Wallace Stevens in a 'Sudden Time,'" in *News of War: Civilian Poetry, 1936–1945* (Oxford: Oxford University Press, 2017), 162–99. And on Stevens's war elegies as both resisting and internalizing the violence of war, see my *Poetry of Mourning: The Modern Elegy from Hardy to Heaney* (Chicago: University of Chicago Press, 1994), 106–19.

13. Wallace Stevens to Leonard C. van Geyzel, in *Letters of Wallace Stevens*, ed. Holly Stevens (New York: Alfred A. Knopf, 1961), 323–24.

14. Stevens, *Letters*, 323n2.

15. Two recent essays survey the extensive scholarship in these areas: see Edward Ragg, "The Orient," in MacLeod, *Wallace Stevens in Context*, 55–64; Glen MacLeod, "The Visual Arts," in MacLeod, *Wallace Stevens in Context*, 187–96. Among the works they reference, see two articles in the international perspectives special issue of the *Wallace Stevens Journal* 25, no. 2 (2001): William W. Bevis, "Stevens, Buddhism, and the Meditative Mind" (148–63), and Zhaoming Qian, "Late Stevens, Nothingness, and the Orient" (164–72).

16. Matterson, "'Whole Habit of the Mind,'" 111, citing Stevens's *Opus Posthumous* and his *Letters*.

17. Jonathan Culler, "The Semiotics of Tourism," in *Framing the Sign: Criticism and Its Institutions* (Oxford: Blackwell, 1988), 155.

18. Stevens, "Adagia," in *Collected Poetry and Prose*, 914. Among other discussions of the subject, see Natalie Gerber, "'A Funny Foreigner of Meek Address': Stevens and English as a Foreign Language," *Wallace Stevens Journal* 25, no. 2 (2001): 211–19; Juliette Utard, "A 'Special Relation'? Stevens' French, American English, and the Creolization of Modern Poetry," introduction to *Wallace Stevens, Poetry, and France: "Au pays de la*

métaphore," ed. Utard, Bart Eeckhout, and Lisa Goldfarb (Paris: Éditions Rue d'Ulm/ Presses de l'École normale supérieure, 2017), 17–28; and Harris Feinsod, *The Poetry of the Americas: From Good Neighbors to Countercultures* (Oxford: Oxford University Press, 2017), 103, 107–8, 114.

19. Roland Robertson, *Globalization: Social Theory and Global Culture* (London: Sage, 1992), 78.

20. Timothy Morton, *The Ecological Thought* (Cambridge: Harvard University Press, 2010), 12.

21. See Lynn Keller, *Recomposing Ecopoetics: North American Poetry of the Self-Conscious Anthropocene* (Charlottesville: University of Virginia Press, 2017), especially chaps. 1 and 5, and "Green Reading: Modern and Contemporary American Poetry and Environmental Criticism," in *The Oxford Handbook of Modern and Contemporary American Poetry*, ed. Cary Nelson (New York: Oxford University Press, 2012), 602–23.

22. Wallace Stevens, *Souvenirs and Prophecies: The Young Wallace Stevens*, ed. Holly Stevens (New York: Knopf, 1977), 134.

23. Robertson, *Globalization*, 179.

24. W. B. Yeats, ed., *The Oxford Book of Modern Verse, 1892–1935* (New York: Oxford University Press, 1937), 1.

25. Gyorgyi Voros, *Notations of the Wild: Ecology in the Poetry of Wallace Stevens* (Iowa City: University of Iowa Press, 1997), 45, 67, 70.

26. Scott Knickerbocker, *Ecopoetics: The Language of Nature, the Nature of Language* (Amherst: University of Massachusetts Press, 2012), 25.

27. Ramachandra Guha, "Radical American Environmental and Wilderness Preservation: A Third World Critique," *Environmental Ethics* 11 (1989): 71–83.

28. See Ramazani, *Poetry of Mourning*, 102–3.

29. Stevens, "Imagination as Value," in *Collected Poetry and Prose*, 730.

30. Bruno Latour, *We Have Never Been Modern* (Cambridge: Harvard University Press, 1993), 2.

31. Bruno Latour, "On Actor-Network Theory: A Few Clarifications Plus More Than a Few Complications" (1996), 6, http://www.bruno-latour.fr/sites/default/files/P-67%20ACTOR-NETWORK.pdf.

32. Gayatri Chakravorty Spivak, *Death of a Discipline* (New York: Columbia University Press, 2003), 72.

33. Immanuel Kant, *Critique of Judgment*, trans. J. H. Bernard (London: Hafner-Macmillan, 1951), 90–91.

34. Knickerbocker, *Ecopoetics*, 9, and Matthew Griffiths, *The New Poetics of Climate Change: Modernist Aesthetics for a Warming World* (London: Bloomsbury, 2017), 59.

35. Morton, *Ecological Thought*, 20.

36. Morton, *Ecological Thought*, 38.

37. Stevens, *Collected Poetry and Prose*, 901.

38. Stephanie (published as Stephen) Burt, "Wallace Stevens: Where He Lived," *ELH* 77, no. 2 (2010): 343.

39. Bart Eeckhout, "Wallace Stevens' 'Earthy Anecdote'; or, How Poetry Must

Resist Ecocriticism Almost Successfully," *Comparative American Studies* 7, no. 2 (2009): 173–92.

40. John N. Serio and Greg Foster, eds., Online Concordance to Wallace Stevens' Poetry, http://www.wallacestevens.com/concordance/WSdb.cgi (also the source for the Stevens word counts below).

41. Robert J. Dilligan et al., eds., *A Concordance to Ezra Pound's Cantos* (New York: Garland, 1981), 546–48.

42. Stephen Maxfield Parrish, ed., *A Concordance to the Poems of W. B. Yeats* (Ithaca: Cornell University Press, 1963), 935–37. The corresponding numbers in Pound are *earth* 54, *world* 27, and *whole* 53 (*Concordance to Ezra Pound's Cantos*, 546, 547, 546).

43. Stevens, *Collected Poetry and Prose*, 663.

44. Morton, *Ecological Thought*, 26.

45. Timothy Morton, *Ecology without Nature: Rethinking Environmental Aesthetics* (Cambridge, MA: Harvard University Press, 2007), 11.

46. Lawrence Buell, *The Future of Environmental Criticism: Environmental Crisis and Literary Representation* (New York: Blackwell, 2005), 66.

47. Heise, *Sense of Place and Sense of Planet*, 10, 62, 9.

48. Heise, *Sense of Place and Sense of Planet*, 56.

49. Rob Nixon, *Slow Violence and the Environmentalism of the Poor* (Cambridge, MA: Harvard University Press, 2011), 234, 238, 235.

50. Morton, *Ecological Thought*, 28.

51. See, e.g., the fine books cited above, by Heise and Nixon.

52. Morton, *Ecological Thought*, 14.

53. Ayesha Ramachandran, *The Worldmakers: Global Imagining in Early Modern Europe* (Chicago: University of Chicago Press, 2015), 4, 6.

54. Walt Whitman, "Passage to India," line 120, *The Complete Poems*, ed. Francis Murphy (Harmondsworth: Penguin, 1975), 432.

55. Whitman, "Passage to India," lines 81–86, *Complete Poems*, 431.

56. Whitman, "Passage to India," line 32, *Complete Poems*, 429. On the (compromised) transnationalism of Whitman's poem, see Kornelia Freitag, "Meena Alexander 'In Whitman's Country'" (2015), http://arcade.stanford.edu/content/meena-alexander-whitman's-country. On the poem's place in modern European thinking about the world, see Eric Hayot, *On Literary Worlds* (Oxford: Oxford University Press, 2012), 92–94. Stevens's debt to Whitman (and Emerson) is most vigorously urged in Harold Bloom, *Wallace Stevens: The Poems of Our Climate* (Ithaca, NY: Cornell University Press, 1976).

57. Ramachandran, *Worldmakers*, 15, 17, 8.

58. Stevens, *Collected Poetry and Prose*, 657.

59. Voros, *Notations of the Wild*, 125.

60. J. Hillis Miller, "When Is a Primitive like an Orb?," in *Textual Analysis: Some Readers Reading*, ed. Mary Ann Caws (New York: Modern Language Association, 1986), 170, 178. See also Joseph N. Riddel, *The Clairvoyant Eye: The Poetry and Poetics of Wallace Stevens* (Baton Rouge: Louisiana State University Press, 1965), 49–50, and

Bloom, *Wallace Stevens*, 294–95 (who oddly sees the poem as a diminished version of Whitman's nationalist ode to America, "By Blue Ontario's Shore" [293]).

61. The trio revises Shakespeare's "The lunatic, the lover, and the poet / Are of imagination all compact" (*A Midsummer Night's Dream*, in *The Riverside Shakespeare*, ed. G. Blakemore Evans et al. [Boston: Houghton Mifflin, 1974], 5.1.7–8).

62. Morton, *Ecological Thought*, 7, 8.

63. Stevens, *Adagia*, in *Collected Poetry and Prose*, 903. On aphorism as a form that is poised between singularity and network, see Andrew Hui, *A Theory of Aphorism: From Confucius to Twitter* (Princeton: Princeton University Press, 2019), 3.

64. Morton, *Ecological Thought*, 28, and *Dark Ecology: For a Logic of Future Coexistence* (New York: Columbia University Press, 2016), 160, 70, 11.

65. Morton, *Dark Ecology*, 160.

66. Stevens, *Letters*, 251.

67. The precise source of this question is unknown, though elements of it appear in Bishop Berkeley's *Treatise*. In a famous thought experiment, Berkeley suggests "trying whether you can conceive it possible for a sound, or figure, or motion, or colour, to exist without the mind, or unperceived," answering that while it may seem possible, the procedure proves only the selective mental habit of "framing in your mind certain ideas which you call books and trees, and at the same time omitting to frame the idea of any one that may perceive them." See George Berkeley, *A Treatise concerning the Principles of Human Knowledge*, ed. Jonathan Dancy (New York: Oxford University Press, 1998), §22, 110–11.

68. Andrew Welsh, *Roots of Lyric: Primitive Poetry and Modern Poetics* (Princeton: Princeton University Press, 1978), and Jonathan Culler, *Theory of the Lyric* (Cambridge, MA: Harvard University Press, 2015).

69. Morton, *Ecological Thought*, 51.

70. Ramazani, *Poetry of Mourning*, 119–34. Among many other self-elegiac readings of the poem, see Charles Berger, *Forms of Farewell: The Late Poetry of Wallace Stevens* (Madison: University of Wisconsin Press, 1985), 178–81, and Helen Vendler, *Wallace Stevens: Words Chosen out of Desire* (Cambridge, MA: Harvard University Press, 1986), 35–39.

71. Barbara Fisher, introduction to *Wallace Stevens Journal* 30, no. 2 (2006): 131, and Joan Richardson, "Wallace Stevens: A Likeness," in *The Cambridge Companion to Wallace Stevens*, ed. John N. Serio (Cambridge: Cambridge University Press, 2007), 12.

72. *The Dialogues of Plato*, trans. B. Jowett, 3rd ed. (New York: Macmillan, 1892), 3:308.

73. Stevens, 240 times; Yeats, 111.

74. William Wordsworth, "Lines Composed . . . above Tintern Abbey," lines 106–7, in *The Poems*, ed. John O. Hayden (New Haven: Yale University Press, 1981), 1:360.

75. See Morton, *Ecology without Nature*, 31, 23, 30.

76. Buell, *Future of Environmental Criticism*, 31, 68.

77. Dana Phillips, *The Truth of Ecology: Nature, Culture, and Literature in America* (New York: Oxford University Press, 2003), 186, 7, 161, 156.

78. Heise, *Sense of Place and Sense of a Planet*, 64.

79. W. H. Auden, "A New Year Greeting," in *Selected Poems of W. H. Auden: New Edition*, ed. Edward Mendelson (New York: Random House, 1979), 292.

80. Auden, *Selected Poems*, 292. I offer a fuller reading of the poem in *Poetry of Mourning*, 209–11.

81. A. K. Ramanujan, "Elements of Composition," in *The Collected Poems of A. K. Ramanujan* (Delhi: Oxford University Press, 1995), 121, 123.

82. Ramanujan, *Collected Poems*, 123. I offer a fuller reading of the poem in *The Hybrid Muse: Postcolonial Poetry in English* (Chicago: University of Chicago Press, 2001), 87–93.

83. A. R. Ammons, *Garbage* (New York: W. W. Norton, 1993), 21.

84. Ammons, *Garbage*, 20.

85. Robert Hass, "The State of the Planet," in *The Ecopoetry Anthology*, ed. Ann Fisher-Wirth and Laura-Gray Street (San Antonio, TX: Trinity University Press, 2013), 305.

86. Lucille Clifton, "the mississippi river empties into the gulf," in *The Terrible Stories* (Brockport, NY: BOA Editions, 1996), 37.

87. Jorie Graham, *From the New World: Poems 1976–2014* (New York: Ecco-HarperCollins, 2015), 330. On Graham's apocalyptic poetry in the volume *Sea Change*, see Keller, *Recomposing Ecopoetics*, 107–20.

88. Graham, *From the New World*, 331.

89. Graham, *From the New World*, 331.

90. Graham, *From the New World*, 331.

91. Juliana Spahr, *This Connection of Everyone with Lungs* (Berkeley: University of California Press, 2005), 8. For readings of Spahr's *Well Then There Now* that draw on recent ecocriticism, see Tana Jean Welch, "Entangled Species: The Inclusive Posthumanist Ecopoetics of Juliana Spahr," *Journal of Ecocriticism* 6, no. 1 (2014): 1–23, and Keller, *Recomposing Ecopoetics*, 39–47, 182–93.

92. Robert Frost, *The Poetry of Robert Frost*, ed. Edward Connery Lathem (New York: Holt, Rinehart and Winston, 1979), 348.

93. Juliana Spahr, "Some of We and the Land That Was Never Ours," in *Well Then There Now* (Boston: Black Sparrow, 2011), 12.

94. Spahr, "Gentle Now, Don't Add to Heartache," in *Well Then There Now*, 124–25. On this poem as melancholic elegy, see Margaret Ronda, *Remainders: American Poetry at Nature's End* (Stanford: Stanford University Press, 2018), 95–111.

95. Spahr, *Well Then There Now*, 131. See Nixon, *Slow Violence and the Environmentalism of the Poor*.

Chapter 8

1. Seamus Heaney, "Alphabets," in *The Haw Lantern* (New York: Farrar, Straus and Giroux, 1987), 1, 2. Ensuing page references appear in text.

2. Regarding Eastern Europe, see Magdalena Kay, *In Gratitude for All the Gifts: Seamus Heaney and Eastern Europe* (Toronto: University of Toronto Press, 2012).

3. Seamus Heaney, *"Anything Can Happen": A Poem and Essay by Seamus Heaney with Translations in Support of Art for Amnesty* (Dublin: TownHouse, 2004). For a reading,

see Jahan Ramazani, *Poetry and Its Others: News, Prayer, Song, and the Dialogue of Genres* (Chicago: University of Chicago Press, 2014), 68–72.

4. I am grateful to Helen Vendler for sharing with me the many heavily rewritten drafts of the poem.

5. Ayesha Ramachandran, *The Worldmakers: Global Imagining in Early Modern Europe* (Chicago: University of Chicago Press, 2015), 7.

6. Richard Kearney, "Dialogue with Borges and Heaney: Fictional Worlds," in *Navigations: Collected Irish Essays, 1976–2006* (Dublin: Lilliput, 2006), 341.

7. In early drafts Latin was its own separate section, before Heaney compressed the Latin and Irish sections into one and centered the Irish in the poem.

8. "I think of the personal and Irish pieties as vowels, and the literary awarenesses nourished on English as consonants." See Seamus Heaney, "Belfast," in *Preoccupations: Selected Prose, 1968–1979* (New York: Farrar, Straus and Giroux, 1980), 37.

9. See Neil Corcoran, *Poets of Modern Ireland: Text, Context, Intertext* (Carbondale: University of Southern Illinois Press, 1999), 79–84, and Helen Vendler, *Seamus Heaney* (Cambridge, MA: Harvard University Press, 1998), 130–33. On the poem, see also Sumita Chakraborty, "Of New Calligraphy: Seamus Heaney, Planetarity, and Lyric's Uncanny Space-Walk," *Cultural Critique* 104 (2019): 101–34.

10. Heaney, *Preoccupations*, 186, 150, 217, 133.

11. Roland Robertson, "After Nostalgia? Wilful Nostalgia and the Phases of Globalization," in *Theories of Modernity and Postmodernity*, ed. Bryan S. Turner (London: Sage, 1990), 50.

12. Mike Featherstone, *Undoing Culture: Globalization, Postmodernism and Identity* (London: Sage, 1995), 92.

13. Anthony Bradley, ed., *Contemporary Irish Poetry* (Berkeley: University of California Press, 1980), 17.

14. Anthony Bradley, "Irish Poetry," in *The New Princeton Encyclopedia of Poetry and Poetics*, ed. Alex Preminger and T. V. F. Brogan (Princeton: Princeton University Press, 1993), 632.

15. Dillon Johnston, preface to *Irish Poetry after Joyce*, 2nd ed. (Syracuse: Syracuse University Press, 1997), xvii.

16. Cheryl Temple Herr, *Critical Regionalism and Cultural Studies: From Ireland to the American Midwest* (Gainesville: University of Florida Press, 1996), 41, 48.

17. David Lloyd, "'Pap for the Dispossessed': Seamus Heaney and the Poetics of Identity," *Anomalous States: Irish Writing and the Post-colonial Moment* (Durham, NC: Duke University Press, 1993), 29, 20, 20–21.

18. Lloyd, 29.

19. Fiona Stafford, *Local Attachments: The Province of Poetry* (Oxford: Oxford University Press, 2010), 2, 4.

20. Stafford, *Local Attachments*, 5.

21. Stafford, *Local Attachments*, 11.

22. Seamus Heaney, "Crediting Poetry," in *Opened Ground: Selected Poems, 1966–1996* (New York: Farrar, Straus and Giroux, 1998), 424–25.

23. Heaney, "Crediting Poetry," in *Opened Ground*, 425.

24. Heaney, "Crediting Poetry," in *Opened Ground*, 425.

25. Heaney, "Crediting Poetry," in *Opened Ground*, 415.

26. Arjun Appadurai, *Modernity at Large: Cultural Dimensions of Globalization* (Minneapolis: University of Minnesota Press, 1996), 34–36.

27. Heaney, "Crediting Poetry," in *Opened Ground*, 416.

28. Heaney, "Crediting Poetry," in *Opened Ground*, 416.

29. Heaney, "Crediting Poetry," in *Opened Ground*, 416.

30. Ian Baucom, *Out of Place: Englishness, Empire, and the Locations of Identity* (Princeton: Princeton University Press, 1999), 32, 4.

31. Heaney, "Mossbawn," in *Preoccupations*, 17.

32. Heaney, "Mossbawn," in *Preoccupations*, 17.

33. Heaney, "Belfast," in *Preoccupations*, 37.

34. Seamus Heaney, "Electric Light," in *Electric Light* (New York: Farrar, Straus and Giroux, 2001), 96–98. Ensuing page references appear in text.

35. Seamus Heaney, "Lux Perpetua," *The Guardian*, June 16, 2001, http://www.theguardian.com/books/2001/jun/16/poetry.features.

36. Cited from *The Boston Phoenix* (1987) by Henry Hart, *Seamus Heaney: Poet of Contrary Progressions* (Syracuse: University of Syracuse Press, 1992), 68.

37. Richard Kearney, "Heaney and Homecoming," in *Transitions: Narratives in Modern Irish Culture* (Dublin: Wolfhound Press, 1988), 102.

38. In a film played for visitors to Bellaghy Bawn, *'Where Are You' by Seamus Heaney*, Heaney states: "People round here have an expression that is both reassuring and questioning. 'There you are,' they'll say, and 'Where are you?,' meaning, whatever notions you have about the world, it might have to be revised if the subject was approached by a slightly different angle by a different person. Meaning also that there is no such thing as a simple answer to any question, even to a question as simple sounding as 'Where are you?'" DVD viewed on April 13, 2014. Thanks to Charlene Small for the transcription.

39. The phrase "straunge strondes," or foreign shores, is plural in Geoffrey Chaucer, General Prologue to *The Canterbury Tales*, line 13, though Heaney singularizes it here to invoke the Thames's Strand.

40. Appadurai, *Modernity at Large*, 33–34.

41. See Marit J. MacArthur, "One World? The Poetics of Passenger Flight and the Perception of the Global," *PMLA* 127, no. 2 (2012): 264–82.

42. Appadurai, *Modernity at Large*, 33–37.

43. Heaney, "Serenades," in *Opened Ground*, 69.

44. Robertson, "After Nostalgia?," 45–61.

45. Heaney, "Viking Dublin: Trial Pieces," in *Opened Ground*, 100.

46. Heaney, "Crediting Poetry," in *Opened Ground*, 417.

47. Isaac Rosenberg, "Break of Day in the Trenches," in *The Collected Works of Isaac Rosenberg*, ed. Ian Parsons (London: Chatto and Windus, 1979), 103–4.

48. Heaney, "Punishment," in *Opened Ground*, 112–13.

49. Seamus Heaney, introduction to *Beowulf*, trans. Heaney (New York: W. W. Norton, 2000), xxvi.

50. Seamus Heaney, *The Government of the Tongue: Selected Prose, 1978–1987* (New York: Farrar, Straus and Giroux, 1988), 165.

51. Bruce Robbins, "Actually Existing Cosmopolitanism," in *Cosmopolitics: Thinking and Feeling beyond the Nation*, ed. Robbins and Pheng Cheah (Minneapolis: University of Minnesota Press, 1998), 2, 3.

52. Paul Muldoon, "Paul Muldoon on Seamus Heaney: The Mark of a Great Poet," *Daily Beast*, August 30, 2013, http://www.thedailybeast.com/articles/2013/08/30/paul-muldoon-on-seamus-heaney-the-mark-of-a-great-poet.html#.

53. Heaney, "Crediting Poetry," in *Opened Ground*, 417.

Chapter 9

1. John J. Gumperz, *Discourse Strategies* (Cambridge: Cambridge University Press, 1982).

2. Most of the criticism on code-switching poetry is culturally or ethnically delimited—Latinx, African Caribbean, Native American, African American, Arab—as indicated by the sampling in the notes below. On the US context, see the overviews in Juliana Spahr, "Multilingualism in Contemporary American Poetry," in *The Cambridge History of American Poetry*, ed. Alfred Bendixen and Stephanie (published as Stephen) Burt (Cambridge: Cambridge University Press, 2015), 1123–43, and *Du Bois's Telegram: Literary Resistance and State Containment* (Cambridge, MA: Harvard University Press, 2018), 28–55; and Mihaela Moscaliuc, "Code Switching, Multilanguaging, and Language Alterity," in *A Sense of Regard: Essays on Poetry and Race*, ed. Laura McCullough (Athens: University of Georgia Press, 2015), 223–32.

3. Carol Myers-Scotton, "Uniform Structure: Looking beyond the Surface in Explaining Codeswitching," *Rivista di Linguistica* 17, no. 1 (2005): 15–16.

4. Penelope Gardner-Chloros, *Code-Switching* (Cambridge: Cambridge University Press, 2009), 11.

5. Roman Jakobson, "Results of a Joint Conference of Anthropologists and Linguists," *Selected Writings*, vol. 2 (The Hague: Mouton, 1971), 561.

6. Steven G. Kellman, "Translingualism and the American Literary Imagination," in *American Babel: Literatures of the United States from Abnaki to Zuni*, ed. Marc Shell (Cambridge, MA: Harvard University Press, 2002), 460–61.

7. Carol Myers-Scotton, "Embedded Language Elements in Acholi/English Codeswitching: What's Going On?," *Language Matters: Studies in the Languages of Africa* 36, no. 1 (2005): 3.

8. Li Wei, "Translanguaging as a Practical Theory of Language," *Applied Linguistics* 39, no. 1 (2018): 23. Another term in linguistics, emphasizing cross-system integration and the inclusion of nonlinguistic communication, is *codemeshing*: see Suresh Canagarajah, "Codemeshing in Academic Writing: Identifying Teachable Strategies of Translanguaging," *Modern Language Journal* 95, no. 3 (2011): 401–17.

9. Michael Meeuwis and Jan Blommaert, "A Monolectal View of Code-Switching: Layered Code-Switching among Zairians in Belgium," in *Code-Switching in Conver-*

sation: Language, Interaction and Identity, ed. Peter Auer (London: Routledge, 1998), 76–98.

10. Gardner-Chloros, *Code-Switching*, 81–82.

11. Helen Vendler, "Poet of Two Worlds," review of *The Fortunate Traveller*, by Derek Walcott, *New York Review of Books*, March 4, 1982, 26.

12. Gary D. Keller, "The Literary Stratagems Available to the Bilingual Chicano Writer," in *The Identification and Analysis of Chicano Literature*, ed. Francisco Jiménez (Binghamton, NY: Bilingual Press, 1979), 269.

13. J. Edward Chamberlin, *Come Back to Me My Language: Poetry and the West Indies* (Urbana: University of Illinois Press, 1993), 99; and Derek Walcott, *Collected Poems, 1948–1984* (New York: Farrar, Straus and Giroux, 1986), 309, 310.

14. Chamberlin, *Come Back*, 100.

15. Helen Vendler, ed., *Poems, Poets, Poetry: An Introduction and Anthology* (Boston: Bedford, 1997), 168–69.

16. Gloria Anzaldúa, preface to *Borderlands / La Frontera: The New Mestiza* (San Francisco: Aunt Lute Book Co., 1987), n.p.

17. Lorna Dee Cervantes, "Poema para los Californios Muertos," in *Emplumada* (Pittsburgh: University of Pittsburgh Press, 1981), 43.

18. Jan-Petter Blom and John J. Gumperz, "Social Meaning in Linguistic Structures: Code-Switching in Northern Norway," in *Directions in Sociolinguistics*, ed. John J. Gumperz and Dell Hymes (New York: Holt, Rinehart, and Winston, 1972). Also pertinent is Carol Myers-Scotton, "Codeswitching with English: Types of Switching, Types of Communities," *World Englishes* 8, no. 3 (1989): 333–46.

19. Cervantes, "Poema," 44.

20. Cervantes, "Poema," 43.

21. Derek Walcott, *Omeros* (New York: Farrar, Straus and Giroux, 1990), 18–19.

22. On the wound trope in *Omeros*, see Jahan Ramazani, *The Hybrid Muse: Postcolonial Poetry in English* (Chicago: University of Chicago Press, 2001), chap. 3. On bilingual jokes, see Doris Sommer, *Bilingual Aesthetics: A New Sentimental Education* (Durham, NC: Duke University Press, 2004).

23. Urayoán Noel, "ode to coffee / oda al café" (2016), The Poetry Foundation, https://www.poetryfoundation.org/poems/89483/ode-to-coffee-oda-al-cafe.

24. Roman Jakobson, "Linguistics and Poetics," in *Language in Literature*, ed. Krystyna Pomorska and Stephen Rudy (Cambridge, MA: Belknap Press of Harvard University Press, 1987), 70.

25. Jakobson, "Linguistics and Poetics," 71.

26. Jonathan Culler, *Structuralist Poetics: Structuralism, Language and the Study of Literature* (Ithaca, NY: Cornell University Press, 1975), 162.

27. M. M. Bakhtin, *The Dialogic Imagination: Four Essays*, ed. Michael Holquist, trans. Caryl Emerson and Michael Holquist (Austin: University of Texas Press, 1981).

28. *OED Online*, s.v. "macaronic," etym., accessed February 8, 2020, http://dictionary.oed.com. On cross-lingual medieval poetry, see Ardis Butterfield, "Why Medieval Lyric?" *ELH* 82, no. 2 (2015): 319–43.

29. Ezra Pound, *Hugh Selwyn Mauberley*, in *Poems, 1918–21, Including Three Portraits and Four Cantos* (New York: Boni and Liveright, 1921), lines 57–60. The Greek line may be transliterated *"tin andra, tin eroa, tina theon."*

30. Paul Drew and John Heritage, "Analyzing Talk at Work: An Introduction," in *Talk at Work: Interaction in Institutional Settings*, ed. Drew and Heritage (New York: Cambridge University Press, 1992), 19.

31. See the rai lyrics cited in Eirlys E. Davies and Abdelali Bentahila, "Code-Switching as a Poetic Device: Examples from Rai Lyrics," *Language and Communication* 28, no. 1 (2008): 12–13.

32. Bernardine Evaristo, *The Emperor's Babe* (London: Penguin, 2001), 204. I offer a more extended reading in *A Transnational Poetics* (Chicago: University of Chicago Press, 2009), 175–80.

33. Cathy Park Hong, *Dance Dance Revolution* (New York: W. W. Norton, 2007), 25.

34. Spahr, "Multilingualism in Contemporary American Poetry," 1124.

35. On the overlapping but more expansive concept of "synthetic vernacular," for language uses that tensely mediate local and global, see Matthew Hart, *Nations of Nothing But Poetry: Modernism, Transnationalism, and Synthetic Vernacular Writing* (Oxford: Oxford University Press, 2010).

36. Edward [Kamau] Brathwaite, "The New Ships," in *The Arrivants: A New World Trilogy* (Oxford: Oxford University Press, 1973), 124–25. On *Masks*, see Robert Fraser, *Edward Brathwaite, "Masks": A Critical View*, ed. Yolande Cantù (London: Rex Collings, 1981).

37. Brathwaite, "The New Ships," 124.

38. Stuart Hall, "Cultural Identity and Diaspora," in *Identity: Community, Culture, Difference*, ed. Jonathan Rutherford (London: Lawrence and Wishart, 1990), 226.

39. Brathwaite, "The New Ships," 125.

40. Myers-Scotton, "Uniform Structure," 16.

41. Craig Santos Perez, *from Unincorporated Territory [hacha]* (Kāneʻohe, HI: Tinfish, 2008), 17.

42. Craig Santos Perez, *from Unincorporated Territory [saina]* (Richmond, CA: Omnidawn, 2010), 14–15.

43. Perez, *"from* sourcings," in *[saina]*, 111.

44. Jahan Ramazani, "Poetry and Song," in *Poetry and Its Others: News, Prayer, Song, and the Dialogue of Genres* (Chicago: University of Chicago Press, 2014), chap. 4.

45. I discuss Armantrout's use of song in *Poetry and Its Others*, 213–18.

46. Charles Bernstein, "The Lives of the Toll Takers," in *Dark City* (Los Angeles: Sun and Moon Press, 1994), 24.

47. Tony Harrison, *V. and Other Poems* (New York: Farrar, Straus and Giroux, 1990), 9.

48. Seamus Heaney, "Clearances," in *The Haw Lantern* (New York: Farrar, Straus and Giroux, 1987), 28.

49. On these debates, see Lesley Wheeler, *Voicing American Poetry: Sound and Performance from the 1920s to the Present* (Ithaca, NY: Cornell University Press, 2008), chap. 1.

See also Charles Bernstein's introduction to *Close Listening: Poetry and the Performed Word* (New York: Oxford University Press, 1998), 3–26.

50. James Merrill, "Self-Portrait in Tyvek^(TM) Windbreaker," in *Collected Poems*, ed. J. D. McClatchy and Stephen Yenser (New York: Alfred A. Knopf, 2001), 669.

51. Robert Lowell, "Commander Lowell," in *Selected Poems*, rev. ed. (New York: Farrar, Straus and Giroux, 1977), 77.

52. Adrienne Rich, "Snapshots of a Daughter-in-Law," in *Adrienne Rich's Poetry and Prose*, ed. Barbara Charlesworth Gelpi and Albert Gelpi (New York: W. W. Norton, 1993), 10–11. Rich describes the poem as an advance over her earlier poetry but "too literary, too dependent on allusion" in "When We Dead Awaken: Writing as Re-vision," in *Adrienne Rich's Poetry and Prose*, 175.

53. Amiri Baraka, *Conversations with Amiri Baraka*, ed. Charlie Reilly (Jackson: University Press of Mississippi, 1994), 176, quoted and discussed in Tyler Hoffman, *American Poetry in Performance: From Walt Whitman to Hip Hop* (Ann Arbor: University of Michigan Press, 2011), 192.

54. M. M. Bakhtin, *Speech Genres and Other Late Essays*, ed. Caryl Emerson and Michael Holquist, trans. Vern W. McGee (Austin: University of Texas Press, 1986), 92.

Chapter 10

1. David Damrosch, *What Is World Literature?* (Princeton: Princeton University Press, 2003), 288.

2. Damrosch, *What Is World Literature?*, 288, 289.

3. Damrosch, *What Is World Literature?*, 291. Among criticisms of "world literature," see Aamir Mufti's application of Edward Said's orientalist critique in *Forget English! Orientalisms and World Literature* (Cambridge, MA: Harvard University Press, 2016); Gloria Fisk, "'Against World Literature': The Debate in Retrospect" (2014), in *The American Reader* http://theamericanreader.com/against-world-literature-the-debate-in-retrospect/, developed in *Orhan Pamuk and the Good of World Literature* (New York: Columbia University Press, 2018); and Francesca Orsini, "The Multilingual Local in World Literature," *Comparative Literature* 67, no. 4 (2015): 345–74. For a staging of the debate over world literature, see Gayatri Chakravorty Spivak and David Damrosch, "Comparative Literature/World Literature: A Discussion," in *World Literature in Theory*, ed. Damrosch (Chichester, UK: Wiley Blackwell, 2014), 363–88.

4. Justin Quinn, *Between Two Fires: Transnationalism and Cold War Poetry* (Oxford: Oxford University Press, 2015), 116, 135 (quotation); Stephen Owen, "World Poetry," *New Republic* (November 19, 1990), 31 (see also his "Stepping Forward and Back: Issues and Possibilities for 'World' Poetry, *Modern Philology* 100 [2003]: 532–48); Rebecca Walkowitz, *Born Translated: The Contemporary Novel in an Age of World Literature* (New York: Columbia University Press, 2015).

5. For the view that style is "the central element in the translation of poetry," see Jean Boase-Beier, *Translating the Poetry of the Holocaust* (London: Bloomsbury, 2015), 31. See also her "Holocaust Poetry and Translation," in *Translating Holocaust Lives*, ed. Jean

Boase-Beier, Peter Davies, Andrea Hammel, and Marion Winters (London: Bloomsbury, 2017), 149–66, and "Stylistics and Translation," in *The Oxford Handbook of Translation Studies*, ed. Kirsten Malmkjaer and Kevin Windle (Oxford: Oxford University
Press, 2011), 71–82.

    6. David Connolly, "Poetry Translation," in *Routledge Encyclopedia of Translation
Studies*, ed. Mona Baker (New York: Routledge, 1998), 171.

    7. Paul Ricoeur, *On Translation*, trans. Eileen Brennan (London: Routledge, 2006), 6.

    8. "Translation in the Affirmative," January 7, 2017, MLA Convention, Philadelphia,
PA.

    9. Peter Robinson, *Poetry and Translation: The Art of the Impossible* (Liverpool: Liver-
pool University Press, 2010), 59.

    10. Robinson, *Poetry and Translation*, 25; Damrosch, *What Is World Literature?*, 288.
See also, e.g., Douglas R. Hofstadter, *Le Ton beau de Marot: In Praise of the Music of Lan-
guage* (New York: Basic Books of HarperCollins, 1997), 138–39, and Lawrence Venuti,
Contra Instrumentalism: A Translation Polemic (Lincoln: University of Nebraska Press,
2019), 109–18. Frost is quoted in Louis Untermeyer, *Robert Frost: A Backward Look*
(Washington, DC: Reference Dept., Library of Congress, 1964), 18.

    11. Matthew M. Reynolds, *The Poetry of Translation: From Chaucer and Petrarch to
Homer and Logue* (Oxford: Oxford University Press, 2011), 28.

    12. On Yeats, see Quinn, *Between Two Fires*, 28, and for Montale's account of Yeats as
"a poet entirely untranslatable," see Robinson, *Poetry and Translation*, 13–14.

    13. Emily Apter, *Against World Literature: On the Politics of Untranslatability* (London:
Verso, 2013). On the recent popularity of the concept, see Saden Tageldin, "Untranslatability," in *Futures of Comparative Literature*, ed. Ursula Heise (London: Routledge,
2017), 234–38. Stringent critiques of Apter include Fisk, "'Against World Literature,'"
and Venuti, "Hijacking Translation," in *Contra Instrumentalism*, 53–82.

    14. Barbara Cassin, ed., *Dictionary of Untranslatables: A Philosophical Lexicon*, trans.
and ed. Emily Apter, Jacques Lezra, and Michael Wood (Princeton: Princeton University Press, 2015).

    15. In addition to the books cited above by Robinson, Reynolds, Quinn, and Boase-
Beier, see Francis R. Jones, "The Translation of Poetry," in Malmkjaer and Windle,
Oxford Handbook of Translation Studies, 169–82; Boase-Beier, *Translating the Poetry of the
Holocaust*, as well as her "Holocaust Poetry and Translation," in *Translating Holocaust
Lives*, 149–66; and Mark Polizzotti, *Sympathy for the Traitor: A Translation Manifesto*
(Cambridge, MA: MIT Press, 2018), 111–28.

    16. Ezra Pound, "A Retrospect" (1918), in *Literary Essays of Ezra Pound*, ed. T. S. Eliot
(New York: New Directions, 1968), 7.

    17. Pound, "A Retrospect," 7.

    18. Pound, from *How to Read* (1931), in *Literary Essays*, 25.

    19. W. H. Auden, introduction (1961) to *The Complete Poems of Cavafy*, trans. Rae
Dalvin (San Diego: Harvest, 1976), xv.

    20. Pound, *How to Read*, 25.

    21. Northrop Frye, *The Anatomy of Criticism* (Princeton: Princeton University Press,
1957), 244, 275; William Frawley, "Prolegomenon to a Theory of Translation," rpt. in

The Translation Studies Reader, ed. Lawrence Venuti (New York: Routledge, 2000), 258. On *lafz* and *ma'na*, see below.

22. Louis Zukofsky, *A Test of Poetry* (1948; Hanover, NH: Wesleyan University Press, 2000), xi.

23. Christian Morgenstern, "Das aesthetische Wiesel," in *The Gallows Songs: Christian Morgenstern's* Galgenlieder," trans. Max Knight (Berkeley: University of California Press, 1966), 18. The literal translation is mine. For earlier discussions, see Jiří Levý, "Translation as a Decision Process," in *To Honor Roman Jakobson II* (The Hague: Mouton, 1967), 1178–79; Ernst-August Gutt, "Translation as Interlingual Interpretive Use," in Venuti, *Translation Studies Reader*, 381–87; and, on other Morgenstern poetry, Hofstadter, *Le Ton beau de Marot*, 392–400.

24. Morgenstern, "Das aesthetische Wiesel," 18.

25. T. S. Eliot, "The Golden Ass of Apuleius: A review of *The Golden Ass of Apuleius, Being the Metamorphoses of Lucius Apuleius. An English Translation by W. Adlington [1566]: Revised 1915–1927. With an Essay by Charles Whibley*" (1928), in *Literature, Politics, Belief, 1927–1929*, ed. Frances Dickey, Jennifer Formichelli, and Ronald Schuchard, vol. 3 of *The Complete Prose of T. S. Eliot: The Critical Edition*, ed. Ronald Schuchard (Baltimore: Johns Hopkins University Press, 2015), 487, Project MUSE, https://muse.jhu.edu/.

26. Ricoeur, *On Translation*, 5, 8.

27. On nonlinearity and hypertext in translation, see Anthony Pym, "What Technology Does to Translating," *Translation and Interpreting*, vol. 3, no. 1 (2011): http://www.trans-int.org/index.php/transint/article/view/121/81, and Augusto Ponzio, "Hypertextuality and Literary Translation," trans. Susan Petrilli, *Semiotica* 163 (2007): 289–309.

28. Auden, *Complete Poems of Cavafy*, xv.

29. Sigmund Freud, *Jokes and Their Relation to the Unconscious*, trans. and ed. James Strachey (New York: W. W. Norton, 1963), 45–47.

30. Julia Kristeva, *Revolution in Poetic Language*, trans. Margaret Waller (New York: Columbia University Press, 1984), 50.

31. Roman Jakobson, "On Linguistic Aspects of Translation," in *Language in Literature*, ed. Krystyna Pomorska and Stephen Rudy (Cambridge, MA: Belknap Press of Harvard University Press, 1987), 430.

32. Jakobson, "On Linguistic Aspects of Translation," 434. For a critique of Jakobson's stance not as richly complex but as contradictory, see Venuti, *Contra Instrumentalism*, 91–93.

33. On the marginalization of Persian poetry in world literature, see the first pages of my essay "Persian Poetry, World Poetry, and Translatability" (which overlaps with parts of this chapter), in "World Poetics, Comparative Poetics," ed. Jonathan Hart and Ming Xie, special issue, *University of Toronto Quarterly* 88, no. 2 (2019): 210–28. Alexander Beecroft briefly acknowledges the duration and geographic reach of Persian literature in *An Ecology of World Literature: From Antiquity to the Present Day* (London: Verso, 2015), 109, 120–21, 190.

On comparative literature as a possible frame, see Nasrin Rahimieh, "Persian Incursions: The Transnational Dynamics of Persian Literature," in *A Companion to*

Comparative Literature, ed. Ali Behdad and Dominic Thomas (Oxford: Blackwell, 2011), 296–311.

34. Jalal al-Din Rumi, Maulana, *The Soul of Rumi: A New Collection of Ecstatic Poems*, trans. Coleman Barks et al. (New York: HarperCollins, 2001), 32. On library book annotation, see Andrew Stauffer, "An Image in Lava: Annotation, Sentiment, and the Traces of Nineteenth-Century Reading," *PMLA* 134, no. 1 (2019): 81–98.

35. Rumi, *Soul of Rumi*, 33.

36. Rumi, *Soul of Rumi*, 29, 31.

37. Jonathan Culler, *Theory of the Lyric* (Cambridge, MA: Harvard University Press, 2015), 307–14.

38. Ahmad Karimi-Hakkak, "Beyond Translation: Interactions between English and Persian Poetry," in *Iran and the Surrounding World, 1500–2000: Interactions between Iran and the Neighboring Cultures*, ed. Nikki Keddie and Rudi Matthee (Seattle: University of Washington Press, 2002), 53, 55.

39. Hugh Kenner, *The Pound Era* (Berkeley: University of California Press, 1971), 199.

40. Coleman Barks, introduction to *The Soul of Rumi*, 9. On Rumi's de-Islamizing, see Annemarie Schimmel, *Rumi*, trans. Paul Bergne (New Delhi: Oxford University Press, 2014), 28; she describes him as "the master of *ishārāt*, of allusions," in her "Maw-lānā Rūmī: Yesterday, Today, and Tomorrow," in *Poetry and Mysticism in Islam: The Heritage of Rūmī*, ed. Amin Banani, Richard Hovannisian, and Georges Sabagh (New York: Cambridge University Press, 1994), 13. More recently, see Rezani Ali, "The Erasure of Islam from the Poetry of Rumi," *New Yorker* Page-Turner online, January 5, 2017, https://www.newyorker.com/books/page-turner/the-erasure-of-islam-from-the-poetry-of-rumi.

41. Lawrence Venuti, *The Scandals of Translation: Towards an Ethics of Difference* (London: Routledge, 1998), 5.

42. Venuti, *Scandals of Translation*, 31.

43. Gayatri Chakravorty Spivak, "The Politics of Translation," in *Outside in the Teaching Machine* (New York: Routledge, 1993), 182, 181.

44. But the equivalence is far from exact, since in Perso-Arabic poetics, verbal euphony in wordplay is typically subordinated to etymological, orthographic, and semantic considerations. See M. G. Carter and J. van Ess, "Lafẓ," *Encyclopaedia of Islam*, 2nd ed., ed. P. Bearman et al. (2012), accessed February 8, 2018, http://dx.doi.org/10.1163/1573-3912_islam_COM_1420. On *lafz* versus *ma'na*, see also Alexander Key, *Language between God and the Poets: Ma'nā in the Eleventh Century* (Berkeley: University of California Press, 2018), 38, and Vicente Cantarino, *Arabic Poetics in the Golden Age: Selection of Texts Accompanied by a Preliminary Study* (Leiden: Brill, 1975), 46–49. On figures of speech and thought in Persian poetics, including *tajnis*, see Natalia Chalisova, "Rhetorical Figures" (July 20, 2009), in *Encyclopædia Iranica*, http://www.iranicaonline.org/articles/rhetorical-figures. For more detailed discussions of the varieties of *tajnis* or *tadjnis*, see Julie Scott Meisami, *Structure and Meaning in Medieval Arabic and Persian Poetry: Orient Pearls* (London: Routledge, 2003), 247–53, and W. P. Heinrichs,

"Tadjnīs," *Encyclopaedia of Islam*, accessed February 8, 2018, http://dx.doi.org/10.1163 /1573-3912_islam_COM_1144.

45. As Annemarie Schimmel writes, Rumi prefers a strong *matla*—as if lightning "strikes him and sets him on fire"; see her *The Triumphal Sun: A Study of the Works of Jalāloddin Rumi*, rev. ed. (London: East-West Publications, 1980), 52. On the *khafîf* meter, see Franklin D. Lewis, *Rumi—Past and Present, East and West: The Life, Teachings, and Poetry of Jalâl al-Din Rumi*, rev. ed. (Oxford: Oneworld Publications, 2008), 332; he scans the (syllabic, long-short) meter thus: XxXX / xXxX / xxX // XxXX / xXxX / xxX.

46. Rumi, Ghazal 1759, in *Say Nothing: Poems of Jalal al-Din Rumi in Persian and English*, trans. Iraj Anvar and Anne Twitty (Washington, DC: Morning Light Press, 2008), 10–11. In my transliteration, *a* as in "stag," *â* as in "straw," *i* as in "steep." For another bilingual translation of Rumi that transliterates some of his quatrains and provides dual translations, see Shahram T. Shiva, *Rending the Veil: Literal and Poetic Translations of Rumi* (Prescott, AZ: Hohm Press, 1995).

47. See Schimmel, *Triumphal Sun*, 52–53, and Lewis, *Rumi*, 330–34. Schimmel's study is devoted almost entirely to Rumi's imagery and theology; on these, see also Schimmel, "Sun Triumphal—Love Triumphant: Maulana Rumi and the Metaphors of Love," in *As through a Veil: Mystical Poetry in Islam* (New York: Columbia University Press, 1982), 83–133.

48. Fatemeh Keshavarz, *Reading Mystical Lyric: The Case of Jalal al-Din Rumi* (Columbia: University of South Carolina Press, 1998), 114–17. On rhythm and sound in Rumi, see chap. 6, 100–117.

49. Amin Banani, "Rūmī the Poet," in Banani, Hovannisian, and Sabagh, *Poetry and Mysticism in Islam*, 39; J. Christoph Bürgel, "'Speech Is a Ship and Meaning the Sea': Some Formal Aspects in the Ghazal Poetry of Rūmī," in *Poetry and Mysticism in Islam*, 57.

50. Mohamad Ali Fatemi, Atefe Sobhni, and Hamzeh Abolhassani, "Difficulties of Persian Learners of English in Pronouncing Some English Consonant Clusters," *World Journal of English Language* 2, no. 4 (2012): 71.

51. Rūmī, Jalāl al-Dīn Moḥammad Balkhī, Ghazal 1759, in *Kolleyāt-e Shams*, ed. Badī' al-Zamān Forūzānfar (Tehrān: Mo'assase-ye Maṭbū'ātī Amīr Kabīr, 1336 [1957–66]), 663. Translation mine.

52. Anne Twitty, "A Guest in the House of Rumi: Doorways to Translation," in Rumi, *Say Nothing*, xvi. On the difficulties of translating the conventions of Persian poetry into English, see Dick Davis, "On Not Translating Hafez," *New England Review* 25, nos. 1–2 (2004): 310–18.

53. A. K. Ramanujan, "On Translating a Tamil Poem," in *The Collected Essays of A. K. Ramanujan*, ed. Vinay Dharwadker (New Delhi: Oxford University Press, 1999), 220.

54. See Natalia Chalisova, "Ihām" (2012), *Encyclopædia Iranica*, http://www.iranica online.org/articles/iham.

55. Rūmī, Ghazal 1759, in *Kolleyāt-e Shams*, 663. Anvar and Twitty give *miân* instead of *aayân*.

56. Rumi, *Say Nothing*, 11; Lewis, *Rumi*, 356.

57. Pound, *How to Read*, 25.

58. See, e.g., Damrosch, *What Is World Literature?*, 22–24. On comparing divergent translations, see Boase-Beier, *Translating the Poetry of the Holocaust*, 78–81.

59. Johann Wolfgang von Goethe, "Noten und Abhandlungen zu besserem Verständnis des west-östlichen Divans," *West-östlicher Divan* (Stuttgart: Cotta, 1819), 530, 531.

60. Simin Behbahani, *A Cup of Sin: Selected Poems*, ed. and trans. Farzaneh Milani and Kaveh Safa (Syracuse, NY: Syracuse University Press, 1999). The ensuing quotes are from the afterword by Kaveh Safa.

61. Ricoeur, *On Translation*, 3–4, 10, 14.

62. Similarly, Forugh Farrokhzad has been said to be less "language-dependent" and so more translatable than Ahmad Shamlou (or Shamlu); see Hossein Pirnajmuddin and Vahid Medhat, "Linguistic Deviation in Poetry Translation: An Investigation into the English Renderings of Shamlu's Verse," *Journal of Language Teaching and Research* 2, no. 6 (2011): 1335.

63. Farzaneh Milani, *Words, Not Swords: Iranian Women Writers and the Freedom of Movement* (Syracuse, NY: Syracuse University Press, 2011), 169, 176.

64. Simin Behbahani, "Koravi Shekl Ast," in *Yak Darīchah-I Āzādī* (Tehran: Sukhan, 1374 [1995]), 129–30; Behbahani, "The World Is Shaped like a Sphere," in *A Cup of Sin*, 57; further references to this poem are to these pages. On this poem, see Marie Ostby, "Genres without Borders: Reading Globally between Modern Iran and the West," PhD diss., University of Virginia, 2015, chap. 1.

65. Davis, "On Not Translating Hafez," 310–18.

66. Mai Der Vang, "Mother of People without Script," *Afterland* (Minneapolis, MN: Graywolf, 2017), 60.

67. Audio can be heard at the Poetry Foundation website (January 2017), https://www.poetryfoundation.org/poetrymagazine/poems/91682/mother-of-people-without-script.

68. See Huỳnh Sanh Thông, introduction to *An Anthology of Vietnamese Poems: From the Eleventh through the Twentieth Centuries* (New Haven: Yale University Press, 1996), 12–14.

69. Robert J. C. Young, "That Which Is Casually Called a Language," *PMLA* 131, no. 5 (2016): 1216.

70. Naoki Sakai, *Translation and Subjectivity: On "Japan" and Cultural Nationalism* (Minneapolis, MN: University of Minnesota Press, 1997), 14.

71. Rebecca Ruth Gould, "Hard Translation: Persian Poetry and Post-national Literary Form," *Forum for Modern Language Studies* 54, no. 2 (2018): 204. Gould criticizes the untranslatability paradigm with the help of Walter Benjamin's and Lu Xun's theories of translation.

72. See Margaret Ferguson, "Poetic Syntax," in *The Princeton Encyclopedia of Poetry and Poetics*, 4th ed., ed. Roland Greene, Stephen Cushman, Clare Cavanagh, Jahan Ramazani, and Paul Rouzer (Princeton, NJ: Princeton University Press, 2012), 1401–7.

73. Stanley Hoffer, "The Use of Adjective Interlacing (Double Hyperbaton) in Latin

Poetry," *Harvard Studies in Classical Philology* 103 (2007): 299–303. On the poem as "an act of *poetic address*," see Culler, *Theory of the Lyric*, 16–19.

74. On the ode's enclosed "*te*," see Steele Commager, *The Odes of Horace: A Critical Study* (New Haven: Yale University Press, 1962), 51–52.

75. H. Darnley Naylor, *Horace, Odes and Epodes: A Study in Poetic Word-Order* (Cambridge: Cambridge University Press, 1922), 14. The translation and highlights are mine.

76. Naylor, *Horace, Odes and Epodes*, xiii.

77. D. S. Carne-Ross, introduction to *Horace in English*, ed. Carne-Ross and Kenneth Hayes (London: Penguin, 1996), 57.

78. John Milton, "The Fifth Ode of Horace, *Lib.* I," in *Complete Shorter Poems*, ed. John Carey (London: Longman, 1971), 96.

79. Lowell Bowditch, "Horace and the Pyrrhatechnics of Translation," *Classical World* 104, no. 3 (2011): 357, 360.

80. Pound to Felix E. Schelling, July 9, 1922, in *The Selected Letters of Ezra Pound*, ed. D. D. Paige (London: Faber, 1971), 179.

81. R. G. M. Nisbet, "The Word Order of Horace's *Odes*," in *Horace: Odes and Epodes*, ed. Michèle Lowrie (Oxford: Oxford University Press, 2009): 400.

82. T. S. Eliot, "Autour d'une traduction d'Euripide" (1916), in *Complete Prose*, 1: 501; "Seneca in Elizabethan Translation" (1927), in *Complete Prose*, 3: 222; "Classics in English: A Review of *The Poets' Translation Series I–VI*" (1916), in *Complete Prose*, 1: 493.

83. Eliot, "Classics in English," 493.

84. T. S. Eliot, "Introduction to *Selected Poems* by Ezra Pound" (1928), in *Complete Prose*, 3: 522, 524.

85. Eliot, "Introduction to *Selected Poems* by Ezra Pound," 3: 522.

86. T. S. Eliot to R. P. Jean Mambrino, SJ, July 24, 1952. My thanks to Ronald Schuchard and John Haffenden for the letter.

87. Haun Saussy, *Translation as Citation: Zhuangzi Inside Out* (Oxford: Oxford University Press, 2017), 20.

88. T. S. Eliot, interview with Donald Hall, "The Art of Poetry 1: T. S. Eliot," *Paris Review* 21 (1959): 56.

89. T. S. Eliot to Paul Valéry, November 6, 1923, in *The Letters of T. S. Eliot: 1923–1925*, ed. John Haffenden (New Haven: Yale University Press, 2011), 2: 266.

90. T. S. Eliot, "What France Means to You" (1944), in *Complete Prose*, 5: 512, 514.

91. T. S. Eliot, "Mélange Adultère de Tout," *The Poems of T. S. Eliot*, ed. Christopher Ricks and Jim McCue (Baltimore: Johns Hopkins University Press, 2015), 1: 41 (ensuing references are to this page). Translations are mine.

92. Jacqueline Guillemin-Flescher, *Syntaxe comparée du français et de l'anglais: Problèmes de traduction* (Paris: Ophrys, 1981), 15. For a deconstructive account of translation that builds on this text, see Philip E. Lewis, "The Measure of Translation Effects," in *Difference in Translation*, ed. Joseph F. Graham (Ithaca: Cornell University Press, 1985), 31–62.

93. Benoît de Cornulier, *Art poétique: Notions et problèmes de métrique* (Lyon, France: Presses universitaires de Lyon, 1995), 47.

94. Eliot, "Gerontion," in *The Poems*, 31; "Burbank with a Baedeker: Bleistein with a Cigar," in *The Poems*, 34.

95. Mark Jeffreys, "'Mélange adultère de tout' and T. S. Eliot's Quest for Identity, Belonging, and the Transcendence of Belonging," *Journal of Modern Literature* 18, no. 4 (1993): 396. See also Michael North on Eliot's feared "lack of identity" in *The Dialect of Modernism: Race, Language and Twentieth-Century Literature* (New York: Oxford University Press, 1994), 84.

96. It is one of Eliot's several French poems in which, as Merrill Turner notes, Eliot "combines seriousness of purpose with levity of tone"; see her "On Not 'Not Knowing French': T. S. Eliot's Poetry *En Français*," *Journal of Modern Literature* 40, no. 1 (2016): 112. She also provides a useful list of Eliot's possible mistakes, 125n7. On the nontransparency of language for Eliot and Valéry, see William Marx, *Naissance de la critique moderne: La littérature selon Eliot et Valéry* (Paris: Artois Presses Université, 2002).

97. North, *Dialect of Modernism*, 84.

98. Polizzotti, *Sympathy for the Traitor*, 68.

99. Evan Maina Mwangi, *Translation in African Contexts: Postcolonial Texts, Queer Sexuality, and Cosmopolitan Fluency*, Translation Studies (Kent, OH: Kent State University Press, 2017), 11.

100. T. S. Eliot, "Preface to *Anabasis: A Poem by St.-J. Perse, with a Translation into English by T. S. Eliot*" (1930), in *Complete Prose*, 4: 135.

101. Goethe, "Noten," *West-östlicher Divan*, 529–32.

102. On the "remainder" in translation, see Venuti, *Scandals of Translation*, 10–12, 95–96.

103. Seamus Heaney, introduction to *Beowulf*, trans. Heaney (New York: W. W. Norton, 2001), xxv.

104. See Jahan Ramazani, *The Hybrid Muse: Postcolonial Poetry in English* (Chicago: University of Chicago Press, 2001), 176–77.

105. Venuti, *Scandals of Translation*, 11.

106. Daljit Nagra, *Ramayana: A Retelling* (London: Faber, 2013).

107. Karimi-Hakkak, "Beyond Translation," 37.

108. Kwame Anthony Appiah, "Thick Translation," *Callaloo* 14, no. 4 (1993): 816.

109. Appiah, "Thick Translation," 817.

110. Agha Shahid Ali, "Arabic," in *Call Me Ishmael Tonight: A Book of Ghazals* (New York: W. W. Norton, 2003), 24. Further references appear in text.

111. Sherman Jackson, "Al-Jahiz on Translation," *Alif: Journal of Comparative Poetics*, no. 4 (1984): 101. For more on this passage, see Abdelfattah Kilito, *Thou Shalt Not Speak My Language*, trans. Waïl S. Hassan (Syracuse, NY: University of Syracuse Press, 2008), 21–37, 41–42. On the question of contemporary translation of Arabic into English, see Robyn Creswell, "Is Arabic Translatable?," *Public Culture* 28, no. 3 (2016): 447–56.

112. Jackson, "Al-Jahiz on Translation," 102; see Michael Cooperson, "JĀḤEẒ." 2008, *Encyclopædia Iranica* http://www.iranicaonline.org/articles/jahez.

113. Ali, "In Arabic," *Call Me Ishmael Tonight*, 80.

114. Eliot, "The Love Song of J. Alfred Prufrock," in *The Poems*, 7.

115. See R. Blachère and A. Bausani, "Ghazal," *Encyclopaedia of Islam*, accessed February 8, 2018, http://dx.doi.org/10.1163/1573-3912_islam_COM_0232.

116. Stacey Chase, interview with Agha Shahid Ali, "The Lost Interview" (1990), *The Café Review* (Spring 2011), accessed February 8, 2020, http://www.thecafereview.com/spring-2011-interview-agha-shahid-ali-the-lost-interview/.

Epilogue

1. Paul de Man, "Lyrical Voice in Contemporary Theory," in *Lyric Poetry: Beyond New Criticism*, ed. Chaviva Hošek and Patricia A. Parker (Ithaca: Cornell University Press, 1985), 55–72; William Waters, *Poetry's Touch: On Lyric Address* (Ithaca: Cornell University Press, 2003); Jonathan Culler, *Theory of the Lyric* (Cambridge, MA: Harvard University Press, 2015).

2. Werner Wolf, "The Lyric: Problems of Definition and a Proposal for Reconceptualisation," in *Theory into Poetry: New Approaches to the Lyric*, ed. Eva Müller-Zettelmann and Margarete Rubik (Amsterdam: Rodopi, 2005), 125–145; Peter Hühn, "The Problem of Fictionality and Factuality in Lyric Poetry," *Narrative* 22, no. 2 (2014): 159.

3. Northrop Frye, "Approaching the Lyric," in Hošek and Parker, *Lyric Poetry*, 31.

4. Eva Müller-Zettelmann, "'A Frenzied Oscillation': Auto-reflexivity in the Lyric," in Müller-Zettelmann and Rubik, *Theory into Poetry*, 125–145.

5. Roman Jakobson, "What Is Poetry?," in *Language in Literature*, ed. Krystyna Pomorska and Stephen Rudy, trans. Michael Heim (Cambridge, MA: Belknap Press of Harvard University Press, 1987), 78, 69. Previously published as "Co je poesie?" (1933–34). See also Eric Falci, *The Value of Poetry* (Cambridge: Cambridge University Press, 2020), chaps. 1–2.

6. Caroline Levine, *Forms: Whole, Rhythm, Hierarchy, Network* (Princeton: Princeton University Press, 2015), 6–11; Werner Wolf, "The Lyric: Problems of Definition and a Proposal for Reconceptualisation," in Müller-Zettelmann and Rubik, *Theory into Poetry*, 34.

7. Hans Robert Jauss, *Toward an Aesthetic of Reception*, trans. Timothy Bahti (Minneapolis: University of Minnesota Press, 1982), 88–89.

8. Gillian C. White, *Lyric Shame: The "Lyric" Subject of Contemporary American Poetry* (Cambridge, MA: Harvard University Press, 2014).

9. See chapter 3 of Gerald Graff, *Beyond the Culture Wars: How Teaching the Conflicts Can Revitalize American Education* (New York: W. W. Norton, 1992); Virginia Jackson, *Dickinson's Misery: A Theory of Lyric Reading* (Princeton: Princeton University Press, 2005).

10. Harold Bloom, ed., *Deconstruction and Criticism* (New York: Seabury Press, 1979).

11. Lyn Hejinian, *My Life* (Providence, RI: Burning Deck, 1980); Hejinian, *My Life* (Los Angeles: Sun & Moon Press, 1987); Hejinian, *My Life* (Los Angeles: Green Integer, 2002); Susan Howe, *The Midnight* (New York: New Directions, 2003); Charles Bernstein, *Recalculating* (Chicago: University of Chicago Press, 2013); Kenneth Gold-

smith, *Uncreative Writing: Managing Language in the Digital Age* (New York: Columbia University Press, 2011), 4.

12. Stephanie (published as Stephen) Burt, "What Is This Thing Called Lyric?," review of *The Lyric Theory Reader: A Critical Anthology* (2014), ed. Virginia Jackson and Yopie Prins, *Modern Philology* 113, no. 3 (2016): 437.

13. Eric Hayot, "Against Historicist Fundamentalism," *PMLA* 131, no. 5 (2016): 1420.

14. Jahan Ramazani, *Yeats and the Poetry of Death: Elegy, Self-Elegy, and the Sublime* (New Haven: Yale University Press, 1990), and *Poetry of Mourning: The Modern Elegy from Hardy to Heaney* (Chicago: University of Chicago Press, 1994).

15. W. B. Yeats, Introduction [1937], in *Later Essays*, ed. William H. O'Donnell, vol. 5 of *The Collected Works of W. B. Yeats* (New York: Palgrave Macmillan, 1994), 204–16. Written in 1937 and first published as "A General Introduction for My Work," *Essays and Introductions* (London: Palgrave Macmillan, 1961), 509–25.

16. Helen Vendler, introduction to *Soul Says: On Recent Poetry* (Cambridge, MA: Belknap Press of Harvard University Press, 1995), 1–8; Kendall Walton, "Thoughtwriting—in Poetry and Music," *New Literary History* 42, no. 3 (2011): 455–476; Peter Hühn, "The Problem of Fictionality and Factuality in Lyric Poetry," *Narrative* 22, no. 2 (2014): 59.

17. Jahan Ramazani, *Poetry and Its Others: News, Prayer, Song, and the Dialogue of Genres* (Chicago: University of Chicago Press, 2014).

18. Culler, *Theory of the Lyric*, 37, 122–23, 216, 275, 336–37, 350–51; Andrew Welsh, *Roots of Lyric: Primitive Poetry and Modern Poetics* (Princeton: Princeton University Press, 1978).

19. *OED Online*, s.v. "ritual," etym., accessed February 8, 2020, http://dictionary.oed .com/.

20. Jonathan Culler, *Structuralist Poetics: Structuralism, Language and the Study of Literature* (Ithaca, NY: Cornell University Press, 1975), 162.

21. Ramazani, "Poetry and Prayer," chap. 3 of *Poetry and Its Others*.

22. Culler, *Theory of the Lyric*, 352; cf. also 5, 65–66, 120, 139, 170–73, 305.

23. Ramazani, "Poetry and Song," chap. 4 of *Poetry and Its Others*.

24. Culler, *Theory of the Lyric*, 305.

25. Culler, *Theory of the Lyric*, 173.

26. Culler, *Theory of the Lyric*, 277–295.

27. Ramazani, "Poetry and the News," chap. 2 of *Poetry and Its Others*.

28. Ezra Pound, *ABC of Reading* (London: Routledge, 1934; New York: J. Laughlin, 1960), 29. Citations refer to the J. Laughlin edition.

29. M. M. Bakhtin, "Discourse in the Novel," in *The Dialogic Imagination: Four Essays*, ed. Michael Holquist, trans. Caryl Emerson and Michael Holquist (Austin: University of Texas Press, 1981), 259–422; M. M. Bakhtin, "The Problem of Speech Genres," in *Speech Genres and Other Late Essays*, ed. Michael Holquist and Caryl Emerson, trans. Vern W. McGee (Austin: University of Texas Press, 1986), 60–102.

30. Ramazani, "A Dialogic Poetics: Poetry and the Novel, Theory, and the Law," chap. 1 of *Poetry and Its Others*.

31. Jahan Ramazani, *A Transnational Poetics* (Chicago: University of Chicago Press,

2009), and *The Hybrid Muse: Postcolonial Poetry in English* (Chicago: University of Chicago Press, 2001).

32. Samuel P. Huntington, *The Clash of Civilizations and the Remaking of World Order* (New York: Simon & Schuster, 1996).

33. Fredric Jameson, *A Singular Modernity: Essay on the Ontology of the Present* (London: Verso, 2002), 12; Franco Moretti, *Distant Reading* (London: Verso, 2013), 60–61.

34. Edward W. Said, *Orientalism* (New York: Pantheon Books, 1978); Ramazani, *Transnational Poetics*, chaps. 1 and 5.

35. Similarly, on the Arabization of poetry in French, see Yasser Elhariry, *Pacifist Invasions: Arabic, Translation and the Postfrancophone Lyric* (Liverpool, UK: Liverpool University Press, 2017).

36. L. P. Elwell-Sutton, *The Persian Metres* (Cambridge: Cambridge University Press, 1976), 66.

37. Pauline Yu, "Chinese Poetry and Its Institutions," in *Hsiang Lectures on Chinese Poetry* (Montreal: Centre for East Asian Research, McGill University, 2002), 57–66; Benjamin A. Elman, *A Cultural History of Civil Examinations in Late Imperial China* (Berkeley: University of California Press, 2000), 266–270, 275, 544–548; Benjamin A. Elman, *Civil Examinations and Meritocracy in Late Imperial China* (Cambridge, MA: Harvard University Press, 2013), 165–68, 295–97; Alfreda Murck, *Poetry and Painting in Song China: The Subtle Art of Dissent* (Cambridge, MA: Harvard University Asia Center, 2000), 51–52; Huỳnh Sanh Thông, introduction to *An Anthology of Vietnamese Poems: From the Eleventh through the Twentieth Centuries*, ed. and trans. Huỳnh (New Haven: Yale University Press, 1996), 3; Wiebke Denecke, *Classical World Literatures: Sino-Japanese and Greco-Roman Comparisons* (Oxford: Oxford University Press, 2014), 182–85; Marian Ury, "Chinese Learning and Intellectual Life," in *Heian Japan*, ed. Donald H. Shively and William H. McCullough, vol. 2 of *The Cambridge History of Japan* (Cambridge: Cambridge University Press, 1999), 367–73; Ki-baik Lee, *A New History of Korea*, trans. Edward W. Wagner with Edward J. Shultz (Cambridge, MA: Harvard University Asia Center, 1984), 118, 180.

38. Huỳnh, introduction to *An Anthology of Vietnamese Poems*, 11.

39. Huỳnh, *Anthology of Vietnamese Poems*, 14.

40. Quang Phu Van, "Poetry of Vietnam," in *The Princeton Encyclopedia of Poetry and Poetics*, 4th ed., ed. Roland Greene, Stephen Cushman, Clare Cavanagh, Jahan Ramazani, and Paul Rouzer (Princeton: Princeton University Press, 2012), 1519.

41. John Balaban, introduction to *Ca Dao Việt Nam: A Bilingual Anthology of Vietnamese Folk Poetry* (Greensboro, NC: Unicorn Press, 1980), 14.

42. Paul Losensky, "Persian Poetry," in Greene et al., *Princeton Encyclopedia of Poetry and Poetics*, 1024.

43. "Raha—Young Iranian Contestant on a Poetry Game Show WITH SUBTITLES!!!," accessed February 8, 2020, https://www.youtube.com/watch?v=62ZU Tb1jApE.

44. Alexander Beecroft, *An Ecology of World Literature: From Antiquity to the Present Day* (London: Verso, 2015), 190.

45. Roger M. A. Allen, "Arabic Poetry," in Greene et al., *Princeton Encyclopedia of Poetry and Poetics*, 65.

46. William Kremer, "Is It Possible to Be a Millionaire Poet?," *BBC News*, May 31, 2014, http://www.bbc.com/news/magazine-27621529.

47. Earl Miner, *Comparative Poetics: An Intercultural Essay on Theories of Literature* (Princeton: Princeton University Press, 1990).

INDEX

Achebe, Chinua, rejects Conrad's modernism, 109

Adorno, Theodor, 60

Africa: Brathwaite "returns" to, 203–4; novel from, fuses with French tradition, 123; and "placelessness" (Eliot), 232–33; poetry from, Eurocentric diffusionism in, 121. *See also* diffusionism, Eurocentric; poetics

aisling (Irish dream poetry), 180

Akan (language), and code-switching, 203–4

Ali, Agha Shahid: "Arabic," 235, 236–38; and Eliot, 119, 235, 236; form/content of, 126; "In Arabic," 236–38; "I See Chile in My Rearview Mirror," 72–74; "Lenox Hill," 13; and place, 13, 72–74; and translation, 235–38

al-Jahiz (Abbasid polymath), on translation, 236

alliteration, 59, 61, 104, 122, 196, 206, 214, 219–20, 240; as stand-in for assonance (Rumi), 221. *See also* assonance; poetics

Amichai, Yehuda, 237

Ammons, A. R.: "Corsons Inlet," 66; *Garbage*, 174

anaphora, 87, 125, 149. *See also* poetics

Ancestry.com, 2–3

Ansari (Persian poet), 57

Anthropocene era, human commonality in, 48. *See also* cosmopolitanism; globalization

Antigua, Kincaid rhapsodizes about, 79–80

anti-Semitism, in Eliot, 232, 233

Anvar, Iraj, 219–20, 222

Anzaldúa, Gloria, on code-switching, 197

apartheid, 91; Press on brutality of, 93–94, 103

apostrophe (in poetry), 31, 43, 88–89, 175, 179; and lyric poetry, 239, 240. *See also* poetics

Appadurai, Arjun, 2; on five levels of global flow, 189; on globalization, 111–12, 156, 185, 189

Appiah, Kwame Anthony: on Afrocentric nativists and modernism, 110; on cosmopolitanism, 15, 28, 29, 31, 32; on Eurocentrism, 109; on globalization, 111; on human commonality, 38, 49; on translation, 235

Apter, Emily, 215

Arabia: and multiculturalism, 142–45; and Yeats, 145

Arabic (language), 142–45; Ali on, 235–38; as language of loss, 235; meters in differ from Persian, 247

Arnold, Matthew, 114

art: Byzantine, Persian influence on (Yeats), 138; global South influences on modern, 13, 120; Japanese, on sword/mirror (Yeats), 148; lyric poetry vs. other forms of, 246

Ashbery, John, "The Instruction Manual," 82, 85–90

Asia: East and Southeast poetics of, 225–26; influence on modern literature, 120; kinship with Ireland (Yeats), 135–36; lyric poetry of, 248–49; Yeats and parts of, 152–53. *See also* Arabia; China, influence on Western poetry; India; Japan, influence on Yeats; orientalism; Persia

assonance, 29, 31, 36, 41, 104, 169, 180; appears in poem (Heaney), 180; in Rumi, 220. *See also* poetics

Aubin, Robert Arnold, on topographical poetry, 52

Auden, W. H., 20; on homophones and translation, 216–17; "In Memory of W. B. Yeats," 44; "A New Year Greeting," 172–73; "Ode to Terminus," 20; on self as landscape, 172–73; "Spain," 44; "Spain," influence on Nagra, 112–14, 115

Bai, Li, 219

Bakhtin, Mikhail, 199–200, 210, 245

Balaban, John, 248–49

ballad. *See* poetry, balladic

Banani, Amin, 220

Baraka, Amiri, 210

barbarians, Persians as (Yeats), 134–35

Barks, Coleman, reactions to Rumi translations by, 218–19

Baucom, Ian, 48, 186

Baudrillard, Jean, 72

Bayly, C. A., 17

Beckett, Samuel, 103

Beecroft, Alexander, 120, 249, 299n33

Behbahani, Simin, 58, 237; *A Cup of Sin,* 223; translating, 234; "The World Is Shaped like a Sphere," 223–25

Belloc, Hilaire, witty epigram of, 217

Bennett, Louise, 109–10, 111; form/content of, 126

Beowulf, 191, 234

Berkeley, Bishop, 169

Bernstein, Charles, 206

Bhabha, Homi, 37

Bible, and tourism poetry, 83, 84

Bishop, Elizabeth: "Arrival at Santos," 77; "In the Waiting Room," 83; "The Map," 73; "Over 2,000 Illustrations and a Complete Concordance," 82–86, 87–88; "Over 2,000 Illustrations and a Complete Concordance," Ashbery praises, 85; "Over 2,000 Illustrations and a Complete Concordance," and tourism, 77, 82–88

Bly, Robert, 57

bolekaja critics, 121

Boorstin, Daniel, 78

Borden, Mary: "The Hill," 47–48; "The Song of the Mud," 47–48

Brathwaite, Kamau, 109–10, 119, 206; on alien, imported forms, 105, 121–22; *The Arrivants,* 203–4, 209; and Eliot, 112, 119, 121; form/content in "Rites," 126

Breeze, Jean Binta, 206

Bristow, Joseph, 89

Buddha, artworks of fuse East and West (Yeats), 136–37

Buell, Lawrence, 163, 171

Bürgel, Christoph, 220

Burke, Kenneth, 20

Burt, Stephanie: defends "lyric" as category, 242; on Stevens's "place-attachment," 162; on topographical poetry, 52

Bush, Christopher, 133

Byron, Lord (George Gordon), *Don Juan,* 200

Callimachus, Yeats on East-West fusion and, 138–39

Canepa, Matthew P., 142

Capildeo, Vahni, "Heirloom Rose, for Maya," 7

capitalism, worldwide: and modernity, 110–11; Nagra on, 114–15

Casanova, Pascale, 118, 213; on Moretti, 119–20, 121

Celticism, and incantatory rhyming, 30

cento, "rearranges found language," 12

Certeau, Michel de, 63

Cervantes, Lorna Dee: on Chicanx code-switching, 197, 209; "Poema para los Californios Muertos," 197–98

Chakrabarty, Dipesh, 48

Chamberlin, J. Edward, defense of Walcott's code-switching, 196

Chamoru (language), asserts Guamanian identity, 204–5

Chatterjee, Mohini (Theosophist), influence on Yeats, 146

Chaucer, Geoffrey, *The Canterbury Tales*, 188

Chi, Robert, 81

chiasmus, 8, 84, 95, 175, 240. *See also* poetics

China, influence on Western poetry, 55–56, 57, 68, 74, 131

Chinese: poetry in as highest form of expression, 247–48; Pound's use of, 200, 216

Christmas truce of 1914, 25–27. *See also* First World War poetry

Churchill, Winston, *A History of the English-Speaking Peoples*, 114

Clifton, Lucille, "the mississippi river empties into the gulf," 174–75

code-skipping, 201–3. *See also* code-switching

code-switching: between English and Hmong, 225; and code-skipping, 206–7; and code-stitching, 201, 202, 204; in everyday life, 195–96, 199, 201, 205, 209; intralingual, 206–8; in linguistics, 194–95; in poetry, 130, 195–211; in poetry, as dialogic, 210–11; in poetry, Latinx, 197–99; in poetry, serves oralist or writerly poems, 209–10; postcolonial, 203–5; precedents for, 200–201. *See also* code-skipping

Coetzee, J. M., 103, 104

conduplicatio, 146. *See also* poetics

Connolly, David, on translating poetry, 214

Conrad, Joseph: *Heart of Darkness*, 113; and racism, 101, 109

Conrad, Sebastian, on globalization, 12–13

Corcoran, Neil, 31

Cornulier, Benoît de, 231

cosmopolitanism: among enemies once dead, 44–45; cross-cultural (suffering, camaraderie, etc. in war), 34–46; cross-cultural, limitations of, 46–48; ecological (in Stevens), 158, 161, 162, 163, 172; etymological, in Hardy and Heaney, 32–34, 191; from below, 37; located, rooted, 28, 192; in Rosenberg's "Break of Day in the Trenches," 31–32; subverts militarist nationalism, 49–50

Creeley, Robert, on form and content in poetry, 124

creole, code-switching and, 202–3. *See also* code-skipping; code-switching; languages

creolization: of form, 60, 121; of language, 106, 125, 158, 194, 202, 228, 230; as model, 111–12, 123, 247. *See also* hybridity, postcolonial, and transnational forms; indigenization; poetics: macaronic

Culler, Jonathan: on lyric poetry, 3, 54, 199, 242–44; on lyric poetry, and ritual, 169, 243; on lyric poetry, and song, 244; on lyric poetry, as truth telling, 218, 244; *Structuralist Poetics*, 243; *Theory of the Lyric*, 3, 54, 242; on tourism, 85, 158

"culturalism," 112

Damrosch, David, on translating world literature, 213

Dante Alighieri, 123

Darío, Rubén, 119–20

Das, Santanu, 29, 48, 264n12

Davidson, Michael, 68

Davis, Dick, 225

deictics, 52, 55, 72, 73, 87. *See also* poetics

Deleuze, Gilles, 4

dialects, mingling, in code-switching, 207–8. *See also* languages

dialogism, 92, 112, 210, 243–45

Dickens, Charles, heteroglossia of, 199–200

diffusionism, Eurocentric: Moretti advances, 119–21; and Nagra, 112–14, 116; "one-way," 23, 108–9, 111, 123; Walcott merges with Caribbean, 122–23. *See also* poetics; poetry, lyric

dinnseanchas (Irish place-name poetry), 52

Dirlik, Arif, 110

"distant reading," Moretti on, 124

Doolittle, Hilda (H.D.), 229

Doyle, Laura, 109

Drew, Paul, 200

Duffy, Carol Ann, "The Christmas Truce," 25–26, 27, 37

Durcan, Paul, 184

earth/Earth: embrace of (Stevens), 163–67; Graham apostrophizes, 175; human destruction of, 172–76; O as (Heaney), 182; poetry on, after Stevens, 172–76; rotation and orbit of, 175; wholeness of, 155–67, 174, 179, 182. *See also* globe

East Asia. *See* China, influence on Western poetry; Japan, influence on Yeats; orientalism

East-West dichotomies, evident in Iran 1981, 224

ecocriticism: developments in, 159, 161–63, 171–72; Stevens and, 161–63, 165, 171–72

Eeckhout, Bart, 156, 162

elegy, 6–7, 44–46, 198, 207, 242

Eliot, T. S., 8, 10, 109, 112, 113, 115, 129; and Ali, 119, 235, 236; as French poet, 230–33; globalism in, 232–33; "Journey of the Magi," 109; "Journey of the

Magi," and Goodison, 105–8, 110, 112; "Journey of the Magi," influences on, 109; "The Love Song of J. Alfred Prufrock," 129, 230, 236; "Mélange Adultère de Tout," 230–33; polyglossia of, 229–30; on translation, 216–17, 228–29; on translation, of his own lyrics, 229; *The Waste Land*, 120, 125, 146, 188, 200, 206

Ellmann, Richard, 147

Engels, Friedrich, 1

enjambment, 5, 6, 36, 93, 96, 104, 113, 130, 165, 174; hard (Walcott), 122; heavy (Moore), 127; mimetic, 31, 240; playful, 96; witty, 113, 128; Yeats's, 135, 148. *See also* poetics

enmeshment: of globalization, 5, 17, 33, 55, 63, 126, 190, 248; of human and nonhuman, 166–72, 173–74; of poetry, 57, 60, 99, 110, 166, 175

Eurocentrism: effect on modernism/postcolonialism, 109; Yeats's, in "The Statues," 134–35. *See also* orientalism

Evaristo, Bernardine, code-skipping in *The Emperor's Babe*, 201, 202

exceptionalism, impossible in culture, 8

Featherstone, Mike, 183

Feifer, Maxine, 87

Ferdowsi, 134

Ficino, Marsilio, 181

film, reversed time in poetry and, 4, 5, 6

First World War poetry: by Borden, 47–48; eliminates human distinctions, 47–48; enemy as doppelgänger or double in, 41–43; global dimensions of, 48–50; by Hardy, 32–36; by Owen, 41–43; by Rosenberg, 27–32; by Service, 36–40. *See also* cosmopolitanism; *and individual poets*

FitzGerald, Edward, 218

Flaubert, Gustave, and orientalism (Said), 151–52

flowers, literary, 7–8, 30–31, 55

form: affordances of, 54; definition of, 117, 125, 279n2; disaggregation of,

124–26; foreign, and local content, 118–24; Latour on, 3; local, and foreign content, 127–30; local, and foreign content, in Moore's "England," 127–28; Persia, Byzantium, and, 138–42; Yeats on, 138, 150. *See also* poetry, lyric

formalism, new, and lyric, 53, 241

Forster, E. M., *A Passage to India*, 120

Foster, Roy, 144

Frawley, William, 216

Freud, Sigmund: defends punning wordplay, 217 (*see also* wordplay); on doppelgänger, 41

Frieden, Ken, on Yiddish vs. European novel, 123

Friedman, Susan Stanford: on *longue durée*, 14–15; on Moretti and diffusionism, 121

Frost, Robert: "The Gift Outright," 175–76; on poetry and translation, 214

Frye, Northrop, on translating poetry, 216

Furtwängler, Adolf, cited by Yeats, 138, 139

Fussell, Paul, 27–28, 30

Gandhi, Mahatma, as "*half-naked fakir*," 114

Gardner-Chloros, Penelope, 194

Gautier, Théophile, *vers de société*, 231

geography: in Ali, 72–73; in Heaney, 183–84; plurality of, 54, 67; in Stevens, 157. *See also* poetry, lyric: topographical

ghazal, 126; of Ali, 235–38; of Behbahani, 223–25; of Rumi, 219–22

Gibbon, Edward: on Persian influence on Byzantine art, 141; and Yeats, 143–44

Giddens, Anthony, 16, 59, 109; on place under modernity, 62–63

Gilroy, Paul, 28–29, 35, 49; on "cosmopolitan solidarity," 37, 38, 40

Ginsberg, Allen, "Howl," 125

"global age," defined, 11–12

globalization: Appadurai on, 156, 189; of culture, in Stevens, 157; of culture, tourism as, 78 (*see also* tourism; tourists); forces of, 12; Heaney and, 190; historicity of, short-term vs. *longue durée*, 12–16; Hopper on, 156; "layers of," in Stevens, 156–59; and localization, 75, 190 (*see also* poetry, lyric); and the modernist era, 16–19; poetry as haven from, 51

global South: poets as tourists in, 91–98; topographical poetry of, 62–66, 119

globe: concept of, in history, 14; "Heaney's," 177–92; as image in Behbahani, 24; O as a (Heaney), 179. *See also* earth/Earth; globalization; Stevens, Wallace

Globe Theatre, 113, 181. *See also* Shakespeare, William

Goethe, Johann Wolfgang von: on translation, 228; and *Weltliteratur*, 218; *West-östlicher Divan*, 234; Yeats quotes, 140

Goldie, David, 45

Goldsmith, Kenneth, 12, 241

Goodison, Lorna, 203; "Quest," 105–8, 110, 111, 112; "To Us, All Flowers Are Roses," 7, 65–66, 74; "Where the Flora of Our Village Came From," 13

Gould, Rebecca Ruth, on translation, 227

Graff, Gerald, 241

Graham, Desmond, 41

Graham, Jorie, *Place*, 175

grammar, and poetics: repeated conjunctions, 82; repeated participles, 104; translating syntax, 227–28; verb modes in, 88; vocative, 96, 227–28. *See also* poetics

Graves, Robert, *White Goddess*, 180

Gray, Thomas, Harrison alludes to "Elegy Written in a Country Churchyard," 207

Greece, ancient, and birth of Europe (Yeats), 134

Greek, ancient: Heaney's study of, 180, 182, 186; Pound's use of, 200

Griffiths, Matthew, 161

Guha, Ramachandra, 160

Gumperz, John J., 193

Habjan, Jernej, 17

Hafez, 15, 145, 218, 223

haiku: poetics of, 149; Yeats's adaptation of, 149–50. *See also* poetics

Hall, Stuart, on cultural identity, 204

hammer, metaphor of: spaces linked by, 4; temporal aspects of, 2, 3

Hammer-Purgstall, Joseph von, 223

Hardy, Thomas, 6; "Geographical Knowledge," topography of, 58–59; "The Man He Killed," cross-national mirroring in, 34–36; "Men Who March Away," 35; "The Pity of It," interlingual weave in, 32–34

Harrison, Tony: *School of Eloquence*, 208; *v.*, 207–8

Harun Al-Rashid (Abbasid caliph): Islamic Golden Age under, 144; preserves ancient Greek works, 142–44

Hass, Robert, "State of the Planet," 174

Hayes, Terrance: "American sonnets," 8–9; "How to Draw a Perfect Circle," 10–11

Hayot, Eric, 21, 242, 289n56

Heaney, Seamus, 13–14, 26; "Alphabets," 177–83, 185, 186, 191; *Beowulf* translation by, 191, 234; "Bog Queen," 191; "Clearances," 208; code-switching in, 208; collocates Yeats and Owen, 44–45, 46; compassion in, 190–91; criticism of, 184; "Digging," 183; "Electric Light," 186–89, 191; *Electric Light*, 186; and globalism/globalization, 178, 189–92; and globalism/globalization, with localism, 190, 191–92; "The Grauballe Man," 43; "In Memoriam Francis Ledwidge," 44–46; "Irishes" Owen, 44; Irish identity of, 184, 189–90; "Mossbawn," 186; Nobel lecture of, 185–86, 192;

Opened Ground, 183; "The Other Side," 191; places written about by, 183–84; "poetryscape" of, 190; "Punishment," 44, 191

Heidegger, Martin, 4

Heise, Ursula, 155, 163, 172

Helgesson, Stefan, 151

Heraclitus, 67

Heritage, John, 200

Herr, Cheryl, 184

historicism, new, and regionalism, 53

Hoffer, Stanley, 227

Hoffmann, E. T. A., discussed by Freud, 41

Hollywood films, as engulfing world, 119

Holub, Miroslav, 213–14

Hong, Cathy Park, *Dance Dance Revolution*, 81; "translanguaging" in, 202

Hopkins, Gerard Manley, 6

Hopper, Paul, on globalization, 156

Horace, 240; *Odes* 1.5, poetics of, 227–28

Hudson River School, 160

Huggan, Graham, 80

Hughes, Langston, 109, 112; "I've Known Rivers," 159

Hühn, Peter, on lyric poetry, 243

Huntington, Samuel, 246

hurricane, as poetic locus (Brathwaite vs. Walcott), 122–23

Huỳnh Sanh Thông, 248

hvarenah (life force of Ahura Mazda): in Byzantine mosaics (Yeats), 142; Strzygowski on bird representing, 140–41

hybridity, postcolonial, and transnational forms, 111–12, 115–16, 123. *See also* poetry, lyric

hybridization, intercultural, Stevens shuns, 158

imperialism: and capitalism, 114–15; and global South, 91

India: Eliot and, 146; importance in Yeats's opus, 145–47; multiplicity of culture of, 147. *See also* Asia

indigenization, 10, 101, 205; of form, 136, 248; as model, 111–12, 115, 116, 203. *See also* creolization; hybridity, postcolonial, and transnational forms; poetics: macaronic

Irele, Abiola, 123

Irish (language), Heaney's study of, 180

Issa, Kobayashi (haiku grandmaster), Yeats adapts haiku by, 148–49

Jackson, Virginia, 3, 53, 56, 241

Jakobson, Roman, 194; on "conative" language, 88; on "poetic function," 107, 124, 199, 240; on translation, 217. *See also* poetics

Jameson, Fredric, 110, 111, 246; Moretti on, 118–19

Japan, influence on Yeats, 147–50. *See also* Asia; orientalism

Jauss, Hans Robert, 241

Jeffreys, Mark, 232

Johnson, Linton Kwesi, 206

Johnson, Samuel, definition of "local poetry," 52, 73

Johnston, Dillon, *Irish Poetry after Joyce*, 184

Jones, William, 218

Joyce, James: *Finnegans Wake*, 129; *Ulysses*, 86, 186

Kalidasa, *Shakuntala*, 146

Kandinsky, Wassily, 108

Kant, Immanuel, 46, 161

Karimi-Hakkak, Ahmad: defends Barks, 218; on types of translation, 235

Kearney, Richard, on Heaney and *transit*, 188

Keller, Gary D., 195–96

Keller, Lynn, 158–59

Kellman, Steven G., 194

Kendall, Tim, 29

Kenner, Hugh, 219

Kern, Adam L., 149

Keshavarz, Fatemeh, 220

Kincaid, Jamaica: *Among Flowers*, 80; on the nontourist poor, 92; *A Small Place*, and varieties of tourist, 79–80, 86

kinship, among wartime enemies (Hardy), 32–34

Kipling, Rudyard, 61; "Epitaphs of the War," globalism of, 49

Knickerbocker, Scott, 160, 161

Kolatkar, Arun: "Breakfast Time at Kala Ghoda," global/local in, 63–64; "The Doorstep," 95; *Jejuri*, 95–98; *Jejuri*, "kaleidoscopically multiform," 95; *Kala Ghoda Poems*, localized but complex, 62–64, 74; "Water Supply," 97–98

Kristeva, Julia, 217

Kusta ben Luka, 143–44

Lacan, Jacques, 181

Lang, Michael, 14

languages: Heaney's immersion in, 180, 185, 186; and lyric poetry, 227, 246–50; porosity of interwovenness, 32–34, 194, 226, 237; Stevens's multiple, 158. *See also* code-skipping; code-switching; Eliot, T. S.; Pound, Ezra

Larkin, Philip: "Sad Steps," 89; "Sunny Prestatyn," and code-switching, 207; "Sunny Prestatyn," and tourism, 82, 88–90

Larsen, Jonas, 78–79, 86, 89, 99

Latin, 182; Heaney's study of, 180

Latinx, and code-switching, 197–99

Latour, Bruno: on bricolage, 2; on form, 3; on global and local, 10, 30, 161; on locality as not self-contained, 56, 60, 63; and the polyspatial, polytemporal, 2–4, 30

Lazarus, Neil, 111; criticizes Said, 110

Ledwidge, Francis, 45

Lefebvre, Henri, 59, 63

Lennon, Joseph, 136

Levine, Caroline, 54, 117

Levinson, Marjorie, 56; on Wordsworth's "Tintern Abbey," 53

Levi-Strauss, Claude, 4

Lewis, Franklin, 220

Lloyd, David, 184

"local," elastic sense of, 119
localization, in poetry: as foil to modernist interchangeability of place, 51–75; Heaney's, 184–86. *See also* poetry, lyric
loco-descriptivity. *See* poetry, lyric: topographical
logopœia, 216–17; lost in translation, 235; in Rumi, 219, 222. *See also* poetics
Loizeaux, Elizabeth Bergmann, on Yeats and Persian art, 138
Longley, Edna, on extranationalism among WWI poets, 48
longue durée, and globalization, 14–15, 32, 189
Lowe, Lisa, 19
Lowell, Robert, code-switching in, 210
Loy, Mina, "Der Blinde Junge," 47
lục bát (Vietnamese poetic form), 248
Luka, Kusta ben, 143–44
lüshi (Chinese poetic form), 248
lyric studies, new: foregrounding factual place, 53; and historical poetics, 241

Macaulay, Thomas Babington, 58
MacCannell, Dean, 90; on tourists, tour guides, and travelers, 78–79, 98–99; on tourist spaces, 86. *See also* tourism; tourists
Magritte, René, 112; *The Treachery of Images*, Press and, 102–5, 109, 110
Mahabharata, 63
Malpas, J. E., 67–68
Mandelstam, Osip, 191
Marchand, Suzanne, on Strzygowski opposing Eurocentrism, 140
Marx, Edward, 148–49
Marx, Karl, 1
Massey, Doreen, on physical space, 54, 56, 61, 66
Mathers, Powys, *Arabian Nights*, Yeats adapts, 145
Matisse, Henri, 108
Matterson, Stephen, 156–58
McCrae, John, "In Flanders Fields," 28, 30–31

McKay, Claude, 119, 121, 156, 276n1; "The Tropics in New York," 60–61, 74
melopœia, 215, 216, 217; Behbahani's, 223; lost in translation, 235; Rumi's, 219, 221. *See also* poetics
Merrill, James, code-switching in, 209
metaphors, 39, 64, 240, 242; and code-switching, 194, 197, 206; of globalization, 19–20; of hammer, 3–4; proliferation of, 11, 165, 167; Stevens's profusion of, 165; as translatable (Auden), 216; and "transport" (Heaney), 188. *See also* poetics
meter: adapting quantitative to accentual, 247; ballad, 38; heptameter, Yeats's, 146–47; hexameter, Walcott's, 122; iambic pentameter, 240; iambic pentameter, Brathwaite on, 121–22; iambic pentameter, Heaney's, 182; iambic pentameter, Larkin's, 207; iambic pentameter, Nagra's, 115; iambic pentameter, Stevens's, 160, 166; iambic pentameter, Yeats's, 137; *khafif*, Rumi's, 220; Persian and Arabic, 247; tetrameter, Stevens's, 118; trimeter, Yeats's, 150; trimeter tercets, Goodison's, 106. *See also* poetics
metrics, in poetry, Vietnamese enmeshment with Chinese, 248. *See also* meter; poetics
Milani, Farzaneh, 223, 225
Miller, J. Hillis, 165
Milton, John: Latin poems of, 230; *Paradise Lost*, 68; translation of Horace, 228
modernism, 48, 51, 276n1; defies form/content paradigms, 127–30; and global South, 112–16; and Nagra, 115; and postcolonial poems (Press, Goodison), 101–16; and postcolonial poems, Kolatkar adapts, 63, 95, 97, 98
monologue, dramatic, 37–38, 143
Moore, Marianne, 8; "England," 127–28
Moore, Sturge, 141
Moretti, Franco, 121, 246; *Distant Reading*, 118–19; on form and literature,

125; on Jameson, 120; limited perspective of, 123, 124; refuted by own details, 123; Stanford Literary Lab, 124

Morgenstern, Christian, translation issues of "Das aesthetische Wiesel," 216–17

Morris, William, on Byzantine art, 138

Morton, Timothy: on ecology, 158, 161, 163, 168, 169; on interconnectedness, 166

Muldoon, Paul, 52, 123; on Heaney, 192

multiculturalism, Arabian, Golden Age and, 142–45

music, in poetry, 215–16. *See also* song

Mwangi, Evan Maina, 234

Myers-Scotton, Carol: and Embedded Language islands, 204; and Matrix Language Frame, 194. *See also* code-switching

myth: within global South poetry (Kolatkar), 95; mingled with WWI poetry (Heaney), 45

Nagra, Daljit, 203; "A Black History of the English-Speaking Peoples," heteroglot *Ramayana* of, 234; "A Black History of the English-Speaking Peoples," influence of Auden's "Spain" on, 112–14, 115; "A Black History of the English-Speaking Peoples," Shakespeare and, 113, 114; "A Black History of the English-Speaking Peoples," Tennyson and, 115; "The Punjab," 128–30; "The Punjab," translocality/ globalism of, 130

nationalism, 10; ridiculed (Stevens), 169; shades into transnationalism (Moore), 128; xenophobic, 50

nature. *See* earth/Earth; ecocriticism

Neoplatonism, and globality, 181

Nerlekar, Anjali, on Kolatkar's *Kala Ghoda Poems*, 63

Nerval, Gérard de, and orientalism (Said), 151–52

New Criticism, 241

Nichols, Grace, "Island Man," 61, 74

Niedecker, Lorine, "Lake Superior": local and global in, 69, 71–72, 74; and notes on geography, places, 69–71

Nietzsche, Friedrich, 147

Nisbet, R. G. M., on Horace, 228

Nixon, Rob, 163, 176

Noel, Urayoán, Latinx code-switching of, 199

Noguchi, Yone, 149

nontranslation, gains in (by Eliot et al.), 230–33

North, Michael, 233

novel (prose fiction): heteroglossia in, 199; Moretti on, 118–19, 120, 123, 124, 125; poetry and, 28, 35, 54, 55–56, 125, 198, 239, 243; translation of, 214, 246; in verse (Evaristo), 201, 210; as West European, vs. poetry as global, 120; Yiddish and Turkish forms of, 123. *See also* prose

Nussbaum, Martha, 28, 35

O (letter): in Hayes's "How to Draw a Perfect Circle," 10–11; in Heaney's "Alphabets," 179, 180, 181, 182, 192; in Kolatkar's *Jejuri*, 96

Odasi, Tifi, "Macaroneae," 200

Odyssey, The (Homer), 77

Okigbo, Christopher, 121

Okot p'Bitek, 109–11, 119, 203; code-switching in *Song of Lawino*, 234

Olson, Charles, *The Maximus Poems*, 67–68, 74, 125

omphalos, links Heaney to Homer, 186

orientalism: Ashbery and, 87; Bishop and, 83; Ireland and, 136, 152; modernism and, 101–2; of *Poetry Atlas*, 58; Said and, 135, 145, 149, 151–53, 246; translation and, 219; Yeats and, 133–54. *See also* Arabia; Asia; China, influence on Western poetry; India; Japan, influence on Yeats; Persia

Osterhammel, Jürgen, 14, 19, 28

ottava rima, 134, 137

Owen, Stephen, 214

Owen, Wilfred, 190; "Strange Meeting," 40–46

parallelism, 85, 181–82. *See also* poetics
pararhyme: Heaney on, 43–44; in Owen, 41–42. *See also* poetics; rhyme
parataxis, 82, 84, 85, 127. *See also* poetics
Park, Robert E., on globalization, 18–19
Parla, Jale, on Turkish novels and Western tradition, 123
Parmenides, preserved in Harun's library, 143–44
Pater, Walter, 84; "Mona Lisa," Yeats's version of, 160
Pausanias, on Callimachus, 138–39
p'Bitek, Okot. *See* Okot p'Bitek
Perez, Craig Santos, 119; code-switching of and etymologies, 204–5
Perloff, Marjorie, 12
Perry, W. J., *The Growth of Civilization*, 113
Perse, Saint-John, *Anabase*, 106–7, 229, 234, 235
Persia: influence on Arab Muslim culture, 142–43; influence on Byzantine art (Yeats), 138–42; Yeats's stereotypes of, 134–35
Persian (language): infiltration into English, 193; meters diverge from Arabic, 247; vast spread of poetry in, 218, 247, 249. *See also* Behbahani, Simin; Ferdowsi; Hafez; Rumi, Jalal al-Din; Saʿdi (Persian poet)
Petersson, Niels P., 14, 19, 28
Petrarchanism, 119, 166
phanopœia, 215–17; Rumi's Muslim, 219; in translation, 236. *See also* poetics
Phillips, Dana, 172
phonology, Rumi's as untranslatable, 221
Picasso, Pablo, 108
Pindar, Pound's use of, 200–201
Piper, Andrew, 118; and "bifocal" reading, 124; and periods, 124
place-names, 162. *See also* poetry, lyric: topographical; tourism; tourists

Plato, Stevens contradicts *Republic*, 170–71
poems: as bricolage, 2–3; digital, 12, 24, 259n35; great house, 64–65; Latinx, mistranslation in, 199; loco-descriptive (*see under* poetry, lyric); "messily eclectic," 116; of place, 75; of place, "entangled," 55–57 (*see also* poetry, lyric: topographical); post-colonial, and modernism, 102–16; temporalities in, 3–4; traveling, 72, 214; use of as literary or oral, 209; "world," 237; "world," Eliot's as, 230–33. *See also* poetics; poetry, lyric
"poeticity," 107, 199. *See also* poetics
poetics, 180; African, 121–22; Aristotle on, 241; in Behbahani, 223; cross-lingual, 200–201; defined, 20–21; macaronic, 195–211; multiple elements of, 8, 122, 125, 196, 202, 214, 246; mulitple elements of (*tajnis*), 219; polytemporal and polyspatial, 1–24; Pound and untranslatability of, 215–16; reflexivity in Yeats's, 149; in Rumi, 219–22; of Stevens's prose, 160; symbolist (French), 119; war poems as ars poetica, 45. *See also* Jakobson, Roman; meter; wordplay; *and individual figures of speech and thought; individual poems*
poetry, balladic, 59, 61, 125, 213, 239
poetry, epic, 125, 162, 213, 219, 229, 239; *The Arrivants*, 203–4; poetic devices in, 86, 89; *Ramayana* (Nagra), 234. *See also* Pound, Ezra; Walcott, Derek: *Omeros*
poetry, lyric: across languages, 246–50; concrete, 97, 209, 244; cosmopolitanism and, 41, 46; critical reactions to, 241–42; defined, 20, 239–41; form and content in, 124; form and content in, interdependence of, 130–31; form/content paradigms of, 125–26; form/content paradigms of, amalgam of (Moore, Nagra), 127–30; form/

content paradigms of, necessary to analysis, 130-31; genres interact with, 245 (*see also* tourism; tourists); globalism in, 128-30, 232-33; and globalization/*longue durée*, 15-16; Heaney's initiation into, 187-88; historicity of, Culler vs. Jackson on, 3; limitations of distant reading of, 124-26; local, as foil to globalized, 51-75; as local and global, 10-11, 120, 183, 184-85, 190, 246; as local and global, with foreign form/local content, 117-24; and locality within totality (Stevens), 155-63; loco-centric, as oversimplification, 121-23; as loco-descriptive, 62-66, 242; love, in tourism advertising, 88-90; modernist, defies form/content paradigms, 127-30; postcolonial, as loco-descriptive, 62-66; as prenational, 247; and ritual, 169, 243; as/against sight marker, 95, 98-100; Sufi, 216 (*see also* Rumi, Jalal al-Din); theorizing, 241-45; topographical, 74-75; topographical, corrective to (abstraction), 54; topographical, depends on global, 56; topographical, gloco-descriptive North American, 66-72; topographical, history of (in English), 52; topographical, loco-descriptive as gloco-descriptive, 62-64; topographical, of global South, 62-66, 119; topographical, one-point readings of, 55-57; and tourism, 77-100 (*see also* tourism; tourists); translations of and cross-cultural understanding, 227; translation within, 237-38; as transnational, 245-46; and travel (Heaney), 187-89 (*see also* tourism; tourists); untranslatability vs. translatability of, 214-17, 228-30, 235-36, 238 (*see also* translation). *See also* novel (prose fiction); poems; poetics; *and individual poets*

Poetry Atlas, 57-62, 99. *See also* poems: of place; poetry, lyric: topographical

poiesis (*poiema, poiein*), 14, 20, 90, 165,

179, 240; and abstraction (Stevens), 164; and globe (Heaney), 183. *See also* poetics

Polizzotti, Mark, 234

polysyndeton, 125, 146, 160. *See also* poetics

poppies, poetic associations of, 30-31. *See also* flowers, literary

"postcolonial," as umbrella term, 21-22, 276n1

postcolonialism: interdependence with modernism, 102-16; interdependence with modernism, Press and Goodison complicate, 110; resists Eurocentrism, 109-10

Pound, Ezra, 108, 112, 131, 244; *The Cantos*, 125, 162; *Cathay*, 219, 229; "In a Station of the Metro," 55-56, 57, 74-75; polyglossia in, 200, 230; on translatable vs. untranslatable in poetry, 215-16. See also *logopœia*; *melopœia*; *phanopœia*; poetics

Presley, Elvis, "Blue Suede Shoes," 129

Press, Karen: *Bird Heart Stoning the Sea*, 102; *Echo Location*, 91-95, 98; *Echo Location*, as "pseudo-guide," 91-92; "Glimpses of Women in Overalls," 93; "Here We Go Again," 93-94; "This is not a riot policeman," and modernism, 102-5, 111; on tourism, 91-95, 98; "The Wedding Was at Paddavlei," 92-93

Pressman, Jessica, 12

Princeton Encyclopedia of Poetry and Poetics, The, 248-49

prose, 54, 55-56, 245; code-switching in, 198; code-switching in, Dickens's, 199-200; lyricity in, 241; lyricity in, Kincaid's, 79-80; lyricity in, Stevens's, 160-61, 163. *See also* novel (prose fiction)

prose poetry, code-switching in (Perez), 205. *See also* poetry, lyric; prose

Qur'an: and Arabic, 236, 237; echoed by Behbahani, 224-25

radio: and global intimacy (Stevens), 157; and Heaney, 185, 187

rai, code-switching in, 201

Ramachandran, Ayesha, 14; on global whole, 163, 164, 179

Ramanujan, A. K.: "Elements of Composition," 7, 173–74; on phonology as untranslatable, 221; "Small-Scale Reflections on a Great House," 65, 74; on Yeats, 147

Rampolokeng, Lesego, 112

Ransom, John Crowe, Heaney draws on, 191

rap, code-switching in, 201

Rasmussen, Matt, *Black Aperture*, 5–6; diction of, 6–7; Latour and, 7

Read, Leonard E., "I, Pencil," 1

Reed, Christopher, 148

regionalism, critical, 53. *See also* poetry, lyric: as local and global

Reynolds, Matthew, on translation, 214

rhyme, 117–18, 169, 182; imperfect, 74, 89, 137; internal, 107, 117, 130, 148, 220, 221, 226, 236; para-, 41–44; parallelism of, 85; slant, 182. *See also* poetics

rhymes, nursery, allusions to, 129

Rich, Adrienne, code-switching in, 210

Richardson, Samuel, 87

Rickard, John, 136

Ricoeur, Paul, on translating poetry, 214, 217, 223

Rimbaud, Arthur: "J'ai perdu ma vie," 57; and "placelessness," 233

ritual, and poetry, 169, 243

Robbins, Bruce, 28, 51, 192

Robertson, Roland, 189; on "globality," 158; on "globalizations," 14, 16, 159; on global within the local, 30, 63–64

Robeson, Paul, 115

Rorty, Richard, 28, 32, 35; on transnational solidarity, 31, 40

Rosenberg, Isaac: "Break of Day in the Trenches," 27–32, 43; and Heaney, 191–92; as Jewish outsider, 32

Rumi, Jalal al-Din, 15–16, 237, 247; Barks

"de-Islamizes," 219; translating, 217–22, 233–34

Rushdie, Salman, 109

Saʿdi (Persian poet), 15

Safa, Kaveh, 223, 225

Said, Edward: Lazarus criticizes, 110; on orientalism, 135–37, 149, 151–53, 246; on orientalism, and sexuality, 145; "Yeats and Decolonization," 152

Sainsbury's (supermarket chain), ad about Christmas truce, 26–27

Saint-Exupéry, Antoine de, 7–8

Sakai, Naoki, on difficulty of translation, 227

Sanskrit, Eliot's use of, 200

Sappho, preserved in Harun's library, 143–44

Sassoon, Siegfried, "Glory of Women," 46–47

Saussy, Haun, 230

Schimmel, Annemarie, 220

Scientific American, 172

seduction, in tourism advertising, 88–90

Seligmann, Kurt, 164

Serres, Michel, 3

Service, Robert: "Only a Boche," 38–40, 43; "A Song of the Sandbags," 37–40, 49

Shahrokh, Keikhosrow, 134–35

Shakespeare, William, 69; adapted Italian sonnet, 15; and diffusionism, 113; on global entities, 14; Hardy quotes, 32; *Henry V*, 181; *Henry VIII*, 188; Nagra and, 113, 114; Niedecker echoes, 69; Stevens echoes, 165

Shammas, Anton, 237

Shelley, Percy Bysshe, 241; "Mont Blanc," 160

Shirinyan, Ara: "Andorra Is Great," 81; *Your Country Is Great*, 81, 86, 87

Snyder, Gary, 98; Chinese influence on, 68, 74; "Milton by Firelight," 68, 69

Solomon, King, Yeats Islamicizes, 145

song: allusions to American, 129–30;

code-skipping and, 206; connective energies of, 25–26; lyric poetry and, 244. *See also* music, in poetry

song thất lục bát (Vietnamese poetic form), 226, 248

sonnet, 8–9, 15, 121, 174, 208. *See also* meter; metrics, in poetry, Vietnamese enmeshment with Chinese; poetry, lyric

Sontag, Susan, on human solidarity/compassion, 40

Soyinka, Wole, 121

Spahr, Juliana, 202; on multilingual poetry, 202; *This Connection of Everyone with Lungs*, 175; *Well Then There Now*, 175–76

Spivak, Gayatri Chakravorty, 109; on globalization, 12–13, 161; on "globe" vs. "planet," 21; opposes translationese, 219

Stafford, Fiona, *Local Attachments*, 53, 58, 184

Stallworthy, Jon, 144

Stanford Literary Lab (Moretti's), 124

Stein, Gertrude, 8, 175

Steinberg, Saul, *New Yorker's View of the World from 9th Avenue*, 183

Stevens, Wallace, 8, 108; "Anecdote of the Jar," 117–18, 119, 120, 130; "Angel Surrounded by Paysans," 168–69; *The Auroras of Autumn*, 168; *Collected Poems*, 170, 172; "The Comedian as the Letter C," 162; "Domination of Black," 168, 175, 176; on Earth as a whole, 163–67, 179; globalization, layers of, 156–59; on interconnectedness, 166; and locality within totality, 155–63; "Man on the Dump," 174; "O Florida, Venereal Soil," 155; "O Florida, Venereal Soil," multiculturalism in, 156–57; place-names in, 162; "The Planet on the Table," 170–72; on Plato and poetry, 170–71; "The Pleasures of Merely Circulating," 167–70, 175, 176; poetic prose of, 160–61; "poetics of the earth" of,

160–61; "A Primitive like an Orb," 164, 165–67, 170, 171; "The River of Rivers in Connecticut," 168; on self and sun, 170–72; "The Snow Man," 160; on world's enmeshment, 166, 169–72

Strzygowski, Josef, Yeats on discoveries of Persian influences, 138–42

symbolism, 119–20, 140, 223

symbols: nationalist, of Jamaica, 111; nationalist, of poppy, 30–31; Pound and, 216; Yeats and, 138–40, 142, 148. *See also* poetics

synecdoche, 85; poem as, 59. *See also* poetics

tanka (Japanese genre of poetry), 150. *See also* haiku

tanku (Japanese genre of poetry), 150. *See also* haiku

technology, globalization and, 16, 17, 88, 111, 157, 159, 163–64, 185, 186–87, 189, 244. *See also* radio

Tennyson, Alfred: "The Defence of Lucknow," 115; "In Memoriam," 42

terza rima, 119, 125, 186

Thomas, Dylan, "Fern Hill," 56

Thoreau, Henry David, "Walden," as model for Yeats, 59

Thousand and One Nights, A, and Yeats, 143, 145

Thrift, Nigel, 67

totality, and environmentalism (Morton), 158

tourism: Ashbery and, 88; changing, 99; evolution of term, 77; negative effects of mass, 88; para-, 94–95; parataxis of (Bishop), 82; poetry and, 78, 84–85, 90–91, 100, 245; and religion, 83–84; semi-, 81; Walcott inveighs against, 80–81; as world's largest industry, 91. *See also* tourists

tourists: advertising seduces (Ashbery), 88–89; comparison with traveler, 78–79; Kincaid as, 79–80; MacCannell on term, 90; poets as, in global South, 91–98; post-, 87. *See also* tourism

trade, international, globalization and (nineteenth century), 157
translation: and cross-cultural understanding, 227; Damrosch on, 213; gains via (Rumi et al.), 218–19, 235, 236; Goethe on, 223; Jakobson on, 217; layered, interactive as solution, 216–17; of lyric poetry as difficult, 213–38; of lyric poetry as difficult, Connolly on, 214; of lyric poetry as difficult, Ricoeur on, 214, 217, 223; Perso-Arabic distinctions in, 216; what lives in, 222–25. *See also* Eliot, T. S.; poetics; poetry, lyric; Pound, Ezra
travel. *See* tourism; tourists
Turkish novel, 123
Twitty, Anne, 219–20, 221, 222

Urry, John, 78–79, 86, 89, 99

Valéry, Paul, and Eliot's French poetry, 230
Vang, Mai Der, 225
Vendler, Helen: on lyric poetry, 243; on macaronic poetics, 195–96, 197, 201; on Stevens, 155; on Yeats's *ottava rima*, 137
Venuti, Lawrence, on translation: as domestication, 219; and heterogeneous discourse, 234
Vietnam, poetic forms of, 226, 247–48
Viswanathan, Gauri, 284n43
Voros, Gyorgyi, 165

Walcott, Derek, 105, 110–11, 119; *The Fortunate Traveller*, 195; "Hurucan," 122; inveighs against tourism, 80–81; *Omeros*, code-switching in, 198–99; *Omeros*, on hurricane, 122–23, 125; "Sainte Lucie," 196; Vendler's criticism of, 195–96
Walkowitz, Rebecca, 214
Wallerstein, Immanuel, 110, 118
Walton, Kendall, on lyric poetry, 243
Wei, Li, 194

Welsh, Andrew, 169
Wendt, Albert, 81
Whitman, Walt, hymns the "vast globe," 164
Williams, William Carlos, 2, 6, 98; *Paterson*, 67
Windfall, 51, 54, 56
wordplay: Baraka's, 210; Freud defends, 217; in Nagra, "The Punjab," 129; as oral and literary, 210; Pound's, between Greek and English, 200–201; in Rumi, 222; Shakespearean, 113; Walcott's, between French and English, 199. *See also* poetics
Wordsworth, William: "The Reverie of Poor Susan," 60; "Tintern Abbey," 53, 171
world literature: Behbahani's work as, 223–25; and inattention to poetry, 2, 24, 214, 222; and migration of form, 117–31; and orientalist critique, 151; Rumi in context of, 217–18, 222; and translatability, 213–38. *See also* Casanova, Pascale; Damrosch, David, on translating world literature; Moretti, Franco
world-systems theory, 13, 110, 118
World War I poetry. *See* First World War poetry
Wright, James, "Lying in a Hammock at William Duffy's Farm in Pine Island, Minnesota," 56–57, 74; Chinese influence on (Bly), 57
"writes back," model of postcolonialism, 109–10, 114

Yates, Frances, 181
Yeats, William Butler, 20, 108–9, 120–21; "Anashuya and Vijaya," 146; and Arabic interests, 142–45; and Byzantium, 138–44; "Byzantium," 140; creates Christian-Muslim dialogue, 143–45; "A Dialogue of Self and Soul," 148, 149; "The Gift of Harun Al-Rashid," 142–45; "His Bargain," 145; "Imitated from the Japanese," poetics of, 148–50

(*see also* poetics); and India, 145–47; "The Indian to His Love," 146; "The Indian upon God," polytheism in, 146; "In Memory of Major Robert Gregory," 45; "An Irish Airman Foresees His Death," 45; on Irish-Asian kinship, 135–36; and Japan, 147–50; "The Lake Isle of Innisfree," 59–60, 74; "Lapis Lazuli," 139, 148; on lyric as "phantasmagoria," 243; "Meru," 137, 153; *On the Boiler*, 134, 135; and orientalism, 133–54; and orientalism, Said on, 152; *Per Amica Silentia Lunae*, 146; and Persia, 134–43, 145; "Sailing to Byzantium," 141; Sanskrit sources for, 146; "Solomon and the Witch," 145; "Solomon to Sheba," 145; "The Statues," 134–35, 138, 152, 153; *A Vision*, 138

Yiddish: infiltration into English, 193; outside influences of, 123

Young, Robert J. C., on point of translation, 226

zeugma, 128. *See also* poetics

Zoroastrianism, influence on Persian art (Yeats), 140, 141

Zukofsky, Louis, 216